Breakthrough Thinking

The Seven Principles of Creative Problem Solving

Revised 2nd Edition

Gerald Nadler, Ph.D.
Shozo Hibino, Ph.D.

PRIMA PUBLISHING

PRIMA PUBLISHING and colophon are registered trademarks of Prima Communications, Inc.

Library of Congress Cataloging-in-Publication Data

Nadler, Gerald.
　Breakthrough thinking : the seven principles of creative problem solving/
　　Gerald Nadler and Shozo Hibino. — Rev. 2nd ed.
　　p. cm.
　Includes index.
　ISBN 1-55958-42-1
　ISBN 0-7615-0648-9 (pbk.)
　1. Problem solving.　I. Hibino, Shōzō.　II. Title.
HD30.29.N34 1994　　　　　　　　　　　　　　　　　93-23559
658.4′03—dc20　　　　　　　　　　　　　　　　　　　CIP

98 99 00 01 AA 10 9 8 7 6 5 4 3 2 1

Printed in the United States of America

How to Order
Single copies may be ordered from Prima Publishing, P.O. Box 1260BK, Rocklin, CA 95677; telephone (916) 632-4400. Quantity discounts are also available. On your letterhead, include information regarding the intended use of the books and the number of books you wish to purchase.

Visit us online at http://www.primapublishing.com

Contents

Acknowledgments

The proposition that we must change the way we create or restructure systems and solve problems is based on far more than philosophy and research. It stems also from the experiences of many people around the world, including the many readers of the first edition of this book who have told us of their subsequent efforts and who now apply Breakthrough Thinking to prevent and solve real problems in the real world. Their successes verified for them and for us that the concepts we presented are eminently sensible for dramatically improving the quality of the solutions sought by all people, everywhere.

We apologize to those whose names do not appear here, simply because it would be impossible to include them all. We especially thank our many clients and students who learned the principles and process of Breakthrough Thinking and then practiced this approach on their projects. Each of them has contributed in many ways.

Where we were given permission to use names of people and companies, the cases in this book contain acknowledgments to them. Where the cases are anonymous, we provide our sincere thanks to those people, who know who they are. We do, however, want to acknowledge those with whom we have worked the most in applying and thus developing Breakthrough Thinking: Art Bond, William C. Bozeman, Andy Fulton, Charles E. Geisel, George Hathaway, David G. Hinds, Nachum Kaminka, Hitoshi Kato, Jacques Lehmann, Robert Leo, Kouji Morooka, David W. Ralston, Gen Sasaki, Alan D. Scharf, E. Michael Shays, Fujio Umibe, Wilbur Walkoe, and Ryuichi Yoshiya.

Several trade and consulting groups have helped to promote Breakthrough Thinking applications for their sponsors and clients. We thank them and hope that this new edition will help expand their effectiveness: The Center for Breakthrough Thinking, Inc.; Central Japan Industries Association; Institute for Healthcare Improvement; Institute of Industrial Engineers; Japan Planology Society; Japan Technology Transfer Association, Japan Work Design Society; The Planning Forum; Project Management Institute; SANNO Institute; and Tokai Research and Consulting, Inc.

Researchers in many disciplines have investigated questions that eventually produced the insights that led to Breakthrough Thinking. For example, in the 1920s and 1930s, Norman R. F. Maier raised questions about functional fixedness that have led to some key ideas. To all these researchers we owe an indefinable, large debt of gratitude.

Our own research is a major impetus behind *Breakthrough Thinking*. We appreciate the funding received in support of this research from the National Science Foundation, Japan Science Foundation, Japan Work Design Society, and many industrial firms. Other research underlying Breakthrough Thinking and many of the sections in this book are adapted from Gerald Nadler's *The Planning and Design Approach* (New York: John Wiley, 1981).

Massaging ideas to make them understandable is a task we asked many people to share. We feel especially indebted to the writers and editors who worked with us on the first edition of this book: particularly, John Farrell and Gladwin Hill, and Catherine Cochran, Gerald Jones, and Janet Kaye, who were very helpful at the right times. John Farrell is the writer to whom we are most grateful for his help on this second edition.

Authors often claim that writing a book is for the benefit of their families as well as the reading public. We must acknowledge that the family also suffers the most in the preparation of such a book. Our deepest expression of appreciation for tolerance and love during the trials of preparing the manuscript go to our wives, Elaine and Shigemi. We dedicate the book to them and to our families as symbols of the individuals and "families" we hope to help with *Breakthrough Thinking*.

Gerald Nadler
Shozo Hibino

Preface

Breakthrough Thinking is "software for the mind," the new principles and new process to plan, design, reengineer, improve, and find solutions to the problems you confront. It leads you to develop a vision of where you need to be and enables you to get there without ponderous data collection.

Breakthrough Thinking extends the creative process to determine the right purposes to be accomplished, generate a large number of imaginative and original options, and develop the systems you need to implement effective solutions. This "full-spectrum creativity" provides structure for the imaginative mind and freedom for the structured mind.

With Breakthrough Thinking, you think smarter, not harder.

There must be hundreds of books available to tell you what excellent solutions and faddish "alphabet-syndrome" programs the best-run corporations and most enlightened people have discovered for the problems they confront. But have you ever really learned from them precisely how you might arrive at the productive pot of gold their rainbows promise?

Many publications of this recent genre—whose popularity coincides with a precipitous decline in American self-confidence—have sold millions of copies in the United States and around the world. Yet these well-written tomes offer only what others have found as answers several years ago, leaving you with the transparent inadequacy of superficial solutions.

Indeed, all such books are primarily descriptive, not prescriptive. Readers are presented with good pictures of lean corporations and successful people doing productive things. Little or nothing is said about *how* they do it, about the methods and the skills needed to become successful.

Alternatively, the books present you with concepts or exercises for becoming mentally tough, quality-minded, and internally changed so that you can be more effective and learn more. As valuable as these ideas may be to prepare you to be better and attain personal mastery, they do little to focus you on what you actually need to accomplish and how to proceed and think in actual design, planning, and problem-solving. Far too often, these books simply present fads that people rush to adopt, one after another, seeking in these "programs of the month" the answer to solve all their problems. The books use sports analogies, speak of quality, extoll outward-bound exercises, promise team-building—the quick-fix laundry list seems endless.

Name a problem; some author has an answer for it. But these answers do not address how to achieve your sense of mission, how to bring out the best in others, how to develop a solution that fits you and your problem (not simply copy someone else's answer), how to adapt to change, or even how to implement a good idea from whatever source.

We enjoy reading these books. They tell us about others' successes. They stimulate thought. They encourage action. They stimulate personal development. But no one seems to say exactly how to go about arriving at an effective solution to the problem that concerns you the most—your own.

On the rare occasion when these books say something about how to actually proceed, they all approach the task with the analytical fervor favored 400 years ago by René Descartes and Francis Bacon, early founders of science and its research approach, arriving therefore at answers that can only be descriptive. All begin by posing the question, What's wrong here? No one asks, instead, What are we trying to accomplish? And none considers data challenging their solutions.

Unlike its predecessors, Breakthrough Thinking offers you a comprehensible reasoning approach, one based on thirty years of research into the intuitive methods of eminently successful problem solvers and preventers—people who seize opportunities and prevent problems. Another book of ours, *Creative Solution Finding*, presents aspects of the history of thinking and problem-solving approaches while providing philosophy and research that explains why Breakthrough Thinking works.

Fundamentally different from conventional solution-finding approaches, Breakthrough Thinking consists of focused principles and a reasoning process that you can learn and apply to master your own environment, which, like that of any human being, is one of constant change. Moreover, this book explains the mental models and techniques needed to make the principles and processes operational.

This constant change creates problems for us. For what is any problem but a need to respond to change, to adapt to our environment, or to seek improvement by regularly changing ourselves? The rapid change of the nineties especially demonstrates the need to rethink our modes of thinking. Our solutions are the changes we effect in ourselves or in our institutional or corporate policies to strike a beneficial, or at least a tolerable, balance between ourselves and our environment. Yet such self-interest still needs to be part of something bigger.

Our burden of self-consciousness as human beings is also our greatest strength. We can suffer agonies of dread—faced as we are with our awareness of the constancy of change, leading as it does to the inevitability of our own deaths. Despite this, we are at least equally blessed in that our consciousness, higher than that of other species, apparently allows us to adapt—not willy-nilly, but willfully, through the directed application of our ability to consciously solve problems, to think.

Our modes of thinking are the issue this book addresses. Other books describe answers and programs others have found—some of which may find their way into your solutions. We show that all of us have to change our way of thinking to develop and adapt the best possible changes now. For example, *Breakthrough Thinking In Total Quality Management,* by Glen Hoffherr, Jack Moran, and Gerald Nadler, (Prentice-Hall, 1994) gives details about how to be successful where so many organizations have failed, translating the worthwhile goals and values of programs such as total-quality management into practice.

We altered our presentation of this book more than once. We had a target solution that guided us, and we have come close to this ideal. Incorporating new research that supports the principles, additional techniques to implement the process, and diverse applications of the concepts, this expanded and re-vised second edition moves us even closer to our improved tar-get. Yet even in our conscious choice to appeal sufficiently to normal instincts so that our book might be published and read, we illustrate one of the crucial seven principles of Breakthrough Thinking and successful problem solving: Each problem is unique and must be addressed on its own terms.

Breakthrough Thinking is a conscious process of thinking that applies seven principles of successful solution-finding to any problem you, your group, or your company may face. Ideal-ly, all seven principles and the process should be used con-stantly. But human beings are, by definition, not ideal. So you don't need to apply all the principles nor follow each process step all the time to be a Breakthrough Thinker.

You must, however, become aware and remain aware of all seven principles and always apply at least two essential prin-ciples of Breakthrough Thinking: uniqueness and purposes. If you don't accept the fact that each problem is unique and ap-proach it in that spirit by always questioning the purpose to be achieved by its solution, you will greatly diminish, if not alto-gether eliminate, the possibility of a breakthrough.

All around us today, problems of immense human signifi-cance beg for solution. These problems are by no means lim-ited to the United States. Japan, Europe, the former Soviet Union, China, India, Latin America, and the developing coun-tries of Africa and Asia struggle with similar issues, which are all too well known to their own citizens.

In the United States, people wrestle with the social prob-lems of diminished productivity, a quantitative and qualitative decline in manufacturing, a tremendous increase in the nation-al debt, the loss of competitive advantage, and a consequent trade deficit of staggering proportions.

After decades of political, economic, and industrial hege-mony, Americans can no longer deny that—even as costs sky-rocket—their health care and education systems are faltering, and must be considered failures in comparison with those of other economically and technologically advanced countries.

Simply stated, Americans today can no longer honestly claim to be the best or to have found the best solutions.

It's obvious that creating or restructuring systems and solutions depends on the availability of an advanced knowledge base if effectiveness, productivity, and competitiveness are to be achieved. The United States has the largest advanced knowledge base in the world. Yet other countries are more effective, productive, and competitive. For the United States, then, the approach people have been following to develop systems and solutions that utilize this knowledge base must be deficient.

In the realm of personal problems, too, all of us could use a fresh start and the confidence that things can work out for the best. Consider the large number of systems of which each of us is a part—home, family, workplace, church, sports teams, personal relationships—and you can perceive the large number of problems needing solutions and improvement.

Today, corporate managers strive to increase quality and productivity to remain competitive in an interdependent world economy. Many corporate managers in the United States have rushed to adopt Japanese corporate culture. Meanwhile, Japan seeks solutions to problems of its own in American and other corporate models. Yet few seem to notice that simply adopting others' ways of doing things is self-defeating.

Simply copying someone else's methods guarantees we will remain behind. For even as we rush to adapt, our competitors are themselves making changes and improvements in their methods, changes certain to put them in front again, just when we assume we have at last become competitive by our rapid implementation of their now outmoded methods. What we need to do is not merely to match the competition, but surpass it—a goal that demands the use of Breakthrough Thinking.

Increasingly, Japanese leaders and foreign observers alike have come to realize that Japan is now facing a turning point. The keyword through the 1970s was the age of the 3C's: copy, control, and chase. The Japanese tried to copy and introduce technology from others or take a "me-too" view. Control of quality resulted in cheaper and better products. Chasing and passing the advanced companies and countries was to be accomplished by high-quality products.

Once Japan entered the 1980s, the situation changed quickly. The chances for finding good models to copy decreased due to severe competition and the high level of Japanese technology. The Japanese faced the fact that they had to create new models beyond quality control.

The 1980s became the age of three I's: identity, imagination, and innovation. Many Japanese companies sought to develop their own corporate identity, often by building research institutes for developing unique products. The 1980s were thus the age of creativity. Breakthrough Thinking in Japan became a key to success in the twenty-first century.

As the entire world moves into an internationally competitive twenty-first century, Breakthrough Thinking will become increasingly essential. Today and in the future, we won't find breakthroughs unless we know how to look for them and how to think differently in approaching every problem.

Despite the challenge of the future, countless people today—workers and students, executives of major corporations, and government leaders—shackle their own potential for success. They repeat outmoded problem-solving methods, accumulating mountains of data, realizing too late their uselessness in finding solutions. Or they try solutions that someone else found successful for his or her own, inherently different situation. Otherwise intelligent people take the same self-limiting thinking approaches every time without realizing they are stuck in time-worn ruts on the road to mediocrity.

Given these circumstances, we have urgent and compelling reasons to offer the principles of Breakthrough Thinking now. All of us can benefit from Breakthrough Thinking in the successful solution of our personal problems. One source of the many gratifying responses to the first edition of this book has been the large number of letters and comments we have received from psychiatrists and psychotherapists who recommend Breakthrough Thinking to their patients.

Beyond our personal lives, however, as members of a global society and as participants in civic and social organizations, in government or business, we all face problems we must solve successfully or perish. The times have changed, and a change in the way we think is long overdue. Today we all must ask ourselves, What am I going to do to help solve these pressing problems that confront us all?

Whatever the problem—whether rising health care costs, declining education test scores, an information management program, a product design, a manufacturing system, or a personal dilemma—how do *you* proceed in finding its solution?

One thing is certain: If, like most people, you have the essentially investigative, adversarial notion that you're going to find out what's wrong, get all the facts, and then "nail the bastards to the wall," that's the most you're ever going to accomplish. You'll nail them to the wall, all right, and, hanging there, they won't do anything to solve the problem. Neither will you.

But there is a better way.

Breakthrough Thinking has been synthesized over thirty years of studying intuitively effective problem solvers, system developers, managers, and designers in a wide variety of professional fields and personal situations, from different cultures throughout the world. We have reviewed the results from hundreds of Breakthrough Thinking projects. What these studies have shown is that the key to an effective solution lies in the *approach* to the problem.

The essential, straightforward process of Breakthrough Thinking organizes the purposes you seek to achieve, identifies the broadest possible purpose level, and develops a feasible target solution from a variety of alternatives. Then, working backward to develop a creative change in the problem situation, you can move toward your solution goals.

The benefits of Breakthrough Thinking summarize the promise of its future and—if you learn and apply its principles and process—your own. Breakthrough Thinking:

- Identifies the right things to do and *then* how to do them right.
- Focuses on solutions in the future, not problems in the past.
- Removes obstacles to simple solutions.

- Requires minimal data collection, thus reducing "analysis-paralysis."
- Produces answers that provide much greater benefits in terms of quality, economic return, and timeliness.
- Requires much less time and cost to provide those benefits.
- Promotes innovative thinking and major changes.
- Provides long-term solutions.
- Emphasizes useful implementation of solutions.
- Builds lasting, natural teams and personal relationships.
- Offers you a rich, multifaceted role in solving and preventing problems.

Moreover, Breakthrough Thinking helps you avoid the eight basic errors most often made in solving problems:

1. Applying the *wrong mental assumptions* to the problem.
2. Taking the *wrong approach* to the problem.
3. Involving the *wrong people*.
4. Trying to solve the *wrong problem*.
5. Addressing the problem with the *wrong timing*.
6. Exerting the *wrong control* over the search for a solution.
7. *Wrongly accepting* a false or incomplete "solution."
8. *Wrongly rejecting* a true and effective solution.

These benefits will come as you apply the seven principles and begin to achieve breakthroughs. But exactly what is a "breakthrough"? The answer is not as obvious as you may assume. In fact, there are three distinct types of breakthroughs.

The first type, of course, is the brilliant creative idea, the blinding flash of absolute insight, the "ah-hah!" moment of epiphany, in which all is suddenly revealed. This is generally what most people understand a breakthrough to be. There are, however, two other, equally valuable types of breakthroughs.

The second type of breakthrough is the solution that produces significantly better results. If you can achieve significantly greater quality and economic returns from the same amount of time and money invested, that's a breakthrough. A similar breakthrough is to realize equal or greater benefits than with conventional approaches with significantly less investment of time and money.

The third type of breakthrough—in many ways the most neglected—is to bring to fruition the "good idea," to make it real, to implement your outstanding system or solution. Even the most excellent idea is useless until it is actually realized, implemented as an effective solution in the real world, and produces results.

Above all, the principles and process of Breakthrough Thinking produce these three types of breakthrough results. Its total approach to problem-solving offers far more than just another set of obvious, generic maxims and enthusiastic, yet elusive, exhortations. Breakthrough Thinking produces specific, measurable, and effective solutions. With Breakthrough Thinking, you will learn to solve real problems in the real world. You will gain the strategic thinking and decision-making skills to make the right new things happen, not just to correct a deviation or maintain the standard performance of a system, product, or machine.

Breakthrough Thinking does not follow a constant pattern of inquiry, a method that is always the same. Indeed, the process that emerges from the principles of Breakthrough Thinking is best understood as a *general flow* of reasoning. In any problem situation, however, this general flow of reasoning is part of a successively more detailed road map that indicates exactly what thinking steps need to be taken.

The Breakthrough Thinking process comprises from three to 24 steps (or more, if you count sub-steps), depending on the nature of the problem you are solving and the level of professional expertise you are applying to the process. Regardless of the number of steps used, however, at almost every step along the way you are guided by a landmark—a result expected from your work at that step. Offering far more than merely a technique or two to apply, each step defines the desired outcome, as well as its purposes.

To the extent you choose to apply its principles and process, Breakthrough Thinking offers a very productive approach to solving and preventing problems. It provides a successively detailed road map to effective problem solving. Following that map anyone, whether a highly qualified professional or an untrained amateur, can successfully use the same concepts. The basic premise of Breakthrough Thinking is that anyone can break out of self-defeating, traditional modes of reasoning and break through to find revitalizing, consistently positive solutions to the problems he or she confronts.

Our work as international consultants in planning and design has often led others to ask us, "Is a good problem solver born or made?"

Our professional experience is that five to eight percent of people are born experts in this regard; that is, not much of anything can ever be done to diminish their innate capacities as effective problem solvers or intuitive Breakthrough Thinkers. These are the "naturals" whose instinctive processes and methods we study. The seven principles and the process of Breakthrough Thinking summarize this research and form the basis of our teaching and applications. They also help the naturally gifted group of Breakthrough Thinkers explain to others how they approach solution-finding so effectively, thus providing "naturals" a means of mentoring and coaching others.

Another five to eight percent are hopeless when it comes to creating or restructuring systems and solutions. The majority of people, however, some 85 to 90 percent who are neither gifted nor bereft, can learn to become excellent problem solvers.

Chances are that you yourself are among that 85 to 90 percent who, by learning and applying Breakthrough Thinking, can greatly improve their own innate capacities for problem solving. As you do, we believe you will inevitably increase your ability to lead in the development of and successful adaptation to change. With that creativity and successful adaptation, you will come to fulfill yourself and flourish as a human being.

Think smarter, not harder.

Introduction

> There is nothing so wasteful as doing with great difficulty
> that which doesn't have to be done at all.
>
> —Anonymous

> The thickness of the proposal required to win a multimil-
> lion dollar contract is about one millimeter per million. If
> all the proposals conforming to this standard were piled
> one on top of the other at the bottom of the Grand
> Canyon, it would probably be a good idea.*
>
> —*Augustine's Laws*

When confronted with a problem, successful people tend to question why they should spend their time and effort solving the problem at all.

A common characteristic of effective people—generally
absent among the less competent—is that they intuitively approach a problem by first questioning the purpose of solving it.
In doing so, they reduce their chances of wasting time and effort on the wrong problem.

Instead, turning their attention to the steps that really
achieve their purpose, they greatly increase both their chances
of success and their personal effectiveness. This approach con-
trasts sharply with the usual approach of focusing on what's
wrong with a problem situation.

In the professional world of systems development, a
related, coordinated method of dealing with problems is called
the Purpose Design Approach or PDA, which we pioneered.
This revolutionary approach evolved over years spent observ-
ing how successful people deal with problems. These studies

---

*Norman R. Augustine, *Augustine's Laws* (New York: Penguin Books,
1987).

1

resulted in the basic principles of Breakthrough Thinking and an orderly way of applying them.

Whatever your problem—whether your aim is to create or restructure a corporate plan, your home, an information system, your commute, a marketing program, a kitchen layout, a regional housing plan, a product design, a factory, or a personal relationship—Breakthrough Thinking significantly increases the probability of your developing and implementing an innovative and effective solution. It translates ideas into action.

Practicing the seven principles of Breakthrough Thinking in concert, you, your group, or corporation can identify problems correctly, reduce the need for and expense of data collection and analysis, minimize uncertainty in decision making, cut costs (both personal and financial), and improve productivity.

Breakthrough Thinking is a holistic approach. It enables you to take advantage of, not merely cope with, the demands of ever-changing conditions. Breakthrough Thinking combines the best of the visionary and the pragmatic approaches to solving and preventing problems. It integrates these components to provide specific, day-by-day methods for relating planning, design, change, and improvement to the real world of individual human lives and human organizations. Jon Elks, a Melbourne, Australia senior manager in the international accounting firm KPMG, says, "Breakthrough Thinking moves people out of their comfort zones. However, this change is managed by the process itself; that is, the results of our work are very positive and thus reinforce the change."

Within a much longer academic and professional tradition of trying to improve the efficiency and effectiveness of human thought and labor, Breakthrough Thinking originated with studies in work design in the early 1960s. At the culmination of this formative, evolutionary period, the first edition of this book represented a breakthrough in Breakthrough Thinking itself: the potentially revolutionary introduction of purpose-directed problem-solving into popular thinking.

In 1990, its publication helped touch off an explosion in effective problem solving. We hope this new edition—expanded and revised on the basis of subsequent research and insights gained as a result of responses to the original edition—will continue to have that highly productive impact. We hope you too will come to use the new "software for your mind."

In one aspect of its philosophy, *Breakthrough Thinking* tends toward an oriental point of view: things are in a constant state of flux, of being and becoming. The solutions to today's problems beget new problems. This inexorable evolution can be harnessed by human reason and constructive action, so that the progression from one solution to the next leads to our ideals.

At the same time, this book is filled with Yankee optimism. You *can* make a difference, and you can enhance your impact by applying a new kind of "common sense." By applying Breakthrough Thinking, you can gain the ability and confidence to work more constructively and more purposefully.

Combining these two perspectives, we often refer to Breakthrough Thinking as "expantegration"—the powerful combination that derives from an awareness of larger ends, bigger solutions, and constant change, while including the people, elements, dimensions, and attributes necessary to arrive at the best results.

You will no longer approach problems with the doubt— or even dread—that comes from dwelling on what's wrong with the current situation. Instead, you'll find the power of belief, of positive action—not by any magic or superhuman gift, but by discovering in yourself and others the ability to take control of current circumstances and direct them toward significant ideals and principles.

In the field of education, for example, applying the principles of Breakthrough Thinking, a dean at a major university developed a more effective registration system; a district school superintendent handled an antagonistic booster club meeting after he had fired a winning football coach; a dean of humanities resolved many difficulties with a curriculum design committee; a high-school principal developed seminars for administrators and teachers in his home state; and a director of instruction developed a drug abuse program for parents and students.

A vice-president of a hospital chain used Breakthrough Thinking to help a team that had been deadlocked for nearly two years decide the allocation of capital improvement money between two hospital sites four miles apart in the same city. The manager of training and management development in a very large insurance company used Breakthrough Thinking to get separate profit centers to cross-market products of the others after previous attempts at such cooperation had failed. A director of total quality management in a manufacturing company adopted Breakthrough Thinking in all training sessions and found that almost all groups produced significantly better results compared to the "analysis-paralysis" of previous sessions.

A federal project director and a high-school principal used Breakthrough Thinking to develop project proposals, design compensatory and remediation programs, plan school activities, design elementary and secondary curricula, and manage task forces.

You can use Breakthrough Thinking to change your situation, meet your present and future needs, and solve almost any problem.

Yet simply talking about change, the future, and emerging needs does not ensure results. Everyone agrees that change is constant, that today's choices create the future, and that we have many options in planning and designing for emerging needs. These maxims are a necessary backdrop for creating or restructuring any solution. But *effective* problem solving and problem prevention involve far more.

The specific methods in Breakthrough Thinking rest firmly on basic scientific theories, research results, and concepts. They establish a context and setting for the nature of reality (metaphysics), set forth methods of knowing and understanding what happens when problems are identified and solutions found (epistemology), and clarify what is meant by change and stability (dynamics). The framework of Breakthrough Thinking is thus the result of intensive theoretical and empirical investigations, as reviewed thoroughly in our book, *Creative Solution Finding.*

By stressing implementation, Breakthrough Thinking prevents planning and design from becoming entangled in utopian schemes. By focusing on *purposes*, it ensures that your solution-finding efforts are directed toward normative goals and values that are workable in the real world yet as close as possible to your ideal solution.

The individual components of Breakthrough Thinking are not new. Indeed, they are natural to the 5-8 percent of people who are intuitive Breakthrough Thinkers. What is new is the integration of these individual components into a holistic, time-line scenario, one that focuses on the "solution-after-next." This focus permits you to concentrate on what is important in effective problem solving and on *how* you can achieve it.

We have compelling reasons to be optimistic about the immensely productive changes that lie ahead. Both in our own work and with reference to that of others, we've articulated the principles of Breakthrough Thinking and watched its successful application in many fields of endeavor—with consistently impressive results.

For many years, as scientific observers, we studied how successful people went about their work. We looked for similarities. We discovered—at first, to our surprise—that there was no real pattern to the solutions themselves. Yes, all the solutions were effective; that much was inherent in our definition of success. Yes, many of the solutions were innovative; but again, there were few similarities in the ways those solutions worked.

Beyond vague statements about being motivated or being persistent, the people we studied often could not tell us *how* they had found such successful solutions. Even when we ourselves achieved exceptional results in our own consulting engagements, we were not certain of what it was we'd done right.

We had much better luck, however, when we examined the research literature (see *Creative Solution Finding*) and particularly the unusual approaches that produced breakthrough solutions. We believe that behind these unusual, and unusually effective, behaviors lie seven basic principles of Breakthrough Thinking. Here are some cases, most of which are explored further in this book, along with the success axioms that each case illustrates.

One case involved a consultant who was asked to design a medical records library system for a major hospital. Although he had only recently worked with a team that had designed a highly successful medical records library system for another hospital, he determined to "start from scratch" in formulating a design for the second client. Despite the fact that both clients had asked for a "medical records library system," the design team in the second hospital discovered that the purposes of the presumably similar systems were in fact different in each hospital.

Question: What was particularly innovative about the consultant's refusal to "clone" the system with which he had recently been involved?

The Uniqueness Principle: Whatever the apparent similarities, each problem is unique, and each part of a solution (setting it up, writing a report, installing a solution, etc.) requires an approach that dwells on its own contextual needs.

Another case involved an industrial engineer called in to design a plant expansion intended to solve problems of late deliveries, low quality, and high costs by doubling the company's manufacturing capacity. Intuitively, the consultant disagreed with the solution proposed by the company's management team. He proposed a "purpose investigation" that led the team to decide that its purpose should not be to expand the plant, but rather to develop more effective management control systems.

Question: What was unusual about beginning his consultation by getting the client company to focus on the aims of the project, rather than on the details of the factory expansion?

The Purposes Principle: Focusing on purposes and their own larger purposes helps strip away nonessential aspects to avoid working on the wrong problem.

In some cases, it was tempting to look for quirks of personality or individual genius behind apparent innovations. Curiously, however, these factors don't necessarily enhance the chances for achieving breakthroughs. It is more important to focus on the "solution-after-next."

A team of systems designers was charged with creating a new tax-collection procedure for a major metropolitan county. They knew that within five years the new system would itself have to be redesigned, upgraded, or retrofitted to keep pace with changing conditions. When the designers felt they had a clear picture of where the tax-collection system—and the county—was going, they proceeded to design a system that could be implemented now but could also evolve and grow to become the system of the future.

Question: Why did the team's design prove simpler, more economical, and more effective than those produced after many weeks of unproductive effort spent thrashing through a plethora of detailed alternative proposals?

The Solution-After-Next Principle: Innovation can be stimulated and solutions made more effective by working backward from an ideal target solution for the future.

On occasion, we wondered why some old truisms appear to hold. For example, why are bureaucratic organizations often seen as ineffective?

In a design project for a large purchasing agency in a state government, the design group wanted to avoid a common problem: conscientious employees who often see their jobs as processing forms, rather than as serving their clients by supplying them with needed items. The group discovered that many forms were initiated just because the original design had failed to anticipate the many interconnections among separate parts of the whole government.

Question: What enabled the design group to develop a breakthrough information structure to greatly minimize paper shuffling?

The Systems Principle: Every problem is part of a larger system. Understanding the elements and dimensions of a system framework lets you determine in advance the complexities you must incorporate in implementating your solution.

We were particularly impressed with a successful group of architects who had won a reputation for functional, useful, and innovative designs. Although each of their buildings was recognized as superior and successful, we wondered why they seemed to have no consistent architectural style—a point of pride for many practitioners in their profession.

Question: Why was their data collection on any project focused mainly on client needs and solutions, rather than on the details and conflicts of the current situation?

The Limited Information Collection Principle: Knowing too much about a problem initially can prevent you from seeing some excellent alternative solutions.

In the 1970s, a huge, federal and state, multiagency, industrial and environmental task force failed in its attempts to control the proliferation of gypsy moths in the United States, a situation that threatened to become a major environmental crisis. Bureaucratic infighting and massive data collection had created a deadlock among the task force experts. They made no progress until an outside consultant showed them that the immediate, essential problem had more to do with organizing the task force itself than with controlling the moths. With hindsight, this realization seems almost self-evident.

Question: Why, despite three and one-half years of previous effort, had this not been realized earlier?

The People Design Principle: The people who will carry out and use a solution must work together in developing the solution with Breakthrough Thinking. The proposed solution should include only the minimal, critical details, so that the users of the solution can have some flexibility in applying it.

The problem of developing a system for dispensing medications in a large hospital was seen in a new light when a concerned nurse persisted in asking when the next step toward the ideal, target solution would be taken.

Question: How did her insistence contribute to realization of the breakthrough idea of automatically distributing physicians' orders for each patient to the hospital departments needed to carry them out as soon as the physician wrote the order?

The Betterment Timeline Principle: A sequence of purpose-directed solutions is a bridge to a better future.

Focusing on purposes, we've found, is fundamental to successful problem solving, but it's just a starting point. In the examples above, it's only one of an interrelated set of seven principles that constitute a formula for success.

Intuitively, you may already be applying some of these principles in your approach to problems. But it's much less likely that you are applying *all* of them consistently and in coordination.

The distinction between principles and process is obvious in other areas of human activity. For example, you probably have a highly developed set of principles (mental assumptions) about the appropriate way to eat. However, the best way to go about preparing a delicious, satisfying, healthy meal is a very different matter. In this case, the distinction drawn is between, on the one hand, the principles of proper nutrition and, on the other, an effective process of food preparation. Or consider the difference between principles of learning and the process of education, of absorbing information or acquiring a skill.

This book tells you specifically and concretely how to combine principles and process, how to apply the seven principles of Breakthrough Thinking to find effective solutions for your problems by following a deliberate, orderly, and yet iterative core process or pattern of reasoning. Depending on your needs, the process of Breakthrough Thinking can be described in as few as three or as many as 24 steps. The 24-step process, as described in *Breakthrough Thinking in Total Quality Management,* is usually reserved for professional applications. The simplest, essential three-step process—purposes, target, results—is represented by the headings immediately below. In this book, which is intended for a well-informed, intelligent, inclusive audience, we propose the following, intermediate nine-step process of Breakthrough Thinking.

Purposes

1. With appropriate others, in specific terms, identify many purposes for solving the unique, immediate problem. Don't ask, What's wrong here? What's the matter? Instead, ask, What are we trying to accomplish here? What are we trying to do?

2. Expand your investigation to examine ever-bigger, more expansive purposes. Develop an array of small to large purposes, from which you select as a focus the *largest* purpose you can practically seek to achieve. A truly effective solution will address both the immediate and the larger purposes. Define measures of purpose accomplishment for the selected level.

Target

3. Generate as many ideas as possible for solutions-after-next or ideal systems for achieving the selected (and larger) purposes. Form these ideas into major alternative solutions.

4. Assess the alternatives and select the solution-after-next target, based on the measures of purpose accomplishment.

5. Within a systems framework, develop a recommendation that fits the real world while coming closest to your target.

Results

6. Detail the recommendation to assure workability.

7. Using the steps of the core process above, develop a plan to install the recommendation.

8. Install the system or solution.

9. Set up dates for its continuing change and improvement.

Following this process, you won't always find a breakthrough, but one of the three types of breakthroughs isn't always necessary. To give your solutions the best possible direction, however, you must continually seek the opportunity for breakthrough. If you're not actively looking for breakthroughs, you probably won't find any.

Perhaps the most remarkable finding of our studies is that Breakthrough Thinking doesn't necessarily require specialized talents, expertise, or genius. Breakthrough Thinking can be described objectively as a process that is repeatable and reliable. Its purpose-directed problem-solving seems to work almost every time, almost always yields better-than-usual solutions, and frequently stimulates breakthroughs.

Following our own advice, we started writing this book by establishing a purpose. Our purpose here is to help people in all walks of life increase their personal effectiveness in dealing with the problems they face every day. In describing the results of our studies in general, nontechnical terms, we hope to extend the power of Breakthrough Thinking problem solving to you—and to anyone who wants to improve his or her chances for achieving successful results.

Though it may sound naïve and hopelessly visionary, our ultimate purpose is to help people build a better world. As individuals, we represent separate cultures: Nadler, occidental;

Hibino, oriental. We have studied and taught in each other's countries, as well as in many other places around the world.

We've found that Breakthrough Thinking problem solving embraces both the oriental wisdom of perpetual evolution toward perfection and the more temporal American ideals of optimism and progress. The exceptionally positive international response to the first edition of this book substantiates our belief that there aren't any cultural barriers to developing Breakthrough Thinking as a natural way to go about planning and directing all types of problem solving in any and all cultures.

As animals, we human beings share a common purpose: to survive. As thinking beings, our purposes become more sophisticated, but essentially they come down to enhancing the quality of our lives. A problem-solving approach that begins and is directed by *purposes* becomes, almost by definition, infused with meaning.

Though certain desired outcomes sometimes elude our grasp, we can control the purposes that we set for our efforts. Thus, Breakthrough Thinking problem solving can be as meaningful as we choose to make it. Far from being merely visionary, Breakthrough Thinking is a sensible way of working toward a better future, regardless of our fields of endeavor or how large or small we perceive our problems to be.

Toward this purpose, the three parts of this book mark a transition from conventional to Breakthrough Thinking:

I. The Conventional You
II. Increasing Your Personal Effectiveness
III. The Effective You

Part I, "The Conventional You," establishes a rationale for using Breakthrough Thinking. Our intent is not to replace methods that have already proved successful for you but to give you a framework for applying these and other methods with greater success.

The stories and cases in Chapter 1 center around three basic ideas. You greatly increase your chances of success if you (1) focus on the *purposes* of the unique situation, (2) structure your approach to actively seek breakthroughs, and (3) obtain agreement about purposes among individuals in order to initiate and motivate effective organization.

Against this background, Chapter 2 takes a longer view of what happens after a solution has been implemented. What happens next? Problems don't go away; they beget other problems. This isn't bad news if you realize that a *chain* of Breakthrough Thinking solutions can lead to the desired future—at least to one that most nearly fulfills your dreams and ideals.

Your solution will be successful and, to that extent, will make you happy. But no solution should ever leave you fully satisfied. Instead, you must adopt the perspective of the existential idealist who always anticipates change and is always looking for and developing the next solution.

Chapter 3 examines the role your modes of reasoning have in solving problems. You don't have to be an expert in the problem area to begin to deal effectively with it. Actually, at the beginning, being an expert can be a liability.

Being expert in the details of a problem can prevent you from seeing some of the better alternatives. Experts best come into the picture once you've identified what your solution should accomplish.

The critical need in preventing and solving problems is to change the way you think about them. The world has a surfeit of information, and the amount keeps growing. The gap Breakthrough Thinking fills is to show you how to effectively convert this knowledge into significant solutions.

Part II, "Increasing Your Personal Effectiveness," moves on to outline the seven specific principles of Breakthrough Thinking that are used intuitively by successful people. These principles are illustrated by cases describing successful people in many different disciplines and personal situations, not just in the professional or business worlds.

Chapter 4 explains why merely copying solutions and fads that have been successful elsewhere in the past or using metaphors, analogies, or stereotypes that assume similarities to other circumstances can be a formula for failure.

Stories in Chapter 5 show that focusing on purposes can strip away nonessential aspects of the problem that may have become barriers to achieving a breakthrough.

Chapter 6 describes how purposes can generate ideal systems and advanced solutions. In this way, the future can shape the present.

The cases in Chapter 7 point out how a systems framework lets you specify the scope of your solution, which is important to the eventual achievement of your ideals.

Chapter 8 examines the uses and abuses of fact finding, data gathering, and other detail-oriented activities.

To help you prevent hasty rejection of your ideas and to generate genuine enthusiasm for your solution among the people who will have to use it, Chapter 9 explores how they can be continually involved with the Breakthrough Thinking principles in developing change.

Chapter 10 rounds out the discussion of the principles by reflecting on entropy—the tendency of everything we make to run down or wear out. All solutions are subject to entropy, and you can either make that fact work for you or against you.

Part III, "The Effective You," brings the principles of purpose-directed problem solving together into a way for you to seek and achieve breakthroughs.

Chapter 11 describes a holistic, total process for finding the solutions to your problems.

Chapter 12 examines the future for you and for Breakthrough Thinking.

A major outcome of developing Breakthrough Thinking may be a basic change in your attitude toward today's problems and toward your own future. In applying the principles, you will also realize that the process of purpose-directed problem solving will evolve further as you continue to apply it.

Developing Breakthrough Thinking is an ongoing challenge that commands our best efforts throughout our lifetimes, throughout generations of growth and change. Having become Breakthrough Thinkers, you who read this book and apply its principles will write its future chapters.

Part 1

The Conventional You

Chapter 1

It's Up to You

A problem is a need for change. A dream or goal you have is a problem. At this moment, you face several problems. This isn't at all unusual; it's the perpetual human condition. Life is an ongoing struggle. The purpose of solving problems and accomplishing legitimate dreams isn't to remove them but to give meaning and direction to the struggle.

Purposes direct the search for solutions in positive ways. Helping you harness the creative, productive energy behind this principle is a major goal of this book. By deciding to read this book, you've already taken a more purposeful approach to your problems. Even if you can't give specific reasons why, you sense that you can be more effective and can take more decisive, personal control of your circumstances.

If you feel this way, you share a sense of purpose with all the people who were involved in shaping this book from a few basic mental concepts to a finished product. You share this purpose with the book's authors, editors, typesetters, proofreaders, printers, bindery workers—the list goes on. If we all got together, we could probably agree on the main purpose of this book: to develop *your* personal effectiveness. You do possess the freedom to shape your life dealing with problems.

It might not be apparent that enhancing your personal ability to deal with problems will have noticeable effects on the world around you. Asserting, "It's up to you," might seem to be little more than empty cheerleading. After all, there aren't many things we do entirely by ourselves. Most of our problems involve some group action, whether at our jobs, with our families and friends, at school—wherever. Ultimately, for almost any type of problem, some organization seems to be in control.

Although dealing with, or within, an organization can be overwhelming, it's not just cheerleading to say that you can make a difference. When you think a bit about group dynamics—the ways people interact with one another—you can see that organizations often—indeed, typically—have trouble approaching problems. At the first sign of a problem, you, as an individual, are likely to be far more effective than the assembled resources of Mitsubishi, General Motors, or any other organization, large or small. The reason is simple: Organization only becomes effective *after, not before,* the purposes of working on a problem are identified.

Think about it. What is the purpose of an organization? Organizations are just groups of individuals whose efforts are structured, through certain relationships, to tackle big jobs. Organization is needed to carry out tasks that are too big for individuals. Each of us supports and is supported by the work of others.

The strongest man in the world could not build a skyscraper by himself, but one person, unassisted, could define the purposes and conceive of the design for a skyscraper. The most powerful computer in the world is between *your* ears; this is the reason Breakthrough Thinking is "software for your mind." Individual human brainpower is the world's most valuable resource. The brainpower of individuals drives all organizational effort.

Initially, before a plan of action has been devised, a large group of people cannot approach a problem. Individuals have to do that. If you have a stake, or concern, in a particular problem, *you* have to take hold of it.

Again, an organization, as a collective body, can't approach a problem. Individuals have to focus the attention of the group effort. An extension of this concept is that, in group efforts, it takes an individual to help organize the group in defining the *purposes* of working on a particular problem.

As basic as this idea is, it's amazing how many people, including influential corporate managers and public officials, don't seem to appreciate its implications. As individuals, we can think of countless reasons not to take action personally. How many times have you read that a committee has been formed to study this or that crisis? Why is it that committees often end up doing little or nothing?

The shortcomings of the conventional committee approach became apparent when a task force of federal and state government officials—including hundreds of experts, professionals, and bureaucrats—and industry and environmental groups attempted to converge on the problem of the gypsy moth.

Gypsy moths are insects that threaten to eat their way into the history books by denuding most of the trees in North America. This problem has been lurking around for more than a hundred years, actually since the creatures were imported to Massachussetts from France in 1869.

Gradually at first, this pest, which had few predators in the area, spread to twelve states in the Northeast. Some of them have been found as far away as Florida, Wisconsin, and California.

Between 1970 and 1976, agricultural experts estimated that the larvae of the gypsy moth consumed one or two million acres of vegetation per year. If left unchecked, hordes of them could gobble up a large portion of the country's forests, woodlots, and suburban greenery.

In 1973, the U.S. Congress finally appreciated the potential anger of millions of taxpayers suddenly deprived of their shade trees. The nation's representatives put pressure on the Department of Agriculture (USDA) to do something before the ungreening of America reached crisis proportions. This encouragement was backed up with about $50 million in public funds to cover an in-depth, five-year program.

In an understandable flurry of activity, groups within USDA started gathering data. They studied the characteristics and behavior of the insect, predicted its spread and impact, identified alternative methods of control, and evaluated the potential damage to the environment that these control measures might cause.

Several years later, the department had amassed huge amounts of information, and groups within USDA had become expert in various aspects of the problem. State governments, industry, and environmental groups had also joined the effort. But factions had formed within the department and the various agencies involved. These factions each had different assessments of the problem, and in some cases, the disagreements had festered to the point of outright antagonism. Since each faction had become defensive about its position and role in solving the problem, a situation of deadlock existed.

No one had the faintest notion of how to coordinate the participants in order to proceed further. Taking action would mean coordinating many federal, state, and private organizations. Consultants had submitted reports on several proposed pest-management systems, but each faction objected strongly to different report recommendations. Since no agreement could be reached on a plan of action, the reports, representing years of effort, were shelved. Meanwhile, the little moths continued to chomp, chomp, chomp their way past the Appalachians.

At this point, one of the more courageous participants put in a call to Nadler, who was then at the University of Wisconsin at Madison. The caller knew that Nadler's research and writing had shown that planning and design methods could be made much more effective than they were at present.

"Gerry," the caller said, "we've been working on this thing for three and a half years. We've got a stack of reports. We can tell you about the biology of the gypsy moth. We can tell you all about defoliation levels. We can tell you about the impact on the social scene when the oak trees are stripped bare. But we don't know anything about how to put together a national gypsy moth pest-management system. What do you think we should do?"

At least Nadler's response was truthful: "I haven't the slightest idea."

Perhaps what the caller expected was something like: "Let's get the Army and convert a bunch of flame-throwers into spray guns and blast 'em right out of the ecosystem!" After all, consultants are supposed to see those obvious answers that have been staring others in the face all along.

Nadler does admit to having a healthy, perhaps even considerable, ego. It's a thrill to get a call from Washington asking you to come up with a solution that millions of dollars and thousands of staff-hours have failed to produce. It would be tempting to toss out an answer, any answer, to let them know that this time they've come to the guy who knows what's what.

Well, he'd been preaching to future industrial engineers and urban and regional planners in his university classes that they should always start a project by questioning the purposes of working on it. Didn't he have the courage of his convictions? He swallowed hard and said: "Maybe what we need first is a project to plan the project."

It certainly didn't sound like an impressive, expert response. In fact, it sounded rather evasive. The real effect, though, was to defuse an explosive situation. Nadler felt he had no business trying to out-expert people who had been studying the problem for years. Instead, he shifted attention from the problem of the gypsy moths to the problem of organizing the group to combat them.

The USDA's immediate problem, it turned out, was not the gypsy moth, but the disagreement among the people involved. The organization was deadlocked because of differences in the biases and perceptions of individuals. Nadler suspected that, though these people disagreed about details of the project, they would have much less trouble reaching a consensus about what the project was supposed to achieve.

He suggested that a starting point would be to convene representatives of the concerned groups and get them to focus not on the details of solving the pest problem, but only on the purposes of working on the problem. So, in July 1977, Nadler and his colleagues from Madison led a group of eighteen key people in a meeting to plan not the pest-management project itself, but a *system for planning the project.*

Disagreements were set aside temporarily as the group thought about the purposes of a project just for planning the larger project. On this subject, there were relatively few existing biases and differences. The group could think constructively about who would be involved in the planning effort, how much it might cost, and how long it would take. After only one day of discussion, the group had selected a planning committee and established a budget and schedule.

Several months later, the short-range project plan was carried out—a general meeting was held to begin the planning of the larger pest-management project. In attendance were twenty-two people representing federal and state agencies, private industry, and university research groups. Each participant came equipped with what the pop psychologists call "negative tapes"—complaints, defenses, and reasons for not participating.

It was apparent that they all wondered who these hotshots from Wisconsin were: "Who are they to tell us what to do?"

The task force participants continued to harbor all kinds of negative feelings toward each other: "Who are the feds to order the states around? Why do we need these peddlers who just want to push their own brands of chemicals? What does a university professor know about getting things done in the real world?"

As you might expect, the planning session was punctuated by heated arguments. The participants argued about levels of concentration of insecticide spray. They argued about timing mechanisms, biological cycles, and impacts on the ecosystem. But, each time bickering broke out, Nadler and his team steered the discussion toward the purposes of these decisions and measures. Attention turned to questions such as, What are we trying to accomplish with the spraying? What's the point of trying biological interventions? Why be concerned with environmental impacts?

On these points, there was much less argument. Discussing purposes was relatively easy to do; it threatened no one and turned attention away from points of controversy and toward common goals. In short, *people usually can agree about purposes.*

The task-force planning group held a series of meetings. The first two or three sessions began with the usual blood-letting, as factions insisted on raising old arguments and reasserting their respective positions. At each meeting, though, the participants seemed to need this catharsis less and less. Purposes began to direct the problem-solving process.

At the first meeting, the group agreed on an overall purpose for the pest-management program: Cope with gypsy moths at all levels of population. This focus was much different than the vague purpose that most people had in mind prior to the first Breakthrough Thinking meeting. People had previously "assumed" their purpose was to eradicate the pest. But the Breakthrough Thinking purposes discussion clearly showed that achieving eradication could lead to many other problems. The group identified ways that the effectiveness of the program could be measured, and even outlined what an ideal pest-management system would accomplish.

At the second meeting, discussion leaders noticed that some of the participants were quick to propose ways that the identified purposes could be carried out. They injected their own ideas about organizational structure and administration. These proposed details of solution just aggravated the old differences. The group was tending toward the political issues that had stalled the program in the first place.

To move the group in more constructive directions, the discussion leaders suggested concentrating on the functions—the planning purposes—of the proposals. The group was encouraged to reserve for later meetings the question of what person or agency would be responsible. Again, agreement on purposes was much easier; and a preliminary plan began to emerge. The group was able to rank the functions it had identified in order of priorities for planning.

By January 1978, the planning group had been able to define what the target system would do. The group was split into committees around each of the functions they'd identified in the planning meetings: operations planning, pest surveillance, environmental considerations, intervention, public communication, and so on.

In short, *successful problem solvers use a target solution as an effective guide in developing details of what others consider breakthroughs.* By this time, the group was working in a highly directed, coordinated way. While exploring the purposes of their work, they discovered their common interests. Essentially, they got into the habit of agreeing. At each point of agreement, positive feelings helped motivate the group toward the next step. In this sense, they began to behave as a truly organized body, rather than as a diverse collection of individuals.

This isn't the end of the story, just the beginning. The important thing is that it was a good beginning—one that eventually produced an effective, nationwide pest-management program. Coming into a confused and unfocused group effort, a few individuals helped it get organized by concentrating only on the *purposes* of solution, not on the problem itself. For the group, defining purposes and developing ideal solutions disclosed points of agreement, encouraged positive feelings, and created a sense of mission. Individuals within the group could see more clearly how they could contribute to a solution.

The idea of focusing on purposes and solutions-after-next isn't always popular, especially when a problem situation becomes urgent. If the members of a group feel that they're facing a crisis, there's a natural tendency to want to get on with it, to do something—anything—before it's too late. In this situation, someone who wants to talk about purposes and ideals can be seen at first as a troublemaker, someone who is standing in the way of progress.

At some time, you've probably been in a meeting that was called to deal with a crisis. The dynamics of the meeting might have been similar to those in the following story.

Not long ago, the tenants of an apartment building became alarmed about a number of break-ins that had been reported in their neighborhood. In one incident, a middle-aged man was killed with his own gun when he attempted to stop a burglar. Later that night, after the ambulance and the police had left, the tenants met to talk about what they could do to protect themselves.

At first, there was no real direction to the meeting. They took turns relating the facts that were known about the incident that night. Others related similar experiences, news items they'd read, close calls they'd had personally. Finally, somebody said, "Let's get on with this! What the hell are we gonna do?"

Of course, no one really knew. That's why they'd called the meeting. Most of them came expecting to be told what to do. No one had any answers, but there were plenty of opinions:

- "We wouldn't be here, you know, if the police would just enforce the law."
- "Yeah, they let criminals off too easy. None of 'em pay."
- "I think the police are doing what they can."
- "You can call the cops, but you could die waiting for them to get here."
- "That's just because people call them every time a dog knocks over a trash can."
- "Call the cops. That's all we can do."
- "No. We can get together and police this building ourselves."
- "Look, I'm all for taking action, but I can't spare much time for this."
- "Some of us here never take part. The same people run the block party every year. What ever happened to pitching in?"
- "Me and my brother can fight 'em. We ain't afraid of anybody."
- "What would we do if we came across somebody dangerous? We can't carry guns."
- "It's drugs. They're all high on drugs."

And so on.

Most of the comments were negative; many were complaints. Most of the people were angry, and it was natural to want to blame someone. The remarks that suggested action seemed poorly thought out. A sense of frustration began to build.

Finally, a young woman blurted, "Just why are we here? This is a waste of time."

It was a hostile remark. The woman was genuinely fed up. The meeting seemed pointless. Other people, who felt they were finally getting a chance to speak their minds, were offended. There was a stony silence from the group.

But the woman persisted, "I've heard a lot about what's wrong. I don't like it any more than you do. But nobody's told me why we're here."

To many in the group, the woman was just being obtuse. One man thought he'd put an end to her objections: "We're here to deal with criminals. It's about time."

The woman wouldn't give up. She genuinely questioned why she should be involved. Whether she knew it or not, she had taken the first step toward dealing effectively with the problem.

She lowered her voice and asked the belligerent man, "Do you really think that we can hope to deal with criminals?"

Someone else answered, "We're here to enforce the law!"

As far as the young woman was concerned, this wasn't an answer. "Can we enforce the law?" she asked.

The reply was, "The police are supposed to enforce the law."

From another corner of the room, a boy, probably not yet in his teens, offered, "We could help the police enforce the law."

The young woman looked hard at the boy. "Now *that* sounds like something we could work on."

The belligerent man confronted the young woman, as if, finding a purpose for the meeting, she now had responsibility for dealing with the problem.

"How can we help the police?" he asked.

At first, the woman's answer sounded as though she wanted to antagonize him. "I haven't the slightest idea," she said.

Then, she thought a moment, and continued: "Why don't we invite a police officer here? Let's ask him what kind of help they need." For the first time that night, she smiled a little. "If you want, I'll even make the call."

Not much later, the meeting broke up—after the tenants had agreed that they would meet again soon with a police officer. The purpose of their meeting, it turned out, had been to gain a purpose in working together. Eventually, they all agreed the purpose was to help the police enforce the law. Once that purpose was identified, the next step seemed obvious.

The young woman in this story didn't solve the problem. Quite naturally, and thinking perhaps only of her own busy schedule, she questioned why she should be involved in solving it at all. Instinctively, she turned the attention of the group to the *purpose* of the meeting. Members of the group resisted talking about purposes at first but eventually realized that a purpose was needed. And it was something on which they could all agree.

The idea that purposes are areas of potential agreement points toward ways that individuals can be effective in group efforts. This is a major advantage of thinking about purposes, but it's not the main reason for starting that way. Even when you're working on a problem by yourself, focusing first on purposes can increase your chances of success.

In other words, *defining the purposes of working on a problem ensures that you will apply your efforts in areas where you can have the greatest impact.*

Thinking about the purposes for working on a problem prevents wasted effort. This approach guarantees that you're not going to be working on something that won't meet your needs. Further, finding the right purpose greatly increases your chances of discovering a breakthrough or an innovative solution.

Finding the right purpose to work on involves thinking about purposes at different levels. For any problem there can be many purposes of solution.

Consider a relatively minor problem: finding a missing bicycle key. You buy a new, expensive bicycle. Since you've had the experience of having a bicycle stolen, you purchase a chain lock for securing the bicycle while it's unattended.

But a problem arises because you haven't made a habit of carrying the key with you and sometimes you forget it. You might say that your problem is to find a missing key. How could it be any more complicated than that?

Well, another, broader, purpose is found by asking, What's the *purpose* of finding the key? A purpose at this level might be to be able to use the bicycle. A series of continually larger purposes can be found by following this progression, asking the purpose of each purpose.

Another way of finding multiple purposes is to write down all the purposes you can think of, large and small. For the bicycle-key problem, you might come up with a list like this:

- Locate the (missing) bicycle key.
- Secure the bicycle.
- Get to school or work.
- Have the key available at all times.
- Use the bicycle.
- Get exercise.
- Keep track of the key.
- Have transportation.

Notice that some of these purposes are broader in scope than others. "Keep track of the key" is a smaller purpose than "have transportation." These different purposes can be arranged as a progression from small to large, from immediate to long-range, from minor to major. This ranking or ordering of purposes is called a *purpose hierarchy.* The reason to think in terms of purpose hierarchies is to find the level at which your efforts will produce the most effective results. Ranking the purposes above from small to large produces the following purpose hierarchy (see Figure 1-1).

One of the important differences among these levels of purposes has to do with the *number of ways* you can find for achieving them. If your purpose is "locate the (missing) bicycle key," you might get a mental picture of searching through desk drawers. One of the problems of working at this level is that the purpose implies that the key will *always* be missing.

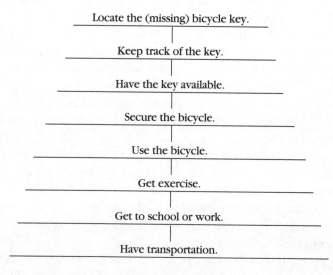

Locate the (missing) bicycle key.

Keep track of the key.

Have the key available.

Secure the bicycle.

Use the bicycle.

Get exercise.

Get to school or work.

Have transportation.

Figure 1-1.   Purpose hierarchy for finding a missing bicycle key.

Moving to a larger purpose level reveals a wider range of solutions. The purpose "have the key available at all times" suggests designating specific storage locations for the key. "Secure the bicycle" suggests alternate ways of parking the bicycle that don't necessarily involve keys. Even larger purposes, such as "get exercise," suggest many other solutions besides riding the bicycle such as swimming, jogging, playing tennis, and so on.

There is no single, correct purpose level for attacking this or any problem. But there is a level, usually larger than the first one, that addresses what really needs to be accomplished for a specific situation. This purpose level suggests a larger number of solutions, some of which may never have been considered in relation to the problem. These solutions represent *break-throughs.*

Coming up with a purpose hierarchy for the bicycle-key problem probably isn't necessary. You wouldn't need to think so methodically to come up with the idea of taking the bus instead. A more striking example might be called "The Case of the Slippery Packing Crates."

A national manufacturer of consumer goods made some major changes in its distribution methods. These changes represented an innovation in the way companies in that industry conduct their business. But the company didn't happen on this breakthrough overnight. It all started when its distributors complained that the company's warehouses were sending them damaged goods.

Company management called in an efficiency expert to investigate the problem. The expert immediately set about gathering statistics on warehouse operations. She studied the nature of the damage, the perishability of the product, the frequency of shipping delays, as well as labor hours and all aspects of distribution costs.

From her study, she concluded that the damage was occurring on the loading docks. Symptoms of inefficiency in this area included damaged crates, chronic delays in shipment, and excessive overtime.

To this efficiency expert, dealing with the problem came down to "fixing what's wrong" with the loading operation. Most of the symptoms had to do with manual labor on the shipping dock. Therefore, a sensible, straightforward approach seemed to be finding a way to automate the loading of trucks.

This expert's approach is typical of the way many people set out to solve a problem. In effect, they make a checklist of what's wrong. Then they go about fixing each item on the list. When they have checked off all the items, they declare the problem solved.

A pitfall of this approach is that you can rapidly become immersed in the details of solving a problem without really understanding either the nature of the problem or the reasons for solving it. In short, focusing on what's wrong ignores the purposes of solution. (This approach also requires the often incorrect assumption that something has to be wrong with the present situation, as in locating a "missing" key.)

Although she never gave it much thought, the expert assumed the purpose of the loading dock was essentially this: Find an efficient way to load trucks. With this starting point, the solution seemed obvious: Automate the loading docks.

The expert, then, came up with an ingenious way to install computer-controlled conveyors for loading trucks. The system she designed would cost about $60,000 per warehouse location, and she estimated that the resulting savings would pay for the new equipment in about eight months.

For major business investments, a very favorable payback period, or time to recoup an investment, is one year or less. A payback period of eight months would be seen as an exceptional opportunity. Feeling that she had an excellent solution, the expert eagerly presented her recommendations to the company's vice-president of operations.

The cost of refitting each warehouse was relatively modest for such a large company. But it owned twenty-four warehouses. Thus, the total commitment for all their warehouses was a $1.44 million decision, one which also could displace hundreds of workers.

Since the company also had staff engineers, there had been little justification for calling in an outside expert. But there's a certain mystique about outside consultants—heavy hitters. The vice-president was inclined to respect the expert's recommendations, but largely for the sake of good politics, he turned to the internal group for a second opinion.

The internal industrial engineering group assigned one of its younger staff members the job of verifying the expert's report. Since no one expected to match the favorable return offered by the expert's plan, the assignment was made almost randomly.

The staff engineer who was assigned to the project was a recent college graduate who had little experience with the company—much less in shipping and materials handling. Undaunted by the expert's opinion, however, the staff engineer took on the job enthusiastically. Here was a chance for visibility at the highest management levels, even if in the end he might rubber-stamp the expert's findings.

The young engineer had little to draw upon except for his previous course work in industrial planning and design. These courses had emphasized purpose-directed problem solving. He therefore ignored most of the fact finding in the expert's report and looked first at the purpose it implied.

To the staff engineer, the purpose "to load trucks" seemed to be one of the smaller identifiable purposes. What is the purpose of loading trucks? That purpose, he reasoned, might be to consolidate shipments to dealers. And the purpose of consolidation might be to transport products to dealers. This line of reasoning proceeded through a number of larger purposes up to the major purpose: distribute company products to the marketplace.

Of the relatively few options available for loading trucks, it seemed that the expert had discovered one of the better ones. But was automating the loading docks the best way of *distributing the company's products to the marketplace?*

Once this larger purpose was identified, the range of choices was much broader. Still larger purposes, such as providing useful products to consumers, were probably too big to be addressed by the study. Yet finding alternatives at the distribution level might be productive.

You don't have to know much more about the young engineer's approach to see how his eventual conclusion grew directly from examining these larger purposes. When his study was completed, he asked to meet with the vice-president.

When the day of the presentation finally came, the young man was confronted by a roomful of executives, including the top managers of distribution and engineering. After some cursory introductions, the vice-president was blunt: "Well, do we go ahead and spend this money?"

The young engineer was on the spot for the first time in his career. The stakes were awfully high if he were wrong. He could barely get the words out. "No, sir," he said.

Startled, some of the participants began murmuring among themselves. Well, the young man reasoned, at least I've won their attention.

The vice-president wanted the bottom line, and quickly. "You've got another way to automate those docks?"

"No," the young man said.

Even as a child, he'd been taught always to speak up, to make all his mistakes in a loud, confident voice. Well, here goes, he thought.

Boldly, he declared, "I think you should sell the warehouses."

His plan, it turned out, was not exactly to sell all the warehouses. He proposed that the company maintain a few regional warehouses, each to be stocked by air shipment directly from the company's manufacturing plants. Eliminating local warehouses would simplify freight transfers so there would be fewer physical handling points for each shipment, more direct and rapid deliveries, and lower inventory levels in the field.

In response to these recommendations of a "solution-after-next," and after considering many other alternatives, the company finally sold twenty of its warehouses, retaining four as regional shipping depots. To avoid firing anyone, alternative employment was found for workers who were displaced by the decision. Most of the company's inventory was maintained at plant locations, and stocking levels were reduced because of the increased efficiency of the new nationwide distribution system. The original problem of damaged goods was resolved by eliminating physical handling steps, not through automation.

The actual savings to the company was hundreds of millions of dollars per year, and the improvements in its effectiveness as an organization were immeasurable. Eventually, its competitors had to restructure along the same lines or face going out of business.

The lesson of this story lies not in the cleverness of the young engineer's solution but in the opportunities that were opened up by the way he *approached* the project. If, instead, he had merely focused on better ways of loading trucks, he might never have considered alternative distribution methods.

The key to innovation in this case—and the engineer's real creativity—came in the initial phase of working on the problem. In this critical phase, he found a purpose level—a position within a purpose hierarchy—to guide the rest of the work. This was the level that held the most promise for realizing a genuine breakthrough.

Finding the "right" purpose to work on doesn't guarantee finding a breakthrough. But it certainly helps the odds. Just knowing that you're working on an effective level, toward a worthwhile purpose, toward a larger meaning in life, can also increase your confidence in approaching a problem.

With this confidence comes a genuine power of positive thinking. This power does not necessarily proceed from strength of will or exceptional motivation. It's just a natural consequence of knowing you're on the right track.

The examples in this chapter illustrate how *purposes* can direct your search toward truly useful solutions. You can also begin to see why organizations have trouble approaching problems. Initially, it takes an individual to encourage a group of people to agree first about *purposes.* Having a common purpose, people begin to feel less isolated and alone.

As purposes emerge, the group can organize itself around them. Arranging these purposes in a hierarchy, from smaller to larger, opens ranges of options, possibly including some real innovations. Working at larger levels of purpose increases the chances for breakthrough and maximizes your effectiveness in dealing with the problem.

Other lessons can be drawn from such success stories. These lessons represent the seven principles of Breakthrough Thinking that are advanced in this book:

1. The most effective problem solvers do not begin by trying to find out what has worked before for someone else; they don't try to clone someone else's solution and impose it on a different situation. They don't initially assume that the

same techniques can be applied successfully to apparently "similar" but inherently different problems.

The first principle, then, is that *each problem (and each part of the process in any problem-solving project) initially should be regarded as unique*. The people involved are always different, the purposes to be achieved are almost always different, and the technology available for a solution may very well be much better in the present moment.

2. The second principle calls for being directed by *purposes* and the context of larger purposes. Several studies show that the quality of such solutions is significantly better than the results from conventional approaches.

3. The third principle states that having an *ideal target solution* for achieving your purpose can lead to innovative solutions and help guide the development of the actual change you will make.

4. Another principle, the fourth, is that problems don't exist in isolation. Each problem is embedded within other problems, and a solution for one needs careful *specification in systems terms* to make it workable in relation to other problems and solutions.

5. In approaching a problem, a great deal of time and effort can be saved by not collecting a lot of information and by not reviewing all the studies that have already been done. The fifth principle asserts that, at the outset, it is actually better to *limit what you know* about a problem. People, even experts, are better able to cope with incomplete and soft data; effective problem solvers know that there is really no such thing as "hard data."

6. As the pest-management case demonstrates, people who may disagree can join in dealing with a problem effectively by focusing initially on purposes. Outstanding problem solvers are *diverse people who seek many different sources of information* in their problem-solving efforts. This is the basis of the sixth principle.

7. The seventh principle refutes the conventional wisdom that you shouldn't fix something if it isn't broken. For a solution to be effective, it has to be *maintained and upgraded continually* toward the target. Even the target needs to be updated regularly. You've got to keep improving a situation or thing to prevent it from breaking down due to entropy, the normal wear and tear of events.

Many people already use one or more of these principles. You may find that some of the principles describe intuitions or commonsense practices that you've already used successfully.

This shouldn't be surprising, since the principles of Breakthrough Thinking are generalizations about effective behavior. But without some means of *coordination,* applying only a few of these principles is like entering your car in a race without tuning its engine. You have the freedom of mind to make the choice to improve yourself and to improve others around you.

Truly creative and productive power can come from applying *all the principles, consistently and in coordination,* to every problem that you encounter. Focusing on them all, rather than on finding out what's wrong or who to blame (almost always a sure formula for decline) is often the critical difference. We call such an approach "expantegration"—expand purposes, solution ideas, target, and interconnectedness in a system that leads to an integration of details and implementation of a solution at the largest possible purpose level.

Harnessing this power is something that you can do personally. It can be an astounding discovery that, initially, organizations can't tackle problems. The thinking power of an individual—you—is needed to galvanize a group to meaningful action. You can also use the power of Breakthrough Thinking to "go for it" on issues, dreams, and problems you face individually. The principles and process of Breakthrough Thinking provide you the competence to focus your intelligence, coordinate your efforts, involve others effectively, and identify meaning in all situations; and, yes, the courage, integrity, and persistence to proceed effectively.

Helping you increase your personal effectiveness in individual and group situations—on the job, at school, at home, in your community—is a major goal of this book. Being effective is never simply a matter of luck. Applying the seven principles of Breakthrough Thinking in a deliberate approach or process that ties together thinking and accomplishment should help you accomplish the following goals:

- Maximize the effectiveness of your recommendations (the breakthrough of "ah-ha!" realizations and significantly better results).

- Maximize the likelihood that your recommendations will be accepted and implemented (the breakthrough of getting good ideas used).

- Maximize the effectiveness of the resources you apply to the problem (the breakthough of minimizing the time and money spent achieving the first two breakthroughs).

As background for presenting in detail the principles of Breakthrough Thinking, Chapters 2 and 3 will help you identify conventional attitudes, assumptions, and techniques that might prevent you from being truly effective. For example, you should get used to the idea that one problem leads inevitably to another. You will either drive, or be driven by, this engine of change.

Chapter 2

Problems Beget Problems (and That's Good)

*N*ot long ago, the World Future Society listed "2,653 problems facing humanity." The list ranged from nuclear war to art forgeries. In 1991, the Union of International Associations issued the third edition of its two-volume *Encyclopedia of World Problems and Human Potential*, replete with 13,000 "world problems" ranging from incompetence to deforestation.

These catalogs were enlightening. But in relation to individuals and groups, rather than "humanity," they hardly scratched the surface. The gamut of problems faced by each individual is virtually infinite.

We tend to think of problems as rocks on an otherwise smooth pathway of life, but the fact is that problems are the *rule* rather than the *exception*. That is because problems are not things, like monkey wrenches and graham crackers; *problems are reflections of states of mind.*

A problem, in its simplest definition, is a condition or set of circumstances that a person or group *thinks* should be changed. Problems are the product of human dissatisfactions and aspirations, including the 2,653 or 13,000 "big" ones.

Because dissatisfactions and aspirations are the driving force of life, consequent problems are innumerable and endless. In solving one, we in effect step through a portal to a landscape that is altered, however minutely. And there another array of problems awaits.

Consider, for example, the wonderful solutions devised for problems of transportation (airplanes), entertainment (movies and television), personal relationships (divorce), communications (satellites), and information handling (computers). Each of these has caused many other new problems.

Obviously, we need an effective way to consider the long-term impact of any solution we may implement. We need a process that ensures that emerging technologies are better suited to achieving human happiness, both in the present and in the future. We need to minimize the negative impact of human advancement by emphasizing the substance of human purposes.

The roots of problems in human dissatisfactions and aspirations are both *subjective* and *relative*. To a man who takes pride in his lawn, crabgrass may constitute a *problem*; his neighbor may not be bothered by crabgrass at all. But if the first man's house catches fire, the crabgrass instantly loses dimension as a problem. Londoners' lamentations early in World War II about shortages of butter and meat were quickly displaced when bombs started falling. Then the big problem became survival.

This is not to say that problems are only a matter of *perception*. Many are intensely tangible—a flat tire, a dread disease, an erupting volcano, a military attack.

But how we look at any problem, how we consider it, plainly is a mental process, and a crucial one.

Numerous books have been written propounding solutions to various problems. The trouble is that problems occur in infinite and unpredictable variety, and the solution to one is rarely applicable to another.

What's the solution to *that* problem?

The great mathematicians of history did not try to catalog answers to every problem. Rather, they expanded the purposes to be achieved and then devised equations and formulas applicable to countless problems. A homely expansionary analog was the wise man's aphorism: "Give a hungry man a fish, and you've given him a meal. Teach him how to fish, and you've given him a living."

In other words, it's the *process* that is paramount. How we look at any problem shapes the way we deal with it.

The premise of Breakthrough Thinking is that how we approach an individual problem or a problem facing humanity, how we come to grips with it, determines whether we will end up with a thoroughly successful solution, an indifferent result, or possibly bigger trouble. A poor solution may leave you with multiple problems in place of the original one. Almost always, the search for a quick fix is a recipe for disaster, leading to even more disasters with still other quick fixes.

Areas of Problems

Although attempting even to enumerate *types* of problems a person may encounter would be an endless exercise, it may be helpful to note some of the major areas in which problems arise. They are major problem areas because each reflects a basic purpose a particular person seeks to achieve. Based on his or her work and interests, a given person will spend more time dealing with one purpose or problem area than with others, but all of us deal with all of them at some point almost every day.

We all deal every day with problems of *survival*, if only to the extent of securing food, clothing, and shelter. Survival may involve anything from an infected finger to the loss of a job.

Then there are problems of *operation and supervision.* Again, everyone engages in these in one way or another. Parents operate and supervise a system called a family. A student operates a study schedule. A mayor oversees the operation of a city.

Professionals tag a vast field of problems with the umbrella label of *planning and design,* which may involve anything from creating the logo on a cereal box to restructuring the plumbing concepts for the city of tomorrow. Obviously, a wide array of specialists—engineers, architects, urban planners, business strategists, and even doctors and travel agents—create or restructure systems or plans. The common thread running through their activities is the exercise of imagination, vision, and ingenuity to arrive at a specific solution. Each of us does planning and design (encompassing all sixteen definitions of "design" that appear in the *Oxford English Dictionary*) whenever we seek to create or restructure anything we are dissatisfied with or aspire to—a vacation, the layout of our kitchen, the traffic flow in the neighborhood, our personal finances.

Another large problem area is *research*. One doesn't have to be a scholar to develop a generalization or collect data about some concern. It may be as simple a matter as trying out different fertilizers for a lawn or discovering which foods affect your allergy. Research is the attempt to satisfy our curiosity about the *why* of some phenomenon—why refrigerators cool and furnaces heat, why earthquakes occur.

There are problems of *evaluation*—weighing pros and cons of how well a previously selected course of action worked out—whether such problems concern a judge's determining how well previous decisions about damages in law suits have fit the objectives of jurisprudence, or a corporate executive's assessing how well the company has done in choosing among alternative factory sites. Ultimately, everyone gets into evaluation because, as we shall see, assessing how well a solution has met the original objective is an essential step in all intelligent problem solving.

Then there is *learning,* the problem of gaining skills or acquiring knowledge. Civilization would be in sad shape indeed if everyone were forced to do original research or obtain personal experience to rediscover all the knowledge and skills previously developed. Solving problems depends on you and others who are prepared with appropriate information and basic knowledge. But effective learning is a problem area all people realize needs new solutions.

Finally, in this overview of problem-land and the purposes we seek to achieve, comes the ultimate category: problems of *achieving personal satisfaction*—use of leisure time, a choice of career paths, a decision about marriage, and so on.

In all of these major areas of problems and purposes, or human activities, the principles of Breakthrough Thinking can be applied to advantage. At the very least, each problem that appears—late delivery of parts for the assembly operation, performance appraisal of employees, the storage arrangement in your kitchen, your need to know the latest about sensors for robots, the poor grades on your daughter's report card—can be explored initially by the experts' approach: What's the *purpose* of working on the problem?

Probably the simplest problem is typified by a jigsaw puzzle. Doing one is largely a matter of trial and error, an exercise even young children can perform.

Unfortunately, the trial-and-error method is applied too often to complex problems that call for a reasoned approach. We have an atavistic urge—perhaps inherited from cavemen's confrontations with animals—to lunge at a problem and grab the first solution that comes to mind. When that doesn't work, we try another and another, and we often wind up in confusion and frustration. Since most problems have a number of possible solutions, the odds of hitting the optimal one on the first stab simply are not good.

For example, people in a select residential development in the Midwest were troubled by the number of auto accidents where their exiting cars made a right turn onto a divided highway. Some residents proposed that a YIELD sign be put up to slow down right-turners. Authorities obliged, but the sign was up only briefly before another faction in the community complained. There was so little traffic on the divided thoroughfare, they said, that it was those drivers who should be admonished to yield.

The controversy may still be going on. The point is that the obvious solution had only created more problems. A traffic problem remained; the community had been split; and relations with local authorities, beset by conflicting demands, certainly had not been improved.

In this situation, some principles of Breakthrough Thinking would have been useful: first, not assuming that the problem was a simple one susceptible to a cut-and-dried answer used in other cases; second, visualizing the problem-beyond-the-problem; and finally, realizing that the problem was not simply logistical but involved people, all of whom had to be considered and whose interests had to be meshed into a viable solution.

The Track Record on Problems

Before going on to look at the individual principles of Breakthrough Thinking in detail in subsequent chapters, it seems worthwhile to take a stroll through our Chamber of Horrors—the contemporary gallery of poor problem solving that Breakthrough Thinking is designed to avert.

THE POLITICAL AND GOVERNMENTAL HORRORS

We couldn't get along without politics and government. But they are the great graveyards of misbegotten problem solving, which is probably why they are perpetual centers of controversy. This is partly inherent and inescapable, but it is also to a significant degree remediable.

Politics and government revolve around the art of compromise, the reconciliation of conflicting interests. Harmonizing diverse interests usually means that instead of adopting a course of action that any single party has envisioned as ideal, reaching an acceptable composite of ideas is the goal. Sometimes this is the optimal solution to a problem, such as a piece of legislation, considering that if all parties are not accommodated, only a stalemate may result.

In the process of give-and-take, however, some basic Breakthrough Thinking principles often get lost in the shuffle. For instance, the concept that every problem is *unique* and must be treated without preconceptions annoys precedent-minded bureaucrats and politicians who are anxious for time-tested solutions that will avert criticism.

Ignoring the uniqueness principle is a major reason why many problems ensue from a solution that is supposed to eliminate a problem. Typically, a law is passed to address the problem *in general,* but the various unique aspects of the problem are treated improperly or negatively, giving rise to many new problems. Or a bureaucrat sets up a system (for example, a telephone hotline for the homeless) that creates more problems (in this case, because the homeless do not have telephones or money for calls).

Also often lost in the shuffle is the vital element of *purposes*—familiarly known as keeping one's eye on the ball.

A classic case of mislaid purposes leading to many new problems was the U.S. Federal Tax Reform Act of 1986. One original purpose was to simplify the Federal Tax Code and the forms taxpayers had to fill out; another was to redistribute the tax burden more equitably according to people's ability to pay.

Yet after countless months of congressional study, debate, and legislative horse-trading, what emerged was, first, a so-called tax guide numbering over 2,000 pages, which even experts were at a loss to digest; and, second, a rejiggered tax schedule that had many middle-income people paying more than they had before, while many upper-income people paid less. Congress, accordingly, found itself confronted with a whole new basketful of problems with which it will be grappling for years, hopefully with a keener eye on *purpose.*

With its 535 members, Congress probably represents the ultimate in management-by-committee; and as we all know, the efficiency of committees varies inversely with their size. Democratic government is not efficient, but Congress could reduce its own inefficiency by attending to the Breakthrough Thinking principles of uniqueness, purposes, solution-after-next, and systems.

Government is further handicapped in making optimal decisions for several chronic reasons. Among these, government is operated mainly by bureaucrats, and bureaucrats' classic criterion in decision making is not fulfillment of project or organizational (legal) purposes but rather the protection of their jobs. In this, they have good role models: Senators and representatives too often seek to maintain their seats rather than accomplish national purposes.

Government's propensity, when confronted with a problem, is to take one of two courses: throw money at the problem (most outlays being dispersed among so many taxpayers as to incur minimum visibility) or appoint a commission to study the problem.

Commissions seldom are authorized to do anything more than make a report. Compiling a report is essentially a fact-gathering operation, and most reports quickly confront the Breakthrough Thinking principle that excessive data collection tends to obstruct rather than facilitate problem solutions. Reports often are shelved, unread and not acted upon, because the report's focus was on massive information collection, no doubt to show how erudite the committee was. By the time the report is completed, everyone concerned is preoccupied with newer problems and more data collection.

Even the activist Clinton-Gore administration is unlikely to get much accomplished in their effort to "reinvent government" since their 1993 report on the subject provides only data and freeze-dried, canned, pre-packaged "solutions." It does not offer a *process of reasoning* designed to get people involved, identify critical purposes, and develop target solutions-after-next. Nor does it recognize that the implementation of even the best of ideas is, in itself, a critical problem that needs to be addressed.

Does this mean that Breakthrough Thinking has no place in government? Far from it. The worthwhile accomplishments of government usually can be traced to individuals who instinctively applied Breakthrough Thinking precepts in courageous defiance of bureaucratic inertia or who called in Breakthrough Thinking facilitators, as was done in the gypsy moth pest-management case.

A bureaucratic whistle-blower will come out of the woodwork and point out several problems because some egregious activity does not accomplish the desired purpose. A commission member will break ranks and leak findings that Congress or the executive branch cannot ignore. A member of Congress will establish a Golden Fleece award for ridiculous governmental expenditures. On rare occasions, an appointee will step forward and suggest that his or her job has lost its originally conceived purpose and should be abolished.

All of these are are heartening testaments to the fact that even the corridors of government are not closed to Breakthrough Thinking.

THE BUSINESS HORROR

Business in its multifarious forms is every nation's most pervasive activity. And while business regularly trumpets its admittedly impressive achievements, its record is perpetually speckled with faulty decision making. One good summary of the factors involved in and the problems characteristic of "the accelerating American decline" is included in Tom Peters's *Thriving On Chaos*.[1] Moreover, recent studies show that corporate bureaucrats and executives use the same decision-making criterion as government bureaucrats—protection of their jobs, not achievement of project or organizational purposes.

Corporate catastrophes that drew much attention in recent years were the Edsel automobile and the "new" Coca Cola. But these are only two of an unending series of misjudgments that constitute a jarring obbligato to business's annals of accomplishment.

Mobil Oil stubbed its toe when, trying to diversify, it took over the Montgomery Ward mail-order house, only to jettison it after a few years. Tenneco, the energy company, went into large-scale farming to its regret. Honda mistakenly assumed a combination with the famous British automobile heritage in its Sterling car would be successful. Exxon, the oil company, made an ill-starred foray into electronics and showed poor operational control in the Valdez–Prince William Sound oil-spill catastrophe. Japanese companies, such as Eidai Industry, Saseho Heavy Industry Corporation, and Yashika, went bankrupt because they did not maintain a flexible mode of operation and were unable to meet the structural changes in their industry in Japan. Both Pan American Airways and Eastern Airlines were for decades highly successful companies in commercial aviation. Both were pioneers in the field—Pan Am the leading international, long-haul airline and Eastern the leading innovator of short, frequent commuter shuttle flights. Despite their early triumphs, both went bankrupt in the 1980s. Giant IBM became involved in collateral activities like publishing and communications, which it was impelled to unload. Lately IBM has come to be considered more a pathetic, hamstrung, self-defeating giant than the trend-setting, industry leader and creator it was considered only 20 years ago.

Some long-term mistakes have been even more spectacular. The railroad industry in the United States lulled itself into near oblivion. Large segments of the television manufacturing and office equipment industries became so ingrown they soon found themselves outgrown by overseas competitors.

The country in which a company is located does not mean mistakes are not made. Problems keep arising in businesses, but companies reduce their risk by keeping *customers' needs* in the forefront. That is one reason why Japanese auto companies are so successful compared to U.S. companies. One Japanese company, for example, risks spending money to help its customers by building twelve prototype cars, compared to one prototype in a U.S. company. The Japanese can almost literally "try out" different cars for their customers. A U.S. company, by contrast, spends its money on market research (vast data collection) and *assumes* it then knows what the customer wants.

Through these and countless other corporate mishaps runs a common thread: disregard of some fundamental principles of problem solving that are epitomized in Breakthrough Thinking.

In the Edsel and Coca Cola cases, there was evidence of misguidance by a plethora of *information,* which turned out to obscure pertinent facts. Both companies relied heavily on consumer surveys that asked the wrong questions or inadequately evaluated the validity of responses. Although the products depended wholly on public acceptance, the involvement of people and their feelings in the effective solution of product development problems was underestimated and misassessed.

The spasm of incongruous corporate acquisitions during the late 1970s and 1980s was likewise characterized by the failure of companies to accurately perceive the *problems* and define the *purposes* of their moves.

The American railroad industry's big mistake was clinging for more than a century to the notion that its mission began and ended with the technology of moving trains from here to there. It didn't realize that the world had moved on, that what had once been an engineering achievement was now taken for granted, and that the industry's modern challenge was competing for customers in the transportation market.

Detroit misconceived its role as catering to supposed public whims about automobile appearance, when the real demand was for technical excellence. Moreover, the industry's big mistake lay not merely in falling behind Japan and other foreign countries in producing high-quality cars, but in losing sight of customers' needs and purposes, thus failing to perceive how times had changed the industry's *purpose*: creating and providing a privately produced public utility, namely transportation, with its specific emphasis on *quality, cost,* and *reliability.*

For example, Ford Motor prospered in the mid-1980s, the time that the company introduced its Taurus and Sable cars and increased its market share from 14 percent in 1985 to 38 percent in 1991. Yet Ford failed to reinvest its huge profits in new models as a means of continual improvement (required by the solution-after-next and betterment timeline principles of Breakthrough Thinking) so that its competitors would have to keep up with an advancing target. Worse yet, the investments that Ford did make in diversification are already creating huge losses. This cultural disease, apparently endemic to the U.S. business community, is repeated far too often.

THE PERSONAL HORROR

Each of us is involved in governmental and business (or organizational) problems because each of us is a citizen and an employee in or customer of an organization. Although it is up to us to take a Breakthrough Thinking role in these organizational problems, the problems that may prey most on our minds are personal.

Statistics about personal problems in the United States show that we are not solving many of them well: The nearly 50-percent divorce rate says individuals are unable to work out relationship problems; the large personal-debt level and low savings rate per capita is a commentary on people's inability to handle their financial affairs; the high death rate due to heart attacks and the high percentage of overweight people reflect an unwillingness to recognize optimal life-styles. Indeed, the rapidly growing number of cases of psychological depression, anxiety, and stress may represent a less-than-stable working environment throughout the United States. Whatever label you may choose for such manifestations of personal and societal failure, they are all problems in need of solution.

Each person faces innumerable less momentous but still nontrivial daily problems. Consider the dropped contact lens, grocery shopping expedition, argument with a spouse, poor school grades, decisions about job offers, vacation plans, housing costs versus commuting time, your daughter's wedding plans, or a broken fence between your and your neighbor's houses.

How you approach finding solutions for these problems affects your sense of well-being and your ability to contribute to the situation. Most people do not give any thought to their approach to such problems, letting their emotions and intuition direct their attempts to solve them. When an individual does ask *how* to go about solving one of these problems, the response is almost always to gather facts, jump to an answer, follow our emotions, maintain our power and position, analyze and subdivide, or do what someone else did.

All this occurs without any reference to the specific principles and process of reasoning designed to answer the question of "how." Exactly *how* do you "stop fighting for your own point of view" or "separate what the two of you can talk about from the things that are too hot to handle" or "treat the other person with respect"? These are all worthwhile goals, but they are usually suggested without any specific framework for pursuing them.

For example, find the contact lens right now (considering purposes might lead you to use your spare until you have time later to look for the lost lens). Or go to the store and buy what you need when you see it (the principles of uniqueness and systems might suggest a list in the order of the aisles). Keep arguing with your spouse to establish who can win (consideration of purposes might show you that the topic isn't worth the emotional drain). Mete out punishment until the grades improve (the principles of uniqueness, purposes, solution- after-next, people design, and betterment timeline might help you develop a study plan your child would "own" and "buy into"). Decide whether or not to take the new job based only on consideration of pay or location or title (the purposes, solution-after-next, systems, and betterment timeline principles might lead to a different decision or to a better understanding of why the initial decision was appropriate). And so on.

Conventional approaches to such problems lead to untold difficulties and traumas. Ineffective solutions also take their toll on the individual in the workplace, not only because of the depression brought on by the effects of a poor answer, but also because the same limited thinking process for solving problems is continued on the job. The conventional way organizations (and governments) solve problems reinforces this behavior—and the problems persist in more or less their original state.

The Track Record on Problem Solving

The horrors that we have related are really only the few most easily recountable. Far more pernicious are the huge number of problem-solving results that are not as effective, thorough, wide-ranging, or long-lasting as they could have been.

Perhaps a problem is solved with, say, a 15 percent increase in productivity, with the two opposing sides in a dispute not fighting, or with the emergence of a new product onto the market. The sad truth, however, is that productivity could have been improved by 40 percent, the opposing sides could have agreed to collaborate on new directions, and the new product could have had many more competitive advantages if only these problems had been approached differently. Unfortunately, we have not had an impressive track record in making optimal decisions.

A century ago, American industry was captivated by "Taylorism," the teachings of Frederick W. Taylor. He carried the Industrial Revolution a major step further by prescribing methods of subdividing production processes into minimal skills, with a major emphasis on management control. His developments occurred as part of the dominant tradition of Western thought, which has three premises: all questions have one true answer, all those answers can be found, and all the answers comprise a compatible whole.

Taylor's approach improved productivity and organizational performance—especially in relation to labor costs—for more than half a century. But, in an age of increasingly complex processes, global competitiveness, greatly elevated educational levels (in the United States in the 1980s, college graduates increased from 21 to 26 percent of the workforce, and those with high-school diplomas rose from 76 to 85 percent), and better living standards dependent on higher wages, Taylorism has outlived its usefulness. Yet many enterprises still cling to its rigid fragmentation.

In the rigorous economic conditions of the 1990s, Taylorism has been extended to part-time or temporary organizations that operate in a so-called "efficiency mode" by avoiding the cost of paying benefits to permanent and full-time employees. "Rent-an-accountant," "rent-an-executive," "rent-a-nurse," or "rent-an-engineer" may reduce costs to an organization, but such reductions are acquired at the cost of diminished organizational products or services and less customer commitment.

Taylor's analytic, numerical approach is geared to short-term solutions that appeal to the executive mentality preoccupied with the next quarter's profit figures yet short-change the more important long term. Moreover, the resulting rigidity in work methods and the separation of management and labor into adversarial camps are major factors in the loss of competitiveness in the United States. For example, until the 1970s, almost all companies assumed it was critical to keep workers and unions out of company decision making. The competitive advantages of labor-management collaboration were lost in the scuffling.

Taylorism gave rise to the label of *scientific management.* But if you follow so-called scientific orthodoxy, dictating that problems are to be subdivided, analyzed, and reduced to their smallest components, you are going to get results that are small, detailed, and not reflective of human capabilities. Although Taylorism was pertinent in its time, the thinking perspectives and concepts of that approach (what we call the "paradigm of thinking" in our book *Conceptual Problem Solving*) are a major cause of our ineffective problem solving today. Indeed, Isaiah Berlin has called such thought processes fallacious and dangerous.[2]

The late industrialist Kounosuke Matsushita, contrasting American corporate malaise with the Japanese economic climate, which remains more vigorous even today, after the "bubble-burst" of the early 1990s, summarized: "Your American firms are built on the Taylor model. Even worse, so are your heads."[3]

The exceptionally successful Japanese company that Matsushita headed (Panasonic) long since subordinated profits as the primary objective in favor of a broader set of standards. These include concern about whether the company's activities serve to improve living standards and the general welfare of society.

Many American business leaders would scoff at such lofty goals as endangering profits or their jobs. But ironically many foreign firms, by shifting attention from short-term profit figures to such elements as sales growth, market share, and employee satisfaction, have enhanced the prices of their stocks more than most American companies.

The recent downturn in the Japanese economy, for example, did in fact significantly reduce the profits of Japanese companies. However, buoyed by the strong yen, these companies still showed fairly reasonable profits. By contrast, U.S. companies (especially automobile manufacturers) showed record-breaking losses when economic adversity struck them in the late 1980s and early 1990s. Improvement in the world economy, which is bound to occur soon, will put Japanese companies back into the very profitable position they previously enjoyed.

Management expert Peter Drucker is reported to have said, "Companies in this country don't maximize profits—they maximize profit *statements.*"[4]

It's a question, says Dr. Drucker's colleague Richard Ellsworth, of how companies define the *purpose* of their existence. In the United States, the dominant objective is serving shareholders. In Japan and elsewhere, the main consideration is serving customers and employees.

This raises the question of the stockholders' purpose. Is it simply to earn an immediate return on investment? Or is it rather to maintain the stability of capital and foster new products and services to keep ahead of the market? If it is the latter purpose, companies concerned with long-term growth clearly serve stockholders best. Preoccupation with short-term profit figures, by contrast, encourages the quick fixes that beget more problems rather than enduring solutions.

Some short-term, quick-fix, panic-button moves are personnel and organizational shakeups, which may accomplish nothing if a system is faulty; throwing money at a problem through ill-considered expansion of facilities or product lines; grasping at gadgetry like automation, computers, and robots (which can have no ideas their proprietors don't); and seizing upon Japanese or other foreign modalities that may not fit the problem at hand. Instead, decision makers should be backing off and determining exactly what the problem is.

Nothing illustrates the "problems beget problems" concept better than two major historical events in the early years of the current decade: the collapse of Soviet communism in 1990 and the Israeli-Palestinian peace agreement of 1993. In their respective arenas, both events represented the "ideal" solutions that Western democracies had been seeking for more than half a century.

Although the approaches followed during those many years of problem-solving effort left much to be desired, based as they were primarily on conventional thinking, the goals and fundamental structure of the solution needed had, in both cases, long been identified. And yet, when the desired end was finally achieved, the quantity of problems (albeit "smaller" in nature) that arose was amazing.

For example, in the case of communism in the Soviet Union and Eastern Europe, resulting problems included the dissolution of Yugoslavia into warring national and religious factions in Serbia, Croatia, and Bosnia-Herzegovina; similar battles between Azerbaijanis and Armenians in the former Soviet Union; and the less-than-entirely cordial reunification of the two Germanys, leading to social and economic tensions that have yet to be effectively resolved.

In the case of the peace agreement between Israel and the Palestine Liberation Organization, new problems include opposition to the agreement by orthodox Jewish settlers on the West Bank of the River Jordan, continuing conflict between Jews and adherents of Hamas and other Islamic fundamentalist groups, and shifting power and security equations between Israel and non-Palestinian Arab nations in the Middle East.

Similar to the constantly fluctuating situations in any organization, family, or society, these geopolitical illustrations demonstrate why even an apparently ideal solution that is actually implemented must include a solution-after-next target to help guide the continuing change that is certain to occur. A Breakthrough Thinking betterment timeline both revises the target every few years and often installs additional, new changes to improve continuously the solution that is currently being used.

These principles apply to business as much as they do to international politics. Nadler was once asked to design a new manufacturing facility that would double a factory's space. But when he asked company executives about the *purpose* of such expansion, they realized that larger purposes were (1) to devise facilities to meet customer requirements by (2) providing space for movement of material and personnel according to (3) a reorganized management control system. Thus, an adequate solution to the problem turned out to have far more ramifications than would have been dealt with by merely tacking on some bricks, mortar, and machinery. The doubling of space proved irrelevant.

We were once asked by a company to evaluate the effectiveness of its 1,300 air conditioner and furnace service centers around the country. The cut-and-dried approach would have produced an answer that on a scale of 100, the service centers scored 65, perhaps because of poor locations, inadequate employee training, sloppy cost controls, or what not.

But looking at the question with the Breakthrough Thinking focus on *purposes* from smaller to larger, the problem became a multilevel one:

1. Provide data about service centers.
2. Determine methods of assessing effectiveness.
3. Apply measurements of effectiveness.

4. Devise methods of improving center performance.

5. Develop appropriate service center procedures.

6. Style service to customers' wants.

7. Arrange for customers' long-term material supply requirements.

In other words, a bottom-line score would have been
meaningless without reference to contributing elements. So
what had started out as an apparent problem in *evaluation*
(levels 1 and 2) turned out to be actually a problem in *planning and design* (levels 5 and 6). Developing Breakthrough
Thinking procedures and service for customers provided a
long-range guide for change in the service centers that far exceeded what management had expected—an evaluation which
would have given a "score" of present effectiveness with some
patch-up suggestions for change.

Short-term approaches—for example, tackling a problem
as stated or "installing" the latest fad program—lead to short-
term or no solutions. Short-term solutions generate more short-
and long-term problems faster. Although problems always lead
to other problems, Breakthrough Thinking leads to longer-term
solutions that often already identify the next change. Thus, the
problem-after-next is one of your own making, based on your
own further improvement of the solution you installed before.
Government, business, and personal problems benefit from
your driving the problems you face rather than being driven by
them. You are in control of the engine of change.

Grounding Problem Solving
in Human Realities

We know that each individual and group with whom we interact is unique. Each has traits and biases that may become involved in problem-solving efforts—different amounts of
isolation, fear, self-doubt, impatience, and tentativeness and different levels of thinking skills. Yet conventional problem-solving approaches often tend to magnify these differences
(concerning how an individual perceives himself or herself)
rather than neutralize them.

Breakthrough Thinking principles, by contrast, *build* on these human realities of individuals and groups so as to arrive at breakthroughs. The integrated approach enables us to avoid self-defeating behaviors, such as pointing fingers of blame at others or relying on the cult of the expert, that undermine the generation and implementation of effective solutions.

Even though expert guidance is occasionally helpful, the people involved in a specific situation generally know more about it than outside experts. They know the bigger picture, what solutions could be considered in the future, and the sources of ideas. No amount of data collection or model-building can ever capture all this wisdom and knowledge.

The long-term information capacity of people is good; yet their short-term capacity is poor. When people have had enough time and experience to deal with a body of information, they develop an intuitive and conceptual indexing framework for it. In the short term, however, people are what some specialists call "poor information aggregators." People deluged by information, usually at the beginning of projects, select and retain only a small fraction of that data: six to seven chunks. Frantic efforts to sort out information leave little time for exploring effective solutions.

Moreover, people are likely to accept a problem as stated, which increases the probability of working on the wrong problem. Individuals tend to *classify* problems quickly and leap to solutions, rather than carefully question purposes and assumptions to find the real problem or purpose.

Functional fixedness—procedural habit—afflicts almost everyone. Conventional problem solving intensifies this tendency by emphasizing data collection and breaking a problem into discrete components. This may result in a functional stereotyping that obscures judgment and interferes with creativity.

An individual's decision making is also very likely to be constrained by the rules and regulations of the organization and the person's position. The likelihood that a manager will accept a solution exceeding his or her budget is close to nil. Relatively poor decisions result from this aversion to taking risks; "satisficing" (taking the first solution that appears to work) and patching it up later are encouraged.

When confronted with information implying something is wrong with their performance, people naturally become defensive. Imagine then their defensiveness if the motivation for information collection, as in much conventional problem solving, is to find out who is at fault or what's wrong.

In conventional problem-solving approaches, the effort is expected to produce the only possible correct solution, by focusing exclusively on "doing things right." By refreshing contrast, the far more productive approach of Breakthrough Thinking helps you to identify first the *right thing to do*. Based on this effective focus, its total approach will then—and only then—guide you in how to "do things right."

Unfortunately, the current educational system, based largely on scientism and its research approach, fosters the attitude that there is always only one right answer. Often, a solution is designed to meet the worst possible circumstances, regardless of how infrequently they occur. For example, federal travel reimbursement forms are long and complicated. They are designed that way, it is said, to prevent cheating by the five percent who might do so. Nevertheless, everyone has to spend an inordinate amount of time on the forms, and an expensive bureaucracy is necessary to process them. Simplified travel expense forms, sample audits, special credit cards, or exception forms to reimburse extraordinary expenses might be better responses to the problem.

People dislike being manipulated and patronized. Professionals are often technicians with academic perspectives. They focus on techniques rather than on people, which easily leads to we-will-take-care-of-you and we-know-what-is-best-for-you attitudes. Worse, such attitudes can lead to a Skinnerian or mechanistic behavioral modification of clients by problem-solving experts "for the client's own good."

The time horizon of most people is short. People are often so absorbed in the now that they seldom consider the future. Conventional problem-solving is often caught between two extremes, proposing incremental patch-up solutions with short time horizons and instant results or long-run utopias that sit on the shelf. Breakthrough Thinking provides for long-run guidelines but effective, incremental, short-run steps to achieve them.

People experience conflicts in selecting solutions. Faced with making a decision, many people hesitate, vacillate, and show signs of psychological stress. This severely constrains acceptance of creative and innovative solutions.

People tend to reject solutions "not invented here" (the NIH factor). People may admire, frequently with high praise, something new, yet contend their own situation is different. Attempts to overcome the NIH factor often conflict with the human realities already presented: Get people to believe a solution or idea is theirs (is it manipulation?), give people extra money or incentives to adopt an idea (bribe?), set up "education" sessions to convince them of the benefits (indoctrination?), and so on.

Those using conventional problem-solving approaches often claim that functional fixedness or resistance to change causes people to reject ideas and recommendations. Such resistance may simply be a rejection of perceived manipulation. Breakthrough Thinking focuses on the development of unique solutions designed to fit the specific circumstances of each client or group. When people discover they can use a machine (or form or component) someone else developed, they will be delighted to save their own time and effort by adopting it.

Also, conventional approaches tend to be confrontational and to demand explanations of why so-and-so is acting irrationally. They assume that once data and analysis are available, everyone will agree that they are fair and accurately reflect reality. Breakthrough Thinking avoids this trap by incorporating "realities" into the understanding of a problem situation and focusing on purposes rather than on data collection and blame.

Individuals have different ways of understanding reality. One typology classifies people in terms of how they become aware of situations.[5] If they rely on specific empirical data they are called sensation (S) types; if they rely on internal data they are identified as intuitive (N) types. Ways of arriving at conclusions are classified as T (logical thinking) or F (feeling). Individuals are various combinations of these types, such as intuitive-thinking (NT) or sensation-feeling (SF). A combination of all types results in a holistic picture of reality. In groups, a combination of these types may result in horrendous conflict. But if properly coordinated with Breakthrough Thinking, groups composed of conflicting personality types may nonetheless arrive at solutions that are both creative and practical.

Each person's interest in or commitment to any issue or change is different. Every individual has a unique profile involving achievement desires, creativity, political attitudes, values, psychological needs, and mind-set, as well as a unique personality profile in terms of style, openness, and concern for others. Because of this diversity, Breakthrough Thinking stresses *purpose clarification, continuous interaction* throughout an effort, and *multichanneled solutions* to meet individual perceptions, needs, and expectations.

People in groups play different information-processing roles: instigator, listener, court jester, nice guy. Sometimes the loudest and most frequent speaker dominates a group to the detriment of the group effort. Furthermore, people in groups respond to messages they agree with and tune out information they don't agree with.

Groups tend to take risks only in the direction of the average pregroup disposition. Group-think can result, negatively affecting the quality of the solution. Group interaction is further complicated by the characteristics of the organization (company, city, neighborhood) from which the groups are drawn.

A high degree of inertia afflicts organizations with regard to change. Inertia is a consequence of self-protection. Self-protection results in reduced risk-taking and concentration on self-maintenance. Conventional problem-solving strategies often retard efforts to overcome inertia; they promote maintenance behavior, fear of risk-taking, and self-protection. Even individuals who may not instinctively have these proclivities are forced to adopt them when confronted by practitioners of conventional strategies. Organizations (that is, the culture nurtured by the individuals in charge) do influence and change the people who function within them.

Organizations tend to hire people similar to those already involved. This reduces the opportunity to obtain competing creative ideas. As a result, the organization's purposes become narrowly defined. Conventional problem-solving approaches then compound this narrow perspective by analyzing and subdividing an already limited problem-as-stated. Although organizations pay lip service to the need for creative, resourceful employees, actually the incentive structure and "tribal ways," as one consultant put it, reward standardized thinking and conformity. Public bureaucracies especially react to the constraints imposed on them: effective and efficienct public employees are not rewarded with increased pay, restrictions on the way resources can be allocated are stringent, and public employees are generally unable to establish the goals of their own units.

A lack of effective communication plagues organizations because of their rigid, authoritarian decision structures, lack of formal and informal channels for employee input, and myths of organizational policies and performance. Problem solving may be disrupted by hidden agendas and personal rivalries, whereas Breakthrough Thinking provides principles that open channels of communications.

The Problem with Problems

This chapter has dealt with a wide variety of topics that, we hope, will be discerned as facets of a single theme. That theme is that life is a great tapestry of problems and that an immense amount of time and effort is squandered in lunging at problems without considering their shape, substance, and implications (opportunities).

For example, tremendous technological advance in computers and the processing and control of information was supposed to advance order in the workplace and improve effectiveness and productivity. Yet in many cases, the vast amount of information and reports now available has had the opposite effect, and the assimilation of information is far too often chaotic. As the oft-quoted phrase has it, "We get more through-put, but no more output." More importantly to Breakthrough Thinking, we get no greater accomplishment of purposes.

Continuing problems are a result of our "humanness" in expressing our dissatisfactions and aspirations. As soon as we think we have solved one problem, we find new problems. Life is one problem (opportunity) after another, and Breakthrough Thinking provides the reasoning process to be satisfied with the breakthroughs, while being dissatisfied enough to anticipate and recognize corollary problems that still require work.

One of the most significant pieces of U.S. legislation of our time, a body of laws that has affected everyone in one way or another, is the National Environmental Policy Act of 1969. Its purpose was to halt the reckless despoliation of our national resources, from breathable air and majestic forests to endangered species and scenic vistas. The act's central injunction was simply that before any sizable project involving a Federal interest was launched, a formal assessment of the environmental consequences must be made. Up to then it had never occurred to anybody to codify one of the homeliest maxims we live by—or should: Look before you leap.

Looking before you leap is a cardinal element of the Breakthrough Thinking process. It provides the insights to address effectively the multiple realities of any situation. It identifies how to look before you leap and yet not waste time and effort.

Initially, it may seem tedious, before tackling a problem, to consider the seven principles of Breakthrough Thinking. Yet we recall that an acquaintance of ours, noted for his sagacity, was known also for having a notoriously clean desk. He never allowed a document or anything else to rest on it longer than absolutely necessary. When we asked him about this habit, he explained that he did it not because he was virtuous but because he was lazy. This, he insisted, was "the lazy man's way" of making life easier.

Think of Breakthrough Thinking, if you will, as the lazy person's way of avoiding untold time and effort on less-than-satisfactory solutions to problems. It also prepares you to keep pressing for continual change as a way of preventing future problems. The dreams encompassed in large purposes and solutions-after-next reflect the road to progress, as more and more parts are implemented. Yet today's dream also needs to be succeeded by a new dream, as implementation continues.

"Problems" arrive in a continual flow. Problems brilliantly disguised as insoluble are the greatest opportunities of all.

An important subtheme of this chapter is that good problem solving is rooted in the individual—namely, you. How well you and countless others think and act is a major determinant of a country's economic performance.

Every good idea starts with one person. A single person with *insight* can galvanize a committee's thinking, avert a corporate fiasco, or shift a government agency or even Congress onto a fruitful course.

There are many avenues to insight, the most common being an alert mind reinforced by prolonged experience. Breakthrough Thinking represents a means of developing insight rapidly—just as quickly, in fact, as you elect to put it into practice.

NOTES

1. Tom Peters, *Thriving On Chaos* (New York: Alfred A. Knopf, 1987).

2. Isaiah Berlin, *The Crooked Timber of Humanity* (New York: Alfred A. Knopf, 1991).

3. Kounosuke Matsushita, quoted in *Engineering Excellence: Cultural and Organizational Factors* (New York: IEEE Press, 1988).

4. John F. Lawrence, "Papering over Problems with Paper Profits," *Los Angeles Times* (November 16, 1986).

5. Carl Jung, *Psychological Types* (Princeton, N.J.: Princeton University Press, 1971).

Chapter 3

Pushing for Breakthrough:
Improving Your Chances for Success

By now, it should be plain that Breakthrough Thinking demands a wholly new way of approaching problems—*a new way to think* about how to cross the gap between the knowledge available to each of us and the systematic employment of that knowledge to develop the artifacts (products, buildings, roads, bridges) and the systems that accomplish our purposes, goals, values, and beliefs.

A breakthrough idea seldom occurs as a "bolt out of the blue." Instead, it occurs most often through *preparation of the mind.* Breakthrough Thinking can be characterized as a way of preparing the mind to increase significantly the likelihood of obtaining a quality concept or "lightbulb" idea, of being able to get that idea implemented, and of doing so in less time, at less cost. It is a way of removing barriers to real progress.

The possibility that there is a different way of thinking is alien to Western tradition. Westerners have long harbored a pervasive prejudice in favor of "scientific" thinking—rational, analytic, compartmentalized, quantified thought. This is so deep-rooted that most people seem innately to consider it the only possible approach to problem solving.

The Judeo-Christian-Islamic religions of the West each claim to provide *the* answer to perplexing questions of life. The firmness of their respective beliefs is illustrated throughout history by their treatment of those holding different views.

Eastern religions, on the other hand, do not presume to have *the* answer. They envision various possibilities and perspectives about contemporary interrelationships. In the East, these flexible outlooks are more dominant than the hereafter-based certainties of Western religions. Because there is no single answer, it is very common among the Japanese, for example, to maintain affiliations and beliefs in two or more religions at the same time. (In the East, mistreatment of people by their rulers has tended to be more overtly power based—that is, openly and without apology a response to political offense—as opposed to the spiritually-based arguments—believe-or-not—made by Western rulers as a cover for the imposition of their temporal sway.)

The mind-set of openness generated by the Eastern approach to problem solving is critical to understanding the continual quest for change within societies and organizations. In its approach to general problem solving, Western society's mind-set is still to seek *the* answer, just as Western religions provide *the* answer to cosmic questions.

Science emerged out of the Western orientation to seek the answers to the manifold questions religion did not probe. Early scientists had to accept religious dogma about the "large" questions as part of a pact that allowed them to seek an understanding of the physical or "small" questions of the world, answers to which they were certain existed somewhere "out there." They also, however, had to commit to and were personally wedded to obtaining *the* single, definitive answer regarding any phenomenon they studied and to believing that all their "small" answers fit together into a comprehensive whole. The methodology they developed—the research approach—provided and came to be characterized by the data needed for finding and supporting *the* answer.

Of course, the multiple goals sought for our modern systems and solutions almost always ensure the emergence of many possible workable and feasible answers. These goals are to develop effective—that is, creative, innovative, high benefit-to-cost ratio—systems and solutions, to assure implementation of the recommendations, and to utilize maximally the resources assigned to solving the problem.

The research approach of science was developed to achieve science's purposes of finding *the* generalization. Even as evidence for the validity of a new generalization emerges, science changes the prevailing truth only reluctantly. Now there must be a different approach for creating or restructuring systems that are not necessarily *the* one-and-only answer. The background and reasons for this assertion are explored thoroughly in our book, *Creative Solution Finding.*

Problem-Solving Approaches

In truth, there are many possible problem-solving approaches. But they are all variations on four basic approaches: do-nothing, chance, affective, and rational.

The first approach, *do-nothing,* we must ultimately dismiss since we assume that people do want to solve their problems. The *chance* approach focuses on the importance of the accidental in problem solving and life in general. *Affective* approaches stress intuition, insight, feelings, and divergent thinking. *Rational* approaches are characterized by structured, systematic, methodical, scientific processes.

Each of the latter three approaches has merit, and each has serious flaws. Some are more applicable to specific types of problems than are others. The total, holistic approach of Breakthrough Thinking synthesizes these three approaches to provide an entirely new way to think.

Everyone uses some kind of approach to solve problems. What is important to remember is that each of the four possible approaches leads to different types of solutions using different kinds of information.

THE DO-NOTHING APPROACH

Although the label sounds pejorative, there are many adherents to this approach. It is characterized by the belief that human beings cannot or should not control events, either because fate is capricious or because a god will provide. There were (and are) great civilizations that have not encouraged problem solving because, in their view, grief, famine, flood, and other events of this world are petty discomforts on the way to the glorious hereafter.

Proponents of this approach, however, are not limited to those of a religious persuasion. There is a genuine moral dilemma associated with the decision to engage actively in solving problems. For example, we must at least acknowledge the possibility that it may be immoral for one person to decide what is good for another.

Without making a claim to definitiveness, we assume that it is right to seek solutions actively so as to realize societal values.

THE CHANCE APPROACH

Probably the earliest humans found solutions to their problems primarily by chance, the likely origins of such institutions as agriculture and the use of controlled fire.

The premise of the chance approach is that the accidental dominates human endeavors. Its methodological implications, however, go in two very different directions.

One chance approach relies passively on flashes of insight or stumbling by chance on the right answer—what Albert Einstein called "finding without seeking."

The second chance approach is closer to a rational approach. It focuses on the constant intervention of accident and surprise in human affairs. Expecting the unexpected leads to an open-ended and flexible approach to problems—for example, contingency planning.

THE AFFECTIVE APPROACH

Affective reasoning involves emotions, feelings, intuitions, and hunches—the characteristics of human nature. Affective problem solvers tend to do whatever comes spontaneously to mind, rather than follow a preestablished, structured approach.

The underlying principle and methods of an affective approach differ from person to person and are difficult to define. However, certain patterns can be described.

Affectively oriented problem solvers are often unable to explain how they arrived at a solution, possibly because the process is too complex and fluid to put into words. Often, the affective thinker, such as Albert Einstein, relates information through nonverbal internal visualizations that are beyond the scope of language.

The elements of this approach include free association, analogy transfers, reliance on heuristics (instinctive shortcuts or "rules of thumb" based on distilled past experience), insight, intuition, and finding unusual connections among bits of information ordinarily considered unrelated. For example, Carl Jung told of the chemist who discovered the molecular structure of benzene when, upon seeing an ancient symbol of a snake with its tail in its mouth, he intuitively sensed that the structure was a closed carbon ring.[1]

Such creativity can likely be both learned and enhanced. Adams emphasizes that "perhaps the most common inhibition to creativity is our usual reliance upon traditional problem-solving routines and the fantasy that creative problem-solving should be easier, rather than more difficult, than producing answers to routine problems."

He then offers four principles to increase creativity:

1. When solving problems, be aware that the information you have in your mind is not complete and is not identical to that of those around you.

2. Be aware that your brain would like to follow a traditional pattern—to simplify your life by applying solutions that have worked successfully before. Be grateful for that, but be suspicious that the creativity you are looking for may not occur automatically.

3. The brain is most efficient in business-as-usual situations when it is able to make use of past experience and apply it quickly and unconsciously. However, the brain may be less efficient in new situations.

4. Conscious effort is necessary to enable people to pursue new directions. Perspiration is, in fact, an excellent investment.[2]

Based on their 15 years experience in the field, management consultants and creativity trainers Ted Coulson and Alison Strickland suggest three ways to develop creativity and foster innovation.

First, they recommend that a person recognize the creativity within and around him or her. Second, to overcome the inhibition and fear that repress creativity, they suggest that one should call himself or herself a creative person because it helps one perform creatively. Third, they assert that creativity can be developed purposefully and systematically because it comes from learnable traits such as thinking skills, communication skills, and problem-solving process.

"The creative problem solving process involves identifying what you have and then imagining what you want in its place. People often get stuck by focusing all their efforts on trying to fix what's wrong instead of working toward what they truly want.

"Creative people think flexibly. They know how to look at issues from many points of view. State your problem in as many different ways as you can. Look at the issue from the viewpoint of an analytical thinker, a procedural thinker, a people-oriented person, and an imaginative, conceptual thinker."[3]

The affective approach can lead to innovative, creative solutions. It does, however, pose certain problems.

1. It may not be particularly effective for systematically *detailing* solutions, which is necessary to implement them. Implementation may also be hindered by the mutual frustration an affective approach may create in groups. A person using this approach cannot explain how he or she arrived at the solution, so others may condemn the solution as unreasonable or irrational.

2. The criteria for weighting factors of importance in making decisions may be random and fluctuate wildly. This poses certain dangers. Consider, for instance, the problems if a postal carrier used an affective approach for delivering mail and some days relied on names and numbers, while on others coordinated the stamp pattern with a house's architectural design.

3. The affective approach can become very elitist, and the absence of standardized criteria precludes checks and balances. Charismatic but unscrupulous leaders can use affective approaches in manipulative and dangerous ways.

THE RATIONAL APPROACH

The rational approach appeared explicitly about 400 years ago, along with the rise of science.

The need for reliable generalizations called for methods that neither the chance nor affective approaches provided. The success of the rational approach in science was so phenomenal that all other fields of human endeavor adapted it, to the almost total exclusion of any other problem-solving approach.

Single-direction and single-factor reasoning, objectivity, structured decision making and systematic logical processes are the hallmarks of the rational approach. Several themes are basic to it.

Positivism. The conviction that science can solve all problems—indeed, is the *only* way to solve problems—pervades the rational approach. "If we can get to the moon, we ought to be able to end poverty," illustrates recent versions of this persistent theme, also known as the "technological fix." This absolutism is a carryover from earlier times when only vociferous advocacy of positivism could counteract prevailing cosmic and faith-based approaches.

Reductionism. Rational approaches are characterized by the extensive compilation and analysis of information and the division of the problem into smaller units. Solve the small problems, and supposedly the larger problem is also solved.

Quantitative and objective data—hard facts—are sought. The existence of nonquantifiable subjective information, such as the human variables of who will implement a solution and how they will actually go about it, is not denied but simply relegated to the category of "unimportant externals."

The Cult of the Expert. Experts who specialize in data collection exist in almost all fields. Only the expert possessing the necessary information is thought to be in a position to arrive at quality solutions. As experts, they are presumed to be unobtrusive and value-free. And despite objections raised by physical and social scientists, data collection is assumed to have no influence on the phenomena being measured. Far too often, experts think they alone are capable of "knowing" what is right or what the effects and risks of alternatives may be. They believe the general public can't possibly know how to assess such weighty matters.

Experts are a result of the specialization penchant that is prevalent in the United States. The cult of the expert leads to a limited perspective on problems, functional fixedness, defensiveness on the part of those to whom an expert's solutions are addressed, and a host of other difficulties.

Determinism. The rational approach assumes that, once the facts are assembled and the data analyzed, one solution will emerge on which all reasonable people can agree. Once this solution is found, presumably the problem evaporates and the solution will always be appropriate.

How firmly this determinism is adhered to varies widely, but it is everywhere in evidence. Architects build buildings as if today's needs will be those of the future, managers assume the personnel practices of 25 years ago are applicable today, and urban planners rely on snapshots of the future extrapolated from the past.

This extrapolation of the present to the future is a dangerous practice. After all, it caused almost everyone in the 1960s and the early 1970s to reject the predictions of the few who were alert to the energy crisis and its impact on every sector of society. The determinism practiced by almost everyone in the 1980s pushed aside predictions of global warming, known as the greenhouse effect. Despite increasing evidence that alternative models may be better, determinism still keeps executives in the 1990s married to the "tried-and-true" command and control management structure of the last 100 years.

Although the rational approach is very useful in developing generalizations and doing research, especially in the physical sciences, it is not necessarily appropriate for other types of problem solving. It is seriously limited in its ability to generate answers to the problems that we confront today. For example, technological systems such as automated factories and nuclear power plants must be designed with a vast and profound understanding of human behavior and roles in what are, in effect, *socio*-technical systems.

Approaches and Personalities

The four different basic approaches to problem solving—do-nothing, chance, affective, and rational—reflect the existence of different personality types, which have been variously described through most of human history.

In modern times, Sigmund Freud, the progenitor of psychoanalysis, proposed that there are two distinct patterns of thinking. The first, he called "primary process" thinking, which he defined as the first pattern of thinking, arising out of frustration that derives from the absence of the mother. Swedish psychoanalyst Eva Basch-Kahre explains that the first representation of this sort of thinking arises in infancy, "when the child hallucinates the satisfaction of his desire, that is, the presence of the mother. Out of this first representation, primary process thinking develops."

The second pattern of thinking Freud identified he called "secondary process" thinking, which he defined as the language of conscious and preconscious thinking. According to Kahre, "it is characterized by logic, concepts of time and space, and by verbal representation."[4] This is the sort of thinking that normal adults are considered to practice.

Over time, Kahre herself and many others have come to challenge and to amplify Freud's perspective, both to refine its assertions and to posit the existence of other patterns of thought. Chief among these was Freud's one-time disciple, Carl Jung, who proposed a wholly different perspective on thinking based on his theory of personality types. In 1923, Jung suggested that four psychological functions—sensing, intuition, thinking, and feeling—comprise the basic attitudes that affect conscious behavior.

According to Jung, people develop dominant preferences for certain types of data in their thinking, preferences for either sensation or intuition. Sensation-dominant people prefer precise, specific data; they see themselves as realists concerned with immediate problems. In contrast, intuition-dominant people seek holistic information that describes possibilities; their decisions use more general data.

Jung also found two main ways that people reach decisions: by thinking or by feeling. Thinking-dominant people emphasize logic and formal modes of reasoning; they generalize and make abstractions. Feeling-dominant people form personal value judgments; they explain things in human terms and emphasize affective and personal processes in making decisions.

On the basis of these ways people obtain and evaluate data, Jung defined four personality types: (1) Sensing-Thinking; (2) Intuition-Thinking; (3) Sensing-Feeling; and (4) Intuition-Feeling. In perceiving and judging, many people exhibit all four personality types at different times. Most people, however, have a dominant, preferred style. This is the style they use more often than the others, across a variety of situations, particularly in situations that are fluid and not firmly structured.

Sensing-Thinking types stress systematic decision making and hard data. They try to establish order, control, and certainty. They focus on tasks and structured information. They take fewer risks than other types.

Intuition-Thinking types tend to ignore specific, detailed information. They prefer to study patterns in data. Their thought takes bolder leaps into the unknown. They emphasize longer-range plans and new possibilities.

Sensing-Feeling types stress harmony, personal communication, and other people's opinions. Facts about people are more important than facts about things. They focus on short-term problems, with human implications.

Intuition-Feeling types rely on their own judgment and experience, often portraying personal views as facts. They prefer holistic, intuitive perceptions over rules in decision making. They focus on broad themes and long-term goals.

From Jung's classic treatise, *Psychological Types*, evolved the Myers-Briggs Type Indicator (MBTI), the test used to measure a person's problem-solving style. According to Myers and Briggs, people who are primarily Sensing personality types tend to be patient, practical, realistic, and good with facts and details. Those who are primarily Intuitive types tend to be impatient, oriented toward theories and ideas, creative, and holistic. The Myers-Briggs test suggests that Sensing types account for about 75 percent of the U.S. population; Intuitive types about 25 percent.

These and other research findings strongly suggest that most people use more than one of the four approaches at the same time. None of these approaches can by itself meet the criteria of a total approach. Chance approaches tend to be fatalistic or merely reactive. Affective approaches, though often creative, cannot assure the implementation of their solutions. Rational approaches, which emphasize experts, measurements, and techniques are not rooted in the human purposes, perceptions, and needs that are the foundation of good solutions.

What is called for, then, is a *synthesis* of the best in all approaches, one that recognizes that each approach to problem solving, each kind of thinking, is a legitimate expression of human knowledge and experience. What is called for is an approach to problem solving that first identifies the right thing to do and then (but only then) specifies how to do things right. This is the wholly new approach of Breakthrough Thinking.

TOWARD A SYNTHESIS OF APPROACHES

The philosophical perspective of Breakthrough Thinking has been given scientific credibility by recent left and right brain discoveries in neurophysiology. As first noted by the Nobel laureate biologist Roger Sperry, there appear to be "two modes of thinking, verbal and nonverbal, represented rather separately in the left and right brain respectively."

The left hemisphere "appears to operate in a logical, analytical and computer-like fashion. Its language is inadequate to the complex synthesis achieved by the right."[5] The forebrain combines both modes of thinking into the process of decision making.

Given these philosophical and scientific perspectives, as well as the obvious fact that human beings automatically use the chance, the affective, and the rational approaches to problem solving, it seems clear that new, integrative modes are called for. In response to this need, a number of "total" approaches have been suggested, with such names as heuristics, bounded rationality, gestalt, cognitive, and doubting and believing games.

The difficulty with most of these so-called total approaches is that they do not go far enough, or that they can be put into practice only in very small problem-solving situations, such as laboratory-administered puzzle tests. An exception to these limitations is the "doubting and believing" games first described by Peter Elbow,[6] each of which incorporates the idea of a method for finding solutions or uncovering truth.

The *doubting game* approach emphasizes arguing and a rigid, reductive, and supposedly objective rationality method: problem diagnosis and definition, problem analysis, presentation and evaluation of alternatives, and solution detailing. Doubting forces one to poke holes in ideas, tear apart assertions, probe continually, and be analytical. It puts people on the defensive, eliciting reactions that protect previous or current positions or decisions.

The doubting game, a specific result of rationality, supposedly makes a person feel rigorous, disciplined, and tough minded. A person who refrains from playing the doubting game is considered unintellectual, irrational, and sloppy. No doubt, you already recognize this doubting game as the mode of choice among Western corporate executives, academic intellectuals, and political leaders. It is the prevailing mind-set of the contemporary power-elite, who, not coincidentally, have generally failed to find effective solutions to the common problems we face today, regardless of how good their solutions appeared in the days when resources were plentiful and global competition was nonexistent. They often form what Robert J. Samuelson has called the "excuse industry" of "it's not my fault," "it's the fault of trade policy, or high taxes, or high health care costs, or Wall Street short-sightedness, or poor public education."[7]

Even in the search for conflict management and world peace—even in our best attempts to solve the gravest of human problems—our approaches to date have been strictly conventional. For example, the first five steps of one ten-step approach all rely excessively on habits of scientific analysis: (1) identify the problem, (2) define the problem clearly, (3) analyze the problem, (4) collect data, (5) analyze the data.[8]

Already, determined peace makers following this prescription have squandered much of their potential. We are inundated with data, data, and more data to the obstruction of real progress toward peace. Nowhere in this approach are *purposes* actively considered.

The *believing game,* on the other hand, is based on an entirely different set of principles. In the believing game, a person initially believes all assertions. To refrain from doubting is the first and foremost rule.

By believing an idea or an assertion, we can see farther into it. We can come to understand its possible working and structure. This is only possible by inhibiting doubt so that no proposed solution, however apparently impossible or wrongheaded, is ever abandoned at the outset. This game causes people to seek ways of achieving the desired ends, thus putting forth positive reactions to questions. The believing posture produces responses such as, How *could* it work? What are the larger ends that particular solution will also achieve? And so on. "All men's gains are the fruit of venturing," the way Herodotus put it in 450 B.C., is an early version of the believing game.

The two games—doubting and believing—are interrelated, and each contains elements of the other. But although problem solving requires them both, they cannot be played simultaneously.

This points to an important aspect of a genuine total approach to problem solving, such as Breakthrough Thinking. Although it must be a synthesis of all approaches, the elements emphasized will depend on the purposes and objectives of the particular problem-solving situation. For example, careful development of generalizations in research requires employment of the doubting game. But creating or restructuring solutions to most problems requires the believing game, in order to devise breakthrough solutions.

The Needed Mental Shift

What is essential now is that you mentally begin to make the fundamental shift necessary to learn and apply the process of Breakthrough Thinking.

Before we can begin to take you through that process and its seven principles, before we can begin to show you exactly how to find breakthrough solutions, you must realize that there is more than one way to think (Chapter 1), more than one type of problem (Chapter 2), and that different ways to think are more effective in solving certain types of problems than they are in solving others.

What's more, even given a certain type of problem, different stages in the process of finding its solution demand different types of thinking. There is a time for each, a place for each. But—and this is all-important—in order successfully to solve your problems, *believing,* not doubting, *must come first.*

Late in his life, Walt Disney, the pioneering businessman and artist who solved more problems than most of us are ever likely to confront, was asked to share his secret of success. Disney's reply was that there were four essential ingredients to success: Think, believe, dream, and dare.[9]

First, he said, people should *think* about their *beliefs and values,* which largely determine the quality of their life. Individuals make choices and decisions in the context of their personal values. The clearer people's understanding of their values, the easier it is to make choices and decisions.

Second, Disney said, people should *believe*: Believe in oneself, believe in an idea, believe in a cause, believe in a purpose, and believe in something, to the point of making a commitment.

Third, people should *dream.* Henry David Thoreau wrote, "If one advances confidently in the direction of his dreams, and endeavors to live the life which he has imagined, he will meet with a success unexpected in common hours."[10]

Fourth, Walt Disney advised, people must *dare* to take action—to make and implement choices and decisions. As Theodore Roosevelt once said: "Far better it is to dare mighty things, to win glorious triumphs, even though checkered by failure, than to rank with those poor spirits who neither enjoy much nor suffer much, because they live in the gray twilight that knows not victory nor defeat."[11]

Think, believe, dream, and dare. As you will see in Chapters 4 through 10, Disney's prescription for effectiveness and success in personal, professional, and organizational development closely parallels the seven principles of Breakthrough Thinking.

What Effective Problem Solvers Do

In order to devise an effective and genuinely total approach to problem solving, we asked ourselves, What are the necessary factors of such an approach, and how can these best be put into practice? A great deal of research into thinking had been accomplished, and some major descriptive insights were available (see Chapter 6 of our book, *Creative Solution Finding*). Yet these research results had not been put into a form that most people could use.

Following our own advice, rather than researching the question to death at the outset and overwhelming ourselves with largely useless data, we took the direct approach and simply asked some of the most celebrated and effective problem solvers *how* they went about it.

We found, not surprisingly, that many of these highly successful individuals—intuitive and self-confident by nature— tended to follow the *affective approach*. Thus, they had difficulty telling us exactly how they went about finding effective solutions to their problems.

Our own observation of their behavior, however, coupled with studies conducted by others, led us to conclude that the following five factors are generally present concurrently, at all points of time in the behavior of successful problem solvers:

1. Pursuing a purpose-based, solution-after-next strategy.
2. Specifying and presenting ideas and the solution in terms of a system—all the factors needed to make it work.

3. Involving people who are directly involved in using the solution, as well as others with a wide range of backgrounds in the problem area, including customers, who are the ultimate recipients of the product, service, or solution.

4. Using a variety of information and knowledge.

5. Arranging for continual change and improvement.

For example, if he had followed the behavior of successful problem solvers outlined above, how might political gadfly Ross Perot have better presented his opposition to the North American Free Trade Agreement (NAFTA) during his 1993 debate with Vice-President Al Gore?

Perot might have challenged Gore concerning the purposes of the agreement. An effective agreement must serve larger, not merely immediate, purposes. It must systematically complement existing and potential U.S. trade agreements, not offer a knee-jerk response to competing alliances. Given the prolonged recession then prevailing, Perot might have questioned the timing of NAFTA. Many of the parties impacted by the agreement had not been involved in its drafting. Private organizations concerned with environmental standards, human rights, and the interests of workers on both sides of the border could have provided knowledge essential to the success of NAFTA. Finally, Perot might have argued that no such agreement should be concluded without inherent provision for its improvement as changing conditions might dictate.

The total approach of Breakthrough Thinking incorporates the five essential problem-solving features. But as we have shown in Chapter 2, because the ends and values of each *type* of problem are different, each requires a different mind-set and method of inquiry to achieve a successful solution.

For example, developing *generalizations* requires detachment; objectivity; tough, piercing questioning; rigid methodology; and challenging old dogmas as well as new ideas. The doubting game assures that new theories are based on evidence and that the status quo is not summarily rejected.

Operating and *evaluating* likewise require a similar doubting game approach. Maintaining a smoothly operating bus system, for example, necessitates anticipating where difficulties may arise, such as finding the "facts" about accidents to eliminate potential causes. Evaluation without doubting and probing would be mere "window dressing." But evaluation can begin by designing the ideal system (believing game) and then comparing (doubting game) what currently exists to the ideal.

The believing game mind-set is most effective for creating or restructuring a situation-specific solution—that is, for problems of *planning and design*—and for *learning* a skill or field of knowledge.

To solve problems of planning and design, you need the believing game's commitment to projection, willingness to explore what is new, flexibility, subjective involvement, deep experiencing, dedication to searching for how an idea could work, determination of how to be larger and more encompassing, working with other people, and listening to and incorporating their ideas.

Learning also is aided by the believing game, which enables us to change or add to our existing knowledge base. Continually believing in the learning process is likely to result in far greater retention and synthesis of knowledge.

Unfortunately, the vestiges of past problem-solving efforts based more on belief than doubt are not at all sophisticated. Rather, they usually are based on historical, frontier-type reasoning in which we attempt to arrive at solutions and changes by means of sheer grit. According to this approach, if we apply enough energy, time, effort, commitment, and money to the problem—the gap between reality and expectation or desire— we can simply overwhelm it.

This may have worked in American society in the past, when so many resources—land, minerals, immigrants—were available. But it no longer works in a world where at least equally energetic nations compete for markets and limited resources. Nonetheless, today we continue in this outdated attitude with the throw-money-at-it approach to problem solving, which does not question *how* the reasoning process should proceed. This means that subconscious, usually research, models will be used.

And so, simply overcoming our research instincts to doubt is not enough—not if we replace these instincts with an equally simplistic prejudice toward belief. What is essential is an advanced, comprehensive methodology to replace the research approach. What is called for is a new formulation of *how to think.*

Following exclusively the research paradigm, critics of contemporary world problems, whether in nations or organizations, point to *products* and *systems* as being at fault, demonstrated by the lack of positive measurable results. Almost no one says a word about the *thinking* and *reasoning* processes of individuals and groups in arriving at these generally poor outcomes. But we believe that past processes of thinking and reasoning are themselves the major culprit.

What needs to be changed is the way each of us goes about finding solutions to problems. This shift—changing our mind-set about how we go about solving our problems—cannot guarantee that we will find perfect solutions. Applying the principles of Breakthrough Thinking, however, will significantly improve the quality and quantity of solutions. The principles of Breakthrough Thinking also meet and indeed surpass a fundamental scientific test: They point the way to how the Breakthrough Thinking principles themselves will be improved in the future.

If, rather than address purposes, you go about it the old-fashioned way and simply ask, What's wrong here? What's the problem? your answer is almost certain to cause more problems. It will be culturally skewed, historically biased, conceptually constrained, and ultimately limiting—precisely because it focuses on problems, not solutions.

A pervasive example of the violation of the Breakthrough Thinking principles of uniqueness and purposes is the widely popular yet inapproriate and untimely use of the medical metaphor in attempting to solve problems. The great advances realized by medical science in understanding and treating diseases have led almost everyone else trying to solve problems to imitate the process or approach used by diagnostic physicians to seek and correct "what's wrong."

Other professionals, notably organizational and systems designers, generally adopt the language of medicine. Thus, they suppose, the first step in problem solving is diagnosis, locating the root cause or source of the problem. Unfortunately, this medical metaphor ignores the insights to be gained by examining a problem in terms of its human purposes.

Using the approach followed by physicians to keep the "human system" functioning well—the purpose of *operating and maintaining*—is not the most effective approach when seeking to *create or restructure* a system or solution, which is an entirely different purpose. With the possible exception of the plastic surgeon, a physician is in no way seeking to create or restructure a system. Yet "change professionals" are.

The change professions (planning and design) are concerned with systems that are malleable—not fixed, as is the human body. Yet reliance on the misleading medical metaphor causes people to assume that the system or solution sought to any problem should be approached as if the arena of its solution were a human body. Such an assumption is patently ridiculous.

In fact, advances in medical technology are largely the result of creating and restructuring the *tools* that can be used to help operate and maintain the health of the human body system. For example, even genetic engineering is the product of continuing planning and design of medical tools. Similar in its conception to the search for artificial intelligence tools, genetic engineering's quest to eliminate human physical flaws seems to us unlikely to succeed (or likely to cause too many serious other problems) because of its scientific perspective; it assumes that there is a direct relationship between human genes and the characteristics of human beings. This seems to us highly unlikely, just as is the possibility that a computer can "think" like a human.

Changing the approach to developing these tools—because such activity *is* in fact creating and restructuring a system— would likely prove more effective than conventional diagnostic approaches in creating medical advances. The conventional approach leads to viewing human body parts (ova, livers, hearts, even rentable wombs) as commodities. This is a very dehumanizing perspective and one that could be in large part avoided if a different approach were followed in developing the tools. Like all systems, the human body is an integrated whole, an integrated organism, which must be considered in its totality by those who would apply to it specific tools.

Similarly, the change professions themselves would benefit from realizing that the medical metaphor is inappropriate. The organizations and systems they seek to create or restructure are tools to larger ends and are not at all similar to human bodies, which are appropriately operated and maintained as needed by physicians.

This does not mean that metaphors themselves are inappropriate, only their inappropriate and untimely use, which can prove dangerously misleading. The crucial factors are when and how we use such metaphors. Certainly, the beginning of the problem-solving process is the wrong time to risk their use. Later in the process, when developing ideas for possible solutions, is the appropriate and advantageous time to employ metaphors.

Another reason to focus on purposes in problem-solving is that times have changed: Today's and tomorrow's world requires a customer orientation, a quality emphasis, a focus on productivity improvement, fast and flexible organizational response, a concern for global competitiveness, and a commitment to excellence. These factors describe our current and future way of life.

The conventional reasoning used to create or restructure solutions worked satisfactorily when we had apparently limitless resources and time and competitiveness were in our favor. Today, the distilled analysis of existing problems is the breeding ground of defeatism. If we use these conventional approaches in our new way of life, we will not be successful. It is no longer simply a matter of hard work. Success today demands hard work with a method that produces breakthrough solutions providing maximum initial improvements and continual changes, rather than just the conventional minimal improvements.

One effect of implementing Breakthrough Thinking as the chief mode of problem solving will be to change the culture, both personally and within organizations so as to accomplish the necessary shift—a change of perspective, a change of mind, a change of heart and habit, a change of attitude and of approach—away from a generally discredited excessive scientism toward a *purpose-based* approach to solving problems.

Lester Thurow, in his popular book *Head To Head: The Coming Economic Battle among Japan, Europe, and America,* provides an excellent conceptual framework to support the idea that personal (and by extension organizational) modes of thinking to solve problems ought to change. He notes that throughout history, one of four factors usually has been essential to the economic predominance of certain countries and societies: natural resources, financial capital, technology, and human skills. Britain, for example, had coal and capital in the early 19th century. The United States had natural resources and technology sufficient to lead in the early and middle 20th century. Japan had technology and human skills in the latter 20th century.

Yet Thurow points out that today, natural resources, financial capital, and technology are available to anyone in any country anywhere in the world. He concludes that human skills are the only major factor that will indicate economic and social success in the present and future. The most effective approach to creating or restructuring solutions is, as we will show, the first and fundamental human skill that every person needs.[12]

The Gap Between Knowledge and Results

Society, organizations, and individuals are faced with an incredibly difficult task: *how* to convert the huge and growing amount of information and knowledge (technology) and the widely available resources and capital into innovative, implementable, effective, and timely solutions for problems. The same difficult task faces each of us as individuals: how best to use all the information and knowledge we possess about personal, family, and societal matters to develop creative and effective solutions to our problems.

This task is not being performed well. Quality and productivity rates of improvement are low; creative products and systems are not being developed; the time and cost of finding even mediocre solutions are higher than those of America's competitors; and personal, family, and societal relationships are growing ever more fractious. Even good ideas, fads, and programs don't get implemented because of conventional ways of thinking.

For example, in the 1980s, we all thought that new computers and communication technologies would produce the answers we needed: the great increases in productivity, quality, and effectiveness. Yet these expected results have not occurred. Clearly now, in order to achieve the breakthroughs of all three types that we seek, we need to ask new and different questions.

The task is to match and adapt bodies of knowledge to human needs, values, beliefs, and purposes, to arrive at the desired solutions (artifacts, systems, creations). The process of moving from here (knowledge and needs) to there (solutions and results) represents a gap that must be bridged more effectively than ever before. The task of bridging this gap is what solving and preventing problems and creating or restructuring solutions are all about. To accomplish these tasks, and ultimately to realize the values we hold, we must shift our internal representation of an effective approach away from excessive scientism and toward the sort of purpose-based problem solving process and the seven principles of Breakthrough Thinking.

Indeed, we do not believe we are exaggerating when we state that to cope successfully with a way of life involving tremendous changes, to solve the problems we confront, and for the human species to advance—quite possibly to survive— we are now called upon fundamentally and radically to change our minds, to *change our way of thinking and seeing,* to bridge the gap between our knowledge and our values.

However compelling, mere exhortation, in the absence of effective methodology, will never bridge that gap. And if we do not bridge the gap effectively, we humans are sure to find ourselves in increasing peril of slipping, plunging, or being pushed into a potentially cataclysmic abyss (low standards of living, low expectations for children, international crises, and so on).

In effect, we must develop "The New Age of Reasoning" to move past Tom Paine's major contribution to structured approaches and scientific processes, *The Age of Reason* (first published in 1794 and 1795).[13] New ways of thinking are needed to perform the task of crossing the gap between our bodies of knowledge—the forms of our information—and our values. New principles are needed to guide our efforts of converting knowledge to practice, to foster creativity in all phases of the process, to make decisions with an understanding of the whole system involved, to "see things" in the mind's eye from a believing point of view, to know how to define what needs to be learned.

In other words, we must disabuse ourselves of a long unchallenged statement that "knowledge is power." As necessary as bodies of knowledge and information are in today's society, we must know that they are insufficient.

Breakthrough Thinking establishes the new credo: *Knowing how to use knowledge is power!*

The old statement was suited to the days when the conventional research approach was used for all types of problems. The new credo applies today in any society because each society must obtain solutions that are the most effective, implementable, and efficient using whatever levels of knowledge and resources are available.

Figure 3-1 illustrates the gap the new credo is fashioned to cross.

Human assumptions and values are individuals' primary concern—whether or not they acknowledge it—because they always appear in the process of solving problems and making decisions. They give rise to the purposeful activities in which all humans engage (Chapter 2). In other words, they shape the perspective and measure of accomplishment each person brings to every activity and system in which he or she works

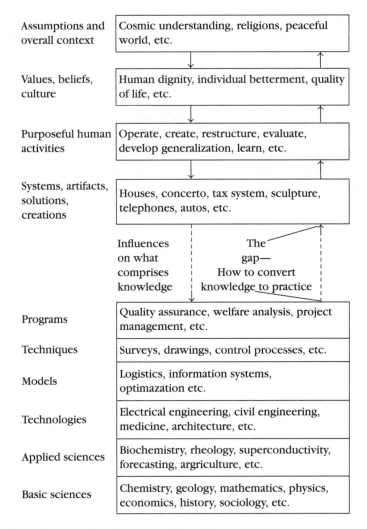

Figure 3-1.   Filling the gap with Breakthrough Thinking

and lives. These assumptions and values differ from person to person, organization to organization, society to society.

The process of Breakthrough Thinking, we propose, is the best bridge available across the gap, the method that best performs the task of converting knowledge to practice. In another framework, it is the method that best converts technology and research results to application as a product or service in the marketplace.

Artifacts, systems, and relationships are the results of converting our knowledge to practice—the manifestations of our society. Whether manifested in a primitive mud adobe, a modern 100-story skyscraper, or the structural relationships in an organization, the interaction of human assumptions, values, and purposes, initially, will lead to artifacts, systems, and social interactions. Then, as we develop bodies of knowledge, a continual interplay between knowledge and values takes place. Knowledge and values move back and forth across the bridge spanning the gap. And this bridge is nothing less than *ways of thinking,* the ways and means we use to convert knowledge to practice.

Thinking Needed to Cross the Gap

More than one reader of this book will no doubt question how engineers can even presume to write about a concept such as Breakthrough Thinking. But the processes of engineering design with which we and our colleagues initially concerned ourselves have always had as much to do with people as with technologies. In addition, our research into what expert and effective planners and designers (not only engineers) actually do is organized to probe the whole sociotechnical process, not just the computer-aided techniques and tools available in these various fields of intellectual inquiry.

Current, excessive reliance on "scientific" mechanisms has clearly failed in the attempt to convert knowledge to effective systems and solutions. The resulting artifacts and systems have been and are still impoverished because of the excessive demand for and reliance upon scientism in their formulation. And yet, the contemporary, pervasive application of scientism still prevails, however self-defeating its attempts to span the gap.

In the field of engineering, for example, general systems theory remains in vogue though it has failed, and failed largely because, as presently constituted, it is rooted in the *natural sci-*

ences—not even the social sciences, mind you, but the natural. Thus impoverished in its potential, it fails to span the gap.

As systems engineer and social scientist C. West Churchman explains, "A number of us have been shouting to our colleagues that their assumptions are either wrong or have nothing to do with rational choices in real (that is, human) systems."[14]

And sociologist William R. Freudenburg concludes: "The social sciences should be asked to provide not just an improved understanding of public perceptions, but also significantly improved quantitative estimates of the probabilities as well as the consequences of important risks.

"This will require, however, that all of us explicitly begin to integrate human behaviors into our thinking about 'technological' systems—and that we begin devoting approximately the same level of resources to understanding the human components of technological systems as to the hardware. Although often overlooked, human and social factors play vital roles in technological systems; real-world risks, far from being free of such inconvenient 'people factors,' are indeed often dominated by them."[15]

Social scientists are beginning to realize that supposedly detached and "objective" analysis of social phenomena cannot in fact be neutral and impartial. Attempting to discover permanent generalizations or immutable laws of nature in the social arena fails to take into account the changing nature of human beings, thus the meaning and interpretation of the necessarily impermanent generalizations discovered. In the social sciences, finding in nature the single "correct" answer in the same way it is sought in the physical sciences is simply not tenable.

A vivid example of the limited thinking that stems from failing to understand the purposes and uniqueness of each problem is the global scramble to apply the emerging technology of artificial intelligence. Intense competition has led to the assumption that a successful, modern firm or organization must base itself on this latest technological answer.

Unfortunately, this belief stems from scientists' assumption that human beings process and manipulate information and symbols in the same way as do computers. At best, artificial intelligence *may* help us make decisions. But such technology certainly cannot capture the human purposes, desires, and emotions that are critical in decision making.

In many ways, however, this attitude of technology fiction—though useful in a different context, as we will show in Chapter 6—has much in common with science fiction. That is to say, most of it does not come true. Even though writers continue to proclaim that human beings do not dominate machines[16] or that humans and machines have collectively co-evolved[17] only human beings are capable of creating or restructuring systems. And we will remain so indefinitely.

And so, the task remains: How do you proceed in converting knowledge (and technology) into practice? What process do you follow? How do you bridge that gap?

All of these questions relate to a *process of thinking,* an approach to the problem. And the real question—as always—is less what you would specifically propose as a solution than *how you would go about solution-finding for the problems you would confront.*

This sort of bemusement is pervasive throughout contemporary American culture, notoriously so within the corporate culture that is supposed to power the economic engine of American society. Business policy strategist Ian Mitroff writes:

> I've seen the mind of corporate America, and what I've seen gives me great cause for alarm. I'm not saying that there is a complete lack of talented individual minds. The problem is that they are few and far between, and they are isolated.
>
> No matter what kind of organization in which they work, they are besieged by three fundamental dilemmas. One, they are faced with issues of strategic importance they have never experienced before.
>
> Two, the issues with which they are struggling are not only new, but come at them faster than before. They barely have time to deal with one issue before it seems like ten new ones are bearing down on them from all sides.
>
> Three, and this is the most bewildering of all, nearly every one of the old tools that they have used so successful-

ly in the past in dealing with problems no longer work. Worst of all, the old tools not only fail to solve current problems, but they actually make things worse.

One of the reasons why our culture is having trouble in shifting from old, standardized industries to new, high-tech ones is because the shift is more than merely a change in our industrial and technological base. Fundamentally, it represents a profound shift in how we think about the nature of the world.[18]

Avoid the Myths of Problem Solving

At this point, it's important that you not get bogged down in an attitude of hopelessness. In chapters 4 through 10, we'll show you not only how to go about preventing and solving your problems but also how, by applying the seven principles of Breakthrough Thinking, you can avoid the trap of finding an apparently excellent solution to the *wrong problem.*

Just as the science of statistics seeks to minimize the probability of rejecting what data should be accepted and of accepting what should be rejected, by applying the principles of Breakthrough Thinking, you will learn to minimize the probability of trying to solve the wrong problem. Once you learn this new way to think, you will no longer fear the fact that problems do not go away, that they are never solved once and for all. Indeed, once you learn how to reach the best possible solutions, you will begin to see your problems not as obstacles but as milestones marking progress on the road to your success.

Above all, by applying the seven principles of Breakthrough Thinking, you will learn how to avoid the seven myths of problem solving. These myths illustrate how, for example, corporate managers are tempted to apply wholesale the techniques of quality-of-working-life programs. Trying to adopt any program others may be using successfully—such as organizational architecturing, strategic planning, or total quality management—entails the same if slightly reworded myths. Quality-of-working-life programs, which are based on Japanese methods of industrial organization, include such innovations as job enrichment and autonomous work groups. They have become increasingly popular among American firms as generic solutions to any and all problems of productivity.[19]

Altruism Myth: Quality-of-working-life programs are for the welfare of workers. Management benefits through the resultant goodwill. But in fact, people dislike being patronized; goodwill is only a by-product of an effective quality-of-working-life program. The direct benefit is that well-designed work enables management to take full advantage of its most important human resource: the brains of its personnel.

Know-it-All Myth: Quality of working life is a quantifiable science that we can entrust to the experts. They will know where quality-of-working-life techniques should be applied and what data to collect so that exact results can be predicted. But in fact, there is a proper balance to be struck between knowing too little and trying to know it all. The methods most appropriate to conduct science may not be appropriate for problems of planning and design. Moreover, the solutions proposed by the usual expert are limited to his or her expertise.

Science demands that data be objective and impersonal, that subjects in experiments be treated uniformly. This is not the best way to implement organizational designs. It is often preferable to use people as participants in planning and design, rather than merely as sources of data—not simply to make them feel good but to ensure that the information gathered is not far removed from its context.

Snapshot Myth: Implementations of a solution (quality-of-working-life program) is an ad hoc process that does not require much planning. To expect a utopian vision to propel its own fulfillment is to ensure that the solution will fail. Whenever we attempt to do something new, especially with a quick-fix program or fad, we must undo something old. Simple before-and-after snapshots of the problem do not provide an order or priority for the doing or the undoing. This uncertainty over means can prevent the ends from materializing.

Snapshot worship can prematurely narrow the focus of attention onto a false or misleading definition of the problem. With everyone's energy directed at the wrong problem, it takes a monumental flash of insight to discover that the right problem is something not visible in the snapshot.

Instant Gratification Myth: Once a quality-of-working-life plan has been agreed upon and implemented, people will quickly be able to carry it out, except for some irrational resistance to change. Acceptance, or at least open-mindedness, by those affected by a new plan is a prerequisite to successful implementation. And it is perfectly rational to reject something whose value one has not come to appreciate.

With a degree of acceptance and open-mindedness, people may welcome the chance to try a new plan; yet this does not guarantee success because only gradually will they understand the full implications of the new plan. Success is not something that can be expected overnight.

Cloning Myth: A quality-of-working-life program that worked well in one organization is almost guaranteed to work well in a similar organization. Most innovations are modified as they are assimilated into a system. A model proposed for cloning exists in the minds of only a few who must sell the proposed solution to the people most affected by it, whose perceptions are likely to differ from their own.

Beware of the prepackaged program. Every technique used to improve the quality of working life is a blunt instrument that can succeed only if adapted to the special circumstances of a particular firm.

Typecasting Myth: People's reactions to quality-of-working-life programs can be predicted by studies that categorize or generalize their behavior. As good as quality-of-working-life principles are, they will not work for everyone or under all circumstances. People cannot predict their reactions to new organizational arrangements until they have experienced them.

Getting people to try something new involves the whole issue of implementation and perhaps a major part of the issue of human learning. It is difficult to predict a future individual case from any generalization based on prior studies or experience. One must give individuals the opportunity to choose, rather than determine their fates according to typecasting.

Department of "Blank" Myth: A department responsible for managing quality-of-working-life programs must be set up to make the program effective. Such departments imbue quality-of-working-life principles with the status of a service that can be introduced and removed at will. This implies that the current organizational style is satisfactory and that only marginal returns can be obtained with the new gadget.

Quality-of-working-life efforts should not be departmentalized or even undertaken until managers are ready to deal with the organization as a whole system. They must be incorporated into an overall *total approach* to planning and improving work structure in the organization.

The total approach of Breakthrough Thinking is far more important to finding and implementing successful solutions than is the choice of any specific generic technique. Breakthrough Thinking incorporates and supersedes all three previous approaches to problem-solving: the chance, affective, and rational approaches.

To reach successful solutions, all three previous approaches are needed. Each individual, each organization, is unique. What the individual or the organization believes (its values, its goals, its methods of adapting to outside forces, its history and style) and what each individual perceives as crucial are the real-world conditions that need to be modified to produce an effective solution and the further ability to change even that.

Leaders understand this. Often instinctively, they formulate their visions, operating methods, and follow-ups to affect those beliefs and perceptions as quickly as possible.

Breakthrough Thinking seeks changes (solutions) that are actually implemented and that incorporate their own continuing betterment, rather than proposals, however elegant, that are not implemented or are viewed as the eternal answer.

Indeed, with all our current problems, the need to make changes, and the new technologies available to us, the *approach* we take in creating or restructuring systems—our mode of reasoning, our thinking process—becomes the single most critical factor in our achievement of success.

There are no quick fixes. Whether the corporate manager is seduced by a wholesale implementation of techniques to enhance the quality of working life, or whether the supposed solution to the problem is to be found in automation or computers, in reality there can be no truly successful generic solutions.

This fact is evidenced with particular clarity in the case of American corporations' head-long rush to increase productivity. According to a special report in *Business Week*:

> Last year alone, [American manufacturing executives] added computers and new process-control equipment to the tune of $17 billion.
>
> The results? Labor productivity in goods-producing industries leaped, pushing the annual growth rate to an average 3.5 percent for this decade, up from the paltry 1.4 percent of 1973-79. Exports are climbing at double-digit rates. U.S. manufacturing is humming again. On the face of it, things are going swimmingly.
>
> Look a little closer, though, and it's clear that a new paradox has emerged: the more corporate America tries to boost productivity, the more elusive that goal becomes.

Furthermore, many organizations lost ground with the new technologies even though a few did accomplish a great deal. The special report points out that:

> General Motors spent "more on automation than the gross national products of many countries," yet had little to show for it, says Stephen G. Payne, chief executive of the PA Consulting group in Princeton, New Jersey. For GM and many other companies, the productivity payoff from automation is nowhere in sight.

[Many people assume that] it's technology, of course, that should do the trick.... So bring on automation, from office PCs to process-control devices. In theory, productivity should soar. In practice, the promise of technology hasn't been fulfilled. [One reason] may be that changes in low tech must accompany the introduction of high tech. The way workers, supervisors, and managers interact may have to change at the same time as new manufacturing systems are adopted."[20]

Similarly, the *New York Times* has noted, despite the fact that fully 42 percent of American workers were employed by companies undergoing down sizing or reduction of their permanent work force:

"Companies that fail to factor in quality-of-employee-life issues when imposing total quality management or 'reengineering,' or any other of the competiveness-enhancing, productivity-improving schemes now popular may gain little but a view of the receding backs of their best people leaving for friendlier premises."[21]

It will come as no surprise to anyone who can recall his or her first attempt to master (indeed, not be mastered by) the potential of the personal computer, that many people spend more time learning how to use such new productivity-enhancing solutions than the labor hours the machines may actually save. Indeed, whenever people simply apply a new technology wholesale, regarding it as *the* solution to their problem, rather than asking first about the fundamental purposes of their productive activity, the so-called solution will tend to do more harm than good.

Those who are charged with finding solutions to the problems faced by public-sector agencies, problems that affect our quality of life, tend to make mistakes similar to those made by their managerial colleagues in private enterprise. In the public sector, too, the first instinct seems to be simply to throw money at the problem, almost always with little if any rhyme or reason, hardly ever with a purpose-based strategy that is well planned and well designed.

Science magazine noted that as the U.S. Congress prepared to pour billions of dollars into fighting a "war on drugs," no provision was made for planning and designing the antidrug offensive, or even for analyzing why previous programs had largely failed.

"Even as the bandwagon starts to roll," said the report, "a few social scientists are troubled by the direction it is taking and by the wobbly steering that guides it. They say that no significant attempt has been made to analyze the government's enforcement record in the past or to gather information that would help guide policy in the future. The emphasis is on action, not analysis. It is time, critics say, to invest in policy research and to target expenditures better."[22]

Yet even these well-intentioned and perceptive scientists focus their concern more on the absence of data relating to past and future efforts than on the crucial factor of antidrug program planning and design. How much better it would be, how much more wisely would the public wealth be spent, if the seven principles of Breakthrough Thinking were applied in the solution of the drug problem. Imagine the impact of applying Breakthrough Thinking to other pressing public problems—depletion of the ozone layer, acid rain, world hunger, the continuing threat of nuclear war.

Competitiveness has become the buzzword replacing *productivity* in our business, government, and media consciousness. It indicates the comparative standing of rivals in obtaining customers and market share.

Like productivity, competitiveness is a *measure* of other things, such as the size of the trade deficit, the percentage of the gross national product that goes to health care, the relative costs of manufacturing automobiles, and so on. But these are essentially measures of how well, or how inadequately, a nation is doing its economic job. They are motivators to take action, but they are not the job itself.

Tinkering with measurements can yield some quick-fix, psychological results—some improvement in numbers. But it does little for the underlying problems. What any nation needs to do is to examine not the thermometer but the furnace. The furnace is a nation's *system* of producing goods and services. And each element of the system—people, machines, material, product designs, service demands, infrastructure, money— needs to be changed in terms of the whole.

What is true for nations is also true for the corporations that largely comprise their economies. For example, the Xerox Corporation, finding itself in a competitive bind versus the Japanese, examined its furnace instead of its thermometer. Instead of focusing on actions that directly affected measurements, like quarterly profits and short-term price-earnings ratios, it pulled itself out of its competitive slump by zeroing in on developing new product lines, market niches, and production processes.

Even desirable actions will come to nothing unless the key purposes of solving the problem are identified. Improving the math and science skills of students, for example, may produce better measures on the standard tests, but unless the new skills are linked to training in better problem-solving methods, the benefits derived will be minimal. Encouraging the development of new technology may produce better innovation rates; for example, the United States produces more Nobel Prize winners per capita than any other country. But leaving in place the current American methods of converting such knowledge to effective and productive practice promises that the United States will face continued difficulties in competitiveness.

Our research, as well as that of colleagues, has shown that successful problem solvers are purpose-oriented, tolerate ambiguity, encompass others' participation, and cope with subjective or soft information.[23] By contrast, we have also found that 85 to 90 percent of American executives are mentally oriented toward dissecting problems, rejecting ambiguity, encouraging isolated and routine work, and emphasizing techniques and hard data. The American educational system also promotes this philosophy at all levels.

Ironically, the principles for an effective approach based on the problem-solving methods of effective people—the principles of Breakthrough Thinking—were formulated in the United States but are used much more by the Japanese to enhance their already positive intuition about problem-solving approaches. This is strikingly reminiscent of Ampex Corporation's breakthrough in the research and development of videotape recorders—created in the United States but successfully manufactured only in Japan.

Yet Japan, too, needs help solving problems. Japan needs to change just as much as the United States. We must all change regularly, solve problems repeatedly, or else fall behind. In 1988, *Los Angeles Times* business columnist James Flanagan reported:

> Japan has made great strides in the 40 years since the postwar occupation of General Douglas MacArthur and his team of U.S. experts reformed its economic and social system. Japan has earned its leadership in many industries.
>
> But there are frightening imbalances in Japan's economy, too—most prominently in land. So inflated is [the price of] Japanese land these days that the 145,807-square-mile land area of Japan is said to be equal to twice the value of the whole 3.6-million-square-mile land area of the United States.
>
> But that's a danger signal, not a sign of strength. Land and housing in Tokyo have shot to such prohibitive prices that it has become a national problem—preventing the development of housing for many of Japan's people and threatening to curb the growth of the domestic economy.
>
> It's no less a problem for being hidden: Japan does not include housing or land in its cost of living index. So while Japan officially showed almost no inflation last year, the price of Tokyo apartments rose 200 percent, to an average of $1.6 million apiece.
>
> Furthermore, sky-high prices on the Tokyo Stock Exchange are based heavily on corporate holdings of such inflated real estate. So Japan appears headed for a crash of stock and land prices.[24]

In fact this predicted crash did occur in the early 1990s. Stock market prices in Japan fell 60 percent. At the same time, evidence of corruption and influence peddling on a massive scale brought the 40-year rule of the Japanese Liberal Democratic Party to a crashing end.

The purpose and spirit of Breakthrough Thinking—and of this book—is in no way exclusive or competitive. We intend to demonstrate that all humanity needs help solving its problems and that sharing knowledge about *how* to do this is good for all of us. Ultimately, individual human beings and how they think are important. To transform individual lives, leaders of organizations must themselves change and demonstrate a new way of thinking.

As one group or nation becomes increasingly able to find better solutions, so too will other groups and nations be able to find other sets of good solutions. All nations should be looking to the future. And in a world increasingly interdependent, the truly effective solution of one nation's problem will contribute to the betterment of all.

This chapter addressed the key question of why we should formulate principles of action and stick to them. It asked you to consider what we are trying to do and to understand the justification for the new behavior.[25] It showed that the gap each of us must overcome needs another concept—a set of principles or assumptions and a process of reasoning to put the principles into action.

Here, then, ends your introduction to the seven principles and "expantegration" process of Breakthrough Thinking:

1. *The Uniqueness Principle*: Each problem is unique and may require a unique solution.

2. *The Purposes Principle*: Focusing on and expanding purposes helps strip away nonessential aspects of a problem.

3. *The Solution-After-Next Principle*: Having a target solution in the future gives direction to near-term solutions and infuses them with larger purposes.

4. *The Systems Principle*: Every problem is part of a larger system of problems, and solving one problem inevitably leads to another. Having a clear framework of what elements and dimensions comprise a solution ensures its workability and implementation.

5. *The Limited Information Collection Principle*: Excessive data gathering may create an expert in the problem area,

but knowing too much about it will probably prevent the discovery of some excellent alternatives.

6. *The People Design Principle*: Those who will carry out and use the solution should be intimately and continuously involved in its development. Also, in designing for other people, the solution should include only the critical details to allow some flexibility to those who must apply the solution.

7. *The Betterment Timeline Principle*: The only way to preserve the vitality of a solution is to build in and then monitor a program of continual change. The sequence of Breakthrough Thinking solutions thus becomes a bridge to a better future.

You need to keep in mind all seven of these Breakthrough Thinking principles as you develop effective solutions to your problems. You may find that using these principles in a different order works best for you. Each principle recurs at various points in any problem-solving effort. One principle may be most important to you at one moment, and then another principle later. Part Two of this book will open your reasoning abilities to the principles of Breakthrough Thinking.

In Part Three, Chapter 11 will show you how to combine and integrate all seven principles into the process of finding solutions to your problems. Finally, Chapter 12 will examine a bright and expansive future, one in which you have mastered, yet continue to seek changes in, the continually evolving principles of Breakthrough Thinking—the new language of successful and innovative change.

NOTES

1. C.G. Jung, *Man and His Symbols* (New York: Doubleday, 1964).

2. J.L. Adams, *The Care and Feeding of Ideas: A Guide to Encouraging Creativity* (Reading, MA: Addison-Wesley, 1986).

3. Ted Coulson and Alison Strickland, "Applied Creativity," *Executive Excellence* (August 8, 1991).

4. Eva Basch-Kahre, "Patterns of Thinking," *International Journal of Psycho-Analysis* (Vol. 66, 1985).

5. R.W. Sperry, "Lateral Specialization of Cerebral Functions in Surgically Separated Hemispheres," in F.J. McGuigan and R.A. Schoonover, eds., *The Psychology of Thinking* (New York: Academic Press, 1973).

6. Peter Elbow, *Writing Without Teachers* (New York: Oxford University Press, 1973), Appendix Essay.

7. Robert J. Samuelson, *Newsweek* (December 11, 1989).

8. Lynn Sandra Kahn, *Peacemaking: A Systems Approach to Conflict Management* (Lanham, MD: University Press of America, 1988).

9. Richard Schikel, *The Disney Version* (New York: Simon & Schuster, 1968).

10. George F. Whicher, *Walden Revisited: A Centennial Tribute to Henry David Thoreau* (Putney, VT: Hendricks House, 1973).

11. Theodore Roosevelt, *Theodore Roosevelt Cyclopedia* (Westport, CT: Meckler Corp., 1989).

12. Lester Thurow, *Head To Head: The Coming Economic Battle Among Japan, Europe, and America* (New York: Warner Books, 1993).

13. Thomas Paine, *The Age of Reason* (Secaucus, NJ: Citadel Press, 1974).

14. C.W. Churchman, *The Systems Approach and Its Enemies* (New York: Basic Books, 1979).

15. William Freudenburg, "Perceived Risk, Real Risk: Social Science and the Art of Probabilistic Risk Assessment," *Science* (October 7, 1988). Copyright © 1988 by the AAAS.

16. Gregory Stock, *Metaman: The Merging of Humans and Machines Into A Global Superorganism* (New York: Simon and Schuster, 1993).

17. Bruce Mazlish, *The Fourth Discontinuity: The Co-Evolution of Humans and Machines* (Yale University Press, 1993).

18. Ian Mitroff, "Teaching Corporate America to Think About Crisis Prevention," *Journal of Business Strategy* (Spring 1986).

19. G.J. Wacker and G. Nadler, "7 Myths About Quality of Working Life," *California Management Review* 22, No. 3 (Spring 1980).

20. Karen Pennar, "Productivity Paradox," *Business Week* (June 6, 1988).

21. Barbara Presley Noble, "Dissecting the 90's Workplace," *New York Times* (September 19, 1993).

22. "Flying Blind in the War on Drugs," *Science* 240 (June 17, 1988). Copyright 1988 by the AAAS.

23. J.G. Peterson, "Personal Qualities and Job Characteristics of Expert Engineers and Planners," unpublished dissertation (University of Wisconsin, Madison, 1985).

24. James Flanagan, "Century of the American is Far From Over," *Los Angeles Times* (July 3, 1988).

25. Robert Nozick, *The Nature of Rationality* (Princeton, NJ: Princeton University Press, 1993).

Part 2

Increasing Your Personal Effectiveness

Chapter 4

The Uniqueness Principle

The board of directors of a $2-billion company with
over 200 divisional profit centers wanted to introduce a
total-quality-management program. The board members
studied various models of TQM—Crosby, Deming,
GOAL/QPC, Juran—and visited companies with a reputation of having successfully implemented one or another of these models.

The board then invited Gerry Nadler to help it decide which TQM model to adopt. To himself, Nadler's immediate response was, "None of them!" Instead, he used
Breakthrough Thinking to facilitate the board meeting and
develop a TQM plan specific to the organization. The plan
that the company ultimately implemented could not be
traced to any one of the pre-existing models.

Although it borrowed something from most of the
models, the plan also included many elements of other improvement concepts, such as just-in-time, reengineering,
self-directed work teams, and strategic planning. The
problem-solving process that the company adopted in its
recommended plan was Breakthrough Thinking.

One of the most pervasive and persistent mistakes in
problem solving, even in planning and design, is to assume that
one problem is identical with another. Why do people make this
mistake? Often, the adage, "don't reinvent the wheel," is used as
their rationale.

A prime tenet of Breakthrough Thinking that we will explain in this chapter is that *each problem is unique*. If an effective solution is to be found, the problem must be treated as
unique from the outset. Propounding this belief in the face of

ages of tradition may seem like an effort to sweep back the ocean, but we hope to demonstrate that the conviction is valid.

The effective leaders and problem solvers we studied were very firm in their conviction concerning the uniqueness of each problem or opportunity situation that they faced. This emphasis on uniqueness held true regardless of their knowledge about what others had done previously to find solutions in apparently similar circumstances.

These effective problem solvers considered uniqueness so important because they knew instinctively that individual human beings involved in seemingly identical situations are *always* different and thus affect possible solutions. Cultural diversity and conflicting values are always present in different organizations, indeed at various levels within a single organization and in all parts of a given project. Each level and every part is unique and must be approached as such from the outset.

Thus, it was clear to the effective problem solvers that they needed to consider their situation and state of knowledge before trying to achieve positive change. These effective people also realized that shortly after a great solution was found elsewhere, new technology might change the solution they should use in their situation.

Finally, they recognized that the purpose of their own system or solution might differ from an identical activity or function. That is, the name might be the same—scheduling, planning, medication administration, entry of purchase orders—but the ultimate purpose of the activity might well differ in different organizations. The effective leaders knew instinctively that force-fitting a system or solution imported from elsewhere into their own unique situation can often cause much more time and money than starting from scratch and developing their own unique system or solution.

No wonder, then, that the effective problem-solvers we studied considered uniqueness to be their first order of business. Indeed, some claimed that their habit of initially viewing every situation as unique is the way they are "lucky." Consequently, some effective problem-solvers suggested that they were naturally able to avoid the pitfalls that routinely plague those others who seek similarities when approaching inherently different problems. Thus, it should be no surprise that we proclaim uniqueness as the first principle of Breakthrough Thinking.

The reason humans, from time immemorial, have tried to liken one problem to an already familiar one is not hard to explain. Everything in nature, from a rainbow or a bolt of lightning to an amoeba or a hippopotamus, instinctively seeks the line of least resistance because it presumably involves the least expenditure of energy. Using an achieved solution to one problem as a model for solving another *seems* like a labor-saving device. It gives a feeling of objectivity, a highly valued but overrated criterion in problem solving and prevention.

Living creatures create paths. In law, the revered object is the precedent. In sports, it's the performance record. In finance, it's the eternal quest for patterns of market fluctuation in the past that will serve as guides to the future. And in everyday affairs, we constantly seek—often subconsciously—to simplify our lives and lighten our burdens (fear of taking a risk, lack of appetite for chaos) by coupling problems with apparently similar situations and deciding that a solution "wheel" that worked once will be equally applicable again.

Yet more often than not, such linkages turn out to be illusory and costly.

It is not difficult to demonstrate that no two problems *can* be alike. No matter how similar two situations may appear on the surface, they almost certainly differ in terms of time, place, people involved, related surrounding conditions, and purpose of solution.

The likelihood of differences in regard to time, place, and people involved is obvious.

In regard to surrounding conditions, we need to recognize that no problem (or organization) exists in a vacuum. Each problem is part of an inevitable web of conditions, which themselves are subject to constant change.

As for purpose, Chapter 5 is devoted to a discussion of this critical variable. For now, however, suffice it to observe that although we may think of our actions as having single, specific objectives, most courses of action also have an array of possible objectives, and that array of purposes is unique for each problem.

This is not to say, of course, that there aren't problems that can be handled in a routine, repetitive manner. Trying to develop a new system for each time you take a shower, get dressed, take a bus to work, or open the mail would be a waste of time and energy. Most of our lives we tend to live by scripts. But even these routine activities should be reexamined from time to time as though they had come up for the first time. Almost no system or solution is as good now as it could be, and a solution that was right five years ago may not be right now, given evolutionary changes in your personal situation or in your organization and its people and purposes.

Theoretically, each time you are to operate a system represents an opportunity for change. But you will most likely be motivated to seek change when you are dissatisfied with a situation because the results do not meet your values and objectives or those of your company or organization.

Every problem situation presents opportunities for Breakthrough Thinking, whether it's a system that is broken and appears to need fixing or replacing, one that works but needs to be updated to improve the accomplishment of its goals, or a system that needs to be invented to attain new ends.

Believing in the uniqueness of your problem at the outset will help you avoid critical errors common to conventional problem solving. For example, if you look at the unique larger purposes you or your organization want to accomplish, you will greatly reduce the probability of working on the wrong problem.

One of the universally recognized ingredients of success is *persistence*. But persistence in essence simply is recognition that today's problem, however familiar in outline, is not identical with yesterday's problem.

The most common example of this is in job hunting. Countless people have had the experience of being told there was no opening at a certain establishment, only to be sought out by the same employer days or weeks later to fill a sudden vacancy—personnel turnover being the predictable rule rather than the exception in most businesses. Such factors can fundamentally alter what seems an immutable problem.

Bernard Shaw, the newscaster, tells how, as only an aspiring journalist, he sought a personal interview with Walter Cronkite, just to get some career guidance. Shaw telephoned the hotel where Cronkite was staying, with no result. But in the next couple of days he phoned *fifty more times*—and finally arranged what proved to be a productive meeting with Cronkite. Shaw's core *problem* had not changed, but an important part of it, the *circumstances bearing on it*, had for one reason or another changed decisively.

If you accept that the framework of your problem is unique and constantly changing in all of its components and interrelations, you will reduce to virtually zero the probability of looking only at the overall system performance to the neglect of errors inside the system, or of looking only at the system components to the neglect of the system's performance as a whole.

If you incorporate in your solution the distinct needs, interests, abilities, limitations, and power of all stakeholders, you will maximize the quality and effectiveness of your solution, increase the likelihood of implementation, and make the most effective use of time and resources.

By considering the uniqueness of your situation, you will be better able to make the problem-solving process real and meaningful to you and all others involved in designing an appropriate solution.

Process Lessons from Effective People

Our studies of effective people show over and over again that they do not assume that previous successful solutions should govern the current problem situation or that analysis techniques and data collection are at first critical. They use, instead, three different sets of assumptions and axioms, which we describe below:

1. *No two situations are alike.* Each customer, company, organization, household, person, student, community, state, and country differs from all others in minor or major ways. Each has a unique history that has brought them to this point in time.

Two hospitals in similar communities—each with 250 patient beds, an emergency room, identical inpatient and outpatient services, and nearly identical patient volume—wanted to improve their medical records library system. The consultant called in to develop the systems was a Breakthrough Thinker, and he did not assume that the system developed for one hospital ten months earlier, however outstanding, would work equally well in the second hospital.

He knew that the *people* who would use the system differed in all their myriad characteristics, their social groupings, their organizational roles, and so on. He knew that the purposes to be achieved in each hospital might well be different. Trying to force-fit the solution from the first hospital into the problem situation of the second hospital, when the purposes of the two hospitals were different, would be a cut-rate prescription for disaster. Without even referring to the initial solution, he set up a team in the second hospital to work on the project.

The first hospital installed a highly acclaimed, automated medical records network where physicians could enter patient information and orders on a dictation system or at a computer terminal on the patient's floor. The orders were dispatched electronically to pharmacy, radiology, or other departments and on to patient billing and medical records. The second hospital had a slightly different purpose to achieve and faced different time, budget, and staffing constraints, so the project team designed a different system using the existing phones and more paper to accomplish their objectives.

The problem solver who sees and accepts *differences* has a much better chance of finding a successful breakthrough solution, no matter how prosaic it may at first appear, than the problem solver who sees only similarities and tries to force borrowed solutions into situations where they are inappropriate. Selling prepackaged solutions—a kitchen layout, a software program, a manufacturing robot—is endemic in contemporary society. Yet even if the solution works, it may not be what would be most effective for the situation.

Researchers, who fuel the early stages of conventional problem solving, love to classify and categorize, most often with either/or labels. Companies are either oriented toward innovation or efficiency. Problems are well structured or poorly structured. Data are hard or soft. Intervention is internal or external. Usually, however, no problem or situation fits neatly into such narrow categories. The erroneous leap of faith, then, is to believe that if my label and your label are the same, the same solution will work for both of us.

Labels, classifications, analogies, and metaphors narrow and limit thinking and bring an air of unreality to the situation. They are abstractions that prove no point. The fact that courts of law can resolve legal conflicts does not mean that the adversarial process is the best way to resolve technical conflicts. If one hospital uses measured allowed times to increase productivity in the radiology department, it doesn't necessarily follow that another hospital's radiology department with productivity 45 percent higher than the industry average should adopt the same strategy. To accept such comparisons, analogies, labels, or classifications is to make reasoning assumptions that obstruct rather than facilitate the problem-solving process. Worse, accepting the assumptions and using the analogies and metaphors may close your mind to the advice and perceptions of others. Openness to the perceptions of all the stakeholders is critical to success and a key component of the uniqueness principle.

A recent fad in industry is competitive benchmarking, in which a company gets all the information it can about the features, costs, quality, timeliness, and production processes of its competitors' or related companies' products or services. The company uses this information as an indicator of how much it has to change and what methods to use in order to achieve the same level as its best competitor. Following this pattern, one company gives the "best" product design to its designers and tells them they have only two choices—develop a better, or at least no worse, design. The likelihood is high that the designers will produce a "no-worse" design because they have studied the competitor's product so extensively. Meanwhile, the competitor has moved ahead so that achieving its benchmark still leaves the other company behind. Also, in trying simply to match its competitor, the company may lose again, because it did not adhere to its own unique characteristics or market niche.

Unfortunately, managements in almost all U.S. companies proceed from fad to fad—quality circles, creativity training, total productivity, and so on—to whatever seductively popular program a current management proclaims to be *the* answer. These are the junk foods on which U.S. managers munch as they seek the quick fix and immediate satisfaction.

As the *Wall Street Journal* so clearly stated in a front page article: " 'The success rate of any of these [fads] is pretty low'. … Employees, as well as customers, rate the effectiveness of these management fads at between just 10% to 20%. …"[1] The uniqueness principle of Breakthrough Thinking explains why these fads fail to work and why each effort at change must instead begin with a clear focus on uniqueness and the other principles of Breakthrough Thinking.

For example, agricultural specialists in a province of Mexico failed to apply the uniqueness principle when they introduced a new variety of maize that produced two to three times more grain per acre than the prevalent strains. They persuaded farmers to plant the new maize, and productivity rose significantly. By the end of the third year, however, the farmers had reverted to planting the old seed varieties. The women who made tortillas from the maize didn't like the new color.

A U.S. factory owned by, say, the Japanese is no less unique. Introducing Japanese-style labor practices—work teams, employee decision making in managing operations, *kaizen* or continuous improvement—has run into a surge of protests in the United States. Workers in these companies now find that job security is not assured and supervisors still have authority at the workplace. Workers feel betrayed by all the promises made about the transferred solution.[2] No matter how worthwhile a solution may be in one location, its transferability is limited.

Minoru Yamada, President of Daikin Industry Corporation, one of Japan's largest air conditioning manufacturers, kept that fact in mind during the 1970s, when his company expanded into foreign markets. Yamada wrote:

> This was a big challenge and a risk for me. I had a strong will to test our technology in the international environment. Made-in-U.S.A. air conditioning equipment had the dominant share of the foreign market, and there was no Japanese-made product at that time. The problem was how to compete with American technology.
>
> American companies shipped their products to foreign countries without thinking about the local conditions in each country. For example, an American company would export left-hand cars without considering the specific country conditions. On the contrary, our company designed products to meet the situation-specific conditions. For example, we change the voltage and volumes of cooling gas, corresponding to the temperature of each country.
>
> We focused on "situation-specific uniqueness principle" production. As a result of this policy, we could not export the specialized product to other countries. So the risk for us would be big if the situation-specific products were not accepted in the country for which they were designed. We had to fight with our back to the sea. We tried to produce the best air conditioners and market them with great efforts in each country.[3]

As a result of these efforts, Daikin Industry Corp. was successful in fifteen countries.

These examples show why the transfer of technology from one country to another does not work, just as it doesn't from one company to another. This holds true whether you are introducing new strains of maize, agricultural equipment, manufacturing equipment, or family-planning methods. It pays to be aware of and assume the unique characteristics of the total situation, just as a successful comedian assays the characteristics of the audience before he tells a new joke, no matter how well it went over with the last crowd.

2. *Each problem is embedded in a unique array of related problems.* "Break the problem up into smaller, more manageable components," advises an old business adage. But this is virtually impossible to do with problems of any complexity. Every problem exists amid a tangle of interrelationships among people and with related systems.

A husband and wife in one family are different from any other couple because they each bring to the relationship a unique set of genes, family traditions, siblings, social and economic circumstances, and so on. These background conditions will influence everything they do as a couple.

In the same way, establishing an inventory system in one company will be different from establishing one in another because the inventory system should be influenced by the larger context of product line, numbers of parts, performance history of suppliers, competitors, the psychological style of the purchasing agent, and numerous other factors that vary from one company to the next.

If you break a problem into smaller components, you fail to see the unique qualities of the system as a whole, and if you only see the similarities between one whole system and another, you fail to see the differences in the components that make the whole unique. You must look at the components individually *and* in their larger context because the system's interrelations will be critical to the successful design and implementation of your solution.

During the early stages of problem solving, don't waste a great deal of time or effort on searching for the equation or "wheel" that solved similar problems or similar parts of problems. Breakthrough Thinking occurs when you initially assume your problem is unique and force yourself to avoid comparisons and quests for similarities.

3. *The solution to a problem in one organization will differ in some way from the solution to a similar problem in another organization.* It is thrilling to see a magnificent operating system, an unusual and innovative product, a state-of-the-art technology, or an innovative organizational system at work.

Like children in a toy store, we want to take the new idea home with us and enjoy it there. But like those same children, we often find that a model train that worked wonderfully in the toy store presents unforeseen problems in the new setting. Indeed, many new computer software programs are difficult to use because they are based on the technical culture of the program authors, not that of most users.

The landscape is white with the bleached bones of impulsive idea borrowing. Billions of dollars worth of agricultural equipment well-suited to farming in the United States lies rusting away in Third World fields. Millions of dollars worth of automated equipment and robots have been scrapped by companies within months of purchase. Failed organizational programs designed to improve the quality of working life, delivery systems, or productivity have left behind a trail of distrust and ill will. Clearly, there is no one best answer. All such ideas are monuments to what we call the technology trap or the cloning myth.

True, it is not always necessary to reinvent the wheel. Solutions that worked for others should be assumed at the beginning to differ from what you will need, but they may be viewed as *alternatives* when you are ready to develop recommendations. This is the way to know if you need a "wheel." After opening up your thinking and really coming to value the unique framework and purposes of your situation, you may decide to use a whole or partial solution that worked elsewhere— almost inevitably, however, with modifications that come from Breakthrough Thinking.

Everett Rogers saw evidence of this reinvention process when he studied the implementation of "Dial-a-Ride," a system developed in Haddonfield, New Jersey. It was a means of reducing the number of cars on the road, a system that grew out of the new computer technology developed in the early 1970s. Computers were used to minimize wait time for the caller and travel distance for the vans. By 1978, about 320 cities had adopted the system, but as it spread, Dial-a-Ride changed with an immeasurable degree of reinvention. Ann Arbor, Michigan, used a manual control system because the city found the computer "too cumbersome." Portland, Oregon, added lifts for the handicapped. Other cities added other specialized uses.[4]

Don't Take Our Word for It

In recent years, other researchers have come to share our sense that not only are almost all problem situations unique but that in each unique problem situation the process of problem solving (thinking) itself is necessarily unique. For example, with reference to Einstein's theory of relativity, Stanford University educational psychologist James G. Greeno postulates the concept of situated cognition:

"We learned in physics," Greeno explains, "that it is meaningless to attribute properties of motion to objects without a frame of reference. We make the same mistake in attributing knowledge and thinking to individual minds without a frame of reference."[5]

According to University of Amsterdam social scientists Jacobijn Sandberg and Bob Wielinga, Greeno's perspective "reflects a major shift in thinking about 'knowledge,' 'information,' 'representation,' and even 'memory.'"[6] In Greeno's view, knowledge can no longer be viewed as a self-contained substance separated from its context. Rather, it is essentially situated; subjective, not objective; embedded in a particular frame of reference; always relative and open to reinterpretation.

Essentially fluid, knowledge evolves continually as it is used. Learning occurs all the time and is situated in the everyday life experiences of individuals. Thus, knowledge can never simply be transferred because it does not exist in transferable form. The context of knowledge, both in its acquisition and its application, is always unique.

Greeno further notes that when we begin to understand thinking and creativity we will need to alter significantly the "framing assumptions" with which research in the field of thinking has been conducted. He proposes that thinking and learning are situated in unique contexts of beliefs and understandings about cognition, contexts that differ between individuals and social groups, and that fundamental properties of thinking and learning are determined by these contexts—the personal and social epistemolgies particular to each individual and group.

Paralleling Greeno's perspective, Japanese mathematician Heisuke Hironaka has proposed the concept of "variable thought" as a key factor in creativity. In this view, thought itself is treated as a variable in the mathematical sense, which implies the discarding of all fixed ideas and preconceptions in all aspects of thought. Moreover, Hironaka suggests that this attitude toward thought leads to creativity.

Hironaka further distinguishes between needs and wants. He defines "need" as existing in a certain time and place, dictated by external circumstances, and based on past experience, knowledge, and analysis of the present. "Want," however, is essentially removed from time and place; it is dictated by the individual's sentiments or aspirations for the future. Consequently, Hironaka interprets "necessity" in Edison's famous phrase: "Necessity is the mother of invention," as referring more to wants than to needs.[7]

Because needs, feelings, imagination, beliefs, and wants will always differ from person to person, the uniqueness of any problem situation where more than one person is involved is going to be even "more unique," if such a description were possible.

Any great creative insight—such as Edison's discovery of the electric light-bulb, which has since come to signify the very concept of a brilliant flash of intuition—will almost certainly partake of both the analytical research approach and the more fluid, intuitive, cognitive processes that in large measure characterize Breakthrough Thinking. Obviously, the search for apparently recurring solution patterns in problem solving is accomplished by means of analytical thinking. Yet it is equally obvious that the exclusive practice of analytical thinking—the Research Approach to solve problems—while possibly increasing one's factual knowledge, is certain to inhibit, if not entirely preclude, the creativity and intuition that are essential to solving problems.

Greeno and his fellow proponents of "situated cognition" maintain that creativity occurs naturally when one's situation is restructured. Changes in the environment, they argue, can cause a reorganization of "conceptual structures."

"The assumption of situated cognition says that all of our cognitive activity is connected with [inherently unique] situations," Greeno explains. "Creativity, in this view, involves reorganizing the connection the person has with a situation, rather than a reorganization that occurs within the person's mind. The situation with which one's connections are reorganized can be physical, social, or conceptual."

Graham Quinton and Brian Fellows, faculty in the Department of Social Studies, Polytechnic, Portsmouth, conducted experiments that tested the problem-solving strategies employed by their 26 subjects. Quinton and Fellows defined "perceptual" strategies as those in which the solver responded to certain constant characteristics of the problems, while more or less ignoring their meaning. They found that subjects using such "perceptual" strategies solved the problems significantly faster than subjects using "thinking" strategies, defined as those in which the problem solver read and thought about the meaning of the premises before answering.[8]

Quinton and Fellows acknowledge that one limitation on the usefulness of perceptual strategies is that their effectiveness seems to depend upon the solver's being able to assume that all the problems presented to him will belong to a restricted family group. That assumption, of course, is the basis of applying pre-existing solutions to new and unique problems. However, since each problem is unique and by definition does not pertain to any family, any pre-existing solution is likely to fail. In other words, shortcuts may sometimes work. More often, they will not. Successful short cuts to effective problem solving are both useful and welcome. But with many problems, perceptual shortcuts will likely lead us into snake-infested swamps.

Getting From Here to There

One of the dangers of adapting someone else's solution is that you fail to develop *transitional steps.* The problem and the solution become like before-and-after snapshots that say, "This is where we are, and this is where we want to be." But the snapshots offer no instruction on how to get there from here. And without that map, you are likely to get lost.

Here are some "red flags" to watch out for on your solution-finding journey:

- "Let's not reinvent the wheel here."
- "This worked for me in the past."
- "This is the way we do things around here."
- "That's the way it's done in our industry (profession, department)."
- "Our competition is doing it; we'd better do it too. And quickly."
- "I've read about a great new technique."

Whenever you hear yourself or others talk like this, immediately stop and practice the uniqueness principle.

Without guidelines, personnel will sometimes take things into their own hands and devise purposeful pathways to reach a goal, as happened at a Midwestern paper mill. Autocratic, hierarchical management policies had undermined labor-management relations at the plant to such an extent that productivity plummeted and the mill was sold as scrap.

The new owners decided to try to keep the plant open. In an effort to get labor more involved with the organization, the new managers purchased a survey-feedback program from a university. They hoped to find strategies for improving information flow, systems, and work relations. But fortunately, the workers broke all the rules. They rebelled against the lengthy surveys, which they saw as another cockamamie management idea with no purpose.

Eighteen months into the surveys, the workers demanded to know, "What are we trying to accomplish here?" They began disregarding the surveys and organized their meetings around specific problems with their machinery. The purposes orientation had entered through the back door and was a significant contributor to the mill's dramatic turnaround. If the managers had started with the assumption that the mill and its people and purposes were unique, the expense and time wasted on the survey, a solution inappropriate for the situation, could have been better used.

Decision makers, once they have subscribed to a solution, must not assume that implementation is an *ad hoc* process. As we saw in the paper mill example, implementation is a process that requires planning. Before we do something new, we must undo something old. Before-and-after snapshots don't establish priorities for the undoing or the doing, and the resulting uncertainty can prevent the "after" snapshot from ever materializing.

That's what happened when an electronic parts manufacturer became convinced that a quality-of-working-life program would be good for his operation. He had his engineers redesign products and processes to promote greater worker autonomy. Then he issued an order stating that the new quality-of-working-life program would be installed, "starting next Monday." The program was ineffective and almost led to a strike.

A solution cannot be bolted in place like a piece of equipment; it should instead be introduced as part of an ongoing process. Due thought must be given to the unique transitional states.

The uniqueness principle encourages problem solvers to value the perspectives, abilities, and limitations of stakeholders in the problem and involve them in planning the implementation of the solution—always, always asking, "What are we trying to accomplish?" This questioning is a constant check to be sure you are working on the right problems before trying to find solutions. The right problem for your organization to be working on may be just outside the frame of the seductively easy snapshot.

Another danger of idea borrowing, or the snapshot syndrome, is that stakeholders presume the utopian image in the "after" shot is eternal, sculpted in bronze, the standard against which to measure all future outcomes. In valuing the uniqueness of your situation, you must also value its life and its need and ability to evolve. As you approach a workable solution, whether new or adapted from elsewhere, people's visions will change and new ideals will come into view, creating fertile ground for other unprecedented problems that will, in turn, create new opportunities for Breakthrough Thinking.

Putting the Uniqueness Principle to Work

Applying the uniqueness principle does not involve a step-by-step process so much as an open frame of mind and a style of reasoning that greets each problem with the conviction that it is different from all others. We offer, however, some specific techniques that will help you and your colleagues think in terms of differences rather than similarities.

- When you first approach a problem, practice identifying its unique features rather than its similarities with other situations. Challenge similes, analogies, methaphors, and so-called successful solutions to similar problems whenever they pop up in discussion.

- Force yourself and others to *not* agree on what the problem is when you first discuss a problem situation. Don't even talk about possible solutions or comparisons with other situations. Make yourself believe your situation is unique, then mentally trace through possible consequences of the unique aspects of your situation. Remain open to all actions that might be appropriate and avoid closure on a fixed problem statement. Try to solve each problem from scratch.

- Ask yourself about the purposes of working on the problem. Thinking about your reasons for considering the problem encourages you to think of a range of purposeful activities in which you might engage. Think also of continual improvement in which these activities might figure. Examining the larger purposes of your unique organization opens your mind to breakthrough solutions.

- Ask yourself what conditions you should have ideally to work effectively on this problem. Try not to let presumed constraints limit your thinking or encourage you to find a quick and easy solution.

- Challenge with the search for purposes both the stated and implied assumptions of the people who present the problem.

Always ask yourself these specific questions:

- Have I approached this problem as if it were unique, even if my first impression tells me it isn't?
- What people, timing, and organizational culture make this problem unique?
- Why am I inclined to force a fit between this unique problem and a "tried-and-true" solution from the past?
- Have I made the mistake of beginning my search for a solution by simply accepting the perceptions or assumptions of the people or person who presented the problem?

If you ask yourself these questions and follow these guiding techniques with every problem and situation you encounter, you will be far better able to make the problem-solving process real and meaningful to yourself and all others involved in designing and implementing an appropriate solution. You will discover the unique array of interrelated problems embedded in your situation. You will avoid the assumption that a solution to a problem that proved effective in one organization will work equally well in your own.

Following the uniqueness principle, you will find yourself engaged in an ongoing process in which the following further benefits will occur:

- Vision and strategic thinking replace limiting and arbitrary solutions.
- Discussions focus on the larger issues and needs that are critical to long-term success, and less time is wasted on useless classification and pairing of problems and solutions.
- Rigid myths about the process of change give way to flexible assumptions that reflect the realties of the problem.
- Solutions fit the needs of the situation and are innovative beyond what you or your group are accustomed to achieving.

- Time, energy, and money are saved and credibility is gained by producing effective results the first time.

- Acceptance and implementation of your solutions become easier because the unique concerns of people involved, who might otherwise have resisted change, have been considered.

- New products and services are competitive because they address unique factors, even if major components of the new product or solution are in fact borrowed.

- Individuals no longer feel isolated, impatient, and tentative, and they begin to listen to others.

- Focusing on the uniqueness of your customers (and their own customers) takes your eye beyond the bottom line to the product or service that predicts future success.

- More tolerance is developed for *ambiguity* (the uncertainties of the present and future), a characteristic of the most effective problem solvers.

- People sense the importance of values, individual preferences, imagination, and hard work needed to accomplish change.

Successful people realize that today's solution may not work next year, so they keep their minds open to change and new options. They expect the unexpected and are prepared for surprises.

As historian G.R. Elton has noted: "The so-called lessons of history do not teach you to do this or that now.... Instead of telling us that certain conditions can be shown, from past experience, to lead to certain assured consequences, history forever demonstrates the unexpectedness of the event.... A knowledge of the past should arm a man against surrendering to the panaceas peddled by too many myth-makers."[9] In his book *The Lessons of History,* Michael Howard states the essential warning about not generalizing from the past: the past is a foreign country. [10]

We urge you to join other effective people in saying, "Our business is different." Realize that each problem is an opportunity to redesign, not just patch, a system. Building on the principle that your problem is unique, you are now ready to initiate

Breakthrough Thinking by examining not the problem, but rather the *purpose* of your efforts—what you are trying to accomplish.

NOTES

1. R. Fred Bleakley, "Many Companies Try Management Fads, Only To See Them Flop," *Wall Street Journal* (July 6, 1993).

2. James Risen, "Japanese Labor Policies Stirring U.S. Rebellion," *Los Angeles Times* (May 20, 1989).

3. Minoru Yamada, "Challenge to the Risk," *Journal of Executives* (August 1985).

4. Everett M. Rogers, with K. McGill and R.E. Rice, *The Diffusion of Dial-A-Ride* (Stanford, CA: Standord University, Institute for Communication Research, Report to the Urban Mass Transportation Administration, 1979).

5. James G. Greeno, in "The Science of Learning Math and Science," *Mosaic* Volume 23, No. 2 (Summer 1992), p. 41.

6. Jacobijn Sandberg and Bob Wielinga, "Situated Cognition: A Paradigm Shift?" *Journal of Artificial Intelligence in Education* Vol. 3 (1992), pp. 129-138.

7. T. Murkami and T. Nishiwaki et al, Nomura Research Institute, *Strategy for Creation* (Cambridge, England: Woodhead Publishing Ltd., 1991).

8. Graham Quinton and Brian J. Fellows, " 'Perceptual' Strategies in the Solving of Three-Term Series Problems," *British Journal of Psychology* Vol. 66, No. 1 (1975), pp. 69-78.

9. G.R. Elton, *Return to Essentials: Reflections on the Present State of Historical Study* (New York: Cambridge University Press, 1991).

10. Michael Howard, *The Lessons of History* (New Haven, CT: Yale University Press, 1991).

Chapter 5

The Purposes Principle

A large Canadian hydroelectric company sought to reduce the costs and improve the productivity of constructing and maintaining its transmission towers. Executives decided to set up a work measurement program to set standard amounts of work for all construction employees.

After the company had spent over $2 million to collect and structure work performance data, implementation of the program was halted by the threat of a strike. Workers objected because the amount of work to be expected from each of them would increase significantly.

Between the start of the program and its scheduled installation, the top executives of the company were replaced. The new management team decided to use Breakthrough Thinking to expand the purposes they sought to accomplish for the work measurement program, within a hierarchy of larger purposes.

They identified the purposes of the program as (1) to set workload standards for construction, (2) to identify the amount of output each worker should produce, (3) to determine the composition of work teams, (4) to produce estimates of the construction work required, (5) to plan construction of towers, (6) to assign the work required to construct the towers, (7) to establish distribution of electricity, and (8) to deliver electric power to consumers.

By selecting purposes 4 and 5 as their focus purposes, the executives decided that agreeing to a trial of the workers' request to set their own work loads was more likely to be effective than insisting on using the standard data developed by the previous management. Within a year, the new management had decided to quietly "bury" that standard data because the workloads being set by

the workers themselves were greater than what the measurement system would have required.

The productivity improvement and cost reduction
developed by the workers were much greater than what
was originally thought possible. Moreover, the huge costs
and long-term animosities certain to result from a strike
were averted.

*T*he word *purpose* has many connotations. It can
mean *utility,* as in "the purpose of pliers is to squeeze things." It
can mean intent, as in "his purpose was benign." It can mean
mission, as in "the purpose of the company is to provide conditioned airflow in enclosed spaces." Or it can mean an *objective,*
as in "the purpose of the bazaar was to raise money."

In Breakthrough Thinking, purpose encompasses, to some
extent, all of these connotations and others, and goes a major dimension beyond. The purposes principle includes the full range
of motivations and results possible in applying change to an existing condition. It states that the exploration and expansion of
purposes provide the opportunity to work on the right problem
within an overall framework of needed personal or organizational purposes.

The effective leaders and problem solvers we studied always placed every problem into a larger context. They sought
to understand the relationship between what effective action
on the problem was *supposed* to achieve and the purposes of
the larger setting of which the original problem was a part.
This led them to develop a hierarchy or ever-expanding set of
purposes for the problem they confronted.

In studying these successful leaders, we began to understand that the expansion of purposes into a hierarchy is a critical
element of effective problem solving. It allows you clearly to understand the wider context of all problem situations. It is the critical beginning for liberating creativity at all points in the problem
solving process, not just for developing innovative ideas.

Most people tend to think of *purposes* in monolithic terms.
We go to the store "to buy bread." We give money to charities
"to help the poor." We do aerobic exercises "to improve our

health." We buy a lottery ticket "to win money." Yet a little intro-spection will show that these ostensibly simple, straightforward purposes have far more complex motivations and results. We seldom come out of the store with only the item we went in to buy. Usually one or more additional things catch our eye. The purpose of our trip has been, unintentionally, expanded. Con-tributing to charities is only partly to help the poor; a subcon-scious purpose is the gratification we get from our altruism. Doing aerobics yields not only physical but also mental and emotional satisfactions. What we really buy in a lottery ticket is, for a brief time, a sense of excitement in being possibly on the verge of riches. In all these instances, apparently simple pur-poses are only the germ of broader purposes.

A core concept of Breakthrough Thinking is that the ini-tial purpose in solving a problem is invariably only the begin-ning, and that a great many more purposes emerge with scrutiny, by looking to customers and external factors. Getting customers to state their purposes can significantly affect the perspective and how your solutions will be framed. For exam-ple, if you ask the attendees at a conference held in a hotel the purposes of a coffee break, their responses are often much dif-ferent from those stated by the hotel beverage service staff. Pur-poses challenge the assumptions and thinking restrictions you and others bring to a problem. The purposes principle pro-vides a guide to expanded thinking, which opens the door to many more possible solutions. Visions begin with these larger purposes.

The structure of this kind of thinking is best represented by a diagrammatic ladder, one that expands downward rather than upward.

The top rung is a blunt statement of the ostensible prob-lem in its simplest form—usually what starts you or a group to work on the project. Successive rungs represent *conceptual ex-pansions* of the purposes of solving that problem as Break-through Thinking is applied.

To illustrate: A manufacturer of plastic bags had a problem with the die-cutting of a sheet of cardboard in a pattern— roughly like a Kleenex box. The pattern was so complicated that misstamping was running as high as 25 percent. Figure 5-1 shows this box design.

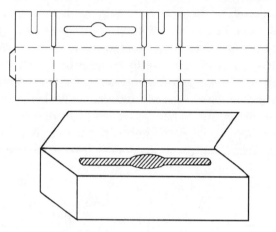

Figure 5-1.   Original box design

Breakthrough Thinking consultants helped the employee-engineer work team to outline the following array of ever-broadening purposes of the die-cutting operations problem:

1. Cut holes in sheet.

2. Provide openings in sheet.

3. Provide openings in box.

4. Package and dispense plastic bags.

5. Deliver single bag to customer.

6. Provide customer with plastic bag.

7. Provide customer with flexible, waterproof container.

By finding progressively bigger purposes for each purpose, the original assumption—that the problem was the difficult and costly task of altering a die-cutting system—was discarded. Consideration was directed, in ever-broadening dimension, to what was to be *accomplished:* a shipping container that would serve also as a dispenser of the bags for consumers (purpose levels 5 and 6).

The Breakthrough Thinking process conceivably might have ended in a perception that customers don't need plastic bags—that some other sort of container might be better. But in this case, plastic bags remained the entity to be reckoned with.

Some constraints or requirements entered into the considerations. The container had to be cardboard, it could not damage the bags, it had to be easy to open, the bags had to be easily extractable singly, and the container had to be attractive and not look complicated.

The result of these considerations (using purposes and other Breakthrough Thinking principles) was a much-simplified container that presented no die-cutting problems and, at the same time, made it easier for users to extract individual bags (see Figure 5-2).

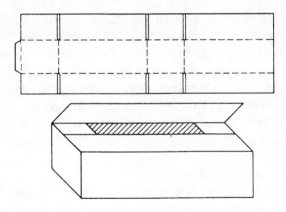

Figure 5-2.   Improved box design serves as package and dispenser.

This example is a microcosm of Breakthrough Thinking. The expanded purpose technique is just as effective in coping with other problems, such as a difficult employee, a hazardous freeway interchange, or even a dying lawn. If you expand your thinking beyond the most immediate, obvious purpose, and think in broader terms of what you want to accomplish, your solution options will mushroom, and the one you select is likely to take you closer to your ideals. For example, depending on the target purpose you choose to work on, the solution to your dying lawn may transcend fixing a broken sprinkler head to re-landscaping with drought-resistent shrubbery to moving to an area where lawns and landscaping are not an issue at all.

Purpose arrays have macrocosmic applications, too. Consider the following example where the purposes were implicit rather than written, but they guided Isao Nakauchi—founder, chairman, and president of DAIEI, Japan's biggest supermarket chain—through years of prosperity and evolution. He relates:

> After the Second World War, I started a small pharmacy in Kobe. I was treating sick people every day at that time. After a while, I started to think about the purpose of selling medicines at my small pharmacy. I realized that the purpose of selling medicines was to protect people from getting ill. I expanded my store and started to sell, not only medicines, but also related goods for promoting people's health. My small pharmacy became a fancy drug store, and we started to develop nationwide chain stores. I continued to think about the purposes of the drug store. Finally I found the purpose of my business was not only to promote people's health, but also to provide a better life. I started to develop the supermarket for that purpose. We are now providing not only physical products for people's better life, but also "software" for human happiness in our worldwide fancy plaza. I have always expanded the purposes of our business and changed our business every year, every month, and every day. "Change" is regularity in this world. Change is opportunity for us. The purposes of our business should be changed in accordance with the opportunity. Systems with unnecessary purposes cannot survive in this business world. We have to try to think of purposes and determine the most needed purposes.[1]

Beyond the Obvious: Transcending Simple Problem Definitions

The purposes principle gives you a mechanism for seizing the opportunity to transform a problem into productive change. It provides a mechanism to avoid working on the wrong problem. But obstacles steeped in historical methods of problem solving must be overcome.

People tend to accept a problem as presented to them and, in doing so, almost assuredly eliminate the opportunity for a breakthrough solution. Accepting the problem as given often leads to an "obvious solution," which is *not* a breakthrough, but which frequently gives rise to other problems. A *purposes* orientation helps you avoid being sold a solution to the wrong problem.

When the national consumer product company described in Chapter 1 was plagued with delays in delivery, excessive overtime, damaged products, and misshipments at the loading dock of one of its twenty-four warehouses, the expert assigned to the case approached the problem in the conventional way, collecting data about all the problems, preparing statistical analyses, drawing flow charts, and so on. Her recommendation to spend $60,000 to automate the loading dock calculated that the cost would be paid back within eight months, thus providing an excellent return on investment.

The supervisor of the warehouse, the manager of warehouses, and the director of distribution all approved the recommendation. Since the automated system would likely be installed in all twenty-four warehouses, entailing an expenditure of $1.44 million, it needed approval from the vice-president as well. The vice-president asked his staff industrial and systems engineer to review the request.

The staff engineer recommended that the request *not* be approved. Rather than setting out to verify the first engineer's data or the workability of her recommendation, the staff engineer examined the purposes, large and small, of the loading dock. The warehouses had been built in the 1920s when a railroad strike had brought the company to its knees. The use of warehouses and trucks for distribution freed the company from its dependence on the railroads. Yet the railroad monopoly condition of the 1920s no longer existed in the 1980s.

The most basic purpose of the loading dock, both in the 1920s and in the 1980s, was "to load trucks." But after discussion with others, the systems engineer expanded the original

purpose to a larger purpose, "to consolidate shipments to dealers." That purpose was, in turn, expanded to "to distribute
company products to dealers." This larger purpose (and those
still larger—to make company products available for sale, to sell
company products, to deliver company products to customers,
and to provide customers with the service of the company
products) provided a wider scope of ultimate ends to be
achieved and many more potential breakthrough solutions than
possible with the limited, basic purpose the first engineer had
assumed: "to load trucks."

Instead of spending $1.44 million to install the automation
system in all the warehouses—the right solution to the wrong
problem—the company sold twenty warehouses and retained
only four distribution centers at the main assembly plants. Using
various forms of transportation, products were shipped directly
to dealers. The company retrained its warehouse employees for
work in other areas of the company.

Accepting a problem as stated invariably means that constraints associated with that area of concern are automatically
accepted as well. If accepted as the problem, "fix the truck-
loading system" makes people assume that the solution has
constraints that include trucks, a warehouse, and inventory.
The larger purpose, "distribute company products to dealers,"
could involve many different forms of transportation, types of
packaging, or even, as we saw in this example, elimination of
unnecessary middle steps in the larger process.

Finding a solution always involves some constraints. Gravi-
ty does exist, day and night alternate on a regular schedule, organizations have structures and resources, actual people figure
in the circumstances, and so on. But identifying the least troublesome constraints and moving beyond them is a major benefit of the purposes principle.

Avoiding the Analysis-First
and Technology Traps

If the uniqueness principle leads the charge against conventional approaches to problem solving, the purposes principle

brings on the reinforcements. Thinking *purposes* is an important defense against the "analysis-first" and "technology" traps of conventinal approaches.

The successful people we studied avoid analytical and subdivision modeling when they first tackle what they acknowledge is a unique problem. They do not believe in launching a vast effort to collect information about a problem area before they talk about what they want to accomplish. Other studies show that successful reasoners devote "more time on global planning than [do] poorer reasoners, but relatively less time on local planning.... The more intelligent problem solvers put more of their time 'up front' in problem solving, in order to enable themselves to operate more efficiently once they get down to details."[2]

In fact, they avoid the conventional urge to start by collecting data and analyzing the situation. Eberhardt Rechtin warns against relying on interpretation of data collected too early in project.[3] Successful problem solvers make sure they have identified the most important purposes first so that they don't waste money by throwing costly technology (robots, office automation, and so on) or program time and effort at a problem before the purposes of the system have been thought out thoroughly.

Nevertheless, the struggle to overturn conventional approaches confronts the weight of history. The success of U.S. organizations during the 100 years of Industrial Revolution helped entrench conventional problem-solving methods. The search for patterns became an obsession. Finding patterns and solutions that worked repeatedly in many different situations was considered the key to efficiency and profits.

Companies began to conduct research to get information about patterns and the nature of problems and solutions. If, for example, incentive plans had been adopted by some seemingly successful organizations, then they considered that they too should use incentive plans. Generally overlooked was the fact that such plans are only short-term bribes that may not be considered useful once the purposes of an incentive plan are expanded to find better ways of obtaining lasting commitment (of executives as well as workers).

Even today, research to discover the *cause* of a problem still drives most change efforts in the United States. When it comes to converting the technology and vast new knowledge created in our research and development departments into practical applications, however, the United States lags behind. We spend a lot of time and energy studying the problem (not the solution) and finding out *who* or *what* is to blame. But so what?

To pull themselves out of the trenches and move ahead, people and organizations need an understanding of the *purposes* they seek to achieve, not the problems they confront. Most corporations, nonprofit organizations, and government entities in this country suffer from a lack of focus on purposes to be achieved. Programs take on a life of their own, and purposes are lost. Consider the U.S. space shuttle program and its ill-fated *Challenger* mission. It took a disaster before the country asked, "Why are we doing this, anyway?" A tragic explosion launched the first serious examination of the array of purposes served by the space shuttle program.

Anyone with a staff would do well to review from time to time the purposes of the group. Mark Bisnow, a former aide to U.S. Senator Robert Dole, said, "Congressional staffers serve themselves or their bosses, but not always the national interest."[4]

In the same fashion, American companies tend to ignore the larger purposes and focus instead on the closest, most obvious, most shortsighted end—the bottom line. When asked to state the purpose of the company, almost every corporate executive says "to make a profit." But profit is only a *measure* of how well the company achieves its actual purpose. Profit is not the company's mission. Purpose can be discovered only by asking the question, "What business are we in?" or "What service are we trying to provide our customers?"

Companies in other countries perceive that they have larger purposes, such as serving customers and employees, which changes the way they operate and usually results in higher profits and market share.

An array of interrelated larger purposes provides guideposts for the long-term growth and evolution of your company or organization. To ensure good answers, you must first ask good questions. With large purposes in mind, you can avoid preoccupation with merely short-term corrections (such as plant closings or layoffs) to the exclusion of larger ends.

Problem Substance and Problem Values

The concept of purposes has an illustrious historical and philosophical frame of reference. Historians seek the purposes of past actions in the total context of motivations, goals, objectives, values, and beliefs.

Philosophers always have sought insights into purpose-related issues—absolute presuppositions, cause and effect, ends and means, modes of functioning, higher levels of meaning, the nature of truth, the essence of reality, and so on.

This holistic perspective is central to the concept of Breakthrough Thinking. We believe that the ultimate reason for successful problem solving is an orientation toward human betterment and that solutions *not* grounded in that belief could fall short of their full potential.

Problems have two primary aspects, substantive and values.

The *substantive* aspect includes all conditions (the who, what, where, and when) of the specific situation you wish to change. The substantive problem of the loading dock is to load trucks or to deliver the company's product to the customers. Throughout this book, when we use the word *purpose,* we are talking about the substantive aspects of the problem, the array of *missions* or *ends* that can actually be accomplished through the activity under consideration.

The *values* aspect of the problem encompasses the desires, aspirations, and needs that have made the substantive aspect a matter of concern. They motivate the desire to work on a problem. Without values, there would be no dissatisfaction and, thus, no problems. Values revolve around the desires of humans to better the world and themselves.

Human betterment is, of course, the broadest of terms, subject to a multitude of interpretations among different people at different times. Robert Nisbet notes, however, that most value systems reflect a "belief in the values of the past, acceptance of the worth of economic and technological growth, faith in reason and in the kind of scientific and scholarly knowledge that can come from reason alone, and belief in the intrinsic importance, the ineffaceable worth of life on this earth."[5]

Our very awareness of the existence of a problem, our consciousness that change is needed, is rooted in our instinctive human desire to realize one or more of these four fundamental values:

• Greater effectiveness

• Higher quality of life and community

• Enhanced human dignity, equality, and liberty

• Individual betterment.

Historically the pursuit of these values has not gone in a straight, ascending line, but in fits and starts of progress and setbacks. For example, the push for effectiveness during the Industrial Revolution entailed sacrifices in human dignity. The era of slavery in the United States represented a grievous regression in human well-being. Wars have incalculably impaired global progress toward a higher quality of life. But over the long term of history, we observe human advancement in what might be described directionally as a spiral, often curving back on itself, seeming to retrace past ground, but always with an overall movement upward.

Few would argue that we are not better off as a species today than we were 200 years ago. Our effectiveness, productivity, performance, individual human dignity—all are greater today, even in the face of the daunting new problems we confront. Indeed, we *must* be better off, *must* keep moving up the spiral of values, for ours is a constant struggle against entropy—the tendency of all closed systems to run down and wear out. Excellence in whatever we do is based on the never-ending effort to move ever higher along the spiral of values.

As your problem solving progresses and you select from your array of purposes the focus purpose or purposes toward which to work, your values or goals will be expressed as specific performance measures or objectives. For example, if you are designing a municipal mass transit system:

- Your *values* or *goals* might be safety, convenient schedules, more jobs, less government, defense preparedness, and passenger comfort.

- Your performance measures (such as time between buses, accident rate, and number of passenger complaints) are the criteria for measuring how well a function is serving a particular value.

- Your *objectives,* then, are measurable performance levels to be achieved in moving toward an objective (for instance, reducing the accident rate by 2 percent in one year).

Recognizing and articulating your fundamental values can lead you to identify problem-solving opportunities and create better alternative solutions. Since values and purposes are fundamentally linked, the motivation for effecting change is very often based on the recognition of values and an existing short-fall in the accomplishment of the purposes that reflect those values. Expanding your purposes also brings to light the often different values realized by addressing larger levels of a problem, an important reason your "solution space" expands as well.

Even though values, goals, and objectives provide the stimulus to do something about a problem, they should be put aside immediately in favor of expanding purposes. Then the correct measures should be identified for the focus (most often larger) purpose on which you will work. Otherwise, you may find yourself pursuing, even more enthusiastically than before, poorly identified purposes or purposes which should not exist at all— "moving faster in the wrong direction."

For example, when Ford Motor Company experienced major financial success with its Taurus and Sable cars in the late 1980s, it made investment decisions based almost solely on financial values and goals—profits, return on investment—not on the actual business purposes the company sought to achieve. Similarly, Wall Street's motivational precedence—"making money" without reference to the purposes accomplished by the enterprise in which money is invested—sometimes leads to innovative ideas. Far too often, however, it leads instead to the destructive greed demonstrated by Charles Keating's Lincoln

Savings and Loan scandal and Prudential's limited partnership travesty in the 1980s.

Incorporating all these aspects of the purpose principle in the early stages of your planning ensures that your decision making achieves more for you, for your organization, and for society than would otherwise be possible. The United States has an ever-increasing base of knowledge and information, but unless we transfer that knowledge into practical application with a clear sense of purpose and strong sense of values, we will not harness that knowledge for its best and highest use.

Several exceptionally successful Japanese companies have long since abandoned profits as their primary goal and have instead imposed broader values: to improve standards of living and serve the welfare of society. Many American executives would scoff at such lofty goals. They must, they say, consider year-end profit statements or answer to unhappy shareholders. The irony, maintains renowned management consultant Peter Drucker, is that many foreign firms have done a better job of keeping stock prices up than have their American counterparts. Concentrating on sales growth, market share, and employee happiness has paid off.

Drucker's colleague Richard Ellsworth says that at the heart of the matter is the fact that foreign firms define the *purpose of their existence* differently. In the United States, the purpose most often is to serve the shareholders. In Japan, it is to serve customers and employees. Serving shareholders too often means too much focus on the quick fix that affects the immediate bottom line. Serving customers and employees generally means a focus on long-term growth.

Application of the principles of Breakthrough Thinking, however, would demand that American executives and shareholders alike ask themselves a fundamental question: "What is the *purpose* of shareholders?" Is it, indeed, simply to earn an immediate return on investment? If so, then, What are the *larger purposes* of earning a return on investment?

Asking these fundamental questions might lead Americans to the conclusion that the purpose of shareholders is to maintain the stability of capital, to invest in companies that develop new products and services, and, thus, to keep ahead of the market. With shareholder so defined, the company that concerns itself with long-term growth (as do the Japanese) would clearly be the company that best serves its shareholders.

This focus on purposes, of course, applies not only to financial and manufacturing entities, but also organizations concerned with education, health care, transportation, agriculture, or anything else. Breakthrough Thinking is the best process for addressing and solving the problems faced by all sectors of society, at all levels. For example, governments should consider their purpose array in deciding what type of action, if any, to take in political or military action abroad—Kuwait in 1991, Haiti and Bosnia in 1993, and so on. Closer to home, expanding purposes provides relative meanings for the personal problems that we all confront in the face of unanswerable questions about the real, sustaining meaning of life.

Table 5-1 illustrates the four concepts included in the word *purpose*.

Using the Purposes Principle

While the uniqueness principle is primarily a state of mind, the expanding purposes concept is both a state of mind and a set of tools for problem-solving efforts. Your mind-set will be continually stimulated and enhanced as you search for ever broader purposes using the tools presented below.

You have just been elected road commissioner of Small County for a four-year term. The two main cities in Small County are Hubsville and Queen City (see Figure 5-3). The two-lane highway connecting the two cities is the main county road, traversing practically flat land. Obstacle Lake is fairly large and deep. You won the election based on your campaign promise to correct the almost continuous bumper-to-bumper traffic on the highway at the least possible cost.

Think through how you would go about trying to keep your campaign promise (find a solution) in the conventional way. Would you try to measure distances? Or would you just

Table 5-1. Illustration of word distinction components of purpose.

Radiology

> Purpose—to produce x-ray of needed body sections
>
> Values or goals—improve diagnostic ability, make people well, increase health care quality, provide patient care (larger level function)
>
> Performance measures—number per day, accuracy, cost
>
> Objectives—30 per day without error
>
> *Example activities*: place patient, turn on machine, interpret x-ray

Building maintenance

> Purpose—to keep equipment in running condition
>
> Values or goals—improve equipment efficiency, increase quality capability, efficient use of resources
>
> Performance measures—% of machines that are operating, number of complaints
>
> Objectives—99% of devices in running order per week
>
> *Example activities*: repair of machines, preventive testing

Personnel Department

> Purpose—to have necessary human resources available
>
> Values or goals—hire capable personnel, reduce turnover, provide employment
>
> Performance measures—% human resources requirements satisfied
>
> Objectives—90% requirements satisfied
>
> *Example activities*: screen, hire, train, fire

Automobile manufacturing company

> Purpose—to produce vehicles for transporting people and objects
>
> Values or goals—make a profit, be stylish, have quality dealers, meet energy requirements, meet customer needs
>
> Performance measures—earnings per share, return on investment, market share
>
> Objectives—20% improvement in earnings next year, 15% in return on investment, 25% in customer satisfaction
>
> *Example activities*: purchase, weld, paint, assemble

try to draw on Figure 5-3 the lines you think would be the answer? Or draw several sets of lines and experiment with them? Or review carefully with someone else all the facts that are provided? Or ask someone else to help define what additional information you need to collect?

1. Identify stakeholders from whom you want to learn about needs and purposes. Talk to them individually, survey them, or bring them together as a group. Schedule appointments or meetings for updating needs and purposes regularly. If you are fairly certain a project will be implemented, neither a group nor a project-management system is likely to be needed, but it is always useful to talk to others about all problems.

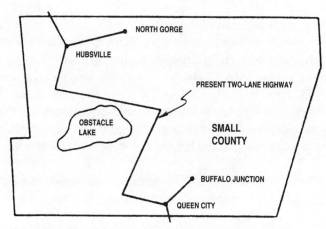

Figure 5-3. Map of Small County main roads.

The group of citizens, politicians, transportation experts, and staff from your commissioner's office agree that the road situation between Hubsville and Queen City must be corrected at the least cost. Beyond the commitment you made to voters during your election campaign, the need is generally considered critical.

You ask the group to identify the purposes that the road between the two cities is intended to achieve. Discussion illu-

minates several purposes: communication link, all-weather surface, accommodation of more people, and so on.

2. Ask questions that expand purposes. To get beyond the problem as it is first presented, ask questions: What are we really trying to do? What "business" are we in? What larger-scope purpose has caused this function to come into being? What are the purposes and needs of the customer and their customers? What is this problem a part of (not the usual, What are the parts of the problem?)? What is the purpose of the project that ensues if you work on the problem?

These questions can help you find appropriate solutions. For example, a company president and several vice presidents decided after an eight-month study that they ought to double the manufacturing floorspace to handle the problems of poor delivery times and cost and quality of product. At the first meeting of a special task group, the consultant asked what the members thought was the purpose of the project. One person pounded on the table and said: "Everyone knows why we are here! We have to design a factory with twice the capacity of this one!" Much to their surprise, after two hours of dealing with the purposes of the project, the group *all* agreed that the purpose really was to develop management control systems!

The next meeting of your group revolves around the development of a purpose hierarchy or array, listing the initial and subsequently identified purposes from smallest to largest. By comparing each purpose statement to every other one, the group decides that "to have an all-weather surface" is actually the smallest purpose. By asking, What is the purpose of having an all-weather surface? the group decides it is in fact "to provide a highway." Then, by asking, What is the purpose of providing a highway? the group decides on its initial purpose array (see Figure 5-4).

3. Create an array of purpose or function statements using the following guidelines. Begin with the perceived needs of the group or organization. If the perceived need is to make the loading dock work more effectively or to double

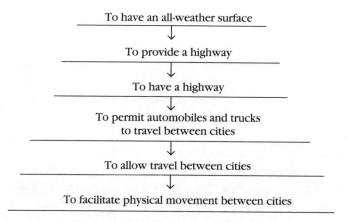

Figure 5-4. Purpose array or hierarchy for Small County roads.

plant size or to set up a paper drive, start there.

Second, select the initial statement for the purpose array. This should be a simple statement describing the smallest, most specific purpose of the problem under consideration. (The purpose of the loading dock is "to load trucks.") One way to start a purpose hierarchy is to create a list of many possible purposes, choose the one with the narrowest scope as the first, then arrange those purposes with successively broader scopes in descending (narrower toward larger) order, as in Figure 5-4. The narrower-scope purposes theoretically will have fewer methods by which they can be accomplished than will the broader, more profound purposes.

Third, compose your purpose statements, using an action verb and a subject. The action verb should be prescriptive and concerned with the total set of conditions (for example, *to provide, to have, to establish*) as opposed to verbs that indicate a measurement of change or incremental objectives or goals *(to increase, to minimize, to reduce)*. Thus, the simplest purpose statement has two substantive words: "to *establish* a *group*." Every added word imposes a limitation and thus reduces the range of possible solutions.

Fourth, expand your purpose array in small increments. If the first-level purpose of a manufacturing company is "to make tables," moving directly to "to have objects supported in space" is too big a leap for the second level. Instead, "to make tables" might better become "to produce tables," or "to have tables available"—smaller incremental expansions leading up to the larger purpose: "to have objects supported in space." Large jumps are undesirable because intermediate purposes are not available for later consideration as a possible purpose level to select for action. The opportunity to work on the right problem may be missed because decision makers are likely to select a smaller purpose. To omit intermediate levels is also to omit opportunities to generate more innovative ideas.

Fifth, in creating your hierarchy or array of purposes, order the purpose statements based on the *scope* of the purpose, rather than on any sequence of activities or explanations. If you have two purpose statements that appear to be equal candidates for the next larger level, list first the purpose that occurs most regularly in your organization. If the scope is really equal, you may arrange them at the same level (see Figure 5-5).

Sixth, expand your purpose array well beyond any possibility for actually implementing a solution. Expand it even beyond your customer, to the customer of your customer. This sets your sights on bigger purposes and goals and helps position your organization ahead of others for the future.

Even though you may select a focus purpose that is small in scope—even the same purpose with which you began your hierarchy—gaining explicit knowledge of larger purposes helps you more effectively make the many minute decisions necessary over the course of the project. Being aware of the whole situation brings focus to the whole project.

You can never know for sure if you have the right array because there is no "right" array in terms of accuracy and precision. But the array is constantly evolving. The first array you make is seldom the final one. It is not unusual to develop two or three arrays and compare them before selecting the one that best captures what most of the people involved in the project perceive and believe.

A. Air passenger services

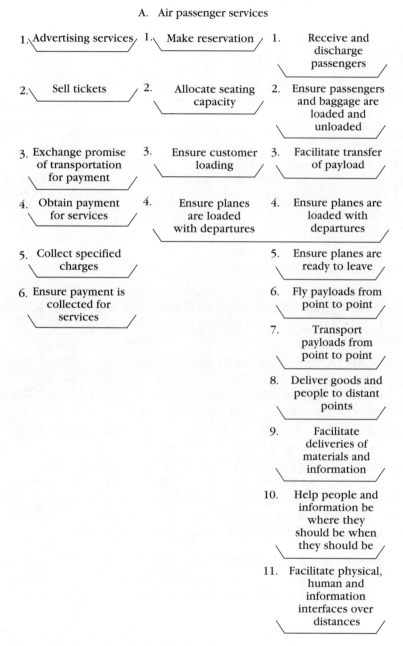

1. Advertising services
2. Sell tickets
3. Exchange promise of transportation for payment
4. Obtain payment for services
5. Collect specified charges
6. Ensure payment is collected for services

1. Make reservation
2. Allocate seating capacity
3. Ensure customer loading
4. Ensure planes are loaded with departures

1. Receive and discharge passengers
2. Ensure passengers and baggage are loaded and unloaded
3. Facilitate transfer of payload
4. Ensure planes are loaded with departures
5. Ensure planes are ready to leave
6. Fly payloads from point to point
7. Transport payloads from point to point
8. Deliver goods and people to distant points
9. Facilitate deliveries of materials and information
10. Help people and information be where they should be when they should be
11. Facilitate physical, human and information interfaces over distances

Figure 5-5. Example of multiple-channel arrays.

B. Performance appraisal systems

To appraise performance
To establish performance
To communicate performance
To inform subordinates and superiors
To provide performance data

| To develop appraisers | To develop employee competence | To reward management of resources | To reward achievement | To make promotion decision |

To...
To...
                To provide resources for management
                To develop employee's achievement of purpose

Figure 5-5.   Examples of mutiple-channel arrays (continued).

Instead of isolating the "right purpose level and array" too soon, a group should spend time discussing alternatives. Members of the group might agree to proceed and see what happens before deciding what array or purpose level to use. As the group views purposes from different perspectives, mental sets expand and contexts come into play. Purpose expansion pushes everyone to consider the seldom-stated assumptions that affect their problem-solving, planning, and design. For example, expanding to include the purposes of the *external* customer helps to assess requests for, say, a new report by a manager (an *internal* customer) in order to determine if it is actually needed at all.

A group may decide that developing a purpose array is not necessary because everyone knows what the purpose is. If the group is adamant about this, one or more of the following tactics can be considered to stimulate broader thinking:

- Get the group to agree on a statement of the purpose that everyone knows, which usually convinces the members that they do not know it.

- Have individuals or the group as a whole develop what they think the system ought to be in five years or less if they could have their own way.

- Identify measures of effectiveness for judging the quality or success of the solution or purpose that everyone agrees on.
- Generate a list of purposes, and let staff members bring alternative arrays to the next meeting.

Any one of these strategies usually leads the group itself to realize that determining the purposes array is necessary before proceeding.

Back in Small County, your highway task group can easily see that the purpose to focus on is neither the smallest nor largest in the array you have developed together. The possible alternatives for "an all-weather surface" are very limited, while the number for "physical movement between cities" is too large for this particular project to consider. The factors the group decides to use in selecting the level for this project include your own desires as the commissioner, the time available to decide, and the prospective cost implications for each level in the hierarchy of purposes you have developed.

4. Set up criteria for selecting the focus purpose. The purpose of setting up criteria is related to organizational needs and available resources that tend to limit the purpose that will be selected to one smaller than the largest. Generate ideas about criteria through discussions, questionnaires, nominal groups, interviews, or other techniques. Then organize and select the criteria by voting, ranking, rating, or other decision-making processes.

The following criteria have proven useful in several, though not all, purpose selection situations:

- Potential benefits of selecting the purpose. Suggestion: Imagine some "ideal solution" options for each pupose to provide a sense of potentiality.
- Management desires. With their intuition and power base, managers may insist that a project not exceed a particular purpose level. Going further might jeopardize their support.
- Political environment. Who is expressing urgency for change. Where are the pressures coming from?

- Time limitations. A project to be completed in six months can involve a bigger purpose than one with a time limit of twenty-four hours.
- Project cost.
- Complexity of action needed to achieve the purpose level.
- Organizational and jurisdictional factors. A project in manufacturing might concern itself with a related purpose in the sales department, yet some organizational units just do not permit crossing departmental lines.
- Control factors. Government, association, or other external controls and regulations may conflict with a particular purpose level.
- Capital factors. Is a particular purpose likely to lead to a solution that requires large amounts of capital? What impact do capital-intensive solutions have on flexibility? (High capital intensity is relatively inflexible.)
- Future resources needs.

Other factors of significance in purpose selection are relationships to other projects, availability of technology within or even outside the organization, workability, actions of competitors, the patent situation, compatibility with company history, liquidity, market position, and adequacy of facilities.

The selection of the focus purpose for the Small County highway solution is accomplished at the meeting where the criteria are identified. Your group selects two levels of purpose as its focus, even though most agree that the smaller purpose, "to have a highway," is closer to the needs of the voters than the larger purpose, "to permit automobiles and trucks to travel between cities."

5. Select the focus purpose. Apply the criteria to the broadest, the largest, purpose in your array. If this purpose is not selected, apply the criteria to the next broadest purpose, and so on, until you come to the largest purpose it is feasible to work on. The selection may be accomplished through group effort, a decision worksheet, outside experts, subjective judgment, or other techniques.

Your focus purpose now defines the *opportunity* to seek, not just the problem to solve.

Although a group usually seeks a single purpose level, sometimes it agrees that two or even three levels of purpose will serve as the foci of the problem-solving effort. This generally happens when the increments between purpose levels are quite small.

Your highway group discusses the measures it and the public will want to use to determine the effectiveness of the solution developed to achieve the selected purpose. Most of the measures are selected at the same meeting where the purpose level is selected. The measures of purpose accomplishment you choose include (1) the cost of the highway is minimized, (2) the average travel time between Hubsville and Queen City is minimized, (3) no slowdowns or delays are due to congestion, (4) a minimum accident and fatality rate is acheived, and (5) the project has minimum political repercussions.

6. Designate measures of purpose accomplishment or objectives for the selected purpose. During the process of selecting a focus purpose, or even earlier, performance measures and objectives begin to surface. In fact, they often are the motivation for starting on a problem-solving foray. These performance measures and objectives will change as larger purposes develop and you gain better understanding of the problem.

When you have selected the purpose level on which you will work, it's time to decide whether specific measures of purpose accomplishment should be established to determine how effectively your recommendations achieve their purpose. Quantifiable objectives are not appropriate for every problem-solving situation—especially personal problem solving, such as planning a vacation or improving relations with your children. Most people don't think in terms of being 50 percent happier. But for most business problems, measurable accomplishment factors—critical success factors, major driving forces,[7] and key performance indicators—are useful in gauging how close your actions are bringing you to the desired purpose level.

Measures of purpose accomplishment should be appropriate for the purpose level you select. For example, measures for possible solutions that "distribute the product to dealers" will be different than for actions that "load a truck."

Objectives usually are specific and quantifiable: We will reduce costs by 25 percent by the end of one year. We will increase citizen involvement in the city's recreational program by 50 percent within two years. We will rehabilitate fifty inner-city houses each year for the next four years.

For such statements about objectives to be useful, you must be able to measure the critical success factors at the beginning of the project, at the conclusion, and at several stages in-between. Measures taken at the end of a project need a base-point taken at the beginning, so you can tell how close your actions have brought you to your desired purpose.

Realize, however, that no measure of purpose accomplishment—benefit/cost, viability, reliability, customer satisfaction, sales demand, process capacity, maintainability, recyclability, and so on—is ever complete, unequivocal, accurate, or precise. Formulating them requires trade-offs among several goals. Sometimes goals are weighted to establish the relative importance of each one.

Goals, performance measures, and objectives are likely to change as other Breakthrough Thinking principles become apparent, but some clear expectations for the problem-solving process should be established at the time a target purpose chosen.

Purposes and Project Management

Trying to solve a problem quite often means you have two problems: (1) how to organize the problem-solving effort and (2) how to impose change on the original problem situation. The purposes principle should be applied to both problems. As you organize the problem-solving effort, ask, What are the purposes of a project plan for working on this problem? Should we work on it at all? This preplanning contributes greatly to the implementation of later recommendations. It helps participants become contributors to the effort and thus, later, implementors of the chosen solution.

For example, the gypsy moth pest-management system was supposed to address the critical question of dealing with the diminutive pest (see Chapter 1). A stack of reports literally four feet high accumulated as massive data collection took place. Earlier in the problem-solving process, a consulting company had been hired to design a pest-management system through which state and federal agencies could attack the gypsy moth. The consultants took a conventional approach, collecting massive amounts of information about the gypsy moth problem from government researchers and compiling that information, along with their recommendations, in a thick report that government officials simply added to their pile of previous reports. Unfortunately, it was just one more report that failed to address the realities of the situation and whose recommended solutions became stalled by political infighting and a diffused sense of purpose.

This data collection continued until the Breakthrough Thinking facilitator helped the group rally around the purposes of the project. He helped them construct an array of purposes to be achieved by the project and finally agree that the target purpose of the pest-management system would be "to manage the gypsy moth at all levels of population." Guided by this larger purpose, the government officials established specific goals and objectives and generated ideas for actions to achieve it.

By highlighting the *purposes* of managing the project before the project began, Breakthrough Thinking brought about results that had been unobtainable before. Breakthrough Thinking helped create an environment where positive, meaningful, and productive working relationships could flourish. Participants were able to create a unique system to fit their special needs and carry out their plans. Instead of spending most of their time collecting and analyzing data, filing reports, and bickering about data, project managers used Breakthrough Thinking to develop feasible targets and the means to achieve them, with provisions for continued planning and improvement.

Watch the Possibilities Unfold

Applying the purposes principle seems risky if you are swimming against a tide of conventional thought, but it is usually more risky not to apply the purposes principle. Consider the difficulties companies, government agencies, service providers, and individuals have had to face because they don't ask about purposes.

Here are some "red flags" to watch out for on your solution-finding journey:

- A directive, including measures, is presented to you as the only solution. For example, reduce costs by 10 percent, lower customer response time by five percent, etc.
- Functional fixedness—ideas, objections, and quick-fix solutions reflect the narrow scope of a particular function.
- "We don't have time. Let's just solve this problem and get on with it." (In this case, ask, "How will we find the time to solve the new problems this solution may create?")

Whenever you confront these situations, immediately stop and practice the purposes principle.

Always ask yourself these specific questions:

- Have I listed my purposes?
- Have I expanded the purposes of addressing this problem?
- Have I further explored the purposes of addressing this problem?
- What purpose am I trying to accomplish?
- What are the even bigger purposes?
- Do I truly know what I am trying to accomplish?
- What are our customers' purposes? And their customers'?
- What larger purpose might eliminate the need to achieve this smaller purpose altogether?

We urge you to summon the courage to ask about purposes. Seek the purposes of everything. What do we hope to accomplish with a toothbrush, fork, tie, doorknob, requisition form, farm subsidy, argument, report, job, or anything else?

Then ask what the purposes are of those purposes. Envision larger ends. Seek awareness of the whole (and larger) situation. If the purpose of a shoelace is to tie a shoe, ask what the purpose of tying a shoe is—and then watch the possibilities for alternative, innovative solutions unfold before your eyes. "It is not enough to just do your best or work hard; you must know what to work on," says W. Edwards Deming, the quality management proponent.[8]

Knowing clearly what to work on is the major benefit of the purposes principle. A dramatic illustration is the following project. Hospital administrators in the thirty-three-member Hospital Council of the Greater Milwaukee Area decided to do something about a shortage of nurses, so they set up a sixteen-person, interdisciplinary team. After preparing a purpose array (Figure 5-6) the committee changed the focus of the project from level 2, how nurses are utilized, to levels 8 and 9, systems for care of patients. It was agreed that if effective systems to serve patient needs were implemented, nurses would be utilized correctly.

The committee was surprised by what this larger view of purposes produced. They ended up without a nurses station because throughout the entire design process, it never became evident that such an area could helps nurses meet patient needs. Instead, patients' care plans and doctors' notes were always to be kept near each patient.

This new solution was tested in a thiry-nine-bed unit. Evaluation of its performance showed that the same number of nurses could care for 48 percent more patients than in the previous system. This percentage is five to eight times higher than that achieved in any previous efforts to "improve nurse utilization." And the nurses were delighted—they could use more of their skills more of the time. This result can be traced directly to the benefits of the purposes array. It showed the group what really needed to be addressed.[9]

1. To obtain information about the way
hospital nurses spend their working hours
↓

2. To determine how
nurses are utilized in hospitals
↓

3. To establish the characteristics and
magnitude of the hospital nursing shortage
↓

4. To identify the critical nurse
characteristics and skills needed in hospitals
↓

5. To define the needed nurse roles in a hospital
↓

6. To relate nursing roles to hospital patient needs
↓

7. To establish a pattern of providing
needed nurse roles in hospitals
↓

8. To establish a system of providing
needed nursing care to hospital patients
↓

9. To develop a system of providing nursing
services that meet the needs of hospital patients
↓

10. To develop a system of providing
services in hospital patient care units
↓

11. To have available services
that meet the needs of hospital patients
↓

12. To give patients hospital care
↓

13. To give patients pre-, in-, and posthospital care
↓

14. To give patients continuing health care services
↓

15. To give patients health care services
↓

16. To produce socioeconomically well patients
↓

17. To provide health care to patients
↓

18. To have a healthy population

Figure 5-6.   A simplified version of the purpose expansion for the nurse utilization project.

If you consistently use the thinking and reasoning aids of the purposes principle, you will develop a flexible mind-set that embraces openness, intuition, and expanded perceptions. You will achieve excellent insights into your own problems. You will tap the minds and energy of your colleagues. You will lend larger meaning to what you do. By bringing other minds and energy into your sphere of understanding, you will ameliorate the isolation each of us experiences as a human being.

Expansion of purposes provides the way to turn problems into opportunities—a comment we often heard from the effective people we studied when they tried to describe the way they were "lucky." Expansion of purposes points the solution-finding arrow toward the right problem to work on, within an overall framework of needed personal and organizational purposes. It helped the effective problem-solvers we studied to understand clearly the risks and uncertainties they faced in determining what purposes to pursue.

An orientation to purposes helps you avoid being sold a solution to the wrong problem. It helps you avoid the lack of focus that could cause you to waste resources by doing the wrong things or trying to do too many things. It determines what does not have to be done to accomplish your purpose. Moreover, finding a solution always involves some constraints. Identifying the least troublesome constraints and moving beyond them is a major benefit of beginning with questions about purposes.

As human beings, we rally with much more enthusiasm around purposes than we do around rules. When you focus on purposes, your products and services are likely to be more competitive because you will develop a keener awareness of the needs of your employees and customers. Even the seemingly routine task benefits from asking about purposes and the purposes of that purpose. The many minute decisions that are made as the task is performed are better made when purposes are clear.

Accept the fact that you have purposes you want to achieve, though perhaps they are implicit. Everyone else also has purposes—a mental model of how they see the world. Why not bring those purposes out into the open, thus dispelling shortcomings and enlarging visions, rather than submerging purposes with data and analytical jargon? Why not expand those purposes into larger ends, thus dispelling the claim that contemporary realities produce lives devoid of direction and meaning?

Even if you do not actually array your purposes in a formal hierarchy, *talk* about purposes and the purposes of those purposes. After all, dealing with even the most technological problem is really dealing with the people who are involved. And purposes are the catalyst that can turn those people into effective contributors to an effective solution.

Purposes eliminate impatience and the faulty evaluation of ideas that we so commonly encounter because purposes teach us to listen to others and answer positively all questions others ask about the ends to be achieved. Arrayed in a hierarchy, purposes help eliminate the tendency of people toward functional fixedness. Visions of creative alternatives are developed by purposes and their expansion. Breakthrough Thinking is a product of people, not machines.

But a breakthrough idea seldom occurs instantaneously as a bolt out of the blue. Breakthrough ideas occur when the mind has been prepared, stimulated, and opened to the possibilities. The purposes principle accomplishes this preparation. Investing time early while you are seeking to find and understand purposes will save a great deal of time, money, and effort later and produce many more of the three distinct types of breakthroughs:

- The "ah-hah!" revelation, an exceptionally innovative idea or solution.
- Significantly better results.
- Implementation of a good idea or avoidance of a bad idea.

With the hierarchy of possible purposes in mind, you have selected the purpose toward which you will work. Now it is time to flesh out the purposeful, innovative solutions that will move you toward your goal. This process will be discussed in Chapter 6.

NOTES

1. Isao Nakauchi, "Catch the Megatrends: Wisdom of Business," *NHK Big Talk,* Japan Broadcasting Corporation (December 7, 1985).

2. R.J. Sternberg, "Inside Intelligence," *American Scientist,* 74, (March-April 1986).

3. Eberhardt Rechtin, Systems Architecting: Creating and Building Complex Systems (Englewood Cliffs N.J., Prentice-Hall, 1991).

4. Mark Bisnow, *Newsweek* (January 4, 1988).

5. Robert Nisbet, *History of the Ideas of Progress* (New York: Basic Books, 1980).

6. Richard Ellsworth, quoted in John F. Lawrence, "Papering over Problems with Paper Profits," *Los Angeles Times* (November 16, 1986).

7. B. B. Tregoe, et al. *Vision in Action: Putting a Winning Strategy to Work* (New York: Fireside, 1989).

8. W. Edwards Deming, *Out of the Crisis* (Cambridge, Mass.: MIT Center for Advanced Engineering Study; 1986).

9. Based on J. M. Kraegel, V. Schmidt, R. K. Shukla, and C. E. Goldsmith, "A System of Patient Care Based on Patient Needs," *Nursing Outlook,* 20, No. 4, (April 1972). E. P. Lewis, Editorial, *Nursing Outlook,* ibid.; J. M. Kraegel et al., Patient Care Systems, (Philadelphia: Lippincott, 1974).

Chapter 6

The Solution After Next Principle

A large, nationwide law firm in the United States focused a sizable segment of its work on intellectual property (patents, trademarks, etc.). As part of its business strategy, the firm decided to revise its procedures to decrease the cost of such cases and the time spent on them, thus being able to provide intellectual property services to a wider segment of the population.

When the partners developed a Breakthrough Thinking purpose hierarchy, the focus purpose they selected proved to be much larger than anticipated: "to provide added value to the client beyond simply intellectual property law." As a result of this focus purpose, many ideas never before considered became the six major alternatives defining how the solution would operate in three years time.

The target solution that now guided the partnership, selected from among the many alternatives they had developed, was identified as Stage Three of the basic elements of intellectual property cases, according to legal and regulatory requirements. That led to spelling out Stage One (recommendations for changes that should be made immediately) and Stage Two (the next set of changes due in eighteen months time) to move actual processes closer to the target, Stage Three.

Moreover, Stage Two included the requirement that Breakthrough Thinking be applied again in two years to redesign the target system and solution. Stage Three would then serve to launch new changes that would further advance the opportunity-solving process, developing additional stages that comprised a new guide for making continuing improvements in the chosen solution.

*R*emember those old cartoons of well-meaning do-it-yourselfers? A man paints himself into a corner of his living room; another builds a boat in his cellar with no plan for getting it into the water; and still another climbs out on a limb and begins to saw, blissfully unaware of the seriousness of his *next* problem.

These are humorous examples of a common failing among problem-solvers—neglecting to look beyond the immediate problem and its current solution to the solution-after-next.

The effective leaders and problem solvers we studied invariably projected a vision of the system or solution they wanted to achieve in the future, even as the current changes they decided upon were being made. Although many of their visions were goal-, quality-, or value-oriented, their focus on "what's next" provided the stimulus for a more detailed "vision" goal—a solution-after-next target, the type of vision elicited by Breakthrough Thinking.

The uniqueness and purposes principles help you construct a framework through which to approach and understand a problem. The purposes array you identify at the start provides a firm foundation on which to construct a workable solution to the problem. Now, the solution-after-next principle helps you develop alternative solutions that take into consideration future needs. This principle states that *the change or system you install now should be based on what the solution might be when you work on the problem the next time.*

After you define purposes, the next step in planning your immediate solution is to think of the future implications of all possible solutions. The painter, boat builder, and tree surgeon in our cartoon examples didn't think beyond purposes—getting the floor painted, the boat built, or the tree limb removed. Had they considered the future consequences of their actions, their immediate solutions almost certainly would have been different.

In any competitive field (and what isn't these days, from manufacturing and road building to education and medicine?), the solution-after-next is *what your competitor is going to come up with after you think you've "finished" a project.* In today's and tomorrow's worlds—whether personal, organizational, or societal—a frequent return to "square one" is a critical way to survive.

The whole history of development is one of somebody originating something: a can opener, a tennis ball, a line of cake mixes. Then somebody else comes along with an improvement: an electric can opener, a colored tennis ball, cake mixes with the frosting included, and so on.

Accomplishing something, then resting on your oars, coasting, and telling yourself subconsciously that your achievement is the living end, is the old-fashioned thinking pattern. Breakthrough Thinking says, "Instead of sitting back and letting someone else harvest the apples you passed up, *preempt* what the other person may do *by standing on your shoulders,* and thus reap a double harvest." One result of the solution-after-next principle is that each successful new product or system becomes the stepping stone to the next.

All problems have implications that extend into the future. By mentally putting yourself at a point in the future when you might have to re-solve your problem, you can save yourself a lot of headaches. The insight you gain will improve your immediate solution and help you incorporate adaptations into your solution to meet future needs.

The solution-after-next principle elevates your thinking beyond the obvious first solution. If you have machinery that isn't working well, an engineer can redesign a gear to make the machinery work better. But you should also ask yourself, Can we improve this solution either by refining the gear mechanism to still further advantage, or even by finding an entirely different way to do the job?

The solution-after-next principle encourages you to envision the ideal solution—one that might not be implementable now, but one toward which you can strive. Your immediate solution becomes not an end in itself but a transitional step toward a better future.

The Importance of Anticipating Change

Just as your problem exists today within a framework of complex interrelations among people and other systems, your problem also exists in the framework of time. It is not an isolated dead-end event but a segment on a continuum that is always subject to change and improvement.

A rash of accidents at a street intersection may call for installation of a traffic signal. Although this may seem like the ideal solution at the moment, it may be only a temporary solution. Increasing traffic eventually may call for a traffic circle or a cloverleaf intersection. Years later, some other stratagem may be called for, such as alternate routes, a public transit system, and so on. Obviously, faced with the probability of such growth, it is wise to keep options open for the solution-after-next by not permitting a cluster of skyscrapers to be built right at the intersection.

All solutions, no matter how ideal they may seem at the time, are merely transitional steps. Time, people, policies, and new purposes inevitably alter the original purpose, so every solution must be formed with the probability of change in mind.

For example, a hospital management system designed to deliver acute care would become instantly obsolete if the hospital's mission suddenly shifted to treating patients with chronic ailments. Administrators who think of the management system as the solution to end all solutions would have trouble adapting to the drastic change in purpose. But if the solution-after-next principle were applied as the management system was designed, the administrators would already have alternative solutions in mind. More important, they would have a mind-set that accepted the management system as a transitional step in an ever-changing world. That mind-set would help them adapt to the inevitable future change in purpose.

Consider, for example, the "solutions" called defense strategy, homelessness policy, or education, as they existed prior to the current decade. Much of the despair in the United States today stems from a lack of focus on the right purposes and the consequent lack of a solution-after-next target or alternatives in these problem areas that could guide us in the world we now face.

Recent research in the field of situated cognition has demonstrated that knowledge itself is not objective but subjective; it is always embedded in a particular frame of reference, always relative and open to reinterpretation. This is why solutions-after-next are critical.

"Knowledge evolves continually as it is being used," write University of Amsterdam social scientists Jacobijn Sandberg and Bob Wielinga. "Indeed, there is ample evidence that memory is reconstructive. The central point is that—there being no 'fixed,' internal representations—knowledge is fluid. [Thus,] knowledge can never be simply transferred, because it does not exist in transferable form."[1]

Just as present knowledge cannot be transferred accurately to the future, neither can a solution designed solely for the present adequately address the needs of an evolving problem situation. The future will always bring change—both to your problem and to its solution.

Okay, the future brings change, but why is it so important to worry about that now, before we have discussed how to apply the other principles of Breakthrough Thinking?

The answer is simple. The solution-after-next, or your ideal system for the future, has a direct bearing on how you think about and shape the solution to your problem today. Asking what is likely or possible to come next, and next after that keeps long-range planning linked to what needs to be done today and today's actions linked to what might be possible in the future.

A plan to modernize a factory that produces a certain kind of paint would be deficient without questioning whether five or ten years hence there would still be a market for that particular paint, and what the technology of paint might be then. The answer would dictate whether the plant should be designed for the long-term with future built-in changes, or as a bare-bones structure easily convertible to something else, such as a bakery.

Although no one can predict the future, having a variety of ideal alternatives in mind is the best anticipatory tool. The purposes array already shows that there is no single end to achieve, and thus no single answer. Your solution-after-next, or what you consider to be the ideal target solution for your future, can be implemented over time as part of an ongoing process, a natural evolution guided by human thought and human values.

People have been conditioned by conventional problem solving to expect an entire change to be made all at once and then be done. How many times have you heard people say, "What! You're changing this again? You just made a change two months ago."

People who consider solutions-after-next are different. They understand that recommendations are being phased in, and they look forward to the next change—perhaps a component of the solution-after-next they helped design.

A Vision for the Future

The solution-after-next principle creates an image of what your system, product, or organization will look like in the future, and joins the daily decision making in your organization to bigger purposes. The successful people we've studied say lofty ideals and vision are essential if one is to enjoy continuing outstanding results.

Makoto Iida, Chairman of SECOM Corporation, one of Japan's largest home security companies, explains his view: "Our company was rapidly expanding and other companies stopped growing, even though they were in a similar business environment. Why did this difference occur? I think this comes from the difference in whether or not you can expand the image of the company's future. This image is not a mere casual idea, but a feasible ideal solution after mature consideration. We have to think about our business after three years, five years, and ten years and imagine what the ideal image of our company will be at those times and how to accomplish this image in the real world. We cannot succeed in establishing a worthwhile company without creating a good imagination for the future of our life and our company."[2]

Developing solutions-after-next requires more than an appropriate mind-set and creativity. It requires knowledge about a wide range of topics, so now is the time to conduct targeted research. But how you use the knowledge you acquire is critical.

Conventional thinkers try to apply the knowledge directly to the problem situation. Innovative thinkers use the knowledge to stimulate new conceptions of ideal target systems.

The concept of thinking about *ideal* systems has been around a long time, but the concept is almost always dismissed as soon as it is mentioned. You've heard comments similar to these: "Well, the ideal method for our office is to get everything computerized, but that is too expensive for us to consider," or, "Our customers like to hear our actual voices," or, "The variety of our parts is far too large, so we just have to forget it."

The problem with such quick dismissal is that (1) no purposes are considered, (2) no sketch of how such a system would operate is prepared, (3) no realistic decision process is used, and (4) rationalizations assume constraints without considering the frequency of their occurrence or importance.

The solution-after-next principle fleshes out the concept of the ideal target solution so that people can understand and support the future vision.

1. It puts a time frame on the ideal solution to be developed. Ask for example: What solution do you think would be recommended the *next* time you work on this problem? In a year? In five years? Such questions stimulate insightful suggestions about what actions to take now. Even if the ideal long-term solution cannot be implemented immediately, certain elements often are usable today. And because they are part of the long view, even parts of the ideal system will serve you better than the short-term, band-aid results so prevalent in conventional approaches.

2. Its future orientation permits you to start fresh. What if we started all over again? is a wonderful question. It frees the mind of the past and unshackles the imagination. Usually, the fresh-start approach is brought into play only when a product or service is being planned for the first time, but it stimulates discussion in any problem-solving situation.

The fresh-start approach worked in greater Milwaukee when that region confronted a severe shortage of nurses. Doctors, hospital professionals, and nurses developed a project team to alleviate the problem. Using the purposes principle, they decided to focus on the function "to care for patients" rather than on the more specific work activities of nurses. A fresh-start option—How would you provide services that meet the needs of hospital patients if you started all over again?—led to a breakthrough conclusion.

The project team developed several patient-care systems based on patients' need for sleep and rest, food and fluids, medication, care, communication, observation, monitored vital signs, hygiene, elimination, material supply, infection control, as well as orientation, education, and discharge from the hospital.

Rather than a central nurses' station, small work groups, each one responsible for a limited number of patients, were set up to provide each nurse with in-depth knowledge of a small number of patients. Standard supplies were kept in each patient's room. A medication profile on the patient was placed on the inside of the supply cabinet, and a timer with a light that went on outside the patient's door reminded the nurse when it was time for the next medication. The innovative nurse utilization system was tested in a 39-bed unit with such success that it was later used, with modifications, in a new 500-bed hospital.

3. It encourages stimulating lines of questioning that lead to alternative "ideal" solutions. Conventional approaches favor selecting the first idea that works. The solution-after-next principle encourages decision makers to ask more probing questions that lead to not one, but many solutions and solutions-after-next. Decision makers who are open to alternatives are more likely to find a breakthrough idea that makes a difference. Sometimes the better alternative becomes the key to survival.

A small but growing computer company in the Midwestern United States felt obliged to double its factory space and hire another eighteen employees to handle a new product and the expanding sales of its current line. The company brought in a Breakthrough Thinking consultant to help review this decision. After the purposes had been clarified, using questions to stimulate ideas (such as, How could it be done automatically?), company personnel suggested several alternative production arrangements. Finally, the company adopted a plan that used the current space and only seven more employees. The alternative solution, adopted in early 1981, saved the company from going bankrupt. The added debt and employee commitments just at the time when the national economy was sliding into recession would not have allowed the company to survive. Instead, it became a strong company that has used Breakthrough Thinking to expand significantly its sales, market share, and corporate and management activities.

Remaining open for as long as possible to various alternatives greatly enhances your chances of arriving at a potentially ideal system. This requires tolerance of ambiguity, a characteristic shared by many effective decision makers.

4. It establishes the concept of regularity as a guideline for designing the ideal system. Solutions-after-next inevitably come up against some unpredictable and infrequent irregularities. But in considering ideal solutions-after-next, don't allow such imponderables, to swamp the project. Focus on regularities of your problem situation rather than on the occasional odd occurrence.

Regularities are the usual, expectable, or most significant eventualities implicit in a problem or system area. *Irregularities* are the exceptional or unpredicatable circumstances that may arise.

In working toward a solution, conventional problem solvers tend to shape a recommendation that covers all foreseeable contingencies. But there are two problems with this approach. First, it is virtually impossible to conceive of all contingencies that may develop out of a particular situation, and the unanticipated ones are always the ones that cause trouble. Second, inordinate attention to the unusual leads to misshapen answers for dealing with the usual and tends to narrow rather than broaden the imaginative field of possible solutions.

You don't tailor a children's picnic menu, for example, to fit the one child who is allergic to milk. Instead, you plan the menu with milk and then modify or add items to provide for the child who has to drink something else.

This may seem ridiculously obvious. Yet it's amazing how similar sorts of irregularities confound people in seeking solutions to more serious problems. Imagine, for example, the frustration of waiting in line at an airline counter, when you simply want a ticket on a commuter flight leaving in ten minutes for a city 200 miles away. Meanwhile the clerk negotiates interminably with someone else who wants two full-fare tickets and three half-fares between Sydney, Australia, and Yokohama, Japan, with a departure date three months in the future.

Why does this happen? Because the ticket-selling operation is structured to handle every request, rather than simply the standard ones with atypical requests being handled separately. The result is inefficient handling of *most* of the traffic.

Preprinted forms are another case in point. Organizations love forms, because they seem to be an efficient way of collecting information. The trouble is that most forms are misconceived; they attempt to encompass all possible irregularities (an impossible task) only to obfuscate the simple information needed in the majority of cases.

In conventional problem solving, when people gather to discuss a proposed solution, everybody tries to find out what is wrong with it, why it might not work. They waste a lot of time initially talking about and making plans for irregularities that occur a small percentage of the time. The time would be better spent discussing regularities.

If you can generate excellent alternative solutions that work under the expected and usual conditions, it is a relatively simple matter to design solutions-after-next to deal with irregular conditions, even if dealing with irregularities requires a separate system.

Consider the following illustrations.

- The design of a medication administration system in a hospital began with consideration of only the regular, most frequently occurring, or most important situations—three times a day, once every four hours, and so on. An advanced system emerged and was adapted to include irregularities (medicines to be administered on patient request, when certain patient conditions arose, and so on). The final system (the solution-after-next) retained most of the ideas developed for the regular conditions with minor adjustments for irregularities.

- A department store adopted a conveyer system for receiving merchandise in cardboard cartons (90 percent of the received merchandise arrived in cardboard cartons) and created a separate receiving area for the other 10 percent—wooden crates and plastic containers not suitable for the beginning of the conveyor system.

- An architectural firm hired to design condominiums did so but also incorporated townhouses and some single-family homes into the development to suit the needs of a mixed market.

The point is, Why throw away what is best for, say, 85 percent of the conditions just because the other 15 percent may not fit?

Considering regularities and irregularities leads to multi-faceted solutions—a breakthrough answer encompassing several alternatives that are ideal for various conditions. Weaving the threads of multiple purposes, multiple needs, and multiple possible solutions into an effective breakthrough recommendation is the challenge of the solutions-after-next process.

Yogi Berra captured the essence of the solution-after-next principle when he said, "If you don't know where you're going, you're probably going to wind up someplace else."[3]

An organization's sense of direction comes from the vision or dream of a good leader. That vision of an ideal future has two components: (1) the expanded purposes array, which portrays the long-term goals, philosophies, driving force, and values of an organization; and (2) the solution-after-next, which describes the directional mechanisms for attaining those long-term goals. For example, Hewlett-Packard Corporation has developed a Manufacturing Research Laboratory to devise models of what would be the "ideal state" for its manufacturing.

Particularly impressive about the two parts of a vision—expanded purposes and solution-after-next—is the opportunity

they provide for customers (the end beneficiaries) to become involved on a nonadversarial basis. For example, the Canada Post
Corporation—Canada's postal system—planned in 1989 to "set
up [Breakthrough Thinking] projects within the corporation and
within corporations that constitute our major accounts.... Our
commercial and retail customers can participate. What better
way to get the feedback we need to institute a customer-oriented
organization?"[4]

Benefits of the
Solution-After-Next Principle

The solution-after-next principle has many advantages in common with other principles of Breakthrough Thinking. Like the
uniqueness principle and the purposes principle, the solution-after-next principle undermines the mental walls or conceptual
blocks that inhibit people from perceiving the right problem or
developing creative solutions. It demands that decision makers
view a problem from various perspectives, putting aside cultural
and environmental taboos and traditions; challenging the propensity to avoid risk; encouraging the generation and growth of innovative ideas; and maintaining an openness to using a wide variety
of tools, techniques, and modes of expression.

The seven principles of Breakthrough Thinking and their
various advantages are so interrelated that it is difficult to allocate certain advantages exclusively to each principle. Nevertheless, the following advantages seem to relate directly to the
solution-after-next principle.

1. *Thinking of the future implications of today's solution
   and imagining an ideal target solution toward which to
   strive improve significantly the quality and quantity of
   breakthrough solutions that can be implemented today.*
   If you are building a house, you must work within your
   current budget. But if you have your dream house in mind,
   you can build it in stages. Your vision will prevent you
   from building something now that will stand in the way of
   your long-range plan.

2. *The trade-offs and compromises inherent in virtually every solution are made in a forward-looking rather than backward-looking mode.* If you imagine an ideal manufacturing system but can't implement it now because of capital or manpower constraints, you can develop an interim solution that will at least take you closer to your goal. Such compromise is more productive and innovative than letting presumed constraints limit your idea generation to short-term, patch-up solutions unrelated to any vision for the future.

3. *Your recommendations for change contain provisions for continuing improvement.* You can look at the components of your implementable solution differently. Components that are part of the solution-after-next can be designed with the ability to adapt and change built-in. Components that are not part of your ideal target can be designed to be phased out or adapted to unrelated purposes as in a paint manufacturing plant that may eventually be converted to a bakery.

4. *You maximize the likelihood of developing creative and innovative solutions by setting aside presumed human, physical, information, and financial constraints that limit your vision.* Often, if you let alternative ideal solutions blossom in your mind, you can then find ways to overcome the constraints either over time or with an immediate innovative solution.

5. *Natural human resistance to change gives way to acceptance and even anticipation of change.* People are taken less by surprise because they understand how the changes fit into the grand design.

6. *You gain valuable lead time for making changes in the future.* With a good sense of where you are headed and built-in flexibility to cope with the unexpected, you can plan phased-in solutions that take you ever closer to your ideal.

7. *Your solutions are easier to implement.* Having a clear image of where you are going facilitates the many minute decisions you have to make as a project develops.

8. *Breakthrough solutions become easier.* The solution-after-next principle dissolves "don't rock the boat" and "let sleeping dogs lie" attitudes that block the generaton of innovative ideas.

9. *You can leap beyond the competition, not just catch up with them.* Conventional thinking would have you copy what your successful competitor is doing, as does the competitive benchmarking concept discussed in Chapter 4. The solution-after-next principle puts you mentally *beyond* where your competition is so you can *surpass* their performance. For example, the NUMMI plant, a joint venture of Toyota and General Motors in Fremont, California, considered a model of the manufacturing technology of the early 1980s. Meanwhile, you can be sure, Toyota was changing its systems in Japan to jump ahead of NUMMI, not just catch up with it.

10. *Your recommendations for change are likely to involve multiple channels developed from many options.* Redesigning schools to lower the dropout rate, for example, would surely involve more than lowering the class size. The complexity of the problem and its web of interrelated problems call for a multifaceted solution with components dealing with class size, teacher training, psychological support, parental and community involvement, crime prevention, supplemental funding, and much more. The alternative solutions you develop to achieve your vision of the ideal school become the various facets of your ultimate target solution.

11. *A creative environment prevails. Defensiveness and conflict over systems and allocation of resources subside as people move cooperatively toward a common vision for the future.* An expanded, continually changing sense of betterment engenders openness to many alternatives. Assuming a long-range perspective makes people more tolerant of ambiguity and the possibility that one or more parts of a problem may have no solution. People become more willing to consider every idea, acknowledging the possibil-

ity that *any* idea may have some merit. These attitudes maximize the likelihood of developing creative, innovative solutions.

12. *You avoid getting bogged down in the myriad circumstances that surround any real situation by initially developing a solution that deals with only regular conditions.* Systems to handle irregularities or exceptions to the rule are developed later at a rate you and your colleagues can handle. Developing a creative, workable solution for ideal conditions eventually leads to the installation of a multichanneled, pluralistic solution that handles irregularities yet retains most of the benefits of the target solution developed for normal conditions. These conditions might be the situation or factors that occur most frequently or those that are most critical.

13. *You do not let current knowledge limit your thinking.* Developing solutions-after-next raises many specific questions that need to be answered before a recommendation is fully developed. These questions will guide your data collection so you can avoid the wasteful, shotgun, get-all-the-facts research used by conventional problem solvers.

Not every solution you implement, however, will be a breakthrough solution. Sometimes your solution will be no better than what you would have achieved with conventional approaches. Sometimes your immediate solution will cause only a small change in desired performance and thus mask the breakthrough quality of your solution-after-next. Sometimes the psychological or political situation surrounding your problem demands a series of small changes rather than one big breakthrough solution, but small wins on the continuum of progress toward your solution-after-next target are bright lights that eventually will transform your vision into reality.

Techniques for Developing Solution-After-Next Ideas

In this section, we describe specific tools, techniques, and processes you can use to develop solutions-after-next, but first, let us emphasize once again the importance of maintaining an open frame of mind.

Our studies of successful problem solvers show that although each has favorite tools and techniques for inspiring creativity, these aids would fail if submerged in the negativism and the limited perspectives of conventional reasoning. An *open mind-set* that nurtures reasoning at a larger level of abstraction (purpose) is the most critical factor in Breakthrough Thinking.

One research project describes the effective planner as one who is purpose-oriented, tolerant of ambiguity, inclined to get other people involved, and likely to search for needed information from a wide range of sources.[5] Other studies of creative thinkers identify additional characteristics: rejection of standard problem-solving formats, interest in many fields, ability to view a problem in multiple perspectives, and an orientation to the future.[6]

Significantly, the thrust of Breakthrough Thinking principles is to get you to always exhibit these characteristics. These are the very characteristics that permit successful problem solvers to use the tools, techniques, and processes we describe in this section. To foster the maximum creativity, this openness must exist in the individual, group, and organization.

There is an old adage that says, "No one ever had an original idea." Indeed, sometimes it seems that *everything* has been thought of before, but the essence of creativity is to combine "old" ideas in new ways.

The Hungarian researchers V. Csanyi and G. Kampis view human society as a complex network composed of human beings, ideas, artifacts, and other living beings exploited by humans. Creative thought, they suggest, does not occur by itself. Rather, it builds on, finds new connections between, and rearranges ideas that already exist.

"A formed, written, or composed idea may be thought of as a sole product of the creative mind," they explain, "but if we consider the entire creative cultural space, the already existing ideas can be identified which provided the necessary information for the creative mind. Ideas are copied, recombined, and only to a lesser extent invented as novel."[7]

Research psychologists Michael Mumford and Sigrid Gustafson note that manifestations of creativity do not just materialize from the ether, however many blank pages were faced by Shakespeare or Beethoven. Even creative titans such as these, they argue, are in fact recombining aspects of their own knowledge and experience in novel ways and forms.

"Koestler's review of the conditions related to innovative achievement led him to argue that it is impossible to create something out of nothing," write Mumford and Gustafson. "Rather, major achievements appeared to depend on the reorganization of existing facts and understandings brought about by the sudden fusion of two or more schemata.

"Although further research is required, this confluence of historic, experimental, and field research suggests that the individual's ability to integrate, reorganize, or restructure existing understandings may play an important role in generating major contributions or new schemata of use in solving a variety of problems."[8]

We have no patent prescription for the mystery of how to generate major ideas, but bisociation[9] is one theory that seems to have merit. Bisociation suggests that breakthrough ideas are born in the brain when two thoughts, two models, or two abstractions intersect. This intersecting of thoughts is at the heart of the process we recommend for developing solutions-after-next.

Use one tool, technique, principle, or perspective at a time to force an intersection with the selected purpose. The various creative, purposeful, alternative solutions that emerge are potential components of the ideal target solution.

One of the greatest advantages of the group process in developing innovative solutions is its ability to expand each individual's creative ideas. Members of the group, however, must overcome their fear of being ridiculed for presenting outlandish ideas. They need to believe that the group values mutual trust, encouragement, and openness. Top-level commitment and policies that support a search for continuing change and enhanced creativity advance enormously the group's problem-solving potential. But the problem-solving team itself can set ground rules and use techniques that inspire group creativity. For example, you might, for example—

1. Prohibit any criticism when ideas are being generated, allowing a later time for judgment and assessment.
2. Encourage freewheeling, however wild the ideas that may emerge.
3. Involve someone who is not a stakeholder in the project.
4. Record all ideas so that each receives due consideration.
5. Pose questions that stimulate or motivate creativity.

   a. What system or value-added services and outcomes would make us an acknowledged world leader?
   b. What would the solution be if we faced no constraints?
   c. What would the ideal system look like if we could achieve all the purposes larger than the one we selected?
   d. What would the solution look like if we started all over again (clean slate, green field, blank piece of paper)?

6. Focus discussion on how to make suggested solutions work, rather than on why they won't work. Play the believing game.
7. In using all of these tools, have fun with humorous activities that stimulate imagination. In generating ideas, humor is a serious matter.

What you really want to do is make the people in the group feel they can break all the rules that confine their thinking. You can do this by using tools or aids that present the situation from different or unusual perspectives. We list below a few of the many tools we've found useful in stimulating innovative ideas.

Principles. Almost every content area (a kitchen, electronic product assembly, taxation, or traffic flow) has a body of knowledge or principles that describe desirable and ideal conditions or solutions for different components of the system (layout, organizational structue, computer system, accident prevention, and so on). Some principles are related to parts of Breakthrough Thinking—eliminate the need for the purpose by considering larger purposes, specify only one input that is low cost (or high quality), specify only one output with the same characteristic(s), do the work automatically, and so on. In your mind, let these principles intersect one at a time with your purpose to generate new ideas. Ask yourself, How could we ideally achieve purpose X by means of principle Y?

If you are designing a kitchen, for example, take the principles that might guide the decisions regarding the floor plan, appliance selection, floor coverings, lighting, and so forth, and force them to intersect in your mind with your selected purpose. Could we achieve our purpose, "to have a low-maintenance, efficient, visually attractive room for cooking," by selecting white ceramic floor tiles?

Analogy and Metaphor. An innovative solution in a completely different field might intersect creatively with your purpose. Select a field in which the purposes may be similar and develop alternatives for that field, then use the solution from the second field as the basis for adaptation in your own field. Or think about how to accomplish the opposite purpose. Or pick unusual objects as a metaphor to stimulate ideas. (How would the system operate if it worked like a dictionary, or a ten-speed bicycle, or a spider web, or a television remote control channel selector.) Or try some unrelated things, such as visiting stores, parks, or museums, or reading poetry, art books, sports articles, plays, or fashion magazines. The exposure may generate ideas about how you might solve an analogous situation related to one or two of your own criteria, such as convenience, quick response, cost, or visual appeal. Ask yourself the bisociation question: How could we ideally achieve purpose X by means of analogy Y?

But beware: Treat analogies and metaphors carefully! Chapter 4 explained why. You're not trying to copy what someone else has already done; you're only seeking stimulus for ideas that are appropriate for your own unique situation and purposes.

Free Association. This technique acknowledges that any thought, object, or vision that occurs can intersect with another thought or purpose as the germ of an exciting idea. Experiment with your mind. Notes and forms drawn on paper can start a chain of associations that may lead to creative ideas. Use words at random from a dictionary to force an intersection with your chosen purpose. Fantasize about solutions with zero costs and zero resource needs—perfect products that satisfy customers 100 percent of the time. Use the projections and forecasts of futurists as stimulators to force an intersection with the purpose. For example, how can the forecast of a decline in birth rates cause purpose X to be achieved ideally?

Technology Fiction. Play the role of the science writer Isaac Asimov on the assignment of how ideally to achieve your focus purpose: *What if* biotechnology could change the molecular structure of the material? *If only* we could slip different computer chips into our heads. *If* current demographic trends *continue* then what will the health care system look like in the year 2035? *If* we had a different business direction?

Imagery. Use one of the measures of purpose accomplishment or critical success factors you selected for your purpose, and envision what the solution might be if that measure or factor were completely achieved. What might a solution look like that would reduce the traffic accidents at a given intersection to zero? What system of handling sales orders would use 100 percent of each resource (workers, paper, computer time, and so on)? Then do the same individually with each of your other measures. The solutions you envision and the measures of effectiveness themselves stimulate ideas about how that ideal future might be reached.

Scenario Writing. This technique can be used at three levels: first, to describe the future when an ideal solution is in place; second, to describe a target solution in place; and third, to describe the actions required (administrative moves, resource acquisition, roles of stakeholders, new core competencies, and so on) to realize the second scenario. The technology fiction tool can also help to develop scenarios.

Pretend. For personal or family purposes, this tool combines some scenario, imagery, free association, and technology fiction. How would you achieve your purposes if you won a lottery that provides you with a one-year release from all obligations and allows you to go anywhere? How would you achieve your community purposes if you were given free advertising on area television channels? If you were your customer (or supplier)?

Historical or Biographical Case. Think of a past event (even one that occurred decades or centuries ago) that had an unusual or outstanding result, and let that case intersect with your chosen purpose to generate new ideas. Or think of a particular bright and effective person whose characteristics you know and understand, and ask yourself, What kind of outstanding solution would he or she have developed to achieve this purpose?

Worst-Case Scenario. This method puts the negatives or constraints that almost every group produces to positive use. A conscious effort to develop worst-case scenarios helps identify possible obstacles to the implementation of an idea, or problems that might arise after the system is in use. It also helps to think through how to deal with variances and discrepancies from desired performance at the points in time and location where they occur. The worst-case scenario stimulates the question, How can an ideal system be developed to do away with this constraint or negative result?

Supplemental Aids. Several of these tools—for example, principles, analogy and metaphors, free association, imagery— have been augmented by specific techniques. Flash cards with specific stimulation prods from these tools are available in Roger von Olch's "Creative Whack Pack." Sets of posters can be placed in a room where ideas are being generated, encourage people to "get rid of your voice of judgment" and "ask dumb questions." Numerous computer programs lead you or a group through the use of these tools. For example, Idea Fisher includes 705,000 words and phrases in many different categories to stimulate the user to generate and capture on the computer unusual ideas.

Variety of Thinking Modes.   People tend to favor one or another of various modeling or thinking styles, most often based on their education or professional training. An engineer, for example, usually thinks with a mental image of a working model. Philosophers, on the other hand, use language and metaphorical images. This means a person may prefer certain of these techniques rather than others. Sometimes, experimenting with a different mode of thinking and its different techniques opens the door to stimulating thoughts.

Among the many modes of thinking that have been identified, the following are particularly conducive to creative thought:

Synthesis puts together parts into a whole, creating a construct that satisfies a goal. Examples of pure synthesis could be a painting made by an uninstructed child or an axe devised by a very primitive man.[10] Synthesis is the kernel of the design of process concerning the *purpose* of a new artifact to statements about its *form* and *use*.[11] A synthesis thinker should use techniques to stimulate many alternatives so the synthesis considers various visions.

Divergent thinking, as originally defined by Guilford in 1950, refers to an individual's ability to generate multiple potential solutions to a problem.[12] Successful divergent thinking results in an abundance of alternative ideas, concepts, and approaches. Thus, a divergent thinker should also use techniques which seek some details (i.e. scenario writers) as a means of stimulating even more alternatives to handle the problems discovered.[13]

By contrast, *convergent* thinking focuses on choosing from among a variety of alternative solutions. A convergent thinker should use techniques which generate many alternatives to assure that the results obtained are based on a large number of ideas, providing a greater probability of a better, more creative solution.[14]

Deductive thinking reasons from the general to the specific. It is usually associated with logical analysis, though not always. It proceeds from existing theories and facts to specific facts or solutions. It seeks an answer to the problem. Deductive thinkers are good with most techniques, and should use many before selecting a solution that can be used.[15]

Inductive thinking reasons from the specific to the general. It is the way that scientific theories are created. When used to solve problems, it often tries to fit a solution into a pattern of solutions for similar problems. Thus, inductive thinkers should use specific techniques (for example, a computer program) to stimulate many ideas before arriving at a solution. This compliments the usual assumptions that there is more than one potential solution, more than one adequate theory. Thus, it is related to synthesis and divergent thinking.[16]

Many other tools exist, and you certainly will develop aids of your own. The important thing is to avoid the conventional approach of analyzing and subdividing the problem. Keep the focus on purposes and solutions, and generate as many innovative solutions as you can for the purpose you have selected.

Using the Solution-After-Next Principle

The process of moving from your purposes array to an ideal target solution that can be implemented is, by its very nature, open and unstructured. Nevertheless, Table 6-1 describes certain steps you might follow in solving and preventing problems so that ideas can incubate and still make progress toward a solution without resorting to conventional approaches.

The steps should be taken in the most nonrestrictive sense. For example, step B may take place before step A at any step of the process. These guidelines are merely crutches to help you make the solution-after-next principle work for you the first few times you try it. They start you with the concept of generating ideas, lots of them, not judging them. Critical judgment is useful and appropriate only in later steps. After a few applications, the principles of Breakthrough Thinking will become second nature to you.

Table 6-1.   Developing a solution-after-next target and selecting a recommended solution.

A. Identify regularities to consider in developing a solution.

B. Develop as many ideas as possible about how you might achieve your selected purpose or a bigger purpose on your array.

C. Organize your ideas into major alternative solutions or systems. Incorporate as many good ideas as you can into each alternative. Each major alternative should be able, on its own, to achieve your purpose and should contain specific strategies for doing so.

D. Add detail and additional ideas to each alternative as needed to ensure its workability and your ability to measure its effectiveness.

E. Select your target solution-after-next by evaluating each major alternative. (Assume conditions of regularity, and assess the solution ideas with the measures of purpose accomplishment you developed for your purposes.)

F. Try to make your solution-after-next target even more ideal.

G. Develop modifications to the solution-after-next target to incorporate the irregularities. Add the details to arrive at a recommended solution.

The Small County highway project group has discussed the two major words in its purpose statement: "to have a highway." "Have" indicates location and direction, while "highway" indicates possible configuration. Discussion about these words and their implications leads to the decision that the group will consider these conditions as the regularities for which to develop a solution-after-next: the surface flat land, with no obstacles between the cities, and a highway with two lanes in either direction.

The first step is to identify the regularities for your target solution. This is not always easy and should be tackled with care when the regularities are not obvious.

Start by reviewing each major word or phrase (verb, subject, modifier) in the selected or larger purpose level. Determine what real-world factors occur most frequently, are most important, or will be constants, basics, or invariables even well beyond the time horizon for the project.

In many cases, the units of regularity are tied to words that represent inputs or outputs of the eventual solution. Inputs and outputs deal with larger systems or the external environment, which are less likely to change for the project, however large or small it may be. For example, 35 percent of orders received in a service center are from the West Coast, 25 percent from the East Coast, 20 percent from the mountain states, and the remaining 20 percent from all other parts of the country and the world.

Another method selects a distant point in time as the regularity. This permits people to think in terms of ideal conditions: How do you think a college of engineering would best be organized ten years from now? What would be an ideal gypsy moth pest-management system for the United States five years from now? How will the downtown area look six years from now after the urban development project has been completed?

Each of these time-based conditions may also require smaller decisions, but these decisions are often easier to make in the context of the longer view. It is relatively easy, for example, to designate which engineering topics will serve as regularity conditions ten years in the future, because people's personal concerns *now* are not at stake.

Another way that regularity factors are used is to assume that each one consecutively constitutes 100 percent of the conditions, and then to determine what ideal or innovative systems might be possible for just that one regularity circumstance. For example, what are innovative ideas for handling service center orders if you assume that all of them come from the West Coast?

Regularities are not an end in themselves, but rather a means of developing a solution-after-next. The regularity concept can lead to a significant breakthrough in actually designing an "ideal" system, but simply listing regularity possibilities does not mean that any of them should be used.

Selecting regularity factors for a specific project often is accomplished through trial and error, and the decisions are often somewhat subjective. During the design of your ideal solution, however, the regularity assumptions may change several times, so this is not a critical decision.

The Small County highway group uses several techniques to develop many ideas to achieve its purposes. Just two of the techniques are noted here.

Question: What solution-after-next or ideal systems would eliminate the need for the selected level, that is, would achieve a bigger purpose?
Answers:

1. *Use piggyback trucks to reduce number of vehicles on the road.*

2. *Put automated carrier tracks in roadway to control traffic flow.*

3. *Install train tracks so piggyback carriers can consolidate trucks and cars.*

Question: What are some best ways (ideal systems) of achieving the purpose level?
Answers:

4. *A completely new four-lane highway in a straight line.*

5. *A new two-lane highway in a straight line for one way and any existing two-lane highway for the other direction.*

6. *Two new lanes, side by side with any existing two-lane highway.*

7. *Requiring everyone to have a four-wheel-drive/dune buggy/land-water vehicle so the shoulders on the road can be utilized.*

The next step (step B, Table 6-1) is to generate as many alternative ideas for solutions-after-next as possible. This is where the concept-building process is critical and where the techniques described earlier will be most useful. Look for more than you know, even more than you can know. You must literally design ideal systems, not just talk about them. You must handle infant ideas carefully. To improve an idea's quality, you must put meat on its bones: *How* can the idea (however wild) actually work?

The ideas you record should be fairly complete. For example, if the purpose is "to prepare invoices," the idea statement might be, "The customer's order is entered into the computer. This deducts the quantities from the inventory memory, adds them to the sales analysis register, and automatically types the combination production order and shipping copy for file, bill of lading and invoice form...."

If someone proposes an incomplete idea, such as "use electronic data processing," you might ask, "What do you mean by that?" or, "How can you make that idea work?" In addition to ideas, this step usually generates a list of questions for which information needs to be collected before a solution can be fully formed.

At the same time, keep this step simple. Don't assume that *ideal* means *complex.* Your ideal system and solution should reflect the easiest and least complex way to accomplish your selected purpose(s). Shape each idea to accomplish your purposes and satisfy your customers in the least cumbersome way.

Once you have generated a suitable set of alternative solutions or options for the future, the sorting process begins (step C, Table 6-1). The ideas you and your colleagues have recorded must now be organized into major alternative solutions.

A major alternative is a broad and complete idea that incorporates as many good ideas from your list as possible. Each major alternative, if implemented, would achieve the selected purpose under ideal or regular conditions. Developing several major alternatives prevents premature closure on one idea and forces the inclusion of as many good ideas as possible into each of the alternatives under consideration.

Major alternatives are relatively mutually exclusive even though a smaller or minor idea may be incorporated in several of them. Eventually, you will select only one major alternative as your target solution for achieving the selected purpose.

To illustrate: A project charged with designing a supply distribution system for the 200 offices of the Los Angeles County District Attorney generated many solution alternatives that were incorporated into three major alternatives:

1. Keep the central warehouse, and use requisition forms and phone orders to be entered on a personal computer.

2. Set up a wide-area communications network that would automate information flow to match the automated storage and retrieval of items in the central warehouse.

3. Have all suppliers of goods ship directly from their facilities to each office when it places an order with the supplier.

A major *component* of a solution may be broad, but it is not a complete solution in itself. It may be part of one or more major alternatives but must be combined with other components to achieve the desired purpose. Using a personal computer to keep track of receipts, orders, and shipments was a major component of each major alternative solution to the supply distribution problem in the district attorney's offices, but a personal computer is not a solution in itself.

As you proceed with your sorting, classify each item on the list of ideas you generated as either a major alternative solution, a major component of a solution, or a detail that might fit into many major alternatives or components. Then combine and restructure these lists into fully workable major alternatives, adding detail and new ideas to each alternative as needed to assure its workability and to permit you to measure its effectiveness (step D, Table 6-1).

Some of the major alternatives might be immediately implementable if only ideal or regularity conditions prevail. Other major alternatives might be implementable only after further developments render it feasible. These present visionary and utopian challenges. They inspire questions for which information may need to be gathered, such as, How *can* the product be distributed automatically? or, How *can* the metal be made to shrink more as it cools? or, How *can* the traffic flow be arranged without any stops?

The Small County highway group has staff members in the commissioner's office gather information it needs to fill in some details of the major ideas and prepare cost estimates and other assessments of the ideas. The group uses each measure of effectiveness to evaluate each of the seven ideas for the regularity conditions. One question surfaces in the process: Is any one measure more important than another? The group decides that cost will probably be the governing factor if other factors were within a tolerable range.

As a result, the group selects idea number 4 as the target solution-after-next. However, idea 5 is also selected as a target system that will work if there is any existing two-lane highway. Since there is such a highway, idea 5 becomes the proxy target system, because its cost will be less than that of idea 4. This target system is defined in Figure 6-1 for the regularity conditions specified.

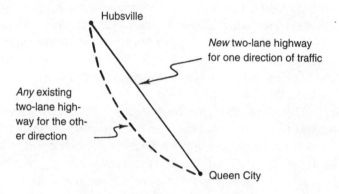

Figure 6-1.   The solution-after-next target system for Small County roads.

Next, you are ready to select your target solution, one that will bring you as close as possible to your ideal and will contain specific strategies for implementing immediate or phased-in changes over time that will bring you closer to your ideal (step E, Table 6-1).

To make your selection, evaluate each major alternative using the measures of purpose accomplishment you developed for your purpose, assuming regularity conditions. And when you have made your selection, ask yourself once again, What can we do to make this better? How can I make it happen? (step F, Table 6-1).

*The Small County highway group now considers the ex-
ceptions or irregular conditions: Obstacle Lake, and the new
two-lane highway's intersecting the existing highway at two
points. Each irregular condition can be treated as a minipro-
ject to develop a set of new ideas: How can we incorporate
the Obstacle Lake exception?*

*Some ideas to cope with the Obstacle Lake irregularity
are (1) use the target system, but with a minimal bend
around the lake; (2) build a smoothly curved two-lane highway, instead of a straight-line highway, to miss the lake; (3)
construct a two-lane bridge over the lake; (4) drain the lake;
and (5) add fill to the lake wide enough for two lanes. These
ideas are evaluated to determine which involves the least cost
(the first idea is best), stays closest to the target (first idea),
and will work (first idea). Therefore, the first idea becomes
the way the Obstacle Lake irregularity is incorporated into
the solution.*

*The ideas that are developed to consider the two-point
intersection exception are (1) have an overpass or underpass
at each point, (2) have a traffic light at each point, (3) have
stop signs at each point, and (4) arrange routing to eliminate
intersections. The fourth idea is closest to the target. It will
also work, as shown in Figure 6-2. The recommendation
modified to incorporate the exceptions is similar to the solution-after-next. Independent evaluation, simulation, and other checks are made to be sure the proposed highway details
are effective.*

Changing a solution-after-next into a recommended system (step G, Table 6-1) involves some smaller projects to find
answers to handle irregularities and a lot of detailing to ensure
workability. In many cases, meetings with other people are necessary to check the information. The result is a solution that is
often a breakthrough, while still noting what future changes
can be expected. In computer terminology, the recommended
solution should be treated as the "current release" or "Version
1.0." The implication then becomes obvious—what is being
done now is but a step toward ultimately hitting a better target.

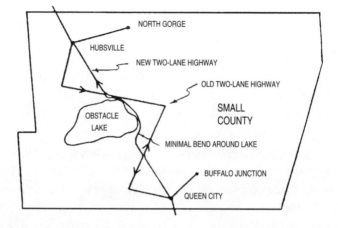

Figure 6-2.   New workable system for Small County roads.

Here are some "red flags" to watch out for on your solution finding journey:

- "We can't go beyond our scope."
- "Stay on your own turf."
- "Don't exceed the local budget."
- "If it looks like it will work, we'll make it work."
- "Let's get on to the next problem."
- "There's only one correct solution for this problem."
- "That's totally unrealistic."
- "Let's get real here."
- "In our department (group, organization), that's not possible."
- "That's just not done in our industry (profession)."
- "It won't work. Ten percent of our customers want *rhubarb* pie."
- "We can't go back to zero."

Whenever you confront these statements or any immediate criticisms when ideas are first presented, stop and practice the solution-after-next principle.

Always ask yourself these specific questions:

- Have I generated many alternative solutions-after-next or ideal systems?

- How should we achieve these purposes if we had to start all over again?

- How do I see this purpose and each bigger purpose being accomplished ten years from now?

- What *regular* occurrences can help us develop the best ideal solution? (Remember to avoid the trap of 15 percent irregularity. Focus on the 85 percent of the time that a solution *will* work.)

- What today is impossible to do but if we could, would fundamentally change the business?

- Am I seeing the right targets toward which our recommendations should lead?

- Have I looked for a second right answer? A third? A fourth?

- Have I remembered to involve in the solution-finding process someone who is *not* a stakeholder in the project?

Conclusions

The solution-after-next principle has the critical role of developing specific strategies to accomplish the mind-opening perspectives of the uniqueness and purposes principles. It forces you to think beyond your immediate problem and its first workable solution and, imagine, instead, what you or your company, system, organization, product, or service should look like in the future. Your imagination can soar, but the solution-after-next principle will bring you back to earth as you seek workable strategies for reaching your target. The principle gives you the freedom to make the right choices for improving "life."

Following the Breakthrough Thinking principle of the solution-after-next—

- Puts a time frame on the ideal solution to be developed.

- Permits you to start from scratch in finding solutions.

- Encourages stimulating lines of questioning that lead to alternative "ideal" solutions.
- Establishes the concept of regularity as a guideline for designing the ideal system.
- Prevents you from building something today that will stand in the way of your long-range plan.
- Ensures that your current recommendations for change contain provisions for continuing improvement.
- Overcomes the natural human resistance to change, which gives way to acceptance and even anticipation of change.
- Permits you to leap ahead of competitors, not merely catch up.
- Ensures that your thinking is not limited by current knowledge.

In essence, you "read the book" of Breakthrough Thinking from the end (the solution) backward toward your problem. As Harold Geneen, former chairman of International Telephone and Telegraph, has written: "You read a book from the beginning to the end. You run a business the opposite way. You start with the end, and then you do everything you must to reach it."[17]

The solution-after-next principle works with any level of background knowledge. Aborigines in Australia may be taught the Breakthrough Thinking principles. Even though they may not be able to design a printed-wire circuit board or a manufacturing and scheduling system, they certainly could use the principles to develop solutions within the frame of reference of their own knowledge base, which would enhance their curiosity to learn new types of information.

The Breakthrough Thinking principles, especially solution-after-next, are needed to turn such knowledge bases into the most effective solutions. The principles stimulate curiosity by dealing with potential futures, enabling knowledgeable people to stretch beyond the present limits of knowledge. They help convert the knowledge base to practice most effectively.

The solution-after-next *target* you select should encompass the following characteristics:

- Be a vigorous presentation of the ideal system you envision to satisfy your purpose. The presentation should include such a clear and frank description of the methods you plan to use in achieving your ends that everyone involved can both understand and draw inspiration from it.

- Have the flexibility to respond to competitive actions. Your competitors are doing their planning and will offer their results to the public along with yours. Your target solution must, therefore, incorporate many points where adjustments and adaptations can be made as the competition changes.

- Contain elements of its own solution-after-next—a solution-after-solution-after-next. We live in a dynamic world. Your target solution should at least be attuned to the forecasts of technological innovation and demographic trends. Many of the forecasts will be correct, but the majority won't—and there is no way of knowing which is which. Developing flexible solutions-after-next for achieving identified purposes is necessary for adaptation as time goes on.

- Represent low risks and high expectation for success—which may seem paradoxical in light of the out-of-the-ordinary ideas this principle urges you to consider. But if you follow all the other Breakthrough Thinking principles, your purposes are clear, you consider the situation unique, and you have constructed sound methods of implementation, the risk of failure should be low. Indeed, the successful people we studied claimed that having in mind a vision or solution-after-next target assured them of being "lucky" as they need to make adjustments over time in the solutions they implement. It does no good to define a vision for an ideal system unless you also build a sense of the possible into that structure.

The solution-after-next principle can thrill you with awareness of *possibilities!* You will never know how much change is possible unless you develop strategies that bring you as close as possible to a utopian situation (perfect quality, zero cost, zero time, perfect customer delight, and so on). The solution-after-next principle is a way of capturing your dreams and furnishing them with action plans for achievement.

"The best way to predict the future is to invent it." Alan Kay

"A man's reach should exceed his grasp, or what's a heaven for?" Robert Browning

"The best way to have a good idea is to have lots of them." Linus Pauling

"If you have built castles in the air, your work need not be lost; that is where they should be. Now put the foundations under them." Henry David Thoreau

"Do not follow where the path may lead. Go instead where there is no path and leave a trail." Anonymous

NOTES

1. J. Sandberg and B. Wielinga, "Situated Cognition: A Paradigm Shift?," *Journal of Artificial Intelligence in Education* (1992) 3, 129–136.

2. Makoto Iida, Adventure Management (4): Power of Information and Imagination, *Journal of Executives*, 85/4.

3. Y. Berra, *Yogi, It Ain't Over....* (New York: McGraw-Hill, 1989).

4. A. Bond of *Canada Post,* personal communication to G. Nadler, February 3, 1988.

5. J.L. Adams, *Conceptual Blockbusting* (San Francisco: The San Francisco Press, 1976).

6. J.G. Peterson, *Personal Qualities and Job Characteristics of Expert Engineers and Planners,* Ph.D. dissertation, University of Wisconsin, Madison, 1985.

7. S.D. Brookfield, *Developing Critical Thinkers* (San Francisco: Jossey-Bass, 1987).

8. A. Koestler, *The Act of Creation* (New York: MacMillan, 1964).

9. Harold Geneen, *Managing* (Garden City, N.Y.: Doubleday, 1984).

10. J.L. Adams, *The Care and Feeding of Ideas: A Guide to Encouraging Creativity* (Reading, Massachusetts: Addison-Wesley, 1986).

11. N.F.M. Roozenburg, "On the Pattern of Reasoning in Innovative Design," *Design Studies*, Vol. 14, No. 1, January 1993.

12. Mumford and Gustafson, op. cit.

13. J.L. Adams, op. cit.

14. Ibid.

15. Ibid.

16. Ibid.

17. Harold Geneen, *Managing* (Garden City, N.Y.: Doubleday, 1984).

Chapter 7

The Systems Principle:
Seven-Eighths of Everything Can't Be Seen

"Strategic planning" captured the attention of the president of a large advertising agency. He decided to initiate the effort by setting up a two-day off-site retreat for the fourteen top executives and himself. The retreat became focused on the values and beliefs of the company—a focus that produced twenty-two statements. All of the participants felt good about the exercise. Within a couple of weeks, however, they all realized that they didn't know what to do next. During that time, the president happened to read the first edition of *Breakthrough Thinking.* He called The Center for Breakthrough Thinking, Inc., to request a facilitator for a day's workshop.

All the top executives attended and wanted to know why their list of values and beliefs had not resulted in a strategic plan. The Breakthrough Thinking facilitator started the day with an introduction to the systems matrix, explaining what its elements and dimensions meant and why a "strategic plan" is actually a system. Then he asked the group to classify each statement on their list of values and beliefs, placing each into the appropriate cell or cells of the systems matrix.

After all the statements had been classified and recorded on the white board in the front of the room, all the participants could see that almost all of their entries were placed in the values dimension. In fact, nothing had been stated about the company's purposes. The fundamental dimension of purposes had not yet been identified, making it very difficult, if not impossible, to develop a strategic plan.

The group began its work again, this time developing a purpose hierarchy for the company, making their customers and their customers' customers an integral part of the hierarchy. They selected their focus purpose or mission statement from the purpose hierarchy they developed. Subsequently, options for strategic solutions-after-next were developed and their rough details developed in terms of the systems principle.

*P*roblems and proposed solutions are often like icebergs: What is visible at first glance often turns out to be only a small portion. And that large hidden part may bring grief, as it did to the *Titanic*.

Breakthrough Thinking's response to hidden problems and solutions is a powerful, precision device called the *system matrix*. If the *Titanic* had had radar and sonar, it might have escaped its tragic fate. The system matrix is like radar and sonar, designed to illuminate the seven-eighths of solution ideas and recommendations that otherwise might be overlooked.

The systems principle states that nothing exists by itself. Successful problem solving and prevention hinges on considering the various interrelated elements and dimensions that comprise every solution. The successful solution-finders we studied had a framework in their minds, one they used to formulate a solution of any sort. Intuitively, they were applying what we call the systems perspective.

First let's deal with that word *systems*. It is certainly overworked but seldom well defined—"This is a lousy system," "You can't beat the system." The word is widely bandied about in many professions and occupations, with a plethora of specialized meanings. We have nearly a hundred definitions in our files. The word is often expanded to "systems thinking," with only a passing reference to "consider all factors."

Basically, a system is (1) a group of related entities that (2) does something—receives inputs, affects them in some way, and produces outputs to achieve some purpose.

Almost anything in the world can be called a system. A sheep can be considered a system. It takes in fodder and produces wool and lamb chops. A volcano is part of a system by which the earth vents excessive internal heat.

In dealing with a system, you could simply list its basic elements or characteristics. Then you could list the factors that might affect those elements. You would now have two lists, or maybe more. Maybe you would want to separate the factors that could affect your system on weekdays from those that affect it only on Sundays.

Obviously with this method you would soon find yourself juggling a lot of sheets of paper and having trouble relating the things in them. To meet this problem, someone whose name is lost to history devised a tabulating method to bring some kind of order out of a jumble of data. That method is called a *matrix*.

A matrix is simply an aggregation of two-dimensional boxes, like a tic-tac-toe blank or the pigeon-holes in a roll-top desk. In the boxes you can write anything there's room for. (If there isn't enough room, you code the box to refer to a separate document.)

A matrix provides both horizontal rows and vertical columns so that several types of information can be graphically related to one another. For instance, if you were planning to locate a new factory somewhere in the country, the options and factors bearing on them might line up as shown in Figure 7-1.

What the figure tells you at a glance, among other things, is that labor availability on the East Coast is something that needs to be investigated before you should select a solution to your problem.

	Climate	Construction costs/sq ft	Labor availability
West Coast	good	$100	100%
Midwest	medium	$150	80%
East Coast	poor	$200	?

Figure 7-1.   Matrix of options and factors for locating a factory.

Displaying the information in this way obviously averts the stiff neck and the confusion you would get in referring back and forth among many sheets of paper.

A matrix can be infinitely expanded and elaborated with adjunct matrices to cover all the factors involved in a problem or solution. A climate column could be a matrix to relate other factors like rainfall, temperatures, and so on. Some practitioners make matrices three-dimensional to encompass a special variable like time. But that is a complexity we can avoid for now.

Figure 7-2 shows how versatile the matrix device can be, how even an Agatha Christie–type crime (Colonel Prothero is killed by a bullet from a gun he had kept for years in his library) might be explored in a matrix format.

Remember that the data in these boxes were filled in bit by bit. With the matrix completed, suspicion obviously points

| | **EVIDENCE** | | | |
SUSPECTS	Location at time of crime	Access to gun	Personal data	Behavior under questioning
Butler	"Walking in woods"	Saw daily in library	Severe arthritis in right (gun) hand	Poised Curious
Maid	Cleaning attic	Never cleaned library	"Afraid of guns"	Fluttery
Cook	At grocery store	Never visited library	20 years with family	Calm Indignant
Gardner	Several versions	Tended library plants daily	Army marksman Gambling debts Hated officers	Defensive Shifty Nervous

Figure 7-2. Matrix of evidence and suspects in a murder case.

to the gardener—a conclusion that, in narrative form, would have taken many pages of text to reach.

The same sort of formulation can be applied to any problem or project. The main point of the matrix is to *correlate* information in an orderly way—and, in the process, to indicate where there are *gaps* in pertinent information: the hidden part of the iceberg.

In the mid-1980s, an Air Force intelligence office was overwhelmed with data flowing in from many parts of the world. The total was so voluminous that it just accumulated in binders and piles of read-out sheets that no one had time to plow through. An officer won a high award for using the *system matrix* by which incoming information was sorted, in effect indexed, and correlated so that its real importance could be extracted readily. A company could similarly find patterns in data about customers, suppliers, or other resources by putting whatever information is available about the topic of interest into the system matrix format.

The basic system matrix, adaptable to many situations, is an arrangement six boxes wide and eight boxes deep (see Figure 7-3), whose labels will be explained individually as we proceed.

The way such a matrix may be applied was illustrated in the planning and design of a huge complex to house the medical school and teaching hospital of a large Midwestern university. Initially, the architect submitted the customary "program statement" delineating the rationales and performance requirements for the complex, for submission to approval and financing agencies.

But the trouble with program statements is that they essentially are idiosyncratic, reflecting a single individual's ideas and preferences. That limitation was conspicuous in this case.

The medical school's dean resolved the problem with a system matrix approach. He tabulated purposes; human inputs and physical items; desired and undesirable outputs; sequence of activities transforming inputs into outputs; environment, in both physical and organizational terms; human agents; physical catalysts (machines such as computers that participate but are not part of the final product); and information aids.

Dimensions

Elements	Fundamental: basic or physical charactistics—what, how, where, or who	Values: goals, motivating beliefs, global desires, ethics, moral matters	Measures: performance (criteria, merit and worth factors), objectives (how much, when, rates, performance specifications)	Control: how to evaluate and modify element or system as it operates	Interface: relation of all dimensions to other systems or elements	Future: planned changes and research needs for all dimensions
Purpose: mission, aim, need, primary concern, focus						
Inputs: people, things, information to start the sequence						
Outputs: desired (achieves purpose) and undesired outcomes from sequence						
Sequence: steps for processing inputs, flow, layout, unit operations						
Environment: physical and attitudinal, organization, setting, etc.						
Human agents: skills, personnel, responsibilities, rewards, etc.						
Physical catalysts: equipment, facilities, etc.						
Information aids: books, instructions, etc.						

Figure 7-3. Systems matrix: agents, catalysts, and aids help process inputs into outputs without becoming part of outputs.

The dean's matrix served as a road map for a planning committee and no fewer than twenty-two subcommittees.

A matrix highlights not only relationships of elements and their interdependencies but, most importantly, provides the best assurance of including all necessary details—that is, not overlooking some essentials. (More than one skyscraper has been built without regard to whether strong winds would blow out the windows.)

This chapter shows how Breakthrough Thinking puts utility into the word *system*. Utility is surely not achieved by appending the word *system* to activities people would understand without the added word (for example, production system, accounting system, railway system, health care delivery system, education system, banking system).

The system matrix formulation has one overarching benefit that makes it most suitable for Breakthrough Thinking: Each element and dimension can be viewed as a system itself of elements and dimensions, and each system matrix can be viewed as a part of one or more larger system elements or dimensions. Since this ability to treat both smaller and larger system relationships continues *ad infinitum,* you are able to include all necessary details in specifying and presenting a solution-after-next target and a recommended solution, while at the same time showing their position and role in the larger systems of which they are a part.

What a System Matrix Does

A system matrix organizes the information about any system, whether dealing with physical items (as in a manufacturing system) or data and information items (as in an accounting system). The complexity of most systems means some way is needed to handle the intangible information about them. Furthermore, the same item of information is usable in more than one other system and is likely to be interpreted differently by various individuals. Developing a solution-after-next (SAN) target or vision and then the recommended system is greatly facilitated by the openness of the ever-smaller and ever-larger perspective of the system matrix.

The Department of Agriculture in a Midwestern state was designing a new data classification and storage system for the many laboratory analyses of crops it receives. Although the SAN could be stated in general terms, the details needed to make the recommendation workable at the same time the broad perspective was maintained would have become a hopeless tangle without the system matrix.

A system matrix on a single sheet of paper is almost never used as a repository of solution details because it is far too limited for almost all Breakthrough Thinking efforts. It does, however, provide the indexing key and flexibility for referencing where the specifications may be found.

A successful change or new solution for a problem of almost any level of complexity requires a great deal of detail and specifications, especially if a breakthrough characterizes the solution. The master professional may have some scheme to help ensure that such technicalities are prepared, but unfortunately most such intuitive processes leave a great deal to be desired. They may suffice most of the time, but there is no way to predict when they are insufficient. Consider, for example, the 1979 near-disaster at the Three Mile Island nuclear power plant. Although the problems were traced to human error, what operational details might a system matrix view of each subsystem have provided that could have eliminated the possibility of such mistakes?

The system idea of wholeness and completeness is so desirable that the word gets used even though it is not fully understood or given a detailed meaning. The systems principle of Breakthrough Thinking captures these desires and add the clarity to meet the many needs of problem solving. For instance, it provides—

1. *A language for discussing and describing solution ideas and recommendations.* Language is only a representation of the images and concepts that occur in our brains. The uniqueness, purposes, and solution-after-next principles are particularly oriented to generate these images. Conversely, knowing the language of the systems principle helps the mind push for a broader and more inclusive set of images. The com-

plexity of most problems requires a systems language you can rely on.

2. *Detailed specifications of the fundamental structure that is to exist after installation and implementation.* Structure refers to an arrangement, configuration, organizational chart of responsibility and authority relationships, or physical portrayal. Structure describes how a SAN target and a recommended solution should look. It also suggests the adaptive routes that may be pursued in moving toward the SAN from its precursor solution.

Even the most detailed checklist (airplane preparation by a pilot, moving from one house to another) is more useful if the factors included are in a broad systems frame, so that each item is in context. Otherwise, just going over the checklist can give you a false sense of security because you think you have covered everything.

3. *Information on how a structure or solution will operate or flow over time once it has been activated.* This scenario of how operations will proceed should include steps to improve the whole solution and to update periodically the SAN guide.

4. *The major activities and events needed to move from presentation and approval of the recommended solution to the time when the structure and its operation are in place.* A commitment to measures of purpose accomplishment and the SAN principle are reinforced with a system matrix format in which values and measures are delineated for all elements of a solution.

Serious problems arise when a solution is not well thought out. For example, U.S. automobile companies might have been much more attuned to purposes, customers, solutions-after-next, and future dimensions—and thus not have lost so much of their domestic market share to Japanese and other foreign competitors—if the systems principle had been followed.

5. *Documentation of the SAN target and the recommendation.* Many parts of a problem-solving endeavor should be recorded to provide an audit trail for complex systems.

6. Protection against the complacency arising from the assumption that the solution or answer is simple. Viewing each solution as a system matrix gives meaning to the exhortation that "everything should be treated as a system." Repeatedly reviewing all the elements and dimensions avoids trouble. Doing this *mentally* while you are in a meeting gives you a great ability to ask pertinent questions when others are "hand waving" away the difficulties of proceeding along a particular course of action.

The questions you ask—about purposes, inputs, values, measures, controls, and so forth—both stimulate the believing game to find how the idea could work and sift details that might be overlooked. The matrix also helps you categorize information that people present so you can locate the cells where information is needed, as in the Air Force intelligence case.

7. Speculation about the future. Solution-after-next forays into possible future events can be explored. People who are asked to project eventualities can be more specific. One person with profound knowledge of, say, tariff history, could be asked to provide system details about future trade opportunities.

Each element can be expanded to continue the generating ideas. That is, you can seek to include the inputs *to* the inputs, the largest products or services that may emerge as a given output is considered. Revealing each element in this way provides continuing insights into the "what if" question.

8. A focus on the important elements and dimensions. Purposes, customers, the relationship between costs and ends to be achieved, people in the system, and so on, are kept at the forefront of the problem-solving process.

The great emphasis in the United States currently is on quality—quality products, services, and customer relations—and on productivity. These desires are obviously universal. But often omitted in all the rhetoric is the consideration that you need to be sure the quality and productivity are obtained *for the most effective items* (the fundamental dimension that is based on the uniqueness, purposes, and SAN principles). *It doesn't make sense to obtain high quality and productivity of items and activities that ought not to exist at all.*

That is, quality and productivity perspectives must be built into the system, not exhorted or managed in later. Some quality and productivity improvements can be obtained from any existing system, but Breakthrough Thinking should be applied initially to the system to provide the effective foundation on which to base the quality and productivity emphasis.

Caterpillar Company's commitment to deliver any part, even an engine, within forty-eight hours anywhere in the world or charge nothing for it requires an extensive set of specifications about how the manufacturing, warehousing, sales, accounting, and other systems must operate to achieve this level of quality customer service.[1]

The systems principle provides the basis for specifying all the needed details so that a quality job can be done. Many quality problems arise because the various dimensions of each element are not sufficiently thought through so that the operators and managers of the system know what is expected. When this is done, they can exercise their best efforts with flexibility and continuous improvement. The interface dimension, for example, shows where and how interactions with and feedback from the customers should be developed.

Spelling out the details of a system, such as air-traffic control, an electric power system, or a nuclear facility, is critical at the earliest stage because technological changes after the system is installed may actually be destabilizing and substantially increase risks.

Problems and their solutions have to be pictured in their wholeness, not in any arbitrary division into "simpler" problems, because all parts affect all the other parts.

A Closer Look at a System Matrix

Any system can be thought of as a hopper—a container with an opening at the top and a controlled opening at the bottom. Inputs of whatever sort go in at the top, are acted upon and altered by various forces, and come out, changed in some way, at the bottom as outputs.

The forces acting on the system include such things as physical catalysts, information aids, human agents, and environmental factors. The operative factor is sequence, the order of steps in whatever processing takes place.

Each system is thus a complex set of interrelated elements. One basic element defines the broad purpose and values of the larger entity or organizational unit within which the system does or will exist. Each system achieves an end. Thus, the purpose, function, or result sought from a system is the first element, and each system has at least one purpose.

Each system receives physical, informational, and human items from smaller, larger, and parallel systems to process into a desired state that will achieve its purpose. Therefore, every system has inputs.

Each system provides physical, informational, and human items or services to its smaller, larger, and horizontal systems. These outcomes represent the means whereby the purposes of the system are achieved. Therefore, each system has outputs.

Similarly, the five remaining elements (rows of the system matrix, Figure 7-3) can be developed: sequence, environment, human agents, physical catalysts, and information aids. The words used for the names of elements are unimportant and can vary, whereas the ideas represented by each are critical.

The hopper model of any system is shown in Figure 7-4. A large hopper can conveniently contain small hoppers. Each large circle or group of circles in Figure 7-4 represents a smaller system level. A hopper drawn around each circle or group shows how the elements in the definition apply to it. The hopper of Figure 7-4 can also be included in larger hoppers, which would thus include other hoppers in parallel. The eight elements from the system matrix (Figure 7-3) and the hopper model (Figure 7-4) are defined as follows.

Purpose is the mission, aim, need, primary concern, function of, customer requirements, or results sought from a system (see Chapter 5 for a detailed discussion).

Inputs include any physical items, information, or human beings on which work, conversion, or processing takes place. These inputs must be part of the output. Physical items could be coils of steel, powdered plastic, money, a floppy disk, or a sales order form. Information could be a bank account balance,

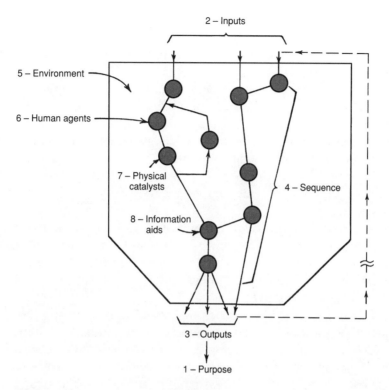

Figure 7-4. Hopper model of a system.

the whereabouts of an executive, knowledge content for a course, or production statistics. The human beings relevant in this context could be sick people entering a hospital, a housewife shopping at a grocery store, a family wanting house plans, a student attending a college, an overweight person visiting a reducing salon, and so on.

The return of previous outputs of the system is also possible input. For example, a system manufacturing airplanes includes the reentry of each airplane for major periodic maintenance. A patient may reenter a hospital after having been discharged. User information about product performance serves as new input to the product design system.

Every system requires at least two of the three types of input—physical items, information, or human beings. A manufacturing system, for example, might require information about alloy, tensile and yield strengths, gauge, and width to accompany the physical input of a coil of steel. A patient entering a hospital system represents human (previous medical history and symptoms), physical (personal belongings), and information inputs.

Outputs include desired and undesired physical items, information, humans and services that result from processing inputs. Desired outputs achieve purposes and meet customer and user requirements by adding net value to inputs. Undesired outputs include such things as human dislocations, pollutants, scrap, and trash, for which provisions must be included in the system specifications.

Sequence concerns the conversion, work, process, transformation, software program, or order and cycle of steps or events by which the inputs become the outputs. The basic steps are the essential "unit operations," or identifiable changes of the inputs that lead to their transformation into outputs.

Environment involves the physical and sociological (psychological, legal, political, economic) factors or ambience within which the other elements operate. These factors are always changing. Many are usually outside the influence of the system itself; others can be specified for the system. Physical or climatic factors include temperature, humidity, noise, dirt, light, colors of machines and walls, and so forth. Ecological physical factors outside the system include spatial aspects, accessibility, and shapes and relationships in the design of the physical facilities and equipment.

Sociological factors include the state of technology within which an organizational unit operates, the cultural and historical determinants of attitudes, and the society's economic conditions. More specific factors concern the attitudes of managerial and supervisory personnel, the operating controls and rules for personnel, the social interactions and communications of the people involved, and cultural considerations. The Japanese, for example, do not build factories or plants with an entrance on the northeast side, which is traditionally considered "the devil's gate." Managerial style and organizational structure set another environmental factor: autocratic, paternalistic, bureaucratic, permissive, diplomatic, or democratic.

Human agents are those who aid in the steps of the sequence without becoming part of the outputs. Human agent activities or methods in the processing sequence include the whole range of human capabilities and intelligence: talking, writing, reasoning, performing tasks, making decisions, evaluating, learning, creating, and acting as monitoring and sensing devices. Human beings may be either inputs and outputs (patients in a hospital), or human agents (nurses). Overlap often exists: Patients can be human agents aiding other patients, and nurses can be inputs into the cafeteria system.

Physical catalysts or resources aid in the steps of the sequence without becoming part of the outputs. Typical items are machines, vehicles, office furniture, computers, energy, buildings, and tools. A chicken on an egg farm is a physical catalyst. Each of these illustrative items could be a physical catalyst in one system, or input or output in another system. A computer, for example, may be a physical catalyst in an accounts payable system, an input in a maintenance system, and an output in a production system.

Information aids include knowledge and data resources that help in the steps of the sequence without becoming part of the outputs. Computer programming instructions, equipment operating manuals, maintenance instructions, standard operating procedures for human agents, and policy manuals are typical information aids. These may also be inputs and outputs in other systems. On occasion, an expert consultant, media advisor, or corporate legal advisor could have this role.

Even a physical object, such as a table, can be described in terms of system elements.

- *Purpose:* to locate objects at a particular height
- *Inputs:* objects
- *Outputs:* objects maintained in position
- *Sequence:* dynamic equilibrium between upward forces of the table and downward forces of the objects, as well as the changes, however subtle, in table strength and object forces and conditions over time
- *Environment:* physical (high or low humidity, and so on) and sociological (for example, careful or careless family)

- *Human agents:* persons to dust or polish
- *Physical catalysts:* wood, metal, furniture polish
- *Information aids:* yield and shear strengths of table materials, abrasive characteristics of objects

Any physical object, information item, or human being can be a different element in different systems. A table, thus, could be the *output* of a manufacturing system, an *input* into a sales system, or a *physical catalyst* in a hotel system.

No model is ever complete, and the hopper model is no exception. Form or structure needs to be added to the elements for completeness. Six dimensions (see Figure 7-3) help specify the conditions for each element in a specific situation: (1) fundamental existence characteristics; (2) values, beliefs, and desires; (3) measures to assess accomplishment of fundamental and value dimensions; (4) control or dynamic methods of ensuring achievement of fundamental, values, and measures specifications; (5) interface relationships of fundamental, values, measures, and control specifications with other systems and other elements in its system; and (6) future existence or desired changes and improvements that can be foreseen in fundamental, values, measures, control, and interface specifications.

The number of dimensions (the horizontal column in Figure 7-3) is not fixed; some can be divided into two or more attributes.

Fundamental concerns tangible, overt, observable, physical, or basic structural characteristics, including the basic what-who-how-where specifications and quality levels.

Values and *goals* are motivating beliefs, human expectations, global desires, ethics, equity, and moral concerns that can be *ascribed in some form to each element*. How people and organizations feel about desirable results in regard to each element is the realm of values and goals. Important assumptions (for example, democracy, civil liberties, justice, profits, aesthetics, environmental issues), quality and productivity, occupational safety and health, human dignity and betterment, and customer preferences are illustrations of possible items to consider. Those values of the internal organization or family are often defined as its "culture," and those in the external world over which your system has no control are often called "societal mores." Values could thus be said to reflect the standards that a solution is expected to continue or establish.

Measures translate the fundamental and values dimensions into particular performance factors and operational objectives (how much and when). In general, measures concern accomplishment, effectiveness, time, performance, cost, and other important factors bearing on the fundamental specifications. They are indicators of success of the eventual solution.

Accomplishment and performance factors are the specific criteria that are considered important measures. Some typical measures of the projected or actual operating system are cost per month, time per service or output per hour, reject rate, index standing (such as the index of innovation or productivity), reliability life, expense, and profit.

Objectives relate to specific amounts and time or cost factors for each measure. If one value is "to improve the department's safety record," a performance measure might be "to decrease accidents," and an objective "to reduce monthly accident rate by 30 percent within a year." Here is another illustration: If the value or goal is to improve manpower services, one performance measure is to increase placement of disadvantaged people; one objective would be to increase the number of disadvantaged placements by 25 percent per year.

Control comprises methods for ensuring that the fundamental, measures, and even value specifications, are maintained as desired (at or within limits around a specified condition) during the operation of the system. Dynamic control of each specification involves (1) measuring the performance of the specification as the solution or system is in operation; (2) comparing the actual measurements to the desired specification; and (3) acting to correct significant deviations through human corrections, automated response, or advance modifications of equipment, by changing a desired specification, or by designing an overall improvement.

All three parts of the control dimension may be carried out within the system itself, or any one or more may become the responsibility of an outside system or group (for example, government regulations). Or all three parts of the control dimension of the system matrix may be an integral part of the fundamental and measures dimensions of a particular element. For example, a part produced by a machine may be inspected by the operator, or inspection may be done automatically.

Interface is the relationships of the fundamental values, measures, and control specifications to other elements and to external systems. Some illustrations of interfaces are inspection of materials received from a vendor, the impact of a changed grading system on parents, shared services with other hospitals, and government reporting regulations related to personnel actions. Illustrations of intrasystem interfaces are process-control interactions with human agents, physical catalysts, and information aids; information systems relationships among inputs, humans, physical catalysts, and information aids.

Interface dimension specifications help avoid difficulties in getting a system to operate well by assessing the possible consequences of negative and hostile interactions. How much more or less work will result for other systems? What costs will the other system incur? Can the other system be modified to let this system be implemented, or even to have the other system take advantage of the ideas? Perhaps a substitute or add-on technological shortcut might be located by such searching for interfaces. What are the risks—and from where—to people, property, and the environment? What possible disturbances and forces from other systems (lobbying, special interest groups, an oil embargo, Supreme Court decisions) will have an impact on this system (delay service, increase cost)?

Future anticipates changes in each specification of the other five dimensions at one or more points of time in the future. The future dimension defines the growth or decay of the specifications. All forecasts (for example, social attitudes, costs, weather, population) express possible future specifications. Also included are specifications on how the dimensions for a specific element will get to their anticipated stages (a transfer function). The arrival at the desired stage (say, the SAN target) may be planned (obsolescence or gradual termination), may be due to learning and duration, or may require a new problem-solving effort.

In addition, the future dimension identifies what research and development (R&D) may be needed to make the solution being installed now become the same as the SAN target. A company may set priorities for its R&D by knowing what the future dimensions are for several systems. An individual can identify what information is needed to permit him or her to reach the target.

The lines denoting the cells or box in Figure 7-3 are *not* firm divisions, for there are both overlapping relationships and interrelationships among the cells. Each cell, rather, connotes the major thrust of an element–dimension intersection.

The representational matrix provides an orderly way of denoting all possible types of information to consider in specifying a system. Not all elements or dimensions need to be specified in a particular system, and it is not necessary to have the same amount of information in each cell. The amount can range from nothing to a very large number of models or data sets. Similar or identical accuracy is not required for the information in each cell. The system matrix is very seldom, if ever, used in exactly this form for recording information needed in designing a system.

The questions raised by probing what specifications should be developed for each cell are almost all-inclusive. They number far more than the usual who, what, why, where, when, and how. They are also much more specific because more than the forty-eight questions the matrix appears to suggest are available. In addition to the sixteen fundamental and values dimension questions, there are at least sixteen measures dimension questions about the fundamental and values specifications, twenty-four control dimension questions, thirty-two interface questions, and forty future questions, or a total of at least 128.

Because everything is a system, each element and dimension of a system can itself be viewed as a system. Picture a full system matrix projecting *behind* the input element. This provides a mechanism for getting as much detail as needed for specifying a solution. Similarly, each cell of a system matrix can itself be viewed as a system.

A system view of an element or dimension could be continued indefinitely, like the picture of a woman on a box of cleanser holding a box of the cleanser with a picture of a woman holding a box of cleanser with a picture of a woman holding a box of cleanser with a picture. Consider the national economy of a country as the basic system: the transportation system would be behind the sequence element, the highway system beneath the physical catalyst element of transportation, a road system behind the output element of highway.

But relax. No need to feel overwhelmed. In practice, only a few (three or so) matrices in one direction or the other are all that are encountered. These detailing and enlarging perspectives, however, do provide operational methods for a project of any complexity to consider simultaneous problem solving on interdependent units as a means of avoiding weak links in the whole system. This ability of effective people to perceive the whole and understand the interconnections and possible weak links through some system framework they have intuitively set characterizes the system principle of Breakthrough Thinking.

Purposes and Goals of the Systems Principle

The systems principle has a wide variety of purposes and goals, nine of which are discussed below. In Breakthrough Thinking, this principle touches on all the other principles by setting up a holistic framework and providing the mechanism for documenting the principles' impact on a problem-solving venture.

1. *To provide a holistic framework for thinking about and describing images of solutions-after-next and recommendations*. Many techniques and tools are available for various aspects of a system (diagrams, charts, equations, pictures, flow charts, organization charts, and so on), but none is sufficient. The system matrix is the setting for interrelating them. Conversely, the matrix is a thorough method for playing the believing game. It furnishes the elements, dimensions, and cells as a stimulus for seeking how the idea *could* be made feasible.

2. *To consider and put into the right perspective all relevant aspects and complexities of the SAN and recommended solutions.* Everyone agrees that most solutions are complex. Proposing anything new or different means all the factors (technical, social, interfaces, individual) should be detailed or appropriately considered. It is especially critical to include specifications that show how to accomplish the many critical objectives and goals each system should seek—the attainment of quality as *part of* the operation rather than inspecting for it after-the-fact; continued productivity improvement of the initial change; the methods of making the customer (or ultimate beneficiary of a problem solution) the prime focus; the development of human resources, where future changes and diversifications of products and services can be phased in; and the appropriate and needed emphasis on costs and timeliness.

The customer is so important that a system matrix of the customer's system ought to be somewhat detailed. Its input element is where your product or service outputs enter the customer's system. Relating your system matrix to the customer's also gives you a chance to understand where improvements can be made in your outputs and purposes, and also where you may be able to develop new products or services. Above all, the system matrix should help you avoid making optimistic assumptions about how your customers will react (or how any people in the system will behave).

The interrelationships shown in a system matrix may also be used to assess the possible impact of other systems on your own—your competitor's system, the service system available through independent companies, the social system that may exist around the outputs of your system.

A pet peeve of ours is the interminable lists of recommendations that end the reports of the vast number of studies so prevalent in our society. Besides being exercises in excessive data collection (see Chapter 8), the recommendations are seldom considered in systems terms. For example, one 1988 report on engineering education and practice had twenty-three recommendations. Many of them were good, but the report did not state how each related to the other or what costs, quality, time, and continuing change factors were associated with each.

Consider how much more effective recommendations would be if they were in some form of a system matrix—the rough ideas of the fundamental, values, measures, control, interfaces, and future dimensions of the purposes, inputs, outputs, sequence, environment, human agents, physical catalysts, and information aids. We can surely do this ourselves; and when we do, we discover many omissions, ideas that could have been included, conflicts, overlaps, and even counterproductive items. Wouldn't it be much better for study groups to prepare their recommendations so that these difficulties would be eliminated and the reports more comprehensible to the reader? Their failure to do so is a prime reason almost all reports end up sitting on shelves without any action being taken.

3. *To organize the details for the SAN target and recommendations.* This purpose stresses *depth* of specifications to complement the breadth and interrelationships emphasis of purpose 2. Successful people provide a firm sense of how all the details are available to show that results can be obtained. This perspective is useful in providing a scenario of gains even as the overall direction is spelled out and guides current actions. In addition, using the system matrix to detail each element, dimension, and cell increases significantly the likelihood of considering all social and human impacts and benefits that will occur with the change and intervention.

4. *To understand complexity.* Although not exactly related to achieving breakthroughs, this objective recognizes that a complex situation may initially need some insights even before any purpose and SANs may be developed. The system matrix is particularly adept at identifying and portraying interfaces and communication links. It is the antidote to the unfortunately correct folklore that says, "Under every rock, there is a snake—and another rock."

Critical to complex situations is an understanding of the nature of the predictions—whether absolutely certain, probable, possible, or uncertain—which are always contained in complex circumstances. These vistas then allow an effective use of the other Breakthrough Thinking principles, while challenging the complexities, interfaces, and future directions. So providing a way to understand the complexity of problems and solutions is in itself an important breakthrough to avoid doing nothing, which often occurs simply because of a problem's complexity.

5. *To obviate failure*. Henry Petrosky claims that the purpose of design, especially the bridges and structures of his civil engineering perspective, is just this: To obviate failure.[2] All of us would agree that that is critical for the solutions he deals with. It is important for all other systems—software, manufacturing, insurance—but an error or failure or two in most designs is not as major as a failed bridge, an explosion in a manned spacecraft, or a collapsed building. A series of these may be catastrophic, so the systems principle purpose of obviating failure means that designers must *anticipate* where failures may possibly occur. Although this will not guarantee that failures will not arise, possible failures must be envisioned. The system matrix provides an excellent vehicle for doing this, giving you the ability to explore nooks and crannies (cells of each level of the matrix) of any system to minimize unintended consequences and unwanted side effects. Consider the impact the system matrix might have had on the 1988 trade legislation in the U.S. Congress. Art Pine noted that "the bill has robbed the U.S. trade agencies of energy that might otherwise have been used to shape broader policy and resolve disputes with other countries.... It's diverting us from our real jobs.... The procedure is also distorting trade policy itself.... The rigid congressional deadlines can frequently boomerang."[3] Similarly, the vituperous debate about the North American Free Trade Agreement (NAFTA), which was underway as the second edition of this book was written, would have been much more informed and intelligible than it was if the system matrix had been used to define the various levels of the proposed pact.

Explication of the system solution also allows gradual and tentative implementation of changes of critical parts.

6. *To avoid overcompensation of controls and corrections due to the system's possible cyclic behavior*. Almost

everyone thinks controls of all sorts *must* be included in every system. For many systems—airplanes, medicines, access to personal information—that is correct. The advantage of the system matrix is the presence of the other elements and dimensions—purpose, interface, values—to put controls in perspective. Letting humans do the controlling where possible may avoid overcompensation with many automated checks. But experiences with nuclear power plant accidents, airline pilot errors, and malfunctioning fire alarms show that humans do "cause" mistakes, so a suitable allocation of controls between humans and devices must be developed. In the design of complex factories, for example, Americans tend to build in very complex control mechanisms, whereas the Japanese put much more control of the factory's complexity in the hands and minds of people (with greater overall success than in U.S. factories).

7. *To avoid unnecessary complexity.* If the system matrix can help you understand complexity and avoid over-controlling a system, then it can also help avoid unnecessary complexity. The matrix helps you to strike the right balance because it exposes all levels of possible interactions. Excessive complexity can only be discerned when the framework (system matrix) permits you to see it.

8. *To increase the likelihood of implementation.* If details are thought out, full perspective included, and failure modes avoided, implementation is more likely. Considering and dealing with possible consequences of the solution specifications are done before decisions are made.

9. *To foster continued learning.* Detailing a system with the elements and dimensions of the system matrix soon makes you a believer in the adage that you can't know everything. Robert Pirsig noted, for example, that defining quality means "we are defining something less than Quality itself."[4] Similarly, setting up the measurements for good management is in fact impossible, because what is important can't be measured and probably can't be expressed. For every feature of a system or control point, the nonquantifiable specifications far outnumber the quantifiable. As Eberhardt Rechtin states, "Be prepared for reality to add a few interfaces of its own." He also points out

that too much detail or at least too many controls may not be satisfactory: "Don't make the architecture too smart for its own good."⁵ There must always be room for humans in the operation of a system (as we will explain in Chapter 9); and every system should have continued improvement built in, for that is the function of the future dimension.

You want to identify as completely as possible in the future dimension what it is that you and others ought to be learning, so that the system can achieve its next level of change. The best organizations today know, in fairly explicit terms, what the system they are changing or installing will look like in three or four years. And next year, they will develop the next solution-after-next target. A system matrix is the great dynamic exposer of what information you should have.

Using the Systems Principle

Like the other principles of Breakthrough Thinking, the systems principle is a mental discipline for all aspects of preventing and solving problems. It is an excellent framework for critical thinking under any circumstance, not just specific projects—committee meetings, political discussions, analysis of a theatrical performance, appraisal of a child's education curriculum, or deliberations about health care. For example, President Clinton's health care reform proposal would benefit greatly from the system matrix understanding of complexity, as well as from the purposes and solution-after-next target concepts.

A mental image of the system matrix can always be called up to provide you with a whole range of questions about any situation. The patterning of the systems principle is a *frame of mind*.

In terms of a particular problem-solving activity, the system matrix is an integrator of all the elements of the SAN target or recommended solution. It provides a language for communicating about the problem or SAN, the recommendation (what the system will look like when it is installed), or the implementation plan.

Here are nine guides for use of the systems principle:

1. *Assume the system matrix is empty when you start a project.* Although there are "given" specifications of the eventual system you will be developing, imagine there are none. Then, just as you would complete a crossword puzzle, "fill in" the matrix slowly and reluctantly as your work proceeds. Perhaps the purposes of the project and of the system will come first. Then there will be some values and measures of several elements. Some components of the sequence or inputs or outputs may come next, to allow smaller groups to work in parallel on parts of the project. Duplicate matrices may then be needed so that alternate SANs can be explored, each matrix with its own additional details for various elements and dimensions. Some of these alternates will be discarded while one SAN target is expanded. Eventually, the recommended solution will be represented by a filled-in matrix along with another matrix detailing the implementation plan.

2. *Understand that filling in a matrix is a figure of speech.* Trying actually to write everything in those little rectangles is patently silly for any real project. The program statement for the large medical school building described at the beginning of this chapter had several pages for each element. Each section of the presentation delineated the contents of the element in terms of the dimensions. The inputs, for example, were described in the fundamental terms of humans, information, and physical items to be expected for processing and conversion at the facility. Additional broad details were then provided about the values, measures, controls, interfaces, and future dimensions.

3. *Think elements (the horizontal row) first, and then expand each element as needed by the dimensions (the vertical column).* This is not a rigid rule, but it usually helps organize thoughts more effectively. It follows from the basic definition of a system as a hopper. As you visualize the hopper for your system, the eight elements are what should be in your mind's eye (see Figure 7-4).

4. *If the complexity of the whole gets too great, transfer any detailing activity from the whole system matrix to indi-*

vidual ones for an element, dimension, or cell. The control of the inputs may need major explication, the quality measures of the sequence may require extensive specification, the values for human agents may demand full understanding, the probability and risk perspectives may be incorporated in the values, measures, and control dimensions, or the test system for the outputs element may need full details. A system matrix view of each gives you the opportunity to get down to the basics without losing sight of the whole.

5. *Establish the system matrix as a language of communications in networks of like-minded people* (CEOs of small companies, administrators of hospitals, engineers of a particular branch). Meetings, roundtables, computer exchanges, seminars, and personal conversations about a particular topic or type of system can be more fruitful with a system matrix guide than with other formats because the matrix elicits full information categories for review.

6. *Convert the system matrix into the format actually used by your organization.* A strategic business plan used by a company can be enhanced by system matrix elements and dimensions. Table 7-1 illustrates the potentials for heightening the usefulness of the strategic plan. Many other patterns can be improved similarly with the system view: policy statements, study reports, feasibility studies, engineering designs, administrative plans, and presentation checklists. Each of these can be treated as a system, and notation of the elements and dimensions can improve them. Note that we recommend modifying what techniques and formats are already used rather than throwing them out and using only the system matrix. The *breakthrough* is in changing dramatically what is already being used as opposed to the almost inevitable rejection of a completely new format.

7. *Find causes and relationships.* This is a form of "reverse architecting," as Rechtin calls it: going backward in time to gain understanding of how events unfolded and failures and successes occurred. "The extreme case of reverse architecting is archeology. Given only a few fragments, what was the system?"[6] Whatever information is available is entered in the ap-

Table 7-1.   How the system matrix can enhance a strategic plan.

Strategic Business Unit Plan Format	Elements and Dimensions of System Matrix	Some Possible Other Items to Include
Mission	Purpose Fundamental, values (assumes hierarchy, but not identified) Outputs Interface, future	How to control mission What future missions or purposes How mission relates to other elements
Key environment assumptions	Environment Fundamental, measures, control, interface Outputs Control, interface	Values of environment Future prospects of environment
Key competitor assumptions	Inputs Measures, interface Outputs Measures, control, interface	Specific fundamental inputs Values of competitors Fundamental outputs, how and future
Constraints	(Government regulations could fit in several cells) Purpose Values	Should avoid, but include only external factors not worth trying to change
Objectives	Purpose Measures, future	Relate to purpose values
Goals	Purpose Measures, future Output Measures, future	Relate to values dimension
Strategy	Sequence Fundamental, values, measures, control	Fundamental and future dimensions of outputs
Programs	Purpose Interface Outputs Interface	Future ouputs Interface purpose and outputs
Resources	(Very broad, could include some inputs, human agents, physical catalysts, and information aids)	(See items in parentheses left)
Contingencies. "What if?"	Inputs, outputs, sequence, environment, human agents Fundamental, control	Triggering mechanism
Financial forecast	Purpose Measures, future Outputs Output, sequence	—

Table 7-1. (continued) How the system matrix can enhance a strategic plan.

Strategic Business Unit Plan Format	Elements and Dimensions of System Matrix	Some Possible Other Items to Include
	OTHER POSSIBLE FACTORS SUGGESTED BY SYSTEM MATRIX TO INCLUDE IN PLAN FORMAT	
Human agents (workers, managers) development		Technological progression
Compensation schemes		Market prospects
Information systems/flow for decision making		Physical Environment changes
Management personnel backup		Management style
Physical facilities projections		New materials to serve as inputs

propriate cells of the matrix, as the Air Force officer did for intelligence data, to permit you to infer what the other cells might contain to make sense of the "hard" information available. Accident analysis also benefits from this use.

8. *Provide an integrating and coordinating framework to handle the many available techniques, tools, and analysis models.* Almost every one of them proclaims that it is *the* tool to use for solving a problem: cause-effect or fishbone diagram, statistical control, critical success factors, mathematical programming, chaos theory, optimization modeling, multiattribute decision analysis, spreadsheets, and so on. The systems principle shows that any such technique cannot be *the* total way of solving problems but can be useful in detailing some aspects of the solution. The system matrix helps to identify what information you need and then serves as a sorting and repository device.

9. *Get people to be quality- and productivity-minded in total systems terms.* Quality and productivity are values and measures (and sometimes control) dimensions in the system matrix. But there are three other important dimensions, especially the fundamental. Fiddling only with measures and values is insufficient. (Changing the scale on the thermostat to have it read 72° when the temperature is really 65°, instead of fixing

the furnace, is the way our colleague Charlie Geisel describes so much of what goes on in quality and productivity programs.) Emphasis on measures and values can be useful if they are put into the context of the whole system. But attaining the most from any focus on, say, measures and values, requires that other Breakthrough Thinking principles be used. Although the system matrix may be the *language of communication* about solutions and specifications, all the Breakthrough Thinking principles together are the *language of attaining* the *greatest implemented results*.

But be careful.

In order to achieve the full impact of these benefits of the systems principle of Breakthrough Thinking, you must beware of certain pitfalls. Among these are overly optimistic assumptions about how people will behave within your system, pie-in-the-sky projections, and others' lack of awareness of what you are proposing to do. Remember too that most projects take longer to accomplish and cost more than most people first assume.

Take care that your action plan expands to include all ramifications of the interrelated system (that is, do not proceed simply to fill in the system matrix one square at a time without considering how each cell of the matrix will affect the others). You must study and learn the sequence of events that your system matrix indicates and strive to protect the key elements in your implementation plan from arbitrary changes that will affect the other elements. At the same time, do not allow the fear of admitting mistakes to delay corrective action when it is needed.

Finally, beware of becoming enslaved by the system you have designed and created. Ultimately, doing things right is always less important than doing the right thing.

Outcomes and Impacts

It is a bit embarrassing to use some of the same terms to describe the benefits of the systems principle that proponents of so-called systems thinking have used in their effusive flag-waving. The only reason we can do it now is that you will have a firm picture of the system hopper and matrix in mind to recall whenever we use the word *system*, as compared to the amorphous "big-picture" view propounded by others.

The beneficial outcomes and impacts are significant:

First, a system view of an element or dimension could be continued endlessly, like the picture of a woman on a box of cleanser holding a box of the cleanser. Infinite numbers of system matrices can be projected conceptually forward or backward in space from any reference system matrix. This provides operational methods for a project of any complexity to solve problems simultaneously on interdependent units to avoid weak links in the whole system. It also allows you to see where simplicity is possible and useful.

Second, the systems matrix is at once holistic and partitionable, capable of being both expanded and divided—characteristics that are important companions to the other Breakthrough Thinking principles. The framework sets up a procedure for evaluating alternatives of the whole system or any of its parts, and for testing prototypes if needed. Would a system matrix have helped avoid the mistake made when a tree transplanted from the White House grounds to the North Dakota state capitol brought the gypsy moth to the Great Plains in the mid-1980s?

Third, continual learning is promoted by the stimulus of the many cells of each of the matrices that a solution may require.

Fourth, the system to be installed is unique and original to meet the unique needs and purposes of a specific problem. The likelihood of all the specifications required for one situation being the same as for any other situation is virtually zero. It does not take much review of the system matrix itself to realize there is truth to the uniqueness principle.

Fifth, a language of exchange in discussions about systems or any other topic is available with the system matrix and hopper model. It allows you to put criticism of a proposal into specific elements and dimensions that can be viewed more dispassionately.

Sixth, errors and careless mistakes in systems specifications, expecially omissions, are more likely to be checked and either avoided or corrected. No one can be certain that *all* details and implications will be noted, but there is a high likelihood of discovering ramifications before moving ahead.

Seventh, key capabilities and resources needed to implement a system are identified and their availability clarified.

Finally, all of these benefits help you explore opportunities (investments, job offers, housing). Instead of rushing into a decision, let the opportunity bubble and boil in the nutritious stew of the system matrix—to be sure all the factors can influence and interact with all the others. Modifying and implementing one specification in one cell can change other cells. For example, an investment in equipment *changes* the environment immediately.

You can prepare yourself for future opportunities by knowing what your basic information is in some of the matrix cells, which will enable you to act more quickly when fast action is required. Your feelings, images, and beliefs about your own abilities can be enhanced by avoiding faulty evaluation of ideas, limited thinking, and failure to listen to others' perspectives about a system or recommendation.

The subtitle of this chapter is the generalized iceberg theorem: Seven-eighths of an iceberg is concealed under water. Until we devised the system matrix, the idea of systems in a prescriptive form was similarly submerged. The systems principle now exposes the whole iceberg of your problem or opportunity, not just its visible one-eighth tip. You can now both avoid its dangers and take full advantage of its awesome size and strength.

NOTES

1. Jay W. Spechler, *When America Does It Right* (Atlanta: IIE Press, 1988).

2. Henry Petrosky, *To Engineer Is Human: The Role of Failure in Successful Design* (New York: St. Martin's Press, 1985).

3. Art Pine, "New Trade Law Has the Makings of a Monster," *Los Angeles Times* (March 26, 1989).

4. Robert Pirsig, *Zen and the Art of Motorcycle Maintenance* (New York: Bantam Books, 1976).

5. Eberhardt Rechtin, *Systems Architecting,* (Englewood Cliffs, N.J.: Prentice Hall, 1991).

6. Ibid.

Chapter 8

The Limited Information Collection Principle:
Don't Become an Expert About the Problem

In 1989, Japan experienced a strong construction boom. As a result, many construction companies and design consulting firms urged Showa Ceramic Company, a well-known manufacturer of wall tiles, to send them samples of tile products. The Showa staff was soon overloaded with urgent requests for sample wall tiles.

Following the principles and process of Breakthrough Thinking, the Showa team did not survey the existing problem situation. Instead, team members realized that the larger purpose of providing sample tiles was not to send the actual tiles, but rather to provide potential customers with a tangible awareness of the various reflective properties, shadings, and textures of Showa tiles.

From the many alternative solutions they had developed, the team selected a completely new and different feasible target solution—a "stick sample." This solution, which revolutionized the conventional concept of tile samples in Japan, was detailed in the information collected, but only after such detail was identified as necessary in the Breakthrough Thinking system matrix.

This "stick sample" solution significantly increased Showa's ability to distribute tile samples. It reduced the cost of material to almost nothing, as very little time or money was now spent in handling and packaging. Since the new sample sticks were so light and compact that they could easily be sent through the mail, shipping and transportation costs were also greatly reduced.

No doubt as a result, the Showa "stick sample" concept won Japan's prestigious Nikkei Advertising Award for 1993.

*T*he successful leaders and problem solvers we studied know that it is impossible for data to be accurate. Realizing that there is no such thing as "hard" data, they know how to cope with "soft" data. They further realize that it is not possible to get all the data.

These naturally expert solution finders recognize that collecting data and information is never a neutral or objective process. Instead, how data are categorized, who makes the observations (their biases and preconceptions influence what is seen), and whether or not the purpose for the information is clear all significantly affect the value of whatever data are collected.

Consider the manufacturer of industrial pumps who woke up one morning with a brilliant idea. Why not branch out into making football, basketball, and beach-ball pumps? He quickly assigned half of his headquarters staff to the quest for "all there is to know" about footballs, basketballs, beach balls, inflation techniques, and recreation in general.

In due course, his staff returned with volumes of information, except for one deviate who ignored his assignment. That staffer spent a few hours corralling figures on ball-pump sales. She learned that the market had been saturated for years and that sales amounted to only a few million dollars a year, compared to the company's industrial-pump volume of $500 million annually. To undertake the manufacturer's "brilliant idea" would thus divert company resources for, at best, insignificant gain.

The volumes of collected information sat unopened on the manufacturer's credenza until they were quietly discarded.

The pump manufacturer didn't apply Breakthrough Thinking to first determine the *purposes* of his information-gathering assignment. If he had, he would have known that, in the absence of a viable market for football, basketball, and beach-ball pumps, accumulating any other information was pointless.

The incident is a composite of the experiences of numerous corporations. It illustrates the need for one of Breakthrough Thinking's basic principles: *the limited information collection principle*. Focus attention on information that is useful and relevant for the other Breakthrough Thinking principles. The indiscriminate amassing of information inherent in "finding out all there is to know" not only wastes time, effort, and money, it can actually impede solution of a problem by burying you under an avalanche of irrelevant, unmanageable detail. In short, it causes, "analysis-paralysis."

A contributing element in the pack-rat approach to information gathering is the subconscious notion that gathering information is equivalent to accomplishing something. Did you ever spend so much time researching a school term paper that you had little time left to write it—even though you knew your grade would be based not on the data you collected in your notes but on the finished paper you turned in?

If you need to do something with your information other than simply possess it, you must learn to gather it selectively. As Theodore Roszak tells us, information by itself is "discrete little bundles of fact, sometimes useful, sometimes trivial, and never the substance of thought."[1]

Heed the warning of our colleague, Alan Scharf: Don't become an expert about the problem. Substitute for the traditional approach of "finding out all there is to know" the limited information collection principle of Breakthrough Thinking. Become an expert about the solution. Find out only what you need to know.

Souichirou Honda, founder of Honda Motors Corporation, told an interviewer:

> An engineer handed me a report on a study of the performance of an assembly line. I told him: "We can understand what is going on by just looking. It is not bad to measure it. However, you have to think of the purposes of measurement and data."
>
> I would like to point out the danger of data gathering. (1) Data are only a tool to understand the situation. However, we tend to fall into a pitfall of the magic of data and tend

to be carried away by data. (2) We tend to confuse whether we need data or not. (3) We tend to miss the point of reasons about where real results come from.... (4) We tend to be satisfied with only the report and tend to be proud of gathering data, without solving any problem.

Another engineer gave me a thick report, saying: "I surveyed the efficiency of our company for six months." I said to him: "You did the most inefficient work, didn't you?"[2]

It is a mystery why people continue to use the conventional approach of inundating themselves with data, facts, and information about the present status of a system or problem area when they start a project. Great quantities of human effort are squandered in learning "everything." People falsely assume that a problem can be solved by throwing data and statistics at it.

It is also a mystery why people adopt the attitude that the process of collecting all the information and the resulting data can't hurt. They often shrug off anyone's questioning of information collection by offering the limp excuse, "Well, we will learn something anyway." The gypsy moth pest-management system project showed the fallacy of that premise. Almost none of the data and reports prepared in three and a half years—comprising a nearly four-foot stack—had anything to do with the solution that was adopted. The data collectors could tell you everything about a gypsy moth, but their expertise completely hobbled them when it came to actually solving the problem.

To apply the limited information collection principle, first identify (in a hierarchy) the purposes of the information you think you need to collect about the system or problem. Awareness of purposes and solutions-after-next for the focus purpose will enable you to recognize what information is relevant. As Ian Mitroff notes, you are looking for the "absolute minimum, essential information to illuminate the broader dimensions."[3]

Honing your information gathering is essential if you are ever to get beyond the gathering stage: In 1988, there were an estimated 86 million books and documents in the Library of

Congress. The reservoir of printed information is said to be doubling every eight years.

Lester Thurow points out that elaborate management information systems are set up because of conventional analysis and centralized decision processes.[4] This lowers the productivity of organizations because of the additional staff needed. But it is clear that you cannot manage by facts.

In a *Newsweek* editorial, Meg Greenfield described such proceedings in Washington as "information overload" and "baloney overload" and asked, "Why is it that we seem always to end up needing boards of inquiry to tell us what just happened— boards, by the way, that often end up needing subsequent inquiries to look into the reliability of their own findings?" [5]

Conventional problem solving that leads to doing research (read "collecting information") will show progress without actually accomplishing much.

Market researchers produce reams of reports supposedly made better by fancy-sounding techniques like Delphi and mathematical models. Edward Mansfield of the University of Pennsylvania told Congress that marketing costs for a new or improved product were twice those in Japan, where companies are adept at developing preferred products. He wondered if United States companies should "spend a little less on marketing studies and a little more on making products well."[6] Sony, for example, claims that it eschews market research in the U.S. mold because it is useless when new products never before available are developed.

Computers, too, are frequently overvalued. In practice, they are far too often a technique looking for problems. Computers produce vast amounts of paper (which was supposed to be reduced by their advent) and provide a new challenge never yet adequately met: how to assimilate all the information they provide. Although they help organize and store needed information, computers are not at all helpful in supplying the ideas and thoughts that must gird problem-solving activities. They do not connect information to cultural issues, the explanation of events, nor the purposes people seek to achieve.

According to *Business Week*, manufacturers in 1987 "added computers and new process-control equipment to the tune of $17 billion." Yet for "many companies, the productivity payoff.... is nowhere in sight."[7] Subsequent reports in 1993 did not refute this statement but did note increasing signs that the corner finally may have been turned.

One apparent exception to the indiscriminate application of computer technology is Wells Fargo & Company, whose chief executive and chairman, Carl E. Reichardt, has stated, "There's nothing worse than selling technology-driven services that do not work." Reichardt was quoted in an article in *The New York Times* that touted the company as "a case study of the effective use of information systems in carving out a strategic advantage over rivals.... It has succeeded in using the technology to pare operating costs...and offer customers new services."[8]

If you are looking for all the facts or whom to blame for the problem, you amass tremendous amounts of data. *What you look for is what you get.*

The Emphasis on Measurement

There is an undue emphasis on accurate measurements in conventional problem solving. The output expectation of a factory, for example, may be set at 1,244.33 units per day when 1250 is all the accuracy the back-up data can supply. Many people assume that measurements are the starting point for everything. The president of $100 million company, for example, insisted that poor measurements of company activities accounted for the company's losses three years in a row. He spent his time improving the measurements, rather than studying the multitude of factors, measurable or not, on which he could act to make the company profitable. After three years of misguided effort, he was fired by the board of directors.

Numbers *can* be a valuable source of information. But too often they are presented divorced from the context in which they were compiled. Take, for example, the statement that "200,000 people a day use the buses." Is that 200,000 individuals? Or does it include repeat fares? What about a statistic that refers to beef imports? Does that mean cattle on the hoof, dressed beef, canned beef, frozen beef, or what?

Seizing on raw statistics without sufficient underlying information can lead one astray. And that's what often happens in a typical, misguided quest for data. Yet, to carefully analyze the context of a statistic may take more time than the information is worth. Recall, for example, the ineptness of the competitive benchmarking information discussed in Chapter 4. Consider, then, how wasteful of cost and time is the attempt to collect all the data.

In today's companies, nonfinancial indicators are necessary to supplement sales, cash flow, and quarterly profit statements. These indicators include such things as lead- and through-put times, flexibility, delivery fulfillments, unscheduled downtime, and use of common parts in different products. Measurements need to be related to the *fundamental* and *values* dimensions of the system matrix described in Chapter 7.

Learning General Knowledge and Collecting Project Information

The United States has the largest advanced knowledge base in the world, yet other countries are better at developing solutions. That means that the process or approach used to convert knowledge to system solutions in the U.S. is deficient. That is what Breakthrough Thinking and the principle of limited information collection seek to correct.

The validity of limited information collection lies in this fact: In any problem situation, factual details are of secondary significance; the framework and setting are what govern possible breakthroughs. The limited information that is actually needed stems from questions that arise from contextual probing of the uniqueness, purposes, solution-after-next, and systems principles.

Put another way, Breakthrough Thinking *does* require information collection, but its principles and process guide you to what information is really needed—purposes, hierarchy, measures of purpose accomplishment, elements and dimensions of the solution-after-next (SAN) alternatives and target, and so forth. For example, detailing solution recommendations with the Breakthrough Thinking system matrix will show that parts of what already exists will be needed. In many cases, sufficient data or measures about those parts may not be available to enable you to integrate them with the rest of the solution ideas. By all means, go out and collect this needed, *limited* information.

Breakthrough Thinking is not designed to limit the amount of general knowledge or technological expertise or even competitive intelligence you can acquire. You should improve your general knowledge base and any particular technological familiarity—through formal education, magazines and journals, computer networks, seminars and literature, organizations in your area of interests, or a personal clipping and reference file. Such contacts provide one with *sources* of information to accompany the openminded mental stance of Breakthrough Thinking. But Breakthrough Thinking is designed so that, for any particular problem, you gather only the information relevant to promote solutions, not submerge them.

Information and Wisdom "in the Heads of People"

The conventional quest for "hard data," "objective facts," and "solid measurements," can inhibit effective interpersonal collaboration. There is an implication that the information people have in their heads is not to be trusted and must be invested with objectivity through someone else's observations and measurements. In response to this implication, those being measured and observed often become defensive. By contrast, studies of successful leaders and experts show that they seek and share information with a wide variety of individuals.

In short, information and data are meaningless without ideas and wisdom to shape their collection.

In Chapter 9 we will expand on the ways you can interact to achieve the ideas, thoughts, and cooperation necessary for optimal problem solving.

Information Needed at the Beginning to Measure Results Later

Thus far, our statements about restricting the amount of information collected for a project assume that you or your organization have a good set of performance measurements concerning your focus purpose. Measures of productivity, costs, quality, efficiency, innovation, and even quality of working life may be needed to assess the impact of various alternative solutions.

Many organizations, however, lack these rudimentary measures necessary to operate their systems effectively. Lack of such information may be a major contributor to the problem actually being investigated. In such circumstances, significant data and information collection about the existing system may be necessary since the ability to evaluate alternatives and measure the effectiveness of final changes is a necessary part of any Breakthrough Thinking project. Just make sure that the questions you ask to gather data are rooted in the solution process (purposes, SAN). Don't simply go off on a data-gathering spree.

There is always a need for relevant measurements, but this is much different than claiming that all the difficulties in a problem need to be measured before action can be taken. The fallacy of such wholesale measurement is evidenced in the current rage for developing mathematical, decision-making, or simulation models. People collect mounds of data to improve the accuracy and precision of the results of such models, whether or not accuracy and precision are needed for their real-life counterpart—the actual problem to be solved.

The measurement process can also be a major source of error. Measuring instruments or methods may be inaccurate or insufficient. Errors can occur whether the measuring instrument is a loosely worded opinion poll questionnaire or a micrometer with one-millionth of an inch accuracy for measuring steel bars.

In addition, the emphasis on measurement can fail to take into account the fact that human knowledge is not accurate and often changes over time. We no longer believe that the earth is flat, for example, or that the atom is the smallest particle, or that all cholesterol is bad. What is judged to be factual is inextricably entwined with human perceptions at particular points in time.

Thus, limited information collection goes hand in hand with the important concept of tolerance for ambiguity. Since total information never can be collected and the accuracy of what is collected is subject to dispute, experts and leaders learn to think of data as a guide to forming their thoughts and ideas. They then fill in with additional information as needed. Since the amount of relevant data collected may be small indeed, this approach is preferable to amassing data and then trying to cull from it what is needed. As University of Amsterdam social scientists Jacobijn Sandberg and Bob Wielinga noted with regard to a research project, "knowledge evolves continually as it is being used. [Thus,] knowledge can never be simply tranferred."9

In one example, a nineteen-member task force in a large Midwestern city had been meeting for a year to develop methods for revitalizing a 200-block section of the city. Many studies were conducted to measure everything and provide everyone with all the information about the area. But a two-foot stack of reports was not digestible, and no one knew what to do until a Breakthrough Thinking consultant helped them through the development process with purposes, SANs, and other Breakthrough Thinking principles. Only five to six percent of the collected data turned out to be relevant.

The following basic ideas about measurements may help you establish guides for effectively attaining Breakthrough Thinking purposes with the degree of accuracy that's warranted:

- Increasing or improving measurements in Breakthrough Thinking projects may lead to some short-term benefits, especially if the current measurements are few or poor in quality.

- Long-term emphasis on accuracy and increased amounts of measurements as a means of pinpointing trouble usually produces poor results because people tend to ignore as unimportant problems for which measures are unavailable and to avoid or underemphasize problems where measures are difficult, if not impossible, to obtain.

- A focus on measurement leads to neglect of useful ideas from other fields (for example, philosophy, political science).

- Measurement is misperceived as an end, rather than a means: When one set of measures does not work, the experts blame the measures, not themselves, and then they simply call for better measures.

- Good measures first need specification of the fundamental and values dimensions of the appropriate system elements (see Chapter 7).

Information Is Based on the Past

By its very nature, information collection focuses on the past and present status of things. This does not qualify it as a guide for the future. Extrapolations are often treacherous because they assume that the underlying data will continue to reflect to-day's supposed reality in the future, whereas information may not truly represent even what exists now.

Extracting information from experts about the way they do their jobs, for example, is filled with problems. Our studies of expert designers and planners show they are consistently unable to recall all the vital details. A gap always exists between the information supplied and the reality.

In sum, the concept "the more information about a problem area, the better" is obsolete. In any case, collecting all the information is impossible. "We don't see everything," William Poundstone tells us, "not even everything implicit in our experience."[10]

Purposes and Goals of Limited Information Collection

Many people imagine that a breakthrough can only be developed with significant amounts of time, personnel, or money. But these are luxuries. Finding the balance between available resources and truly necessary information is what this principle is all about. Using this principle, solutions are found quickly with fewer development costs. For example, other countries are offering high-quality products and services in the United States 20 to 25 percent faster and with 15 to 20 percent lower development costs than are Americans. The limited information collection principle is a major contributor to such reductions of time and cost.

The specific purposes and objectives of this principle are—

1. *To focus efforts on collecting only the necessary information for a particular project.* Too much information obscures important issues and does not help make the most effective decisions.

2. *To provide meaning to the existing information.* Leaders develop the cohesiveness and effectiveness of their groups by shared meanings and interpretations of the real world, according to Warren Bennis and Burt Nanus.[11] Since, as we've discussed, information is only today's perception of reality, this purpose encourages mutual understanding. Because a number standing alone is subject to many different interpretations, any number used in Breakthrough Thinking must always be tied to something specific (the fundamental and values dimensions of appropriate system elements).

3. *To encourage networking for obtaining information, contacts, and results.* Achieving breakthroughs depends far more on interaction than on the amount or accuracy of information.

4. *To avoid disorganization.* The second law of thermodynamics holds that all entities tend toward disorganization, called entropy. Combatting that natural tendency requires energy. An overload of information saps energy.

5. *To lessen the preparation of many unneeded and unread documents and the arguments over differing measurements, interpretations, and analyses.* Surveys and questionnaires are especially suspect techniques for information collection. "Many of the questions are worded so that either their meanings are ambiguous or.... the issues are prejudiced, [leading to] undue emphasis...on relatively unimportant issues when the analyses are reported."[12]

6. *To avoid the institutionalization of information collection as an end in itself without regard to purposes.* For ex-

ample, corporate data gatherers attend seminars on what competitors are doing, what new products they are offering, what facilities they are building, and so on. But how valuable can such programs be for most problem prevention and solution? If your competitors have new products, services, and facilities, you are already behind!

The '90s rage for collecting competitive intelligence far too often gets stuck on techniques and accuracy of data and models (company X has a model that can calculate the quarterly shipments of competitor Y to an accuracy of one percent) rather than purposes (financial analysts could have supplied the "one percent accurate" number if company X really had a purpose for it).

7. *To maximize the use of time, effort, and resources.* Information limitation can minimize costly studies that emphasize the past. The search for failures and its symptoms—the who-struck-John syndrome—governs too many data collection activities.

Often, people will agree this is so once they recognize the syndrome. For example, the executive vice president of a large retail distributor of magazines and books wanted to reduce delivery time to provide better service and decrease operating costs. She told us she wanted "to get all the facts about what's going on so I can make inroads on our objectives."

By asking purpose questions and suggesting that a view of the ideal would lead most directly to achievement of the objective, we were able to show her that the information we should gather pertained to what the eventual system might be rather than to what was going on now. An advanced technology system was installed, and the project was done in less time and for less money than originally allocated. All the personnel from the previous system were involved and committed to the new one. Our client was so enthusiastic she put a poster on her wall: "FACTS = PURPOSES, SOLUTIONS-AFTER-NEXT, AND SYSTEMS!"

Why the Limited Information Collection Principle Makes Sense

Because the principle flies in the face of the accepted "need" to collect all the facts, explaining its underlying assumptions may make it easier for you to use with colleagues. Play the believing game with them. Apply the Breakthrough Thinking concepts to all information.

Assumption 1. Information is only a representation of the real world. We've all heard about the man who drowned in a stream with an average depth of two inches. We've all seen signs: "Binksville—Pop. 2,453." Does anybody really think that if you counted noses you'd come out with 2,453? A zoologist reports that "coyotes have never been known to attack human beings." Is the reality that coyotes don't attack humans or just that they've never been seen to do it? Ivory soap was long advertised as "99 44/100ths percent pure." Pure what? An airline advertised that in a survey "75 percent of passengers said they had enjoyed their flight." Did that mean that one in four was very dissatisfied? We are shocked by a report that "150 people were killed in auto accidents over the Labor Day weekend." But although it appears to be an absolute statement of reality, its meaning is not clear until we know how many people die in car accidents on an ordinary Saturday, Sunday, and Monday. Such are the fallibilities of information.

This assumption means that all information must at first be viewed as incorrect, or at least viewed skeptically. Although people tend to reject information anyway when it differs from what they "know," this first-pass skepticism must also be applied to your current knowledge in the face of new information.

The reality information is supposed to represent is not a fixed entity. "Real is what a sufficiently large number of people have agreed to call real—except that this fact is usually forgotten; the agreed-upon definition is reified (that is, made into a 'thing' in its own right) and is eventually experienced as that objective reality."[13]

However, pertinent information, models, and analysis of a system or situation that accept certain facts as true do have benefits in Breakthrough Thinking. They enable you to:

1. Manipulate or "play" with relevant solution parameters, variables, conditions, and assumptions to assess the impact of a change without affecting an actual system.

2. Predict specifications and performances (costs, interactions, time, yields).

3. Identify critical factors.

4. Assist the thinking process by organizing, recording, and stimulating thought and visualizations.

5. Facilitate communications.

6. Control project activities (a model of a solution process can indicate how well the steps are being performed).

7. Educate and train.

Yet, however valuable these benefits may be, it is also important to remember the potential dangers and limitations of information collection, modelling, and analyses. Some of these dangers include:

1. Incompleteness. The only information that can ever be the same as real life is real life itself—an obvious impossibility.

2. Mistaking the information or model for the system in question. The system is then assigned "properties which belong to [the] model but which are irrelevant.... The price of the employment of models [and data collection] is eternal vigilance.[14]

3. Errors.

4. Wrong viewpoint. The information collector's perspective may not correspond to the real-life situation. A chemist models a tree, for example, in terms of basic elements and molecules; a forester in terms of cost, board-feet, and method for removing it; a poet as a descriptive word-picture.

5. Communications gap. Detailed information collection formats are likely to be complicated. Most decision makers and managers want the whole project summarized on one sheet of paper.

6. Information collecting mind-set. There is a danger that every problem will get translated into a data collection model (a manufacturing problem means a flow chart is

necessary, an information system bottleneck means a programming check must be made, and so forth.)

Assumption 2. The future cannot be predicted from "perfect" knowledge about the present. Specialists in probability recognize this as fundamental. Yet even this assumption has a finite probability of being wrong very slightly above zero ("never say never").

The average of a set of data can never predict the value of a future specific performance or occurrence. At best, the average should be reported with its range of values and various odds of occurring.

There are those who prefer to ignore this assumption. Lee Dembart, a book reviewer for the *Los Angeles Times,* counts economists among them. He describes them as "unwilling to give up their effort to describe and predict human behavior mathematically though their efforts have met with virtually no success.... [They] will tell you it's just a matter of gathering more data and refining their formulas and they will be able to make accurate forecasts."[15]

Ivar Ekeland points out that "there are a great many computations that cannot be performed now or in any foreseeable future."[16] This notion is recognized in most of the sciences as well. Physics formalizes it in the uncertainty principle and in quantum mechanics. A biologist stated it another way when he was discussing a grant he received for a ten-year study of one bacterium found in the intestine of a particular species of Australian goat. Of course, he commented, "we won't know all we should after the ten years are over."

Assumption 3. Relevant information is more important than accurate information. Some sort of projection of possible events and activities and their performances is definitely required for working on a problem. In the face of assumptions 1 and 2, however, relevance is pivotal. There is some truth to the adage that statistics can be more misleading than enlightening. Scenario writing (Chapter 6) and the elements and dimensions of a system (Chapter 7) illustrate methods that result in relevant information that may lack some accuracy.

Interestingly, since data are often inaccurate, they can create a subconscious push to incorporate more data. One of Norman Augustine's humorous laws posits that "the weaker the data available upon which to base one's position, the greater the precision which should be quoted in order to give that data authenticity." He cites as an example an estimate by the Federal Education Data Acquisition Council that, in a given year, "9,495,967 man-hours will be spent filling out forms."[17] Information and data should have their variability noted so that useful interpretations can be made. Treating a single curve on a graph as a statement of reality is neither useful, accurate, or relevant.

In effect, getting "correct" information is not possible. All decisions are made on the basis of information that has accuracy gaps, yet decisions need relevant, purposeful information to become effective. The uniqueness principle of Breakthrough Thinking plays a role here—see to it that people who "know the business" in their heads are involved in deciding what information is actually relevant.

Assumption 4. Collecting information about a system or problem is not a value-free or neutral process. Society places a high level of importance on "just the facts, Ma'am." But, alas, it's questionable whether there is any such thing. Information exists only as part of a larger whole.

Journalists, for example, are told to go out and "cover the story." But *when* they arrive at the scene, *who* they interview, *how* their own point of view shapes the questions they ask their interviewees, *what* information they choose to include in the article, and *where* they place which pieces of information all shape the story that appears. It is never possible to collect all the information about any topic. What is collected thus reflects what someone decides is important, and this is not at all a neutral process.

Any information has a structural set of values or biases or inclinations. Eliminating them is difficult or impossible. What you can do is be clear in identifying the values and biases that flavor the data. (The journalist, for example, can be aware of his or her bias and strive to cover all aspects of the story, presenting it in value-neutral words. To write that someone "said" something, for example, has a far different connotation than to write that someone "admitted" that same thing. To report that a cup is "half-full" has a decidedly different tenor than to report that it is "half-empty.")

The systems matrix and the purposes principle encourage this type of disclosure.

Using the Limited Information Collection Principle

To apply the limited information collection principle, treat every information collection situation as a problem. Whenever someone proposes doing a study, collecting data, building a model, making a library search, running an experiment, developing mathematical relationships, writing a report, conducting a survey, introducing a computerized information system, measuring performance, or any other information-related activity, a purposes array (see Figure 5-6) ought to be developed, so that the prospective data will accomplish needed ends. Develop at least a sketchy solution-after-next about the way the information, if needed, would be obtained; and put together some of the details in a system matrix (see Figure 7-3) for a realistic informational endeavor based on the SAN target.

This mental reasoning puts a forward-looking cast on the adage that what you look for is what you get—asking about information for purposes and SAN gives you effective results.

Information limitation is, by definition, a decision-making process. The following cases may give you an idea of how to decide how much information to amass and how much is relevant, and how to limit information collection:

1. Pat Murphy was given the assignment of coordinating changes in the sixth-grade social studies curriculum for a medium-sized school district. The first impulse people have for decision making ("What do I do now?") is to set up a data-collection task force to find out everything now being done. Instead, Pat used Breakthrough Thinking, first asking about the purposes of

the project. He then began to collect information relevant to those purposes. When a team member suggested conducting studies on the problems of the present curriculum (student and teacher complaints, student grades, external review team to point out shortcomings), Pat asked about the use for such data if it were available in six months. That discussion focused the team toward significant issues. The group decided to seek information about them from teachers, students, principals, and curriculum specialists, and to continue the development of purposes. They also agreed to then use their knowledge for developing SANs to identify what specific information was necessary—Are these books available to do A? Movies or videotapes to do B? The use of Breakthrough Thinking techniques worked. The principal and superintendent gave the team members certificates of appreciation for the extraordinary quality of the installed curriculum and especially for the exceptionally fast time—ten months—from beginning to end of the project.

2. Rosemary Makradokus wanted to redesign the clothes storage arrangement in her bedroom because she felt there wasn't enough storage space for everything and she wanted to save time in the morning in identifying what she wanted. The usual decision at this point is to detail the current storage arrangement, find out what friends do to solve the problem, and so on. Rosemary spent a little time on her purposes to put them in context and much more on ideal systems for herself. This exercise led to the search for quite specific information: Could she obtain small front-loading drawers? What equipment was available for use in a very limited space to hold the clothing she wanted to lay out the night before wearing it? How and in what order of selection did she decide what to wear? Her rearrangement impressed visitors. Nevertheless, Rosemary told them not to copy her solution but to follow the Breakthrough Thinking principles.

Within this overall framework, there are some specific aids and suggestions for using this principle:

1. *Develop purposes and a purpose hierarchy for any request, suggestion, or hint that information should be collected.* What is the purpose of the report (even if requested by an

executive) is the opening toward limiting the information that is collected. Focus on what needs to be obtained if you want to "win" in the problem-solving and design game.

2. *Answer questions raised by the development of solution-after-next options for the problem.* People are much more willing to accept information if they know the purpose for the data.

The questions also help put prospective information into a bigger picture. Purposes and SANs help illuminate the big picture and basic "facts." They require you to integrate information and provide an awareness of what the information might mean.

There will be differences in the amount of information needed from project to project. A project based on a new need or a nonexistent system will require far more information than a project started as a planned change in the absence of current difficulties or as an improvement (fixing something wrong within the system).

3. *Use the information and knowledge in the heads of many people doing different work.* They know the present situation and can be called upon if the solutions need their expertise. Get them involved in supplying information about the purposes and SANS of the information collection process itself: What are the purposes of the information someone says we need? What are the ideal ways of achieving the selected purpose to which the information will be put? This exemplifies what some researchers claim is essential aspect of valid information: "Design situations or environments where participants can be origins (sources of information) and can experience high personal causation (psychological success, confirmation, essentiality)."[18]

Simply calling meetings is insufficient. What you do in the meetings is critical. Pose questions effectively. If you ask questions about the problems—What's wrong with what exists?—you will get what you asked about. But what you should be seeking is based on purposes of the information, SANs, and so on. The objective should be to collect "blameless" data—information that is then used without finger pointing or implicit threats. Successful managers and designers start solving problems by mulling over the purposes and information they can recall or have nearby. Instead of collecting large amounts of data, they reason plausibly. They know when to collect information and do research to answer solution questions.

Use the knowledge and heuristics—simple rules of thumb—you already have in your head, and then expand them to define where you can strip away painstaking studies and reports.

4. *Ask how an idea or SAN could be made operational.* This raises directly the questions that need to be answered by information collection, research, modeling, and other means. Questioning helps pinpoint the proper place for possible use of the large number of available techniques.

5. *Ask if the information were available in, say, three months, what you would do with it.* Sometimes called the law of preposterior analysis, this question forces you to probe the relevancy, consistency, understandability, flexibility, and efficiency (cost, time, quality) of the data. The amount of foolish information collection stopped by this simple question is amazing.

6. *Have a prepared mind, not an empty head.* A wide range of background knowledge is a big help in utilizing all the Breakthrough Thinking principles. Learning new topics and gaining different technical skills are always desirable, both for vocations and avocations. Keeping up with the many books and journal articles predicting future technological developments is stimulating, can provide you with breadth of vision, and is a worthwhile way to garner broad market and competitive intelligence while still enabling you to avoid excessive information gathering on any one problem.

7. *Share information with everyone, not just an elite coterie.* The results of collected information can be interpreted more fruitfully if many people involved with the project share their different perspectives. Ideally, all of them would have been involved in the information collection activity as well. Letting each of them have information gives them the opportunity to make active contributions to the project based on their own insights rather than requiring them to be the often-reluctant and resentful followers of supervisor's orders.

8. *Seek needed information from a wide variety of sources.* One recurring characteristic of the creative people, experts, and leaders we and others have studied is that they talk to people in, read materials from, and attend meetings in a wide variety of disciplines relating to a specific topic. They do this for general learning purposes to better prepare their minds. They are then able to find relationships among many more factors than those who think they have the information at hand in books or friends or data banks. One way to implement this method is to force yourself to list the disciplines or experiences you know are related to a problem. Then you can more easily force yourself to search out a person or group to whom to ask your questions.

9. *Study the system matrix of the SAN target or recommended solution.* When a project has reached this stage, information has been accumulating to the point where the prospective system or change is fairly well delineated. The specific types of information yet to be obtained are clearly identified by the gaps in the systems matrix stipulations already stated. Even when the information may appear disorganized to an outsider, the system matrix gives you a basis for finding the relationships.

10. *Use models and quantitative techniques.* When you do identify a question for which information is needed, explore the range of techniques available for the class of question.[19] For example, if your question concerns the analysis of alternative options or programs, three of several available techniques are contingency analysis (where you attempt to think in advance of all the difficulties that could occur), gaming (where you simulate probable actions), and scenario planning (where you write out a script of how the system would operate if it were installed).

Take care, however, not to believe too easily the models and their resulting computer aids. Some studies show that people using computer aids fail to recognize that using the program actually led to poor decisions. Their love affair with the computer and its models made them overconfident. Note also that use of such ready-made computer models violates the uniqueness principle.

11. *Use computer bibliographies, networks, search routines, and databases.* Computer inquiries generally provide more up-to-date data than do handbooks and encyclopedias. As of mid-1989, there were about 4,200 publicly accessible bibliographic data bases.

12. *Decide what information to collect.* Eberhardt Rechtin, retired president of Aerospace Corporation, provides an appropriate rule of thumb: "The efficient architect, using contextual sense, looks for the likely mis-fits, and designs the architecture so as to eliminate or minimize them." He also notes that when choices in a system design have to be made, as is generally the case, "with unavoidably inadequate information, make the best apparent choice and then watch to see whether future solutions appear faster than future problems.... If not, go back and change the choice."[20]

The same reasoning applies when deciding what information to collect. Once you find that certain information is needed, go directly to the experts for it. Get outside professional help, seek out the most knowledgeable persons, use the most advanced tools and techniques. When the purposes of the information you need are clear and the method to get it is well-defined, then do your collecting effectively, quickly, and simply.

Outcomes and Impacts

Like the uniqueness principle, the limited information collection principle achieves its greatest impact through the discipline it places on your reasoning processes. The examples throughout this chapter illustrate the mental frame of reference needed to achieve the purposes and objectives of this principle, as well as providing some specific demonstrations of inappropriate information collection. Negative examples—such as the excessive information gathered in the gypsy moth pest-management system and in the project to revitalize a 200-block section of a Midwestern city—illustrate the importance of the principle.

To adopt the mental toughness the principle requires, you must always inquire about the purposes of the information collection and about the ideal way to accomplish those purposes. This will require steadfastness on your part because of the fantastic pressures in our society to "get all the facts"—particularly at the beginning of a project.

What about the moguls who gruffly growl that they don't want to be bothered with these new theories about limited information, who pound a fist on the desk and order you to go out and "get the facts"? The appropriate response is to ask about the purposes for which they want the "facts" and then about the purpose of that purpose, and the purpose of the second one, and so on. This response with the Breakthrough Thinking principles works most of the time, but it needs commitment to the principles to be effective.

Remember that you are not disagreeing; you are actually displaying an intelligent extension of his or her remarks. Even if the response is "I want to nail the bastard whose fault it is," the question about the purpose of doing that is still appropriate. It gets him or her thinking about the statement, something that wasn't done before. (If you are kicked out of the office and told, "I gave you your instructions," you should consider the purposes of continuing to work there.)

Some of the positive results you can look forward to if you remain adamant are:

- Less total time spent collecting information and analyzing data. Even if you consider the slightly increased time for thinking through initially what your information needs are, the total time spent is less, primarily because you avoid analysis-paralysis.

- Less total cost for data and information collection. These costs are critical in determining overall product or service costs and timeliness. You learn to listen to others.

- Less energy involved in data collection and attempts to assess what all the information means. You learn to listen to others.

- A higher quality of information appropriate to solution and project needs, not just accuracy and precision for their own sakes alone. You avoid faulty evaluation of ideas.

- Better interrelationships among people working on a project and those who will be affected by it. You avoid being impatient.

- A focus on developing and implementing systems and changes rather than on techniques of information collection and model building. This lets you know when to back off from the data collection process, comparing what's done to the purposes and recommendations.

- Far fewer reports to store.

The limited information collection principle of Breakthrough Thinking warns you always to beware of people who are mindful of measures at the expense of the solution-after-next. These misguided souls believe that producing a thick report is more important than actually proposing solutions to the problem.

Such people are likely to say:

- "Get me all there is to know about..."

- "I can show you research that supports my conviction that our solutions can't possibly work (or...my recommendations can't miss)."

- "If we only had a little more data, we'd know for sure whether we're on the right track or not."

- "Let's find out how it works for them."

- "Let's begin by identifying the industry (competitive) standard."

Conclusions

The thrust of this chapter is the process of gathering information for a particular problem or project. But receiving and consuming such information is also a problem of consequence. Solutions are thrown at you, urging you to adopt this, that, or the other way of organizing your paperwork or information flow. The "information age" has caused an explosion in available information, and you are truly inundated and overwhelmed.

Don't be intimidated. As an information receiver and consumer, you have a problem that can be addressed by Breakthrough Thinking. What purpose do you want to achieve? What purpose expresses your primary need? What ideal systems would accomplish the purpose(s)? What solution-after-next could you use as a target for your system? Answering these questions enables you to design a way of handling and coping with information, especially in determining how to retrieve what you receive and how to relate it to other sources you may need to tap. Let the questions you *need* to answer "pull" the information and the technology from the vast resources that are available. Don't let all of it be "pushed" into your process for creating or restructuring solutions.

Just as Breakthrough Thinking principles focus on the "customer" for most systems and problems on which you will work, they serve you well when you are the customer.

Kounosuke Matsushita, the founder of the company that makes Panasonic products, puts information into a valuable perspective: "It seems that knowledge has overpowered wisdom. Although it is very important for a human being to have wide and profound knowledge, it is more important to have the wisdom with which we can utilize knowledge as our tool for our human happiness...."[21]

Wisdom about working on a problem starts with recognizing that there is no single gem of information to be collected. The closest one can come to a magical prescription is the focus on gathering broad wisdom and insights about the purposes of collecting the projected information.

An omnipresent temptation is to go scrambling after information that "might help" on a project, even when there is abundant information at hand. Extensively analyzing all of it has traditionally been considered a way of learning "something." An admonition we have found serviceable in such situations is simply, "Don't make a mountain (or a chart) out of a molehill."

"Curiosity killed the cat" is another apt adage for the believer in "getting all the facts." In so many cases, curiosity is the only purpose that might exist for gathering information. Curiosity is a valuable trait, an avenue to learning new things. But in a specific problem-solving effort, unfocused curiosity is a pitfall.

Rather than asking yourself questions that reflect all-encompassing curiosity, ask instead:

- "Am I wasting time learning 'all there is to know' about the problem?"
- "Do I have too much information? Is it confusing me?"
- "Am I wasting my time looking for all the facts or whom to blame?"
- "Have I weeded out excess information?"
- "Am I gathering information necessary to promote solutions, not bury them?"
- "Are other team members gathering limited data to support their belief that some of the proposed solutions won't work?"

"If an [information collection] project is not worth doing at all, it is not worth doing well."[22]

The breeding ground of defeatism is the detailed analysis of what exists. "Information" is a reasonable substitute for "regulation" in Augustine's thirty-ninth law: "The ubiquitous regulation [information], created as a management surrogate, takes on a life of its own and exhibits a growth pattern which closely parallels that of selected other living entities observed in nature; most specifically, weeds."[23]

NOTES

1. T. Roszak, *The Cult of Information* (New York: Pantheon Books, 1984).

2. Saburou Shiroyama, "100 Hours with Mr. Souichirou Honda," (Tokyo: Kodansha Publishers, 1984).

3. I. I. Mitroff, "Correcting Tunnel-Vision," paper delivered at the School of Business Administratin, University of Southern California, September 5, 1985.

4. Lester Thurow, "A Weakness in Process Technology," *Science*, 238 (December 18, 1987).

5. Meg Greenfield, *Newsweek*, (August 10, 1987).

6. Edwin Mansfield, quoted in Annette Miller and Dody Tsiantar, "A Test for Market Research," *Newsweek* (December 28, 1987).

7. *Business Week* (June 6, 1988).

8. B. J. Feder, *New York Times* (June 4, 1989).

9. Jacobijn Sandberg and Bob Wielinga, "Situated Cognition: A Paradigm Shift?" *Journal of Artificial Intelligence in Education* Vol. 3 (1992), pp. 129-138.

10. William Poundstone, *Labyrinths of Reason: Paradox, Puzzler and the Frailty of Knowledge* (New York: Doubleday, 1988).

11. Warren Bennis and Bert Nanus, *Leaders: The Strategies of Taking Charge* (New York: Harper & Row, 1985).

12. R. A. Frosch, "A New Look at Systems Engineering," *IEEE Spectrum*, (September 1969).

13. M. J. Adler, *Philosopher at Large: An Intellectual Autobiography* (New York: Macmillan, 1977).

14. R.B. Braithwaite, *Scientific Explanation* (New York: Harpers, 1960).

15. Lee Dembart, Review of Ivar Ekeland, *Mathematics and the Unexpected, Los Angeles Times* (Dec. 20, 1988).

16. Ivar Ekeland, *Mathematics and the Unexpected* (Chicago: University of Chicago Press, 1988).

17. Norman Augustine, *Augustine's Laws* (New York: Penguin Books, 1987).

18. Chris Argyris, Robert Putnam, and Diana McLain Smith, *Action Research* (San Francisco: Jossey-Bass, 1985).

19. G. Nadler, *The Planning and Design Approach*, (New York: John Wiley & Sons, 1981).

20. Eberhardt Rechtin, *Systems Architecting*, Englewood Cliffs, N.J.: Prentice-Hall, 1991).

21. Kounosuke Matsushita, "Matsushita Saying," (Nami Shobou, 1979).

22. Anonymous.

23. *Augustine's Laws*, ibid.

Chapter Nine

The People Design Principle

In Japan, the International Family Society (a member organization of the International Voluntary Circle) plans, designs, and develops all of its programs based on the seven principles of the Total Approach. Particularly active in central Japan, the IFS was established in 1981 to promote international understanding by providing a familial atmosphere and environment for visiting foreigners, as well as offering Japanese members the opportunity to share values and experiences with members of other cultures.

Under the leadership of Mrs. Kazuko Toyoda, wife of the former chairman of the Toyota Motors, and others, IFS members in Nagoya City utilized the Total Approach of Breakthrough Thinking to develop the motto of "SAN KI SHUGI," which suggests three fundamental principles for voluntary activities of all kinds throughout Japan: (1) Kirakuni (act with ease spiritually); (2) Kinagani (act steadily over a long period of time; once started, don't quit); and (3) Kimochiyoku (act with pleasure).

Today, the International Family Society has grown to become one of the most active voluntary circles in all of Japan. Its successes have been repeatedly commended by the Japan International Cooperation Agency, the Aichi Prefecture Government, and Nagoya Training Centers. The number of IFS member families has now reached more than 350 and continues to increase rapidly with branches established in Tokyo, Toyohashi, and Ina, all on the basis of Breakthrough Thinking principles.

When a friend was in the fifth grade, she won first prize in a poetry recitation contest for her impassioned delivery of the poem "Invictus" by William Ernest Henley. "I am the master of my fate: I am the captain of my soul,"[1] she recited, with all the fervor of her ten-year-old being.

The audience response was so positive that the next year she entered the contest with a second poem celebrating autonomy, Rudyard Kipling's "If." She told the assembly of parents, "If you can keep your head when all about you are losing theirs and blaming it on you,... You'll be a Man, my son!"[2] She won again.

She wasn't that good an orator, but they were wonderful poems with a lot to teach us about the importance of building on our strengths and adhering to our principles. And the poets' words, implying as they do the sense of "going it alone," strike a responsive chord with Americans raised on a creed of rugged individualism.

Applying that philosophy alone to problem solving will not result in optimal solutions, however, because the isolation inherent in the approach leaves out an indispensable resource: each other. Even on the American frontier of the nineteenth century, settlers relied greatly on one another, whether "circling the wagons" against Indian attacks or joining together for mutual "barn raisings." In essence, the people design principle is based on the premise that life means nothing apart from other people. Their concerns and ideas should be treated as the basic fabric of problem solving.

Imagine, for example, that you are playing a game of Scrabble. You're staring at your seven letters unable to see even a three-point, three-letter word. In defeat, you show the letters to your fellow players. To your surprise, they quickly come up with several high-scoring words you could have made.

Although you may not always want to show your hand so literally, odds are you can do so more often than has seemed permissible given the strictures of conventional problem solving. When it comes to planning, design, and problem solving, it's best to apply the adage, "Two heads are better than one."

Think, for example, of the worst oil spill in U.S. history. Attributed to the negligence of the captain of the *Exxon Valdez*, it occurred in Valdez, Alaska, on March 24, 1989. Community members would say that, at a public meeting held just weeks before the spill, they had been warned that excessive drinking by oil tanker crew members could lead to just such a disaster. And management itself had the captain's history of hard drinking and treatment for alcoholism on record.

If a management system had been in place to listen to and apply the knowledge so readily available from so many individuals, the disaster almost certainly would not have occurred.

The fact that vital information was known to community residents willing and anxious to share it—and not just to the employees—points out another important Breakthrough Thinking tenet: *Anyone* has the potential to become a valuable contributor. The object is to create an atmosphere that fosters the optimal contribution each individual can make.

To do that, you must first throw away any preconceptions about who is qualified to offer what solutions and really listen to what each person has to say. If you do, you'll see the fallacy in the seldom-challenged premise that people don't like change.

It's not change we resist; it's conventional change.

Andy van de Ven, professor of management at the University of Minnesota, summarizes the relevant social science research: "People resist change when it is not understood, is imposed, is perceived as threatening, has risks greater than its potential benefits or interferes with other priorities."[3]

The people design principle gets people to work on change from the center (themselves) out rather than only from the outside (others) in.

With Breakthrough Thinking you can learn to minimize imposed change and turn risk into opportunity.

Consider the example of trucking deregulation. When the federal government began significantly to ease trucking regulation several years ago, many company executives balked. They cited the "If it ain't broke, don't fix it," philosophy. But the fact is that, broken or not, the industry was changing.

Still these executives refused to change with it. They made very few alterations in company practices—and they generally suffered for it—losing profits and, sometimes, the companies themselves.

By contrast, other company executives entered into a dialogue with the officials who were designing and implementing the eased regulations—a dialogue that helped them influence and understand the changes. Meanwhile, they viewed the change as a chance to provide potentially lucrative services they'd been prevented from adding under the old, stricter regulatory scheme. These executives urged their employees to elicit and be responsive to customers' needs: What new services were required? What old ones could be eliminated or enhanced?

They then used the answers to revise company operations. Service, pricing, and pickup and delivery schedules all changed in response to customer feedback.

Under deregulation, most of these companies prospered. By consulting with government officials, employees, and customers, the executives were instinctively applying the people design principle. The principle holds that the prospects of a solution's success are enhanced in direct proportion to the involvement of those individuals who stand to gain or lose as a result of the solution. This is especially true when the purposes and solution-after-next principles guide your efforts to involve others.

Such consultation need not be formal. Kounosuke Matsushita, founder of the Matsushita Electric Corporation (Panasonic) was a believer in participatory management. But, he cautioned, " 'Two heads are better than one' does not mean frequent meetings.... [Instead] we have to...try to establish the free environment for suggestions from employees and try to listen/adapt the people's ideas. If we have this kind of attitude in daily work, we could decide by ourselves without having a meeting because people's ideas are included tacitly."[4]

Applying the people design principle in accord with the other Breakthrough Thinking principles resulted in nurses willingly designing a new patient care system that increased their workload by 48 percent. And the nurses were delighted with the change. Other nurse utilization studies with conventional approaches are lucky to obtain a three to five percent improvement, reluctantly accepted.

In another case, a Chicago-based corporation with 150 factories nationwide used employees' expertise to increase quality and productivity.

The company sought to develop standard operating procedures (SOPS) for all machine operators. SOPs are full-size books or loose-leaf notebooks containing procedures or rules and regulations for operating equipment. The books are usually intended to cover all potential occurrences, but since nothing can do that, they generally collect dust on shelves and in drawers.

Yet when a Breakthrough Thinking consultant put together groups of people from several of the factories to work on the project, they devised a solution called Operator Guides (OGs)— booklets that would fit in a back pocket. When the guide was open, one page was printed and the facing page was blank. The operator could write in his or her own notes about system and equipment operations. In periodic updates, the written comments were incorporated and new blank pages were provided to continue the process.

The result is that OGs are used throughout the corporation, and quality and productivity have been significantly improved.

This concept of including many people in the solution process is not new. Yet in a 1986 report on human resources practices, researchers noted that they found it difficult to identify organizations where people are used effectively. Researchers concluded that most organizations are woefully behind the leaders in doing it.[5] Another study showed that only five percent of companies had given employees any training in group decision making or problem solving in the past year.[6]

One reason may be that there is little incentive to involve people since doing so using conventional techniques has not been successful. In fact, customary tactics exacerbate the human and group realities reviewed in Chapter 2. Functional fixedness and acceptance of the problem-as-stated are promoted by detailed analysis of what exists. Defensiveness is increased by asking people what is wrong. People's search for one correct solution is encouraged, group inertia is increased, and people's knowledge is utilized only for data collection about the existing situation rather than for setting up guides for major change.

With Breakthrough Thinking by contrast, involving people does work. Breakthrough Thinking enables you to work with the realities rather than to defend or ignore them—two practices that inevitably lead to failure. The ostrich approach of the crew and management of the *Exxon Valdez* is a good example of this.

Here are some other realities important to acknowledge:

1. The great need for creative and innovative solutions in any organizations is matched or exceeded by the need for fast implementation and use of the solutions. Installing change thus requires the active involvement of those who will operate it. Their commitment is built by understanding what the solution is and how it was developed. Implementation of solutions starts at the beginning of a project—by getting related people involved.

2. Obtaining the quality and productivity needed in organizations requires different programs and precepts than most organizations have used previously. The growth of human relations programs has led to various techniques that are at best short term. Often they are patronizing, an insult to our intelligence.

A colleague was present for one such example, when a management consultant hired to increase morale among employees at a federal agency told them to write their fears on a piece of paper and then rip the paper into shreds and flush it down a toilet. And our colleague heard—and agreed with—the employees' comments that morale would have improved much more had the agency taken the money it lavished on the consulting fee and divided it up among the employees!

3. The people design principle works on projects regardless of almost all corporate management styles and pay and reward structures. Both of these may be quite restrictive and represent problems in their own rights. Each of these problems can be worked on with Breakthrough Thinking.

4. Bringing people actively into design and problem solving is a need, not just a desirable social value. Conventional approaches assume that, as you work on a problem, it is possible to separate the technical aspects from the human, social, or learning aspects. The supposition is that experts should design the best economically justifiable technological solution and then workers should accept it.

The people design principle should demolish any linger-
ing belief in a presumption so at odds with both common
sense and human nature. Even the engineering design process
is best considered from the perspective of "the social nature of
designing."[7]

In fact, the people involved in designing a solution should
extend to your customers and suppliers as well as including direct stakeholders. Your organization will benefit from the resulting variety of technical and socioeconomic backgrounds
applied to its problems. Learning from one another is much
more likely to produce better results than merely imposing
rules, terms, and solutions. The people design principle emphasizes the need for mutually respectful relations to obtain mutual
benefits.

5. Individuals with diverse cultural backgrounds and different kinds of intelligence in design and problem solving
should be consulted. Why? In part because, as Stanford University educational psychologist James G. Greeno explains: "We
learned in physics that it is meaningless to attribute properties
of motion to objects without a frame of reference. We make the
same mistake in attributing knowledge and thinking to individual minds without a frame of reference."[8]

Greeno notes that research on general thinking abilities—
productive, higher order, critical, and creative thinking—has
progressed slowly compared with the rapid progress that has
been made in the study of cognitive structures and procedures.
If we are to make significant progess toward understanding
thinking and creativity, says Greeno, we should significantly alter the "framing assumptions" with which research in the field
of thinking has been conducted.

Greeno proposes three new fundamental assumptions
about thinking. One of these is "situated cognition," which
Greeno defines as thinking that is situated in physical and social
contexts. He says that cognition, including thinking, knowing,
and learning, can be considered a relation involving an agent in
a situation rather than an activity in an individual's mind.

Obviously, there are numerous categories of intelligence.
For example, some people are repositories of knowledge about

particular topics ("gatekeepers"); others have an idea a minute without concern for possible utility ("creative"); still others have a strong political and contextual insight into situations ("street smart"). Some people like to jump right into taking action—do anything, but do it now. Some are detailers of ideas to get to implementation right away. Others are intuitive and concerned about feelings.

However you classify people, be sure to involve them. Not only will doing so increase your odds for optimal design and problem solving, it will prevent those individuals from becoming the reluctant, often resentful victims of imposed change. Each type of person may also learn more about the other and become more adaptive in future activities.

6. Employees should know not only when to push a particular button on a piece of equipment but also why that button exists (purposes). Knowing how the system operates enables workers to handle crises that arise during operations, thus keeping decision making where it belongs for efficiency: at the lowest possible level of the corporate hierarchy.

Greeno's second new assumption about thinking is what he calls "personal and social epistemologies"; thinking and learning are situated in contexts of beliefs and understandings about cognition that differ between individuals and social groups, and fundamental properties of thinking and learning are determined by these contexts.[9]

7. In business, systems must be customer-based for companies to remain competitive. The best equipment in the world by itself is not sufficient to do this. Even if only a few people in your organization deal directly with customers in the marketplace, never forget that most of your work problems affect them. Employees must be aware of the needs of the customers, not just those of their supervisors. Think of the transportation deregulation example: The successful companies are those that listen and respond to customers' needs. They must continue to do so if they are to continue to succeed.

8. Individuals look for meaning in life. The benefits of the expansionary views of the purposes and solution-after-next principles are brought together in the people design principle

to provide at least some relative meaning for all. Because each person's aloneness is a given in psychology and philosophy, mutual involvement is needed for mutual support. This also provides each individual the opportunity to improve his or her capabilities and position.

Unfortunately, human beings naturally tend to feel negative about themselves and their abilities. They often exhibit several negative characteristics—apathy, fear, self-doubt, isolation, impatience, faulty evaluation of ideas, tentativeness, and failure to listen to others. Worse yet, the conventional mental model of how to approach problems exacerbates these negative characteristics. Fortunately, when the Breakthrough Thinking principles provide the basis for action, the set of questions posed to and by each person involved in the solution-finding process is virtually certain to ameliorate this instinctive human negativity.

Where the People Design Principle Fits

We found that the successful leaders and problem-solvers we studied took pains from the very beginning to involve in all phases of a project or effort to effect change all of the major stakeholders in its outcome. These naturally expert problem solvers recognized intuitively the principles of uniqueness, purposes, solution-after-next, systems, and limited information collection. Viewed from another perspective, involving people with the principles of Breakthrough Thinking is beneficial not only to the problem-solving process, but also to the individuals involved.

People instinctively respond negatively and defensively to questions about the nature of a problem, searches for who is at fault or whom to blame, and analysis and subdivision of the existing problem situation. By contrast, people respond positively and eagerly to questions that recognize their uniqueness as individuals, probe and expand their particular purposes, seek solutions-after-next, and ask how they would ideally accomplish an identified purpose if they could start all over again.

Conventional thinking views people as "hands," objects to be manipulated at management's desire, available for physical rather than mental activities, unable to comprehend the overall situation. Douglas McGregor called this "Theory X" and defined it as "the assumption of the mediocrity of the masses."[10]

Logic (as well as our studies of successful people) tells us this is a prescription for workers' underutilization, resentment, and drudgery. We all want to be involved in making decisions that influence our lives. And we accept and feel good about implementing a solution that we help to devise. That's the premise of the people design principle. Breakthrough Thinking allows you to maximize individuals' participation and secure their commitment to the solution even before it is fully known.

In some instances, the benefits of group participation in creating a solution can be more important to the company than the solution itself. For example, one company used Breakthrough Thinking to develop a much better system of cost allocation for both regional and headquarters offices than either of the two feuding groups had proposed before. Yet, according to the vice-president of human resources, the most important benefit to the company was the team building that occurred.

When applying the people design principle, remember the following:

1. People touched by efforts in creating or restructuring solutions and affected by the results eventually realized should be given continual opportunities to participate in the problem-solving process. There is no way to predict just who will contribute at what point. But without the *opportunity* to do so, people feel snubbed. Worse, they may let negative feelings take over their attitude toward the whole project. When provided continuing invitations to participate, a previous decision not to take part is not an obstacle to the individual's future contribution. All of us know people who do not speak up until the third or fourth meeting while others dry up after the first one.

2. People are the source of information. Much fewer data need to be collected when "it is right here in the room with us."

3. People *can* understand intricate techniques and complex situations. There is no reason to claim that those affected

cannot really grasp the sophistication, beauty, and elegance of your proposal: The burden of explaining your new technique, model, or complex idea is on you.

4. Meetings *can* be productive. True, conventional meetings do not generally produce creative, timely, cost-effective, and implemented results. But "participative discussion has a greater effect than mere information presentation [because] the subject must actively reformulate, or rehearse the information ... received in order to internalize an attitude change."[11]

5. People enjoy working on and accepting responsibility for projects. Surveys show that 75 to 85 percent of people in most organizations feel they would be able to handle more responsibilities. In one case, workers at a plant chose to get involved in designing a new department for a new product. They felt so positively about one alternative that they challenged the engineers who favored another product to a trial run. The workers' alternative was shown to be much better.

6. The individual is the source of ideas. Although group processes may stimulate creativity in some people, such activity alone may stifle it in others. Some people do not participate well in groups but have tremendous capabilities that need to be tapped. Individual follow-up can help you to do this if the stimulus of the group fails to elicit ideas from a particular individual. At the same time, appropriate group activities can increase the creativity and productivity of an individual over what that person would generate alone. In fact, sometimes only a group can meet an individual's needs—for example, the need for recognition.

The Definition of People Design

We've given you the definition for the people design principle: Give people related to or affected by change the continual opportunity to take part in operating or restructuring systems and preventing or solving problems. By continuing to review purposes, solutions-after-next, and systems changes in the future as a means of encouraging people to ask questions and suggest improvements, the opportunity can even be extended to the time when a change or new system is installed. But actually accomplishing these ends is another matter.

First, you must determine the identity of the affected individuals. You and your problem may at first appear to involve no one else, but that's probably not true. Organizing your desk? What about your secretary and colleagues. Preparing your resume? What about your spouse, secretary, prospective recipients, friends, and those you do not want to receive it? Writing a speech you are to present at a meeting? What about your colleagues, the prospective listeners, and support personnel?

Not everyone who stands to be affected will be interested in getting involved, but if you are expecting them to change or to adopt something new, their involvement in the project activity should be considered. Sixth- and seventh-grade children developed many unusual and excellent contributions (poems, skits, debates, panel discussions, exhibits) when they designed with Breakthrough Thinking their own study plans for reading a book.[12]

Categorizing by role is another way of considering the range of people to be included: Worker, manager, gatekeeper, maintenance specialist, designer, and customer may all be directly involved in the problem area. In addition, those who fill a role, such as an expert in a particular field, may need to be included. Furthermore, each function or person could be involved at different phases or steps of the Breakthrough Thinking process, as described later in this chapter and in Chapter 11.

Of course, all of these roles are only nominal titles because each person or group plays other roles as well. Factory workers, for example, may also be spouses and parents, service club members, and churchgoers. Frequently, the knowledge these individuals have gained in their other roles can be useful in solving your seemingly unrelated problem. But by the same token, to assume that experts, factory workers, and others will deal with an organizational project only on its objective merits without considering their other roles is foolish.

Even if all the affected people cannot be involved due to logistics or sheer numbers, identifying who they are gives you the opportunity to do something about them—through subgroups, newsletters, videocassettes, talks, conference calls, and so on. The gypsy moth pest-management system case illustrates this carefully crafted method of dealing with the number of people related to or affected by a change.

The gypsy moth case also illustrates another important Breakthrough Thinking tenet: Treat the planning of how you will approach a problem as a problem in itself for which Breakthrough Thinking principles are to be used.

Although it is true not everyone will or can participate at every step of a project, the key is to provide a never-ending occasion for response and contribution. This means more than the usual admonition in companies to "communicate with your employees," as important as that is to helping the organization. It's an admonishment to have them *take part in* the desired result. It means presenting the project as a desirable challenge, rather than just something to be left to the experts in the field.

Today's job market generally offers employees very little job security. So how do you obtain their commitment to a solution? Actually, many studies (*Leaders, In Search of Excellence, The Leadership Challenge*) show that some form of autonomy and entrepreneurship is essential to achieving the quality and productivity organizations need. Many Breakthrough Thinking examples of solution finding (factory managers and personnel, nurses, gypsy moth specialists, and engineers and workers in the box die-cutting project) show that participation and commitment can be generated with or without job security.

In addition, the commitment to customers and their customers inherent to Breakthrough Thinking requires an important ingredient that organizations often fail to recognize—the need to be committed to employees. Invest in developing people to use Breakthrough Thinking for problem solving, planning, and design—it's your best investment for the future. Improving the quality of service to your customers will be achieved by employees at all levels *if* they feel they have the respect, preparation, and support to practice a customer-first orientation. This is the way to compete from the inside out. Each employee understands these needs when he or she is involved in the Breakthrough Thinking process.

Also, keep in mind one other thing: A solution should specify only the minimum number of critical details and controls. Flexibility in operating the installed solution should be given to the people working in the system. The appropriate amount of such flexibility will depend on the situation. Clearly, monitoring a nuclear power plant or controlling a shuttle flight requires very specific operating constraints. But all systems need people who are well prepared to cope with both the expected and the unexpected.

Purpose and Goals of People Design

As conventionally practiced, efforts to include people generally fail because they accentuate the negative. For example, a project meeting will start with participants being asked to describe the problem, where the difficulties occur, and who is to blame.

This conventional probing of difficulties is likely to produce a feeling of helplessness to the detriment of present and future projects. Conversely, a group starting with purposes, "ideal" systems, solutions-after-next, and so on maintains enthusiasm and commitment. *How* participation is carried out is thus as crucial as the actual involvement. Initial actions or statements cast the die. Groups lose hope for success and even stop trying if some success is not attained almost immediately.[13]

By increasing significantly the likelihood that a breakthrough solution will occur and be implemented, the people design principle:

1. *Copes with the realities of individuals and groups.* Classic problem solving exacerbates the mind-set that usually exists (see Chapter 2): acceptance of problems as stated, functional fixedness, protection of the status quo, the search for one correct solution, and so on. It is precisely this type of setting that the people design principle, with the other Breakthrough Thinking principles, is able to overcome. Why reinforce functional fixedness, for example? Why even let fixedness appear? Ask nonthreatening questions based on the Breakthrough Thinking principles.

2. *Shares meanings and interpretations of reality.* Warren Bennis and Burt Nanus point out that leaders need to provide a "social architecture" that conveys a corporate creed or culture if cohesiveness and effectiveness are to occur.[14] Much of the need for this social architecture stems from the divorce of social purpose from actual work when the industrial revolution dramatically changed occupational structures. The people design principle provides the concepts of purpose arrays and solutions-after-next as a mechanism for sharing the larger meanings and vision of the organization and customers in society.

3. *Develops champions and a winning attitude.* The breeding ground of defeatism is the detailed analysis of what exists. It takes unusual energy and commitment by one or two people to overcome the usual growing frustration in groups in the face of such information. The conventional approach calls for a champion—to wield influence, to "break down the doors" to change.

Breakthrough Thinking's focus on purpose and solutions-after-next emphasizes constructive change. And with Breakthrough Thinking, just as many individuals can become contributors, many contributors can become champions. Any number of people can be in the forefront "carrying the ball."

4. *Develops the capabilities of each individual.* People generate creative ideas when the setting encourages them. Even though one-third of the ideas are produced by 10 percent of the people, there is no way to know who these idea-producers will be unless everyone is given the opportunity to contribute. Thus, encouraging more people to get more ideas is critical. Japanese companies, for example, obtain from fifty to ninety ideas from each worker per year, whereas U.S. companies get less than one quarter of an idea per person.[15]

In the United States most programs that seek to get people involved—self-managed work teams, quality of working life, suggestion systems, total quality management, incentive systems—flounder in reaching the goals because they emphasize techniques, not individual human beings and their contributions to understanding purposes and solutions-after-next.

Greeno supports this perspective in his third new assumption about thinking, what he calls "conceptual competence."

Children, he notes, have strong potential capabilities for cognitive growth through complex and subtle processes of constructing knowledge and thinking skills. Thinking, learning, and cognitive growth are activities in which children elaborate and reorganize their knowledge and understanding rather than simply applying and acquiring cognitive structures and procedures.[16]

This sort of growth extends potentially throughout a human lifetime. Thus, each individual's creativity can be tapped to form a collective intelligence for the group or organization. The future of any organization will depend on the development of the core competencies of its people—technical, team, social, and strategic.

The real need is illustrated by statements in the mission, values, and guiding principles of the Ford Motor Company: "Our people are the source of our strength.... Involvement and teamwork are our core human values."[17] Breakthrough Thinking frees each individual who stands to be affected by a change to generate ideas that could influence the shape of that change. It also allows people to engage in effective decision making at lower levels of the organization, a characteristic of critical importance in the '90s and the century to come.

5. *Builds the teamwork capabilities of each group.* Group members can rapidly process and simulate the possible solutions, deciding whether to explore each one further. When, on complex projects, subgroups are necessary, each of them can work effectively with the main group because of the common Breakthrough Thinking language. Applying the Breakthrough Thinking principles and process to the problem or opportunity on which a group is to work means that team building becomes an integral part of the effort, not an afterthought or add-on set of exercises.

Establishing a high level of performance for individuals and groups is a hallmark of Breakthrough Thinking. Why? Because people generally perform the way you expect them to perform.

6. *Secures needed information from a wide variety of sources.* The people involved in a project are those most likely to know what questions need to be asked. But finding the answers often means tapping additional sources and resources.

Answers are much more useful when both those queried and those asking the questions are given the background information regarding the purposes, the alternative SANS, and so forth.

7. *Increases creativity in planning, design, improving, and problem solving.* Breakthrough Thinking principles facilitate your own creativity, and it is equally crucial to get other involved individuals to use theirs. Paul Hare summarized a creative person as "a nonconformist with the capacity to pursue nonconforming and creative ideas."[18] The Breakthrough Thinking principles assuredly give each person the opportunity to be nonconformist—that is, not adopting the usual societal pressures to see things as others have seen them (uniqueness), expanding the purposes, seeking ideal systems, solutions-after-next, and still other solutions after that.

8. *Increases the likelihood of accounting for the human factors.* The human ingredient is a key part of most systems. Even satellites and space launches fit this characterization since humans are so involved in the preparation, launching, and control of the flights.

Involving many people with the Breakthrough Thinking principles increases significantly the chance that the solution devised will fit the humans who operate the system. The involvement of people in a project is itself a way of fostering the autonomy and entrepreneurship that is considered an attribute of excellent organizations.

9. *Overcomes the arrogance over who is in charge.* According to Shoshana Zuboff, managers continue to embrace the authoritarian perspective that inhibits the development of workers' knowledge about advanced technology, even when it is to the managers' disadvantage to do so. Organizational effectiveness is thus subverted.[19]

Part of the difficulty with managers is traceable to the short-term outlook that afflicts the American approach to solving problems. Managers think it will take less time if they alone develop solutions. That's short-term thinking. They forget the myriad illustrations of sabotaged solutions for which the people affected by a change were not consulted.

Another difficulty is that managers, like the rest of us, remember the response of people to conventional approaches to problem solving—placing blame, for example—and they expect that to happen even if they are using the other Breakthrough Thinking principles.

10. *Avoids past mistakes.*

11. *Overcomes emotional, cultural, and environmental blocks.* Jim Adams points out several blocks that keep people from developing creative ideas.[20] Many of these take the form of taboos, such as the Japanese aversion to building a door or opening on the northeast side of a building, the "devil's gate." Others take the form of decision criteria, such as the Iroquois Indians' admonition to consider the impact of any action today on the seventh generation from now. Still others take the form of language and expression preferences, such as for or against mathematical models in projects. These blocks are often difficult to work with because they are so ingrained.

The people design principle is critical in the process of working with, not putting aside, whatever beliefs exist. When combined with the other Breakthrough Thinking principles, people design allows group members to express their own values, enabling them to push forward within their own contextual framework. This is the major reason Breakthrough Thinking is used successfully around the world in many different cultures.

12. *Avoids the tendency to overcontrol systems.* This refers to the unfortunate tendency of the rationalist approach to problems to impose various controls on workers, often just because the technology is available to do so. Robert Howard describes the horrors of overcontrol:

> Monitoring often does not even serve the narrowest ends of economic efficiency that are its ostensible justification. One Citibank supervisor, for example, tells the story of a two-minute "average working time" placed on all calls to customer representatives at the bank's bank-card processing center in South Dakota. What happened was that, as workers anxiously approached the end of the time limit on each call, they would hang up on their customers whether the conversation was completed or not.[21]

Several other purposes and goals of the people design principle are important enough to mention here but similar enough to those already noted that elaboration is not needed.

- Increases the long-term commitment of those involved to assure the workability and continued improvement of the solution.
- Gives acceptable answers to questions that bother people, such as Why change? What's in it for me?
- Provides the individual with insights on how to exert some control over what is to be done. Each person can use the principles and process for personal problems (as psychiatrists have noted), for problems at the office or at home, for setting up performance expectancies with a manager or direct-report, for mentoring and coaching other individuals, for evaluating a person's performance, for considering requests for equipment expenditures, and in effect, for all "standard" problems. Each person can thus do a great deal to practice quality in all his or her future endeavors.
- Adds an important intellectual source of satisfaction to most people's work by teaching them to use Breakthrough Thinking ideas, thus increasing their self-esteem and sense of accomplishment.
- Develops a cohesive work group to decrease long-term uncertainty and ambiguity. External team building and internal relationships are built.
- Avoids the "group-think" process of rationalization when team members begin to accede to a manager who doesn't tolerate dissent or refuse to take seriously a leader who encourages everyone too much. Breakthrough Thinking's emphasis on developing many options at each step of the way greatly reduces this danger while still resulting in a group that is able to disagree and yet work together effectively.

Using the People Design Principle

If you think and act as if a person has real ability, the person will consistently do better than previously thought possible.

Applying this positive approach to each individual's participation can add an intangible yet invaluable asset to problem solving, particularly when applied with the following additional two levels of insights into how to use the people design principle.

The first level of insight includes suggestions that are almost out-and-out exhortations, and reasonable methods that might be useful in many contexts. The second level identifies five considerations regarding how to implement the people design principle for the problem on which you are working.

SUGGESTIONS

a. Try it. Use the believing game. Talk to people. Educate them in the Breakthrough Thinking Principles. Adopt the language of Breakthrough Thinking in your discussions—purposes, measures of purpose accomplishment (customer satisfaction, costs, timeliness, productivity), solutions-after-next, and so on.

b. Ask questions. The questions should be about the purposes, ideal systems, etc. These are nonthreatening questions, whereas conventional questions tend to confuse rather than clarify the issues.

c. Hold an informal team meeting during, say, a usual lunch grouping, an organizational athletic meeting, or a community's weekly service club meeting. This will provide an opportunity for a positive and nondominating exchange.

d. Set up a one-time meeting with people who might have constituted a good long-term project team had it been possible to establish one. They may then be able to carry the solution-finding process forward with small group meetings and individual interviews.

e. Set up a one-time meeting to plan the problem-solving system using the Breakthrough Thinking principles. (This is illustrated in the gypsy moth case discussed in Chapters 1 and 5.)

f. Allow for the catharsis of finger pointing, superficial diagnosis, turf protection, and other defensive routines people are likely to engage in when they first meet on a project. (This, too, is illustrated by the gypsy moth case.) It's part of the "unfreezing" that Kurt Lewin defined in 1964.[22] Meanwhile, keep on track with the Breakthrough Thinking process agenda as much as possible.

g. Get the people you involve to be customer-driven and market-oriented through the larger purposes in the array. The trucking deregulation example given earlier in this chapter illustrates this need.

h. Involve different people, depending on whether your purpose is to improve an existing system that is in trouble, better a system that is in good shape, or create a new product or service.

i. Include a person or two previously successful at "breaking the rules." The processes they used—thinking patterns, sources of information, people queried—may be useful.

j. Include a person or two with a liberal arts bias. This assumes that the project is technical, as most are. (Conversely, an arts, cultural, or religious project should include a technical person or two.) This will give breadth to the insights.

k. Use existing groups. Organizations that have a commitment to teamwork are well positioned to change to Breakthrough Thinking. Although new groups will also be necessary, members of existing groups may have valuable observations since they often have already considered what they would do differently if they were to start all over again.

l. Keep the energy level high for the Breakthrough Thinking principles, not for initial judging. Conventional reasoning pushes evaluation and choice far too early.

m. Seek ways to get recognition for individuals and groups who have made major breakthroughs. Such visibility is important to many people and may motivate others. Other forms of appreciation should be provided for those making smaller gains.

n. Use some guidelines to determine how well the group is working together: Are members open, confiding in each other, focusing discussion on purposes and the other principles, having fun, practicing the believing game, following through on assigned tasks, eager to attend meetings, and, of course, getting results?

METHODS

The five considerations regarding how to implement the people design principle for the problem or project on which you are working are shown in Table 9-1. All five parts may not be important in all situations.

Problem-Solving Phases or Steps. The purpose to be achieved by the phase or step should determine who, when, and how to involve people. Different groups of skills, influence, and knowledge are likely to be needed at different points.

Keep in mind that people's concerns and interests change. Some people who were initially interested may not be as involved later, for instance, as they perceive that they are not threatened by the project (which may have motivated their initial participation). Furthermore, people transfer jobs or terminate employment, or new people are hired as the project proceeds.

Don't be dismayed if the project experiences difficulties not linked directly to a specific activity. Projects almost inevitably have one or two muddles that occur along the way. You're probably personally familiar with some of them: Some project team members may "say they think the whole project is a waste of time; [important people] get into an embarrassing argument in the middle of a meeting; a previously uncommunicative and uncommitted [person] suddenly starts crusading for a cause you thought had been killed off;...meetings are getting unruly;...there is a general moroseness and sinking feeling that the [organization] is going down the tubes unless [the project] does something about it; there is a general understanding that the big ideas that surfaced in the first few meetings were naive, even childlike."[23]

A return to a prior phase or step may help. Or additional resources (human agents, money), time, or political support may be needed. Another course of action is to redesign the planning system.

Level of Organizational Participation. Trying to get many people involved in a project can backfire if the organization has a pattern of authoritarian processes and styles. It is difficult to imagine, for example, how workers and first-line

Table 9-1. How to involve people in Breakthrough Thinking*

A. Phase or Step
Obtain employer's go-ahead
Train others in Breakthrough Thinking
Develop the planning system
Determine type of problem
Determine criteria for decision making
Determine which group members should do what
Determine purposes and hierarchy of purposes
Generate ideas
Consider solution-after-next
Select target
Detail
Obtain approval
Install
Make a betterment change

B. Level of Organizational Participation
None
Persuasive autocracy
Consultation
Reactive control
Bargaining
Anticipatory control
Joint determination
Supportive collaboration
Permanent work groups
Complete self-determination

C. Roles of Involved Individuals
Advisor
Advocate
Analyst
Client/owner
Conciliator
Consultant expert
Consumer, purchaser, or user
Customer's customer

•Use the phases or steps (consideration A) and the level of participation (consideration B) to determine which items you select from each of the other three considerations.

Table 9-1. (continued)   How to involve people in Breakthrough Thinking.

Decision maker, source of power (resource controller, politician, board member, etc.)
Designer/innovator
Educator/expert
Evaluator
Lobbyist
Manager
Organizer
Owner
Representative(s) of affected group(s)
Researcher

D. Group Processes
Brainstorming
Brain writing
Debate
Decision worksheet
Delphi method
Game or simulation
Idea writing
Interacting
Interviews of individuals in the group
KJ Method (person card)
Media-based balloting
Multiattribute utility assessment
Nominal group technique
Opinion poll
Pay for performance
Quality circles
Questionnaires and surveys
Role playing
Sensitivity training
Shared participation
Suggestion system
System matrix
Team building
Telecommunications

E. Meeting Conditions
Room
Location (on or off site)
Lighting, noise level, temperature, and ventilation

Table 9-1. (continued)   How to involve people in Breakthrough Thinking

Table arrangement (round, oval, etc.)
Group size (7 plus or minus 2)
Seating arrangement (random, alphabetical, etc.)
Identification (Name tags, place cards)
Supplies (paper, pencils, easel, chalkboard, etc.)
Space per person (2- to 4-foot minimum)

supervisors in an autocratic organization will ever get involved in meetings to design a new manufacturing facility.

Column B, Table 9-1, lists ten overlapping management styles, from no participation to complete participation. The different participatory styles can be defined as follows:

1. None: There is no participation and involvement. People express surprise if the "boss" asks them a problem-solving question. People are paid to "work," not "think." Managers "send down" decisions.

2. Persuasive autocracy: There is some recognition that an effort to "sell" the project or the solution has been considered and will be incorporated "if there is time and money."

3. Consultative: Responsible managers ask people many questions and seek to obtain as many ideas as possible, but establishing criteria, weightings, and details are left entirely to managers.

4. Reactive control: The organizations do involve others with measuring, comparing, and assessing the performance of a satisfactory system. Citizen groups, regulatory boards, peer review, and so on, are means whereby participation is obtained. Policy formulation matters arise only occasionally.

5. Bargaining: More adversarial or at least structured formal involvement is built into normal operations.

6. Anticipatory control: The organization consciously scans the horizon to become aware of possible future occurrences. Groups are allowed to report intelligence that could indicate developments. They can also develop alternatives for responding and "controlling" the future.

7. Joint determination: Although decisions are usually joint, there is a relatively continuous interchange of ideas among those charged with the responsibilities for operating a system and those working in it. Management operates this way because it thinks it's desirable, and workers have no assurance of its continuation. Most other stakeholders also may not be included in the participatory effort.

8. Supportive collaboration: Efforts are likely to be more formalized, with some decision responsibilities spelled out (for example, advisory group, citizens' commissions).

9. Permanent work groups: Employees and managers meet regularly (usually during working hours) and seek to solve all types of problems that emerge in any area of concern.

10. Complete self-determination: A joint worker/management board of directors or several joint groups share key decision-making responsibility (budgets, new products, acquisition and divestiture, personnel policies and practices, and so on.)

Payment and reward systems are also a factor in considering each of these levels of participation. A strict piece-work incentive structure is likely to be used in level 1 through levels 4 or 5, whereas group bonuses or gains sharing are more likely in levels 7 through 10 (even though the '90s do not appear to offer security to anyone). The Breakthrough Thinking principles and process can be used to create or restructure these systems, thus avoiding the temptation to force-fit the "broad-banding" method or fad of reducing the number of pay scales from, say, 30 to 8.

Roles of Involved Individuals. The number of people who ought to be involved by role and position is usually large, whether or not they are formally in the group. Some should be included throughout the project, others only during certain phases or steps (column A, Table 9-1).

Most of the different roles and functions you should consider for a group to ensure its top performance are included in column C. None is a "pure" role; the boundaries of each are flexible, and you may need to adopt more than one role at a time or to ask others to take on some of these roles. If you are working independently on a problem, you may want to adopt several or all of them yourself. Projects where the key executive served as a "change agent" or catalyst by taking on such role(s) were found to have a 100 percent success rate.[24]

In general, the variety of roles and skills needed for a project should be identified before individuals are considered. The fact that each fulfills many roles must be taken into account when considering individuals for group participation. For example, a person selected for a citizen or consumer role in a health care planning council may be biased if the job assignment involves selling medical supplies. A person selected for a consultant role as an expert in a particular area of knowledge should have a facilitative style to help move the group toward understanding and utilization of the information.

In addition, you may want to choose participants based not only on their knowledge, abilities, and brand of intelligence ("street-smart," for example), but on social competencies, emotional evenness, or even ethical values. The major criterion for selecting people should always be to improve the probability of arriving at an effective, innovative, and implementable solution while using available resources. This almost always means that "social homogeneity as a selection criterion...[and] social conformity as a standard for conduct" are inappropriate for a good group.[25]

A "good" group, on the other hand, is dependent on its size, representation, and longevity. Try for seven people, plus or minus two. In larger groups, interchange is restricted because people do not listen, form small coalitions, hide and do not speak, or else make speeches. A few aggressive individuals predominate, and the chance for consensus and a quality solution decreases. Fewer than five is usually too small a group for adequate representation and dynamics. Odd numbers tend to promote productivity, to avoid coalitions, and to result in effective outcomes. Next, every relevant perspective should be included. Convergent and divergent thinkers, bureaucrats, and free-thinkers—all should be there. Finally, select people for ad hoc groups who are likely to stay with the organization through in-stallation of the change.

Group Processes. Having a group does not necessarily mean that meetings will be held. Several techniques (opinion polling and telephone conferencing among them) enable groups to "meet" without meetings.

Using a group and having a meeting require serious con-sideration. Choosing people and roles is vital, but by itself it is not quite sufficient for successful application of the people de-sign principle. Getting people to take part in a meeting can be-come a disaster without appropriate methods and techniques. Some useful techniques are listed in consideration D, Table 9-1; each technique is described in Table 9-2 in terms of its basic purposes and what you should expect as a result of using it. From these, you should be able to determine if it is suitable for your situation.

Note that many of these techniques can now be enhanced by computers. For example, brainwriting, nominal group, and suggestion systems offer computer software that can be used by individuals or groups in a meeting, if each group member had a computer terminal networked to the screen projection computer.

The following are some of the characteristics of groups that you should consider when designing a project planning system:

1. Its purposes, hierarchy of purposes, and objectives.

2. To whom it is responsible and its degree of autonomy.

3. Who became a member how, what group authority each member desires, and the relationship of each member to the others.

4. Whether group operation is formal or informal.

5. The friendliness, frankness, and freeness of the discussion atmosphere (whether communication cuts across ranks or proceeds through them).

6. Cohesiveness of the group (whether it is effective and com-mitted as a team) and the comfort-level with using comput-ers in the group decision-making process.

7. The degree of control of the facilitator and the source of decision making.

8. Physical resources available (computer terminals, conditions in meeting rooms, and so on).

9. Information resources available (library and database facilities, experts, and so on).

A permanent group (for example, product development) needs some additional characteristics, among them, modes of interrelating with other organizational groups.

There can be disadvantages to groups: The pressure to conform can cause lower-quality solutions, or groups may settle too quickly on a solution, avoiding even high-quality ideas once a tentative solution has been reached. Breakthrough Thinking principles help group members themselves learn to push beyond, and even make use of, the negatives.

Meeting conditions. Because meeting conditions usually make a difference, meetings should be held on neutral turf, in a nonconfrontational seating arrangement to avoid subgroups seated by rank or faction (see consideration E, Table 9-1). Many factors need to be determined before a meeting; and some, such as the amount of light, heat, and ventilation, always need to be checked.

The following leader's guidelines for meetings should also prove beneficial:

- Stick to a previously distributed agenda where topics are purpose-oriented. Many research projects show structured group activities are far more effective and take no more time than unstructured ones.

- Err toward covering a little too much for the available time on an agenda rather than too little. There is truth to the saying that work expands to fit the time available.

- State on the agenda how long the meeting will last.

- Within each agenda topic, control only the process, not the content. Give everyone a chance to contribute by a leader-arranged, round-robin process; call on nonspeakers; use techniques that assure everyone's participation and state the rules of order.

Table 9-2.   Some group process techniques.

BRAINSTORMING and BLUE SKY IMAGINING
Stakeholders openly discuss and exchange ideas on an improvement problem to come up with a combined solution that best suits the situation.

BRAIN WRITING
This technique is basically the same as brainstorming, except each person writes each idea on a separate card. The cards are either passed to the next person seated at the table or placed in the center of the table for distribution to other members. Each person who gets a card adds ideas and suggestions to make the idea more workable.

DEBATE
Two groups formally debate proposals. A committee of decision makers assesses and rates each group's performance to determine the best proposal.

DECISION WORKSHEET
Crucial characteristics of alternative solutions are ranked by the participants on a decision worksheet to arrive at the best one.

DELPHI METHOD
Questionnaires are sent to respondents for the generation of ideas; the responses are summarized by a staff group. Subsequently, a second questionnaire is sent to the same participants who independently evaluate earlier responses and vote on priority ideas included on the second questionnaire. The staff team makes a new summary of the evaluations and votes, and a decision-making group decides on the most suitable ideas.

GAME OR SIMULATION
Computer programs simulate the possible processes that follow implementation of each alternative. Outcomes of simulations determine the final decision.

IDEA WRITING
Ideas are developed and their meanings and implications explored using four steps: initial organization of problem-solving subgroups of a large group, initial written responses, written interaction among the participants, and analysis and reporting of the written interaction.

Table 9-2.   Some group process techniques.

INTERACTING
A group meets to discuss problems in an unstructured way. There is minimal direction by the leader, although a trained leader can provide increasing degrees of structure.

INTERVIEWS OF INDIVIDUALS IN GROUPS
Ideas and decisions are facilitated by interviews of individuals who offer their opinions independently without interacting with other members of the group.

KJ METHOD (PERSON CARD)
Each person in the group writes one idea per card. The group places them all on a board or face-up on a table. The members sort the cards into piles, each one representing "one person" in the "family." The result is a chart of relationships of the "persons" or groups of cards in whatever structure or order the group decides (hierarchy, balloon diagram, outline, etc.).

MEDIA-BASED BALLOTING
Balloting through media (e.g., TV or conference calls) allows decision making through voting and avoids direct interaction among the participants.

MULTIATTRIBUTE UTILITY ASSESSMENT
The utilities of various attributes of different alternatives are assessed mathematically to reach a decision.

NOMINAL GROUP TECHNIQUE
Individuals meet and silently generate in writing ideas that are subsequently reported, one idea per person, one person after another, and recorded on a flip chart. Discussion of each individual idea follows, and each individual prioritizes the ideas. The solution selected is mathematically derived through rank ordering or rating.

OPINION POLL
Individuals express ideas and preferences of a problem situation through a poll of opinions without having to interact directly.

PAY FOR PERFORMANCE
Individuals are rewarded based on the performance results of their team rather than individual results.

Table 9-2.   Some group process techniques.

QUALITY CIRCLES OR WORK TEAMS
Small informal groups of employees meet voluntarily to discuss and provide solutions for productivity improvement problems. Quality circles are part of the Japanese participative management philosophy.

QUESTIONNAIRES AND SURVEYS
Participants respond to questionnaires and surveys to provide ideas on problems without interacting.

ROLE PLAYING
Individuals "play" various roles in the decision-making process, thus becoming aware of their attitudes and effects on others and learning how to become more effective problem solvers.

SENSITIVITY TRAINING
This process helps individuals develop self-awareness whereby they can become more sensitive to their effects on others and can learn by interacting with other participants of the group.

SHARED PARTICIPATION
Group members are encouraged to share opinions and ideas openly in a shared participation manner; everybody participates in the decision-making process.

SUGGESTION SYSTEM
Individual suggestions for improvement of the workplace productivity and quality are obtained. Suggestions are often dropped in boxes. A committee assesses if the recommendations are worthy of implementation.

SYSTEM MATRIX
A solution framework guides the problem-solving group through the development of its solution. The system matrix forces members to think holistically and thus consider interfaces and future dimensions of the recommendation.

TELECOMMUNICATIONS
Voice messages, E-mail, or video images are sent back and forth among participants, allowing the exchange of ideas without direct face-to-face interaction of idea and decision makers.

- Start with a statement of achievements anticipated by the end of the meeting.

- Inform the group of developments since the last meeting. Use displays. Individuals responsible for interim activities should inform others of progress.

- Summarize what the meeting has accomplished, what is to be done by the next meeting and by whom, and what the next meeting will concern.

- Use majority voting only as a last resort when differences are so pronounced that consensus is not really possible. Use the telephone and computer to get information.

- Be enthusiastic about the group's work if you expect the group to be interested and enthusiastic.

- Put any decision that narrowly achieved a majority on the agenda for the next meeting as a means of gathering new information, obtaining ideas from experts and persons with other roles in the organization, heeding warnings of moral and ethical consequences, and getting greater group concurrence.

- As needed, repeat the overall strategy and total approach within which the meeting's agenda topics fit to reinforce the overall perspective as a basis for decisions. "Listen with your whole being." Emphasize purposes for all deliberations and decisions. Check and recapitulate to assure broad understanding among members.

- Avoid spending too much time on a conspicuous idea or the first alternative. Look for other alternatives and broadening information. Avoid the dangers of "group-think" pressures toward conformity and uniformity.

- If possible, have someone other than a group member take the minutes and circulate them before the next agenda is distributed. Record ideas initially in the way the individual states them.

- At the meeting, avoid handing out material not previously reviewed by the group. This may be difficult to adhere to because the nature of Breakthrough Thinking causes new information to appear spontaneously.

- Adhere to time limits and plan future activities based on a timeline.

- Maintain some flexibility so informality is not cut off when group members seem to need it for building openness, creativity, and trust. Discussion can be encouraged if a hot topic arises that affects the project, even if it is outside the agenda or from outside the group. Avoid self-censorship.

- Maintain a positive tone: Ask questions rather than give answers, rephrase ideas positively, offer one or more interpretations, cut off name calling, and establish civility and respect among members, irrespective of differing viewpoints.

- Recognize that each group is different. Some start as a collection of individuals and others as an affiliative group from the same organization. Within these guidelines, each group should develop its own methods of operation.

- If status (organizational level, experience, power, reputation) is highly variable, talk with the high-status people before the meeting to get expressions of willingness for equal treatment of all in the group (advocate first-name basis for everyone; avoid introduction of any status words such as *expert* or *doctor*; avoid criticism of ideas during idea-generation steps; seat people at random or alphabetically, rather than by position or representation).

- Conflicts that arise should be put into a win-win form that aids rather than disrupts the process. Creativity can emerge from conflicting viewpoints. For example, move to larger-level purposes in the array (see Figure 5-4), get an individual to explain another person's position so it is acceptable to the other one, focus on achieving the purpose and the results rather than on defeating a person, give everyone all information to avoid coalition formation, and take a little more time rather than moving directly to voting.

- Be alert for and appropriately responsive to problems and difficulties. Some people may act bored or may attack the chairperson, attendance may be low, time may always seem to run out, the team may lack skills and mutual respect, facilities may not be good, and so on.

- After completing a question, wait at least three seconds, even if there is complete silence, before saying anything. Continued talking or a shorter delay after asking a question greatly minimizes the likelihood of getting responses.
- Be neutral in responding to members' ideas. Avoid saying, "okay," "good," "great idea," "fine," and so on. Instead, try a phrase such as, "Let's expand that idea." The additional questioning and probing stimulates more and better responses because people do not become subconsciously smug and satisfied, as they may with the complimentary words.

Red Flags

Beware of people and organizations that convey information only on a need-to-know basis. In such cases, you're likely to hear one or more of the following warning signals:

- "We'll tell them when the time is right."
- "They wouldn't understand the complexities."
- "They don't have the training to participate in this level of decision making."
- "They'll do what they're told."
- "The key here is the sales job we do on these people."
- "He's an unrealistic dreamer."
- "She's too stuck on details to help."
- "They drive me crazy with questions."
- "Let's just cut to the heart of the matter."
- "It takes less time for us (management) to develop solutions."

The assumptions reflected in such phrases are sure signs that the value of the people design principle has not yet been recognized, much less been put into practice.

Outcomes and Impacts

The advantages of applying Breakthrough Thinking principles extend beyond any particular problem and any team or group effort. Indeed, a "group" is not always needed. The people who are involved in the group can learn to apply Breakthrough Thinking to their own problems. When they do, their ability to perform on the job can improve dramatically, because they can more easily understand why and how the system is put together. This in turn leads to an increase in confidence that enhances their contribution and enthusiasm in all work situations.

People involved in the group also learn how to become effective team members in future assignments. This skill is essential in today's world. As organizations shrink and layers of management are eliminated, an individual's success will not be recognized by promotion to positions that no longer exist, but rather by his or her ability to make lateral moves, to show a solid basis for performance pay increases in whatever position he or she may occupy, and achieve the flexibility elicited by purposes, hierarchies of purposes, solution-after-next options, systems understanding, and particular uniqueness. The personal capacities developed by Breakthrough Thinking do make for good leadership, but they are also critical to developing effective and contributing followers.

These benefits are not guaranteed, but the thinking patterns of the people design principle, applied in conjunction with the other Breakthrough Thinking principles, significantly increase the likelihood that the benefits can be obtained. People will implement solutions and execute procedures that they help to develop. Indeed, with Breakthrough Thinking, what they propose becomes a self-fulfilling prophecy. Thus, your continual interaction with those you have encouraged to get involved makes installation a natural action rather than a sudden change, for you and for them. Some additional benefits result.

- Restrictive, egotistic thinking is minimized. Your pride in authorship is mitigated by the ideas of others who are also trying to solve the present problem while preventing future ones. More people end up with "ownership" of the solution. People primarily considering their own success will be less effective (and less successful) than those who focus on the purposes and assignment.[26]

- Regularly scheduled groups such as quality circles, action teams, department committees, or self-managed work teams become increasingly responsive to needed changes rather than existing for their own sake. Breakthrough Thinking adds to, as well as creates, substantive participation arrangements. Problem-solving or system design groups start to replace layers of bureaucracy, saving time and money while increasing quality.

- The focus on job satisfaction and meaningful accomplishment leads to higher quality and greater productivity in day-to-day work, as well as in special projects. The people design principle enables workers to help design their own participation scheme. People have an opportunity to "work with the heart," to learn and care about the work they do. Change and continual improvement are likely.

- Performance evaluation is handled positively and developmentally. The conventional analysis, one that emphasizes what has been done wrong, is inherently destructive. By contrast, a discussion based on Breakthrough Thinking principles allows the person to arrive at his or her own discovery of what your criticism might be.

- Flexibility in work activities is attained. Knowledge of what's coming next, group activities, and project involvement build a breadth of understanding that lets each individual adapt quickly to changing needs while avoiding past mistakes.

- Workers involved in the design can add many of the details needed to operate a changed system or new solution that has been specified only in broad terms. They can keep improving and moving toward the solution-after-next target. One company found its operators doing quality checks, performing regular machine maintenance, and going to the customer's plant to discuss product and quality problems.

- Psychological and often physiological costs of work are reduced. Robert Karasek and Tores Theorell have demonstrated that stress-related conditions (heart disease, high blood pressure, and so on) are reduced when workers have a high level of involvement and job control. Employee turnover rates are also lower.[27] Some studies suggest that negative (conventional) thinkers have weaker immune systems, contract more infectious diseases, are more likely to suffer depression, and develop more health problems after age 45.[28]

- The time needed to adapt to change is lessened when those who are affected are helping to design and implement the change.

- An awareness of solutions-after-next helps prevent problems. Knowing what is coming keeps people from misperceivng the current change as *the* answer.

- Because the solutions that are installed consider the human factor, they are likely to be successful.

In order to achieve these and other benefits of the people design principle of Breakthrough Thinking, remember always to ask yourself:

- "Have I acted on the certain knowledge that 'two thinking heads are better than one'?"

- "Am I including all the stakeholders or their representatives in defining purposes and generating solutions?"

- "Have I given people on the team enough time to understand the change?"

- "Do they perceive the benefit?"

- "What groups or segments need to know our solution?"

- "Am I including a good mix of minds on the team—experts, doers, and creative thinkers?"

- "What is the best way to communicate information? Small groups, newsletters, memos, staff meetings, audiovisual methods?"

- "Who should communicate our recommendation? Team members? Supervisors? Top management?"

An organization has no presence beyond that of the individuals who bring it to life. You can't create a learning organization. But you can enhance people's capacities to learn and to align their individual activities in creative ways.[29]

Many ideas grow better when they are transplanted into another mind than the one from which they sprang.
No one is as smart as all of us.

NOTES
1. William Henley, "Invictus," *Poems* (New York: Scribner, 1898).

2. Rudyard Kipling, "If," *Kipling's Poems* (Chicago: G.M. Hill, 1899).

3. A. Van de Ven, comments to the National Academy of Engineering/Commission on Behavioral and Social Science and Education Symposium, "Designing for Technological Change: People in the Process" (March 13-14, 1989).

4. Kounosuke Matsushita, "Practical Management Philosophy," *PHP* (1978).

5. "Changing a Factory's Culture Is Not Just Wishful Thinking," *National Research Council News Report* (October 1986).

6. Gerald Ledford, Jr., quoted in Jonathan Weber, "Workplace Democracy More Talk Than Action," *Los Angeles Times* (July 25, 1989).

7. Louis L. Bucciarelli, "An Ethnographic Perspective on Engineering Design," *Design Studies,* Vol. 9, No. 3, (July 1988).

8. James G. Greeno, in "The Science of Learning Math and Science," *MOSAIC,* Vol. 23, No. 2, (Summer 1992).

9. Ibid.

10. Douglas McGregor, *The Human Side of Enterprise* (New York: McGraw-Hill, 1960).

11. D. G. Myers and H. Lamm, "The Polarizing Effect of Group Discussion," *American Scientist,* Vol. 63, No. 3, (May-June 1975).

12. M. Norton, W. C. Bozeman, and G. Nadler, *Student Planned Acquisition of Required Knowledge* (Englewood Cliffs, N.J.: Educational Technology Publishers, 1980).

13. A. Rosenfeld, "Learning to Give Up," *Saturday Review,* (September 3, 1977).

14. Warren Bennis and Burt Nanus, *Leaders: The Strategies of Taking Charge* (New York: Harper & Row, 1985).

15. *Productivity* Brochure, 101 Merritt 7 Corporate Park, Norwalk, Conn. 06851, on "Total Employee Involvement" conference (October 24-26, 1988).

16. Greeno, op. cit.

17. Ford Motor Co., Mission Statement as of August 1989.

18. Paul Hare, *Creativity in Small Groups* (Beverly Hills, Calif.: Sage, 1982).

19. Shoshana Zuboff, *In the Age of the Smart Machine* (New York: Basic Books, 1988).

20. J. L. Adams, *Conceptual Blockbusting* (San Francisco: The San Francisco Press, 1976).

21. Robert Howard, *Brave New Workplace* (New York: Viking, 1986).

22. Kurt Lewin, *Field Theory in Social Science* (New York: Harper & Row, 1951).

23. N. H. McMillan, *Planning for Survival* (Chicago: American Hospital Association, 1978).

24. P. C. Nutt, "The Tactics of Implementation" (Ohio State University, 1985).

25. R. M. Kanter, *Men and Women of the Corporation* (New York: Basic Books, 1977).

26. Robert Karasek and Tores Theorell, *Healthy Work: Stress, Productivity, and the Reconstruction of Working Life* (New York: Basic Books, 1990).

27. R. J. Sternberg and J. Kolligian, Jr., Eds., *Competence Considered* (New Haven: Yale University Press, 1990).

28. M.E.P. Seligman, *Learned Optimism* (New York: A.A. Knopf, 1991).

29. Gareth Morgan, *Imaginization: The Art of Creative Management* (Newbury Park, Calif.: Sage Publications, 1993).

Chapter 10

The Betterment Timeline Principle:
Know When to Improve It

Canada Post Corporation (the Canadian national postal system) undertook a project to design administrative systems that would support a single clothing store for postal personnel, rather than the three stores that were then in operation. A project team of first-line supervisors from various locations across Canada was established.

The design project began with a five-day workshop attended by the project team, which utilized the Breakthrough Thinking process. Their work resulted in a purpose expansion and purpose hierarchy for the project, the selection of a design level (which represented the mission statement for the project), a solution-after-next (which was the vision or target toward which the team designed the immediate solution), and an action plan (a betterment timeline) to implement the immediate solution and solution-after-next systems that the team had selected.

Their immediate solution consisted of a detailed manual system designed to satisfy the needs for a single clothing store. Within three months, this immediate solution was successfully implemented.

The solution-after-next target envisioned by Canada Post was to provide a nationwide retail organization, such as Sears, Bay, or Eaton, with standards for official Canada Post uniforms. The approriate Canada Post employees would then be given credit vouchers to purchase their uniforms directly from the selected firm. This long-range solution eliminated entirely the need for a postal system

clothing warehouse and the associated distribution system. Following its agreed betterment timeline, Canada
Post Corporation is now in the process of implementing
this long-range solution.

"*I*f it ain't broke, don't fix it" and "fix it before it
breaks" are two contradictory mind-sets. The "if it ain't broke"
school is widely accepted. But Breakthrough Thinking takes the
opposite perspective and goes one crucial step further.

The chance of a system's "breaking" can be virtually eliminated by scheduling the installation of further changes based
on the solution-after-next (SAN) and the betterment timeline
principles. When you first implement a solution, plan for
changes. No action is ultimate; solutions exist on a continuum
yielding ever-more gratifying rewards.

"If it ain't broke" is a false rationale invoked far too often.
Politicians love it. They believe it gets them off the hook on a
lot of issues. Managers use it to discourage subordinates who
propose changes before a system becomes a problem. Sometimes the expression is used to explain or justify decision makers' arbitrary priorities; too often the issue is not priorities, but
laziness or smugness.

Executives of General Motors probably used this rationale
in explaining why they did not tinker with an executive com-
pensation plan that paid them huge bonuses even when GM's
market share was decreasing, profit ratios were low, and their
cost of manufacturing cars was the highest in the industry. The
purpose of the plan was to reward performance, and that purpose was not being achieved. The company finally did stop
such bonuses after Ross Perot made it one of the issues that led
to his termination as a company director.

"Fix it *before* it breaks" is the clarion call of the modern
competitive world. Hosts of programs claim they provide a set
of guidelines or organizational structures or techniques or educational sessions that achieve this end—"total quality management," "total employee involvement," *kaizen* (Japanese for
continuous improvement), quality of working life, productivity
improvement, "quality first," and so on.

Organizations such as People Express (an airline operating from 1981 to 1987) practiced participative management to a degree almost unheard of before; they had only three levels of management, everyone was called a manager, jobs were rotated, and so on. This was supposed to increase creativity, efficiency, motivation, and commitment to the customer. The problem with this adoption of participative management, as with the other types of programs, is that it was assumed to be *the* permanent solution of problems. This outlook, oblivious to the SAN principle, ignored the fact that no solution is suitable at all future points in time; thus, redesigns of the area of concern must be scheduled frequently.

Success with any product or system should be viewed with a deliberate betterment perspective, even a complete revision starting with the Breakthrough Thinking process. Success may be your major failure. Ford Motor Company, for example, scored very highly with its Taurus and Sable cars in the mid-1980s. But the company squandered its advantage by forgetting the purposes and possible SANs *of the cars*, instead investing its huge profits elsewhere, not in the betterment of its cars and systems. As a result, by the mid-1990s, Ford had lost a competitive opportunity. Peter Drucker put it well: "The winner in a competitive world economy is going to be the firm that best organizes the systematic abandonment of its own products."[1]

"Fix it before it breaks" is closely allied to the "do it right the first time" perspective of the quality-first movement. One of the few ways of doing a job right is to be sure the equipment, methods, customer specifications, information flows, materials, and other essentials are "fixed" before work is done. Then, paying close attention to the whole system affecting your work is a good way to fix things before they break. This is done in organizations with problem-solving groups or work teams or quality circles for constant improvement to fine-tune an existing system.

Most of the "fix it before it breaks" programs in organizations are quite good at inception. The Leadership Through Quality program at the Xerox Corporation is one of the best we've observed, yet notes for employee training sessions use conventional approaches (gather information, analyze, and so on) within the current job environment, thus building in thinking limitations. The operational aspect of the "fix it before it breaks" aphorism is apparent in your home life when your spouse uses it to chide you to fix the fence before it falls down, change the washer before the faucet leaks too much, put in the storm windows before the snow falls, and plan your vacation before good locations are booked.

An expansion of the "fix it before it breaks" idea is "know when to improve it." Scheduling the next change based on the SAN target provides assurance of successive improvements, as well as a mechanism for incorporating projects that arise and valuable "solutions" people think of on the way. Could People Express have saved itself by scheduling its own betterment to replace the system that it is now obvious should not have continued to exist?

The gypsy moth pest-management system (GMPMS) included a planning committee to schedule built-in changes; determine how to handle problems and problems-in-the-making; assess the utility of people's suggestions; and plan the revised SAN target, as well as the overall recommended GMPMS, every two years. This process is made much easier because the uniqueness, purposes, SAN, systems, limited information collection, and people-design principles guide the process. Other "fix it early" programs using conventional approaches inhibit significant success because of their large data collection requirements and detailed analysis perspectives. Moreover, the improvements that are developed may fix what ought not exist at all (based on what a SAN target would show) or may not focus on important needs, only because someone had a random idea about some part of the system. "Know when to improve it" helps prevent problems before they arise.

Breakthrough Thinking's betterment timeline principle epitomizes the "know when to improve it" concept. We need this principle to keep a good system, healthy company, or effective solution good, healthy, and effective. Why? Because not only do problems beget problems, solutions do too.

The collapse of Soviet communism, with its eruption of ethnic wars, shows why even an ideal solution requires a solution-after-next target to help guide continuing change toward improvement. A formal betterment timeline revises the target every few years and installs often new changes to improve continuously the system or solution that, once it is actually installed, becomes the system currently in place.

Consider the possible impact of the betterment timeline and other principles on congressional legislation during the late 1980s to rescue the failing savings and loan companies. Paul Craig Roberts claims that "legislation to drastically overhaul our financial system is moving from start to finish in three months.... Such a rushed job leaves the bill's architects little time to ponder the possible results [and negative outcomes]. The bill is trying to do too much at once.... The bill's basic goals are sound.... However, the unrealistic deadline for meeting the capital requirements and contradictory provisions could result in an even greater crisis."[2]

Besides the obvious benefits that the purposes, solution-after-next, and systems principles would have brought to the bill, attention to the betterment timeline principle would have spotlighted *needed* changes over time to approach the SAN target. It just does not make sense "to quickly dispose of the issue and 'get the crisis behind us' " when the measure itself is to be in operation for such a long time.[3]

This principle shows another important aspect of Breakthrough Thinking: *A real breakthrough is not only the "big bang" or major-change solution but also the assurance of continual change and improvement in the area of concern.* A solution-after-next target may actually entail exciting and innovative ideas that you think ought to be installed right away. But attempting such a major change, such as installing first computers throughout an office or later trying to network them all, is filled with many pitfalls and obstacles.

With a SAN target in hand, sequential smaller changes contributing to the whole system may be the procedure to follow. Small wins, each as big as possible at one time, provide reassurance of direction and afford optimum visibility of the benefits of the change and its succeeding improvements. Each one is a test or experiment that produces insight toward making the recommended whole system more likely to work well. Moving toward the SAN target represents the journey of a thousand miles that the oriental sage said has to start with a single step.

The learning curve of improvement—the more often you do something, the easier it gets, the less time you spend doing it, and the less it costs to achieve your desired result—is simply the normal, expected outcome of change. Then, however, the next change should propel your system toward the next learning curve. Baseball fans, for example, know well that hitting a series of singles and doubles is often more effective than trying to slug home runs all the time.

Similarly, the successful leaders and problem solvers we studied sought to move as quickly as possible to achieve their ultimate vision (solution-after-next target). Therefore, change was continual through all of their efforts and was intuitively based on the previously stated principles of Breakthrough Thinking, not on some ready-made, pre-existing, generic program of continual improvement that was simply added on.

A Simple Concept

The short and simple definition of the betterment principle is *Prepare a schedule for change and improvement of a solution when you are implementing it*. Identify the elements of the change you are installing that could be changed later to move it toward your solution-after-next target. The new clothes-storage system you are installing in your bedroom does not include all the features of your ideal system. Schedule review in six months to determine if you could possibly use the tie rack or drawer shelving or whatever included in your SAN. Schedule a review in four months of the newly installed hospital patient admission system to determine if the parts of the SAN target are now feasible: Are computer costs lower? Are office layout changes now possible? Can forms be simplified without affecting the rate review procedure?

A second part of the definition is *Prepare a schedule for starting all over again to expand purposes and develop a new solution-after-next target using the other Breakthrough Thinking principles*. Decide that you will solve the problem (actually prevent the future problem) of storing clothes four years from now. Your changed financial circumstances, body size, relationships with a significant other, or interests in clothing styles will affect what the ideal system ought to be to guide you to long-term changes. Decide that you or your department will solve the problem (or prevent future problems) of the hospital patient admission system three years from now. A changed patient mix, insurance plan provisions, data-processing equipment, or health care provider arrangements will mean that the solution-after-next guiding major changes should then be changed.

The two parts of this definition apply to all systems or solutions, whether a bill passed into law, an international agreement, a drug-enforcement scheme, an educational plan, a neighborhood watch program, a printed-wire circuit board manufacturing system, or breakfast preparation in your kitchen. It's obvious that you are not likely to set up such schedules for "simple" or personal systems. What we are saying is that the concept still applies to all systems and is available to help in any system. What's more, the concept will permeate all problem activities to emphasize that no change is permanent whether or not actual schedules for future change are prepared.

How you feel about yourself and your abilities can be improved if you incorporate this principle. If you feel you failed to choose the right goals, or you get impatient with results, or you used a faulty evaluation of ideas, or you failed to celebrate in some way the success you did achieve, the betterment timeline principle (along with the other principles) provides the basics for improving yourself and your perceptions of yourself.

The basic thought behind this principle is *There is no such thing as a solution*. This may come as a shock to you after reading about solutions throughout the book, even in this chapter. After all, if there *is* a problem, there must be *a* solution that makes the problem disappear. We hope, however, that the other principles and the introductory concepts in Part 1 of this book provide eminently sensible explanations for boldly exclaiming that there is no such thing as a solution. The effective people we studied retain their effectiveness by knowing the scenarios for future changes, even as their "big" change is made now.

Such an assertion is better understood when the word *solution* is defined as "a change that includes the seeds of its own later change." This definition stems from the use of the purposes and solution-after-next principles because of their expansion and long-term perspectives. The definition, however, is still applicable even if you claim that you are using a conventional approach. You will just find a smaller variety and level of significance of the "seeds" in the initial change as long as you really apply the betterment timeline principle.

What this definition does is supply a missing ingredient we delayed describing until now because it would not have meant as much earlier. Every time you see the word *solution* anywhere in this book, especially in Chapters 4 through 10, use this definition. (There are several points at which reference is made to *the* solution, as used by conventional problem solvers. They mean the definitive answer that makes the problem disappear, a notion that is far removed from our own definition. The context of a sentence and section provides the distinction about when this definition makes sense.)

Defining a solution as "a change that includes the seeds of its own later change" gives operational meaning to Warren Bennis' statement that "change is the metaphysics of our age."[4] What you install today is only Version 1.0, or the Current Release of your solution. Future "versions" or "releases" are expected—and built-in.

Purposes and Goals of the Betterment Timeline Principle

The betterment timeline principle expands the objectives of the other Breakthrough Thinking principles—to increase significantly the likelihood that a breakthrough solution will occur and be implemented when you are working on a problem—by adding a key ingredient: A breakthrough can occur *over a period of time*, not just at a single point in time.

Two people who had an advanced idea (a breakthrough) about an information system structure were each promoted to executive positions in two different divisions of an organization. One started immediately to promote the idea with his new division. After three months, he found that the people in his division were adamantly opposed to the idea. He had to drop it.

The other executive started immediately to organize a small task force to work on the information-processing "problem." She talked about finding the purposes of the system, identifying the long-term solutions, and considering all aspects of the possible change. Some early changes were made in four months, and more every couple of months thereafter. Within a year, almost her entire original idea was installed.

Is the breakthrough only the idea or the implementation? Which approach represents leadership for change?

Within your overall goal, the betterment timeline principle has several purposes and objectives:

1. *To take advantage of the long-term perspectives of the purposes, solution-after-next, and systems principles*. Everyone knows that a change must often be made quickly, even with the guidance of purposes and targets. But the insights provided by these guides can motivate a continuing change mode as well as ensure that the early change is both as good as it can be and can still be adaptable to further improvement. Through these principles, change becomes your ally. The real benefit of the other two principles is that they provide a concrete base to work with rather than simply the amorphous statement that "change is the only constant."

The key ingredients to knowing when to improve are the SAN and systems matrix specifications that presumably will succeed whatever is being installed today. This knowledge should never be lost. The end sought by the betterment timeline principle is the scheduling of the next modifications toward your SAN target.

2. *To provide a basis for realistic planning*. Far too often, at both corporate and shop-floor levels, planning is an exercise in futility—or worse, in juggling numbers to induce a "good feeling" about the strategic orientation of the participants. Unfortunately, as John F. Lawrence points out: "In theory, [planning] should be a useful exercise. It frequently isn't, because

the strategy setting often takes a back seat to making certain the bottom line comes out according to some preconceived notion of how big the profits should be.... The numbers become more important than the assumptions used to arrive at them.... Five-year planning takes the place of continuous assessment of conditions. In effect, the plan substitutes for the real world."[5]

The path to and timing for specific improvements and investments are clear when purposes and solutions-after-next are the recognized basis for strategic and long-term planning. The future dimension of the system matrix also spells out the configurations to be expected and the research and development required to move toward the next "version" or "release." Planning in this way provides the opportunity to identify, say, the top five technologies to investigate, the specific information to seek, and the prospective skill levels needed.

3. *To ensure the success of a system.* The timeline impetus to review a system for the next change also serves the critical need of paying attention to the previous change. Occasionally, the scheduled new change may not be feasible: the new device is not ready, the cost is still too high, the workload is so heavy that it is not possible to stop the production or offering of the service, or a person with a critical skill is sick. Checking the performance of the activity, even a procedure you may have set up at home (household chores, paying bills, servicing your car), is constructive. In addition to knowing when to change again, success can also mean knowing when to back off or delay a change.

4. *To maintain the push toward being a fast-response organization.* The other principles have focused on the "customer," the larger purposes, the quality and timeliness questions, and the longer-term view of your systems, all of which make an organization able to adapt quickly to new demands of the marketplace. A scheduled change (education for some people to increase their capabilities, lowered level for some decision making, new equipment) can keep you ahead of the competition.

The idea is to help overcome "Bennis's First Law of Academic [or organizational] Pseudodynamics: Routine work drives

out non-routine work and smothers to death all creative planning, all fundamental change...in any institution."[6] The concept
is to create an exciting organization. The betterment timeline
principle provides the framework for identifying just what is
meant by a learning organization. With the future dimensions
and planning characteristics noted above, you and the organization are always learning and improving. For yourself as an individual, the notion is to create an exciting life by viewing
everything in terms of opportunity rather than simply in terms
of the status quo.

5. *To learn continuously in a rapidly changing environment.* A scheduled change, as firm as you think it may be, is a
chance to learn about new developments. It is never too late to
explore options for a change. Reassessment is one way to learn
continuously. For example, have people attending meetings
bring with them at least two ideas about what steps to take
next, what new improvements can be made, or what current
solutions might be replaced with better suggestions. If the
change contemplated is a mistake, it is best to learn about it as
soon as possible and thus get it out of the way—a capacity of
leaders described by Bennis.[7]

Today, even more than in meeting customers' needs, the
main impetus for effective problem solving, planning, and design, is most likely to be found in external factors.

6. *To avoid the "surprise" of a crisis.* Ian Mitroff, director
of the Center for Crisis Management at the University of Southern California, documents how crises, such as product tamper-
ing, oil spills, terrorist attacks, and computer viruses, are
occurring at an increasing rate and are quite likely to have global impact. His call for "total redesign of our institutions...not
only [to] react but prevent these crises from occurring in the
first place"[8] is another reason for keeping alert with scheduled
changes in systems. The redesign he calls for is particularly suitable for a Breakthrough Thinking approach.

There are other more common types of surprises in any
system—breakdown of equipment, late delivery of parts, poor
quality—and they should be considered in the design of the
whole system. The systems principle allows conceivable sur-

prises and their prevention or possible responses to be built into the system, and a scheduled betterment timeline review offers the opportunity to build in more defenses against these and unpredictable shocks. This prepares us to overcome Bennis's Second Law of Academic Pseudodynamics: "Make whatever grand plans you will, you may be sure the unexpected or the trivial will disturb and disrupt them."[9]

There is no foolproof solution to any problem. As H. L. Mencken is said to have put it: "There's an easy solution to every human problem—neat, plausible, and...wrong." Breakthrough Thinking shows that the easy solution is almost always wrong for many reasons: It provides only a patch-up change, omits critical system specifications, ignores the reactions of other people, does not ensure that the system should exist at all, relies on too much data collection, does not provide for built-in change, and so on. Breakthrough Thinking principles ensure that surprises will likely be minimal.

The Need for the Betterment Timeline Principle

Debate in the world, the United States, and each organization about our problems is based on two widely separate foci—the nature and severity of a problem and the great solutions to the problem. Competitiveness is described *ad nauseum* in terms of trade balances, productivity statistics (for example, the ratio of the number of U.S. versus Japanese labor hours to produce a variety of products), quality, product or service innovations, customer satisfaction surveys, and so on. Solutions are broadly stated: fast-response organization, cost reduction, participative hierarchical culture, quality improvement, favorable research and development tax laws, differentiated product or service functions, trade barrier modification, customer service improvement, and so forth.

In the same way, the drug problem is described in reams of data about the average age of users, level of corruption, dollars involved, relationship to foreign policy, tons of illicit drugs, and so forth while solutions entail decriminalization, money for law enforcement, fields of drug plants to be sprayed in foreign countries, U.S. borders to be sealed, massive educational programs, and so on. The design of your home office is inadequate because of the large amount of mail you get, the space needed for your writing, the number of books to store, computer space, insurance policies, supplemental clothing, and so on while the possible solutions include moving to a mini-office, installing clothes arranger closets, file cabinets, book shelves and so on.

Unfortunately, the debate seldom touches on how to get from here to there, even for the problems where a "there" or a SAN target is relatively easy to develop. When the "there" is still an unknown (as in the drug problem), there is even less discussion about the *process* of problem solving—just when the need is the greatest. Surely, the approach followed in the gypsy moth pest-management system (Chapter 5) could be used for such complex problems. At the very least, this approach would result in a system based on the stages of a betterment timeline of continual changes rather than on a definitive SAN.

In all cases, the betterment timeline principle emphasizes defining when additional changes should be made or a new project begun or different people brought in or a transfer of technology attempted. This principle is a critical wrap-up for the other principles, putting their contribution within an appropriate philosophical continuum, yet it is able to stand on its own as a tool in solving and preventing problems. Needs in Society, government, organizations, and your own life can benefit from this principle alone, even if you don't use the others. The needs are significant.

First, the law of entropy, or the tendency of systems to move toward disarray and lack of order, means that energy and effort are needed just to stabilize the system. Thus, to make advances, additional effort and energy are needed, especially if you want to avoid the crisis that occurs when the system is really perturbed (product or service is not produced, quality is not acceptable, an accident occurs). Unfortunately, society rewards problem solvers and not always problem preventers—those who use a betterment timeline to know when and where to apply energy and effort. Yet the need to retain a technological, organizational, and competitive edge and keep your eye on the customer's (or end beneficiary's) requirements should be more than sufficient reason to set up betterment timelines for yourself and your organization.

Second, time tarnishes even the best solutions. Successful products and services need to be probed at regular intervals to determine if betterments are possible and, occasionally, if a new SAN target is desirable. The old SAN target was the advanced system that had been worked out as both the guide for what was installed, as well as the replacement for what was implemented. It too gets tarnished and needs replacement. Everyone tends to take for granted the framework within which they work, not questioning the conditions often enough. Organizational structures need continual adaptation to meet transitions and changes in the marketplace. The performance of a newly installed system or solution usually goes up and then goes down, and the need is to catch the upward performance movement and improve the system so that performance continues to go up rather than becoming negative or reaching crisis status before something is done.

Consider rewriting the scenario for a given SAN target by re-doing the problem-solving project using the Breakthrough Thinking principles and process. Remember the uniqueness principle if a new fad program, technology, or system stimulates you to start over.

Third, there are no easy answers. Regardless of how much technology is available, the quick-fix attitude of many organizations is not really viable. This remains true even though computers are thought to be so "bright." However much we develop computer intelligence, computer data are subject to continual improvement.

Two illustrations show why easy answers aren't readily available. The problems in primary and secondary education, documented in several national reports, produced recommendations that businesses form alliances with school districts. The gap between the two is enormous, and the usual quick-fix business solutions aren't always applicable to the fundamental problems and structure of education.

The second illustration concerns the major attention given to benchmarking, a comparison of one company's performance with that of other leading organizations. The comparison is supposed to lead to changes in the organization designed to close the gap. The problem is you never can get ahead because while you think you are closing the gap, the leader is getting better. And even proponents of benchmarking point out how difficult it is to get all the data. The need for all the Breakthrough Thinking principles—especially the betterment timeline based on purposes and SAN—is clear when reviewing such situations.

Fourth, continual improvement is a concept that today is emphasized to seek better *performance levels in an existing system.* The betterment timeline principle extends the concept to the *specifications of the system itself.* For instance, improving performance levels (reduced errors, increased output, lowered cost per unit) in the operation of a company's purchasing department is a critical need. At the same time, this principle also emphasizes changing the structure of purchasing itself (inputs, outputs, sequence, computers, human agents, and so on, as indicated by the systems principle).

Performance improvement is seeking greater efficiency and timely *corrective* actions, while changing the system specifications is seeking greater effectiveness. Even in seeking performance improvements and corrective actions, the use of Breakthrough Thinking significantly increases the benefits obtained. A survey of forty-eight manufacturing companies with productivity improvement programs found that the economic savings per year with Breakthrough Thinking ideas were over twice the amount developed with conventional problem-solving methods.[10]

This principle makes performance improvement, as well as system design and remodeling, a pleasant chore. Each cost saving, time reduction, or quality improvement assignment within an existing system is a Breakthrough Thinking opportunity, not a data collection or analysis nuisance. The culture and character of an organization, family, social group, or community activity are much different with the betterment timeline principle applied to their modes of operation.

Fifth, the management of technical people and technology is a most critical endeavor in organizations. The amount of technical information and the number of technologists are increasing at great rates. An organization's competitiveness depends on both the availability and effective utilization of technology. The cycle time of projects must be reduced. Organizational systems need to be designed, operated, redesigned, fine-tuned for performance improvement, and redesigned again.

There is no single solution for this problem, as Breakthrough Thinking points out. Looking for the single answer (or even the small group of "solutions") is going to prove elusive and not useful. It is quite conceivable that, in this highly complex area, with so "many individual differences among organizations,"[11] the improvement for tomorrow may be a return to an organizational structure previously put aside for what is in existence today. Technology changes so rapidly that a new system that is "old" can easily be imagined as being more effective now than it was five years ago and thus be a breakthrough for tomorrow. Obviously, this idea applies to all systems or solutions, just as the *process* of the betterment timeline principle is the major need in this extremely critical area.

Using the Betterment Timeline Principle

There are various ways of applying the betterment timeline principle. For you or your organization, the need to set up a system to schedule changes to each project is a problem calling for Breakthrough Thinking. What purposes should it achieve? What ideas can you create to lead to a betterment systems SAN? And so forth.

Another way of using this principle is incorporating the concept into the overall planning process of the organization rather than treating betterment activities project by project. The principle can guide planning for new products and services, new technologies and skills to be available to the organization (the "technology platform"), and new and better systems and processes. The technology platform idea would make certain "that new technologies are well enough understood by [people in the organization] for new product, [service, and process] development to proceed smoothly and quickly."[12] This type of complete planning leads to the consideration of the solution after the solution-after-next as the best type of Breakthrough Thinking.

Responsibility for betterment timeline activities can be delegated and decentralized. Applicable primarily in organizations, someone closer to the system initially installed can be assigned the duties of paying attention to and scheduling the coming changes. This also transfers some of the excitement about forging ahead to other people in the department, section, division, or subsidiary. Delegating is comparable to lowering the levels of operational decision making (quality, maintenance, customer relations for all questions) strongly advocated in today's organizations, yet now for planning and change efforts as well.

Training and educating people about the responsibilities and methods of continual improvement and betterment activities for changed systems are a good supplement to the delegation method. In addition to learning about Breakthrough Thinking, the individuals also have an opportunity to learn new technical content and skills by working on particular projects incorporating the new technology. This may lead to other technical training for employees—an area in which writer and management consultant Tom Peters reports that Germany, Switzerland, and Japan each outspend the United States by three times.[13]

Performance evaluation methods and associated reward structures may need to be revised to emphasize betterment activities, as well as involvement in Breakthrough Thinking projects. Few methods today provide any satisfactory answer to the person who asks, What's in it for me? In addition to identifying the factors to consider, the process must also indicate how performance will be measured, how and how often feedback will be provided to each individual, and how the reward will relate to what each person does.

Another direction for betterment planning is preventive maintenance (PM) for *all* systems or procedures. PM schedules each piece of equipment for regular servicing whether or not it needs it, just as you take your car in for service on a regular time schedule. Under Breakthrough Thinking, all major systems and procedures or problem or functional areas or program (such as Total Quality Management) would be scheduled regularly for a complete review, automatically incorporating any intervening betterment.

This is probably the best way of institutionalizing the precept that you should challenge everything that is being done in the organization—jobs, units, departments, products, services, policies, and so on. Seeking to better any one of these systems will also result in an assessment of whether or not the system itself ought to exist, knowing what we know now. The PM view of betterment doesn't leave to chance what is being challenged; it prevents defensive questions such as, Why are you studying what I'm doing?

The idea is to motivate a cycle of change in the organization, resulting in an exciting company or an exciting life for yourself. The PM perspective is based on cyclic activities, and the betterment cycle is oriented specifically to prevent problems and, in organizations, to keep you ahead of the competition, rather than just trying to catch up.

One specific technique that might be used for time scheduling is an operations wall board, similar to those used for scheduling production or service activities. For a year or more, time in weeks or months is marked off along the top, and the various systems or projects down the left side. Markers or tabs are placed on the project line at the desired time to indicate what then needs to be done. A complete overview of all betterment activities, as well as the timing for each system or project, can thus be seen at a glance.

Another specific technique is the set of tickler folders used to contain material you want to hold for review later. Each folder is marked with a specific date and holds the documentation describing the specific work to be done for betterment of a system. All time-related schemes should also state the time for redevelopment of the SAN and do this repeatedly for the cycle adopted—for instance, every two years for the gypsy moth pest-management system.

Techniques similar to the operations board and tickler files are available for the more sophisticated: time horizon charts, timeline scenarios, and the like. Try the simpler ones first. You can graduate to a more elegant scheme when you find it necessary. Also remember that estimating times for updating any system is subject to the usual errors in time estimation. According to Augustine's twenty-second law: "Any task can be completed in only one-third more time than is currently estimated."[14]

Each time the betterment timeline prompts you to do something about the system, it may be worthwhile to evaluate the performance of the system to date. It should have been subject to continual assessment anyway, but some sort of review would usually be desirable before starting in motion the next change, which may not be workable if the system is not performing as expected. (One version of Murphy's law is appropriate here: It is impossible to make anything foolproof, because fools are so ingenious.)

The criteria or measures of effectiveness were established with the system specifications, and data in terms of these factors should be assessed. But beware: Ed Lawler notes that "the people in the organization tend not to use these 'scientific' data when they evaluate the success or failure of the effort.... In many cases, the evaluations are based on odd pieces of circumstantial data or happenstance."[15]

A manager's predisposition colors his or her interpretation of a remark, say, from a worker who says nothing much is happening. If not in favor of the change, the manager may use the remark to offset any favorable evaluation data. The opposite situation may exist. The life of making betterment changes is not always easy, but evaluation data should in most cases be helpful.

It may be useful to calculate a value-of-change to cost-of-change ratio at that time to determine if the planned change is worthwhile. Performance may be so much better than anticipated that the ratio is smaller than what would have been expected, indicating that a change may not be necessary. Or it could be the opposite, indicating that the change may need to be accelerated.

Last but not least in the methods of using the betterment timeline principle is the believing game. You and others must do everything to exhibit the belief that the betterment change can be made; that the solution-after-next *is* achievable in the planned steps; and that betterment of policies, product, service, quality, productivity, and cost is *always* possible. Commitment to continual change is an outcome of such efforts. Betterment is too important to be left to those who play the doubting game.

As you seek to apply the betterment timeline principle, you'll find it helpful always to ask yourself these questions:

- Do we think there is only one ultimate solution and this is it?
- Do we have plans to "fix it before it breaks?"
- Have we prepared a schedule for initiating change and improvement?
- Does our solution include the seeds of its own later change?
- Have we designed our strategic and financial plans with the needed betterments integrally included?

Betterment: Some Reflections

The idea of betterment has its paradoxical aspects. On the one hand, each of us has a gut feeling that progress is inexorable; it keeps changes occurring in our lives and presents us with more and more options for almost everything. On the other hand, each of us gets very comfortable with the activities we perform or the systems we operate—our home, a sports program, visits to relatives, the standard operating procedure for our job, the rituals of our community. The latter situation is indeed fortunate as a means of establishing a base of life around which the former situation can take place.

Societies in general reflect this ambivalence, expressing a belief in the values of the past while seeking and accepting the benefits of economic and technological growth, and in the worth of humans and life on Earth, while adopting faith in the advances in science and technology brought about by our deliberate search for new knowledge. The desire for a good or better society is a predominant motivation for the human actions incorporated in these beliefs. It is also the motivation for designing and developing systems, for solving and preventing problems. Even the methods of maintaining past values and the worth of humans require problem solving and prevention.

What does better entail? Professor of management and organization Jim O'Toole, executive director of the Leadership Institute at the University of Southern California, uses a four-direction, static compass model to determine what values can help a person to move through life in these turbulent times: liberty, equality, efficiency, and community.[16] Yet no definitive answers can be given because there are nearly six billion people in the world with differing notions of just what this means. On the other hand, society in general has capsuled some dynamic perspectives on the elements of better that can provide background for this principle and the reasons you can use it to your benefit.

One element of better is the desire to achieve greater *effectiveness* or to harness limited natural and human resources to do more. Several terms describe specific ways people refer to this: greater productivity, increased efficiency, higher profits, improved services, improved quality, increased market share, improved relationships with constituencies, improved capacity for producing goods and services. Although this could be an end in itself, inquiry into its result or value reveals another component of better.

The aim of seeking greater effectiveness is a higher *quality of life*. Often, greater effectiveness is associated primarily with the physical goals of life. Overemphasizing them engenders a materialistic attitude, which may be detrimental to other values. Ideas associated with attaining a higher quality of life include peace among nations, a sense of community, a comfortable standard of living, universal health care, efficient transportation and mobility systems, economic security, law and order, national defense, full employment, safe working conditions, availability of leisure time and resources, longevity, a clean environment, and concern for those less fortunate.

Again, a higher quality of life can be an end in itself. But doesn't it result in the enhancement of *human dignity?* Associated with enhancing human dignity and individual liberty for each person are beliefs that each human being has inherently unique capacities and qualities and that each person has many rights and freedoms: a person's private time for a human permits the pursuit of unique activities, each human life has a high value, greater individual justice is available, work can be humanized, individual privacy and freedom of information can be enhanced, and opportunities are available to learn for learning's sake alone.

What is the result of enhancing human dignity? The result is *individual betterment*—each person is equal in having a capacity to grow, each can choose a unique path in life, and each must have the protection of individual rights. As with the other elements of a higher quality of life, the desire for individual betterment is an end in itself. But if we ask, What is its primary result? the answer seems to be to enable societies and individuals to achieve greater effectiveness.

The relationship of the four elements of "better" can be expressed in a circular pattern (see Figure 10-1). Any element could be selected as a starting point. But the continual search for a better condition in the other three elements leads back to the first. This circularity means that concentration on any one affects, intentionally or not, the entire set.

This circular array of elements can be portrayed with time as a third dimension. Assuming an upward improvement scale produces the spiral effect shown schematically in Figure 10-1. A historically accurate spiral would show unevenness of movement along the spiral. Trade-offs and imbalances among the elements are historical facts. The spiral suggests that both the definition and realization of better conditions expand over time. The "amounts" of a single element, human longevity for instance, are greater now than 150 years ago. Progress for any society may in fact be defined as a relatively smooth upward movement along the spiral.

As reasonable as these elements and their dynamic spiral relationships are in explaining why the betterment timeline

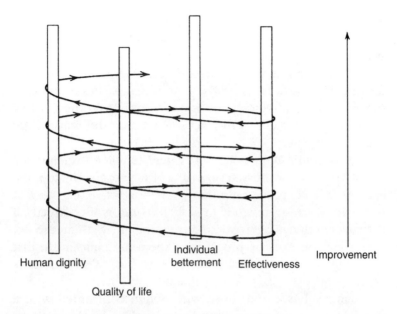

Figure 10-1. The spiral nature of betterment.

principle makes sense, one other ingredient is needed to illuminate why you should set up a schedule for continual change for every project or system you design.

There is no certainty about the longevity of current change. The most basic scientific field of physics has its principle of uncertainty to denote the inability to describe exactly the position and momentum of a particle, nucleus, or molecule. When it comes to systems that humans organize and operate, the principle takes on real meaning—the law of entropy will definitely cause any change in a system to deteriorate quickly, unless effort is expended both to improve the system's performance and to update the system at regular intervals. The timeline is the mechanism for translating our hopes and wishes for betterment into a reality of schedules and effort.

As you seek to apply the betterment timeline principle, always beware of those whose attitude towards systems and solutions is the simplistic perspective, "If it ain't broke, don't fix it."

These are very often the same people who will reject a proposal to improve an existing system or solution simply out of laziness or to protect their own self-interest.

Often they will strive to appear dynamic and forward-looking: "We solved that problem months ago. Let's move on to more productive issues." Or they will insist that the existing confusion about corrective actions is just "the way we do things around here."

Those who ignore the betterment timeline principle are usually people too busy trying to do things right to stop and ask, "Are we doing the right things?" Beware of getting stuck at this point because someone insists, "It *would* work correctly, if only we did things right." Alternatively, they may attempt to dismiss your concerns by proclaiming them insignificant. In that case, you are likely to hear such responses as, "That problem's not a big enough deal to waste time on now."

Finally, beware of those who, when confronted with a problem, dismiss its inherent complexity with the simplistic assertion, "This is a real no-brainer." If that were actually the case, they would no doubt be the perfect people to solve the problem.

Conclusions

This odyssey through the betterment timeline principle ties Breakthrough Thinking to the general goal of society to improve everything we do. This solution is not the last. Yet the journey illuminates the critical need, if we are to be effective, to change the way we go about the effort to improve.

The value of the other Breakthrough Thinking principles becomes clear when you consider how the current methods for improvement are random, chaotic, and lacking in focus without them. It is not sufficient simply to proclaim that change is good or "fix it before it breaks." A whole mind-set of different principles is necessary if betterment is to be as successful as it needs to be.

A continuous cycle of change is an expected outcome of this principle. Successful organizations look to change (effective development of new products and services, refinement of systems before they break, and improvement of problem situations) as their *modus operandi*. To paraphrase Benjamin Franklin, diligence to continual betterment and improvement is the mother of good luck. Kounosuke Matsushita notes:

> Human beings tend to fall into the easy life when we are doing well or everything is going well. We live in the easy life and lose the enthusiasm to seek a new life. I agree that this is quite natural as human psychology. However, by this way of thinking, we cannot follow the dynamic change of our society and our improvement or growth will stop.
>
> So we never forget the attitude that we always try to seek new life and do what we should do by ourselves. As long as we can continue to have such a positive attitude in usual work or daily life, we can see the big change between now and one year ago. Moreover, we can establish new life and new work within five years. The advance and improvement come from this daily continuous effort.
>
> An old saying goes, "A wise man changes his mind three times a day, a fool never—the wise adapt themselves to changed circumstances." Changing his mind three times a day means that he can find a new thing or create new ideas three times a day. A fool cannot change at all because he cannot create anything.[17]

The betterment timeline idea is a key ingredient of efforts to focus on value-adding management (VAM). Integrating many so-called techniques for continual improvment proposed by experts—just-in-time component supply, quality of working life, total employee involvement, total quality control, quality circles—is necessary for every organization. Yet calling in an expert to help with your problem results in proposals limited to his or her own expertise. The betterment timeline brings all these experts together in a synergistic way so that each contributes to the eventual recommendation rather than simply promotes only his or her own answers.

Don't get stuck in the mud of assuming the continued viability of a system installed even a single day ago. "True openness means closedness to all the charms that make us comfortable with the present."[18]

The systems in our lives require the dynamic consistency of change. Constantly seek perfection, even though it can never be attained.

You must build a new model at the peak of the success of the current. Although it may appear to many that organizational rules are being broken, Breakthrough Thinking is a way for you to learn how to break the rules effectively.

Climb on the Happy BUS (Happy *But UnSatisfied*).

NOTES

1. Peter Drucker, as quoted in *Focus,* monthly publication of the National Center for Manufacturing Sciences, Ann Arbor, Michigan, October, 1991.

2. Paul Craig Roberts, "Rushing to Rescue Risks a Panic at S & Ls," *Los Angeles Times,* (April 24, 1989).

3. Ibid.

4. Warren Bennis, *Why Leaders Can't Lead* (San Francisco: Jossey-Bass, 1989).

5. John F. Lawrence, "5-Year Plans Often Ignore the Real World," *Los Angeles Times* (May 11, 1986).

6. Bennis, *Why Leaders Can't Lead,* ibid.

7. Ibid.

8. Ian Mitroff, "In a Modern World, Our Responses Are Way Out of Date," *Los Angeles Times* (March 31, 1989).

9. Bennis, *Why Leaders Can't Lead,* ibid.

10. Gerald Nadler, *The Planning and Design Approach* (New York: John Wiley & Sons, 1981).

11. Albert Rubenstein, *Management Technology in the Decentralized Firm* (New York: John Wiley & Sons, 1989).

12. Gary Reiner, *New York Times,* (March 12, 1989).

13. Tom Peters, *Thriving On Chaos* (New York: Alfred A Knopf, Excel, 1987).

14. Norman Augustine, *Augustine's Laws* (New York: Penguin Books, 1987).

15. Ed Lawler, *High Involvement Management,* (San Francisco: Jossey-Bass, 1986).

16. J. O'Toole, *The Executive's Compass: Business and the Good Society* (New York: Oxford University Press, 1993).

17. Kounosuke Matsushita, *"Practical Management Philosophy,"* PHP (1978).

18. Allan Bloom, *The Closing of the American Mind* (New York: Simon and Schuster, 1987).

Part 3

The Effective You

Chapter 11

The Holistic Process:

Coordinating the Seven Principles

Someone once asked the great symphony conductor Arturo Toscanini, "Why do you change the arrangement when the musical tradition precludes such an interpretaton?" Toscanini replied, "And what is tradition but a collection of bad habits?"

*B*y now, you may well be saying to yourself: "All right, so I've read all these other books, and I still don't succeed like competitors. Now I've read your book too, and I know the seven principles of Breakthrough Thinking. I understand they are the important assumptions I need, the new 'software for my mind.' "I know a 'solution-after-next' when I see one. I know what it means to 'expand purposes.' I know what it means to develop a systems matrix. But now what do I do?

"How do I get started using Breakthrough Thinking? What do I do with an actual problem or opportunity or request?"

It may help to recall that, basically, there are three ways a problem or an opportunity to create or restructure a solution comes to your attention: (1) a serious difficulty in which you need improvement as soon as possible, whether through an incremental change or a major redesign (unsatisfactory existence of a system or situation); (2) a situation that's currently working or a system that is running well enough, yet you want to better it, whether through a radical redesign or a managed evolution (satisfactory existence); and (3) a situation where no solution or system yet exists, but you have a need that you want to accomplish with the lowest cost and time, which is the most effective solution that is likely to be implemented (future existence).

You want to get started using Breakthrough Thinking to find solutions. This involves a different process of reasoning, a new mode of viewing how to proceed, a revised pattern of thinking, a holistic set of steps to guide your use of the Breakthrough Thinking principles. They change your basic assumptions about finding solutions.

Relying now on Breakthrough Thinking, you leave behind the old attitudes and perspectives. From "copy-what-the-Joneses-are-doing," you move to the Breakthrough Thinking principle of uniqueness. From the single problem-as-stated, you now ask about and expand purposes. From *the* once-and-for-all solution, you move now to the concept of a solution-after-next.

Discarding the attitude that "my experience tells me I know how it will work," you move instead to the systems principle, based on the new certainty that seven-eighths of everything can't be seen. From "get all the facts," you move to the principle of limited information collection. From "find out who's at fault," you advance to the principle of people design. Finally, dispelling the misguided belief that "once we solve the problem, it will go away," you act upon a new appreciation for the necessity of a betterment timeline.

The question then becomes, What process will I now change to that matches and utilizes my new basic assumptions, the seven principles of Breakthrough Thinking? We certainly want to dispense with the conventional problem-solving, planning, design, and solution-finding process. We want to get away from gathering data, building models of what already exists, finding the model's difficulties, comparing difficulties to what others have done, generating ideas about eliminating the difficulties, setting up a solution, selling the solution, and installing the solution.

To answer these questions of process, you must seek guidance from the Breakthrough Thinking principles themselves.

The Principles in Review

In applying the principles of Breakthrough Thinking you have learned, the first thing to remember is that problem solving is synergistic: The whole is greater than the sum of its parts. Therefore, trying to apply one principle at a time or one after another in a preset order may not be the best way to deal effectively with the problem.

Current trends in holistic medicine, for example, focus on the total interactions of mental and bodily functions rather than on specific organs, as in traditional medical professional specialties. In Breakthrough Thinking, a holistic process sets up a dialectic interchange among the principles, the process, and you. If adverse developments occur during the process, you will have an instinctive sense of what steps to fall back on.

The holistic approach has been shown to be effective. On the basis of a 25-year longitudinal study of his students at the Massachusetts Institute of Technology, psychiatry professor Benson Snyder concluded that there exist two distinct modes of thinking, which he identified as "numeracy" (Mode One) and "literacy" (Mode Two). He further discovered that professional and personal creativity was dramatically associated with the use of both modes of thinking.

Snyder concluded that "Mode One alone is not sufficient for dealing with the ambiguity and complexity of the human condition." He noted that Albert Einstein liked to underscore this micro–macro partnership in effective thinking with a remark from Sir George Pickering that he chalked on the blackboard in his office at the Institute for Advanced Studies at Princeton: "Not everything that counts can be counted, and not everything that can be counted counts."[1]

Stanford University educational psychologist James G. Greeno has sought to do for cognitive theory what Einstein's theory of relativity did for physics. Greeno maintains that knowledge and thinking are also relative, dependent upon a person's frame of reference. Thus, cognition is "situated," learning is a function of the thinker's personal and social epistemologies, and conceptual competence requires a context in which children (or adults learning to "think anew") are free to elaborate and reorganize their knowledge and understanding, rather than simply applying and acquiring existing cognitive structures and procedures.

Greeno asserts that creativity occurs naturally when a person's situation is restructured. Changes in the environment, he argues, can cause a reorganization of "conceptual structures." He states that creativity involves reorganizing the connection a person has with his or her situation, rather than what occurs within the person's mind. The situation with which one's connections are reorganized can be physical, social, or conceptual.[2]

This chapter takes a coordinated view of the seven principles of Breakthrough Thinking so you can deal with your situation as a whole.

It incorporates the research of Snyder, which shows that effective people combine all modes of reasoning, and that of Greeno, which shows that a broad frame of reference is essential. If you use all seven principles of Breakthrough Thinking at the same time, adopting the attitude of the "believing game," your approach to problem solving will be similarly holistic.

The effective people we studied had a good sense of how to expand their thinking before integrating the responses they received; how to diverge and converge in their thinking several times while following their solution finding process; and how to practice the believing game most of the time and yet know when they had arrived at the appropriate, effective moment to engage in the doubting game. Along with the available research showing how effective thinking differs from conventional thinking, a review of the Breakthrough Thinking principles will show how those principles help shape the process.

Fundamental to your success is the uniqueness principle— a constant awareness that at the beginning of the problem solving process, *each and every problem is unique.* Each part of a project is unique. Each activity is unique. Each problem may require a unique solution. Consequently, "me-too" solutions almost always fail, wherever and whenever they are applied.

Adapting an existing solution to a current problem can cost two to three times as much as starting from scratch with your own unique solution. If each problem is not treated initially as a unique entity, time is bound to be lost, money squandered, and competitiveness diminished.

Even if a particular solution worked before, there is no guarantee that it will fit a new problem. If nothing else appears different, the people and the time are now different. Your search for each new solution must begin with opening wide the opportunities, which can be seen only if, considering the uniqueness of people and of time, you drive out preconceived notions and mistaken assumptions.

Moreover, every step in a project, every activity in which you engage, every discussion you have, every meeting you attend, is unique. This means that the Breakthrough Thinking principles and process can prove useful every time.

Breakthrough Thinking is an *organized and flexible thinking process,* not a rare and random moment of revelation. Although it encourages and sometimes does include flashes of insight and intuitive understanding, the process itself provides a way of applying the seven specific principles in a coordinated and holistic way.

Furthermore, although one or another of the seven principles may seem more important to you at a given moment in the problem solving process for a particular situation (this will sometimes be true, as later illustrations will show), you must remember to keep all of the seven principles available all of the time throughout the process.

First among equals, however, is the purposes principle. This principle especially must be applied.

At each step along the way to your solution, remember to ask yourself, What is the *purpose* of working on this problem? What are we trying to accomplish with this information? What are we trying to do with the system matrix? What *purposes* would this group of people serve on the task force?

Your problem will be solved with the many small decisions that comprise the synergistic thinking process. Just as the smallest gear in a machine must be designed in terms of the purpose of the larger engine that it serves, each decision you reach in the process of solving your problem must be based on the correct premise: the expanded *purposes* of your working on the problem.

Almost equally significant is the solution-after-next principle. Having in mind a target solution for the future gives direction to near-term solutions and infuses them with larger purposes.

Stimulate your creativity by allowing for several alternative solutions and keeping them viable for as long as possible. You have to apply pressure so that you focus on the search for new ideas, not on the acceptance of the first solution that comes along.

By avoiding premature closure of the problem, you'll be more likely to identify the information that will be critical to achieving the optimal breakthrough solution. Also, when you pursue the solution-after-next rather than simply asking what's wrong with the current solution, more people at all levels are likely to get involved.

An ideal solution provides a completely fresh start to what once was a problematic situation. Focusing on your *challenge*-after-next directs your efforts toward solutions that remain valuable long into the future, solutions that may even resolve some of tomorrow's problems before they arise.

According to the systems principle, seven-eighths of everything cannot be seen. Your problem is not necessarily so immense as to be beyond your ability to solve effectively. It is, however, part of a *system* of problems that includes related issues and challenges that may or may not affect you. You have to be constantly aware of this larger context, or you might find that your solution is incomplete or only temporary.

There is a difference, however, between recognizing complex interrelations and being overwhelmed at the outset by the details of your problem. The system matrix puts order into what used to be a morass of details.

Without some criteria for limiting your investigation, you'll fall victim to information overload. Excessive data gathering may make you an expert in the problem area, but knowing too much about it probably will prevent you from seeing some excellent alternatives.

Most people assume that, to solve a problem, they first must gather all the relevant data, call in an expert in the *problem* area, or themselves become an expert in the problem. According to the limited information collection principle, however, what is really relevant are the data that pertain to a *solution* for the right purpose, not those data that pertain to the problem itself. Examining the purposes of information collection often leads to the problem's turning into an opportunity for accomplishing significant changes.

It is possible to know too much about a problem. It then becomes too easy to dwell on "facts" about what's wrong with the current situation rather than first to take an objective look at information on what *should be* and then to get the experts on your solution.

People who have a stake in the problem area must feel responsible for dealing effectively with the solution and its continuing changes. If these people don't participate in developing the solution, they are not likely to welcome the changes necessary to bring it about. Breakthrough Thinking gives people a positive way to get involved. People enjoy defining purposes and expansion of purposes, finding ideal systems and target solutions, and designing systems definition to assure effective interrelationships. Most people do not like to gather information about how bad the problem is.

According to the people design principle, those who will carry out and use the solution can thus be intimately and continuously involved in developing it. In designing for other people, you should include only the *critical* details in your solution. You have to allow some flexibility to the people who must implement your solution.

The betterment timeline principle reminds us not only to fix it before it breaks but also to know when to improve it. Like everything else in the physical universe, human beings—and human solutions—are subject to entropy.

Eventually, everything runs down or wears out. As living organisms, however, we enjoy relatively long life-spans because the human body renews itself continually. Similarly, the only way to preserve the vitality of our solutions is to build in and then monitor a program of continual change. In effect, rather than merely seeking solutions, Breakthrough Thinking seeks changes that include the built-in seeds of future changes.

The features revealed by this review can now be put together into a set of core steps for any problem, opportunity, assignment, part, or phase of any project, request for resources, planning assignment, design requirement, interaction with anyone else, and any "standard" or repetitive activity.

Despite the necessity of intuition in its application—an instinct learned and developed best through experiencing many different solution-finding projects—Breakthrough Thinking generally follows this *strategic thinking* pattern or core process[3] to define the opportunity for you.

The Breakthrough Thinking Process: Core Steps

1. Identify many purposes for the system or area of concern, whether a problem, opportunity, program, project, or activity.

2. Expand the purposes from the smallest in scope to the largest, placing them in a hierarchy or array, then select the focus purpose(s) and related measures of purpose accomplishment.

3. Generate many solution-after-next and ideal system ideas to achieve the selected focus purpose(s) and larger purposes, then group these ideas into major alternative options.

4. Assess these options to determine your solution-after-next target (for regularity conditions).

5. Develop the recommended solution that stays close to the target (incorporating irregular conditions).

6. Detail the recommended solution to ensure it will work.

7. Design the installation and transition plan.

8. Install your solution.

9. Set up dates for betterment to attain larger purposes and more parts of the target (and to redesign the target).

Notice how various principles play a more prominent role in some of the steps than in others. Uniqueness and purposes are useful in almost every step; solution-after-next is the leader in steps 3, 4, and 5; systems guide steps 6 and 7 (with early use in 4 and 5); betterment timeline appears in step 9; and limited information collection and people design work in most of the steps.

In steps 1 through 4 or 5, the believing game predominates. The doubting game takes over in steps 5 and 6. Divergence is the thinking mode in steps 1 and 3; convergence in steps 2 and 5.

In other words, these core steps embody most if not all of the concepts that various people use to describe ways of thinking, yet they do so in a prescriptive format that provides guidance in action, not mere exhortation. That is why Breakthrough Thinking is rightly called "full-spectrum creativity."

These core steps of "expantegration" provide guidance through the huge array of decisions and risks entailed in any type of solution-finding or planning effort. The nine steps can be expanded to 24, with many sub-steps for use by the professional Breakthrough Thinking facilitator, as described in the book *Breakthrough Thinking in Total Quality Management.*

It is not necessary, however, to use even all nine steps listed above for the many other activities and situations where Breakthrough Thinking is needed. So, here are three basic words to keep in mind. Along with the seven principles, they summarize the essence of the Breakthrough Thinking process:

Purposes >>>>>>>>> **Target** >>>>>>>> **Results**

With the seven principles of Breakthrough Thinking, these three key words will equip you to tackle your world, its problems, and its opportunities with Breakthrough Thinking. P > T > R is certainly a short and sweet rule of thumb, but we hope you will also acquire insight into what these three guiding lights entail by learning about some of the more detailed steps of Breakthrough Thinking. That background is sure to help you, even as you apply this most simple, basic Breakthrough Thinking process.

At the least, P > T > R is a reminder of the "full-spectrum creativity" of Breakthrough Thinking. Purposes and their expansion provide the chance to be creative in finding the real problem to address. Targets offer the frame of reference with which to generate creative solutions. Results give you the mechanisms for creatively staying as close as possible to your target while achieving the implementation of changes.

The PTR Process Used Everywhere

One of our major reasons for writing this second edition was the feedback we received about the wide range of areas where people applied Breakthrough Thinking and found it very useful. Psychologists had shown their patients how to use Breakthrough Thinkjng for solving personal problems. Strategic planners used it to develop the process for strategic planning in a company. A board of directors designed its own total quality management program on the basis of the Breakthrough Thinking principles and process. Reengineering project directors developed project work programs with Breakthrough Thinking, incorporating the core process steps as the basis for the project time schedule. The president and other officers of a company based their efforts to change the organizational culture from regulatory to entrepreneurial. Breakthrough Thinking managers handled requests for expenditures, and executives set up performance expectancies and accomplished performance evaluations with each of their direct reports. Parents dealt with children in developing specific study plans and educational programs. We could go on and on.

All of these situations seek to create or restructure a system or solution—the realm of Breakthrough Thinking. This demonstrates that the principles and process embodied in Breakthrough Thinking's "software for your mind" should be in constant use. They show you what information needs to be collected; teach you to address purposes, not what already exists; seek solutions-after-next, not simply a patch-up or interim band-aid; specify only those elements and dimensions that need to be specified, not pursue the accuracy of all data; identify the areas where risk assessments are needed, not apply wholesale generalizations about the behavior of people and technology.

For example, as you begin using Breakthrough Thinking, ask yourself the *purpose* of getting started on a particular project or problem situation. Just as we did to overcome initial obstacles in the case of the gypsy moth pest-management system, you might begin simply by planning the planning system.

When hospital administrators in the 33-member Hospital Council of the Greater Milwaukee Area decided to do something about their difficult nurse-shortage problem, they set up a project on nurse utilization (see Chapter 5). The Council agreed that no real benefits had been obtained from the many existing nurse-utilization studies. The question of how to get started had to be resolved.

The group members asked themselves to define the purposes of a nurse-utilization study. As a result, the group changed the focus of the project from how nurses are utilized to a system for care of patients. It was agreed that if effective systems to serve patient needs were implemented, nurses would be utilized correctly. Getting started meant getting the right *purpose for the project* and setting up the planning system to achieve it. (When the purpose of the system to provide needed nursing care to patients was found from that expansion, it turned out to be "to observe, interpret, and regulate patients' physical and sociopsychological functions to meet their needs.")

The idea of process introduces the dimension of time. To plan, design, or solve problems means that, as time goes on, certain things must be done in some order. These steps imply both a sequence of activities and a progression toward some result. The principles of Breakthrough Thinking form the assumptions by which you are guided in taking these steps.

Thus, the principle that obviously occurs repeatedly is people design: Which people should be involved at each step?

Who are the stakeholders in the situation? Who are the decision makers? The opinion leaders? The sources of specialized knowledge, the customers, the suppliers, the operators of the system, the government actors or regulators? And so on.

Even though you identify all the possible stakeholders, do they all have to be involved all of the time? When they are involved, *what purpose is to be served?* When should they be involved? How should they be involved—in a project team, on-call as needed, interviewed, through a computer decision-support system? How long will it take for each person to accomplish his or her participation?

We can provide no answers to these questions, at least no answers that will fit all situations. (True to the uniqueness principle, you should have said this to yourself when we first began to pose the questions.) Instead, what we have developed for ourselves and our colleagues is a Breakthrough Thinking Process Worksheet (Figure 11-1). It summarizes the questions we've raised and places the steps in a time-oriented perspective to guide you as you set up your unique planning, design, re-engineering, improvement, or solution-finding effort.

The worksheet could also be used to solve a personal problem—laying out a kitchen, developing a personal career plan, writing a book report, arranging a community homeowners meeting, working on a voters' petition drive, settling an argument with a neighbor—though to use it that way might well be overkill. Nevertheless, it should still serve you as guide, even in solving less complex problems.

The five boxes in the upper left corner of the worksheet remind you that the core steps of the Breakthrough Thinking process can be used over and over again for various types of efforts and each project phase or step. Just check one of the boxes to keep you focused on what project or problem that specific worksheet addresses. Then start to work on both the stakeholders for each step or group of steps (in P>T>R) and the purposes of their involvement at that step. The last two columns—how and when to involve stakeholders—should be considered next; and they could affect the first two columns. Some people may not be available when desired, or the distances involved may require a different type of step arrangement.

Table 11-1. Breakthrough Thinking Process Worksheet

Core Steps	Who Needs To Be Involved	Purpose of Involvement	How To Involve	When To Involve
Use Core Steps for each need and opportunity ❑ To set up a program ❑ To do a project ❑ To solve a problem ❑ To do planning ❑ To perform an activity or any step or phase	Stakeholder Analysis	Generate ideas, communicate, make decisions, gain approval, get expert opinions	Presentation, one-on-one interview, brainstorm, survey, computer group support	Dates, milestones

P	1. Identify Many Purposes 2. Develop Hierarchy, Select Focus Purpose(s) and Related Measures of Purpose Accomplishment	
T	3. Generate Many Ideal and Solution-After-Next Ideas and Group These in Major Options 4. Assess Options to Determine SAN Target 5. Develop Recommended Solution	
R	6. Detail the Recommendation to Assure Workability 7. Design the Installation and Transition Plan 8. Install the Solution/System 9. Set up Betterment Date for Solution and for SAN Target	

At the start, most worksheets become fairly detailed, especially the first two or three steps of the core process. The rest of the worksheet steps may be sketched out because many changes are typically made in later steps based on what results are obtained in the first two or three. For example, the loading-dock problem, the nurse-utilization project, and the effort to double factory capacity all illustrate why this occurs: The project changed so dramatically after step 2—when the purpose to be achieved was selected—that it would have been a waste of time to pre-judge what people and methods might be needed for the later steps.

The identification of stakeholders at various steps is a main reason that Breakthrough Thinking is able to make it very likely that your solution will be implemented. In addition to involving the stakeholders throughout a project, their participation in determining purposes, solutions-after-next, and even systems gives them a positive perspective to support what they developed, not simply defend what already exists.

Practice Makes Perfect

The core set of steps or actions *guides* you in applying Breakthrough Thinking to your particular problem. Although you must keep in mind the unique nature of your problem, the purposes of its solution, and the need to seek the largest feasible solution at any stage of planning and problem solution, there is more than science to Breakthrough Thinking; there is art.

The art of solving and preventing problems is based on making a series of minute decisions, each one affecting all the others, regardless of how insignificant you may consider any particular decision. The uniqueness and purposes principles must be the start of each point of making decisions—what to name the project, how to arrange the room for a meeting, how to shape the statement about which you want to elicit ideas from others, what criteria to use for selecting a purpose level, which technique to use in evaluating alternative criteria, and so on.

The buildup of purposes and solutions-after-next from previous decisions, in whatever order they may have been made, is background influencing the current point of decision. At each point, the Breakthrough Thinking principles are used over and over again to significantly increase the likelihood that the result of your countless decisions will be a breakthrough.

A key feature of the Breakthrough Thinking process is its ability to have you identify many options at several points— purposes and their various hierarchies, solutions-after-next, and options assessment—and to keep those options open as long as possible. Identifying them makes you more knowledgeable about a variety of sources of potential action. Keeping them open as long as possible allows you to find what might make an innovative idea actually work.

Not only must you keep all the principles in mind at all times, you must also come to know instinctively *which princi- ples to concentrate on when*. Indeed, this is essential to the successful application of the Breakthrough Thinking principles. In this regard, all of us are on our own. There is only one guide now: Practice makes perfect.

When we first consult with a prospective client, we don't immediately speak from a position of intellectual certainty. Even though we *know* the principles of Breakthrough Thinking inside out, even though we *know* that following the principles greatly increases the likelihood of finding the best possible solu- tion to any and all problems, we never begin by saying: "The first thing we're going to do is define the purpose of your pro- ject. The next thing we're going to do is…" If we talked like that, we'd get kicked out more often than not.

For example, a Breakthrough Thinker worked with a col- lege of engineering at a large public university to help the facul- ty develop the engineering curriculum for use ten years in the future. He worked with the dean and steering committee in de- veloping a schedule of activities. Since the committee felt the faculty would be offended if someone assumed they didn't know the purposes of an engineering curriculum, developing a "curriculum-after-next" or ideal curriculum options became the first part of the project.

In the first steering committee meeting, many ideas were developed. By the second meeting, however, the faculty members themselves said that they needed to define their purposes before proceeding.

The availability of the core steps of the Breakthrough Thinking process allows you to know what needs to be done when and in what general order, not simply resort to the lame "get more information" instinct of the conventional approach.

Sometimes, in a particular project, we may appear to violate a given principle, especially the limited information collection principle. For example, we want our clients to know if the project is successful when the work is ending. If they are not able to measure the impacts and results because there are no good data at the beginning (most organizations do have more than enough), then we suggest that the initial purpose to achieve is to obtain reasonable indicators of the key factors which will signify the project's success. In other cases, such as the nurse-utilization project or the factory expansion project, purposes need to expand before the needed factors or measures of purpose accomplishment can be identified.

Even knowing all the principles inside out—as we do, and as we hope by now you do as well—it is far more important at the initial stage to be sensitive to, react to, and interact with the client—whether the "client" is yourself, another individual, or a group—to search for what he or she is trying to get accomplished.

We are aware at the beginning—and at all points—of the purposes principle, but more important when starting is the people design principle, as already illustrated in Figure 11-1, the Breakthrough Thinking process worksheet. More than once, we've said to ourselves, "This guy's really got to let loose about all the bad things that are going on. All the problems that he has. If we try to stop him now, it'll be the worst thing in the world."

So if the corporation president (or spouse) is ranting and raving about how bad this or that department is performing (how bad the relationship is going), we recommend that you let him or her go right on complaining for a while. After years of experience, we know we can't just stop people at this point and say: "Wait a minute, we (and you) don't need to know this. Start with the purpose of solving your problem, and with the purpose of the problem area." Instead, just sit there and listen. Maybe they need the catharsis.

On the other hand, sometimes we go into an initial meeting, and within the first three minutes, the client says: "We've got these data and they clearly demonstrate performance failure in our marketing division. We're not achieving sufficient penetration of the market, and we're paying too much overtime. So what do you think we should do?" In this case, experience tells us we must respond immediately with an insistence on the purposes principle for the marketing system or, most likely, the planning structure to put in place to work on the marketing system project.

As we have said, Breakthrough Thinking is not a rigidly ordered process. Indeed, it requires an intuition that can generally be learned and developed best only through repeated application of the principles and process in a variety of different projects.

For example, arranging for the resources needed in step 6 may have to be done for a change effort even before steps 2 and 3 have been "completed." If so, you or the manager are recognizing a framework for a likely solution and deciding to take somewhat risky action to get the resources and framework started before the project is "finished." Conversely, knowing about underutilized resources already available in the organization, resources obtained in some cases to be prepared for strategic opportunism,[4] will probably affect the identification of purposes and solution ideas for a project.

In addition, many efforts to make significant change—reengineering, changing organizational cultures, developing new products, investing in economically disadvantaged sections of cities—are dynamic, iterative, and large-scale projects. They involve many stakeholders, are enmeshed in a variety of criteria, and are usually poorly structured. In such cases especially, flexibility in using the Breakthrough Thinking process is the only way to handle the heavy flow of activities and negotiations required to obtain group decisions and the most effective results.

Applying the principles of Breakthrough Thinking holistically, we can bridge the gap between our values and needs and the bodies of human knowledge and technologies available to us. As we develop new knowledge and express new needs and aspirations, the gap will always remain. Indeed, the gap is what compels us to progress as a species. The key to human happiness is, in large measure, success in traversing this gap.

That individuals, organizations, and countries are not doing very well at converting knowledge to practice is well known in the United States. MIT economist Lester Thurow notes that the advances in technology found in the United States have not prevented it from lagging behind in devising methods of using the technology.[5]

Thurow uses another frame of reference[6] to show how important *your role* has now become in turning around this situation. He points out that, in the past, the economic leadership of a given country could be credited to one or two of four basic factors—the availability of natural resources, capital markets, technology, or people skills.

Britain was the economic leader until the early 1900s because of its natural resources and capital financing. The United States led through the 1970s because of resources and people skills. From the 1980s on, Japan has led, largely because of people skills. However, now and in the future, the first three factors have become available to anyone, anywhere in the world, almost instantaneously. Thus, the singular factor for differentiation in the future will be people skills—*you.*

Consequently, in order to succeed, we will all need to go beyond our own particular technology and interpersonal abilities. We will need to understand how to think creatively, solve problems, see things in our mind's eye, learn, adopt a systems point of view, and make effective decisions. In other words, each of us must now learn to become a Breakthrough Thinker.

Today, the task of creating or restructuring solutions or systems is to efficiently develop effective and innovative recommendations that can be implemented to better cross the gap. Knowing how to cross the gap—to use knowledge—is power. The *how* of Breakthrough Thinking is the invisible power now available to each of us.

Motivation to Succeed

It's not wishful thinking to change your way of thinking. In fact, essential to the success of Breakthrough Thinking is the winning attitude that it develops in those who practice it. The more you do it, the better you get. The more you do it, the more likely you are to develop the winning attitude that is essential not only to your own success but also to the further development of the Breakthrough Thinking process.

As Breakthrough Thinkers, we aim to change the way that people everywhere go about finding solutions. We aim to change the corporate and organizational cultures that are based on outmoded, unsuccessful ways of thinking. We aim as well to change our personal problem solving attitudes and outlooks, and so to change our lives.

If you're a corporate manager, at this point you probably need little more motivation than to look at your figures for market share and to examine your bottom line. You *have* to *succeed.* You *have to make a profit.* You *have to outperform* your competition. If you do not, you won't have many more opportunities.

As individuals, we may have a wide range of interests and motivations. Some people seek money as an indicator of success—a greedy characteristic often ascribed to Wall Street financiers. Others seek satisfaction from helping their fellow human beings. Most of us have the more modest goals of survival, operation and supervision, planning and design, research, evaluation, learning, personal satisfaction, and the four goals of society: greater effectiveness, higher quality of life, enhanced human dignity, individual betterment. Yet all such motivations need to be converted to effective processes if our real purposes are to be accomplished, the purposes for which our motivations are measures of success.

But as either individual citizens or corporate executives, we must frequently ask a question that relates to the source of problems to solve or prevent: How do you identify what you should start looking at as a potential Breakthrough Thinking effort? Some specific factors may cause you to sense that an opportunity is available or a problem needs to be solved or prevented and where you can begin to apply the principles of Breakthrough Thinking (see Table 11-2).

Pick one or two of the opportunities or problems that Table 11-2 stimulates and get started. Although some time might be spent on identifying the problems, stop when you have a few and select a couple of them.

If you're more concerned with problems in your personal than in your business or professional life, your motivation may come in the form of a painful loss—a failure so difficult to bear, an outcome so frightening to contemplate—that you will be motivated to make the difficult but ultimately less painful changes that will eventually lead to your success.

Planning a vacation, designing your house, or developing your educational plans are all opportunities that may start your application of Breakthrough Thinking. Consider, for example, a personal problem as necessary and as difficult as quitting smoking or going on a diet. The doctor tells you that you must quit smoking or that you're too heavy or that your cholesterol count is too high. The way to solve your problem and prevent its recurrence is not simply to will yourself to quit smoking, lose weight, or lower your cholesterol intake. First, ask yourself the purpose of these acts.

For example, the purpose of eating chocolate is to satisfy your taste for chocolate. The purpose for that is to satisfy your sweet tooth. What's the purpose of satisfying that sweet tooth? Pleasure. What's the purpose of pleasure? To enjoy life. Soon you realize that you can't enjoy life at all if you're dead. And soon after that, you'll find it relatively easy to dispense with your once beloved chocolate.

In this way, you can begin to compare levels of purpose. You may thoroughly enjoy smoking and drinking, eating the "wrong" foods such as chocolate, and not exercising. Your purpose in these pursuits may be pure and simple pleasure. But what is the purpose of pleasure?

When you realize that the pursuit of certain pleasures puts your life itself at risk, life becomes a greater purpose than pleasure—at least the pleasures of tobacco, food, drink, chocolate, and lethargy. At that point, your decisions to quit smoking, minimize drinking, go on a diet, and exercise become more than an exercise of willpower; they become conscious purpos-

Table 11-2. Sensing opportunities or problems to which you might apply Breakthrough Thinking.

Human Perceptions and Feelings

Intuition
Mood
Values and ethics
Perceived gaps between present and desired circumstances
A sense of inequalities
A sensitivity to needs
Dissatisfactions (e.g., balance work and outside life)
Curiosity
Questioning your own role in a system
A drive to search for areas of change
Expectations
Critical event(s) or unexpected happening(s)
Exploration of current assumptions
Motivation to be a leader
A desire to be up-to-date
A desire for benefits (money, time, etc.)
Tension
Shame/humiliation
Internal pressures, perplexity, discomfort
Frustrations
The sense of a vicious circle

Signals and Stimuli

Consumer, user, or process needs or complaints
Large budget variance
Activity or department with largest budget allocation
Lack of priorities
Inefficient operations or procedures
Needs assessment
A worrisome situation (e.g., interdepartment strife)
Unresolved conflict or conflicts
Barriers and intentions
Fad program follows fad program
Scouting and reconnaissance
A crisis or incongruity
Poor index indicator (productivity, quality, market share, delivery times—someone tells you to reduce costs by 25% or time by 30%, etc.)

Table 11-2. (continued)   Sensing opportunities or problems to which you might apply Breakthrough Thinking

---

Signals and Stimuli

Unreachable value, objective, or goal
A challenge or the unexpected
Demographics
Someone insists that a "constraint" is fixed
Competitor's lower prices or higher quality
Yearly planning cycle
Another phase in the product life cycle
Noisy systems (difficulties, poor performance,
    bottlenecks in a program such as Total Quality Management)
Quiet systems (good results but good potential for betterment)
Nonexistent systems or unmet needs
Informal group discussions
Tapping existing information sources
Organizational continuity (growth, acquisition, divestiture, communi-
    cations, products services, performance, financing, structure, peo-
    ple developer)
Industry and market arrangements

---

es of which you approve, purposes even more supportive of your essential values than your previous pursuit of self-destructive pleasures. The solutions to your problems become easier to implement and last longer.

In the case of a close "chocoholic" colleague, the comparison between purposes was precisely that dramatic. His older brother had to undergo open-heart surgery. He warned our colleague that he had learned that almost all their relatives had suffered some form of heart trouble.

These facts compelled our friend to compare the purpose of staying healthy and alive to the purpose of enjoying chocolate. Comparing the pleasures and comforts of chocolate (even Godiva chocolates) with the pain and perils of open-heart surgery soon led him to forswear the most delectable bon-bon in favor of an even more enjoyable and reassuring strong heartbeat.

Though often difficult, the solution of our personal problems is usually less complex than the solution of problems in our business, professional, and public lives. In these realms, our lives are affected not only by our own beliefs actions (which by now include Breakthrough Thinking), and values, but they are also affected by our peers, our managers or executives, our own responsibilities for the work of others, as well as by external parties that influence us directly (government relations, family pressures).

For example, it's one thing to know you must focus on purposes. It's another thing entirely to be confronted with the demands of a recalcitrant superior who is less than receptive to "new-fangled ideas."

You want to get started with Breakthough Thinking, but you need to know what to do when your manager pounds on the table and proclaims: "I don't give a damn what book you read. All I know or care about is that the billing department overtime is up, costs are high, quality is low, and our mailings are always late.

"Don't waste my time with fancy theories. I want you to go out there and get the facts on that department. Gather all the information. I want to subdivide this problem into its component parts and analyze the data you come up with. That's the only way that I can make an informed decision."

It probably won't get you anywhere to reply: "Well, sir, I'd really like to try this other, new approach." Instead, you've got to pick up on whatever the boss says at the time. Only later should you begin to probe the purposes of solving the problem.

So if your boss says, "Get out and work on that billing department!" do so. But do it in the most effective way. Apply the principles of Breakthrough Thinking. Ask yourself: "What's our purpose here? What are we really trying to accomplish with the billing process?"

Focus on what purposes you want to achieve, which purpose of the many you identify expresses your primary need, what ideal systems would accomplish that purpose or purposes, which solution-after-next you could use as a target for your system. These questions enable you to design a way of handling the plethora of information your boss demands.

The recommendation you present him will have to have plenty of support to justify it. The information may not be exactly what the boss thought would be forthcoming. But if you can demonstrate that the solution you propose produces the services cheaper, better, and faster, even the most stubborn boss will be satisfied with the information you did collect and may soon admit that nothing succeeds like success.

Breaking the manager's rules may sometimes be appealing. But you are better off knowing *how* to break them.

Some Insights into Organizational Problem Solving

Getting started requires diligent work. Breakthrough Thinking is a simple idea about how to think. Although adding another way to think is difficult, it is certain to provide the best possible solutions. Yet Breakthrough Thinking does not replace hard work.

In American business especially, corporate leaders seem desperate for new ideas. Too often, what they really mean is new technologies—ready-made, off-the-rack, ill-fitting solutions of the sort that they would hesitate to wear but which they are more than willing to drape across the back of corporate enterprise.

Most consultants, unfortunately, emphasize conventional modes of thinking. They sell expertise in data collection, previous solutions, and previous report writing, thus violating most of the Breakthrough Thinking principles. They want to collect and analyze data. They want to show how expert they are by proposing *the* solution to be imposed. They assume that once their solution is known, its logic and beauty will cause everyone to adopt it.

Most American corporate leaders think in new ways only to the extent of recognizing that the culture of corporate decision making must change. The change they are willing to accept, however, is merely an exhortation to make changes within the old methodologies—for example, finding "new" solutions by applying outmoded methods, the same old ways to thinking.

At best, they will tolerate change in the criteria by which success is measured. Instead of simply asking about economic trade-offs, they may now talk about the impact of their solutions on the timeliness of orders, the impact of self-service on customers, and similar considerations. The criteria by which success is evaluated may be changing, but solutions are still sought within the same old self-defeating framework, the same old crippling straitjacket of approaches that has failed time and again.

Although corporate leaders are looking everywhere for answers, especially the fads or programs they believe will give them a quick fix, few have yet broken through to make the critical leap to change their thinking processes—the leap that takes them beyond merely looking for new answers to looking for new ways to *think* about looking for answers. If they are to achieve the paradigm changes required in their organizations, what they really need is a paradigm shift in thinking.

For example, strategic planning in many corporations is focused on the answers to three basic questions: Where are we now? Where do we want to be? How do we get from the first answer to the second? The questions are asked yearly or biannually to keep strategic plans current.

It sounds good. It's simple, direct, and attainable. What this method fails to recognize, however, is that to think about *Where are we now?* is to bog down an entire corporation in a morass of details, one that is unlikely ever to be resolved by finding the best possible solution. One obvious drawback to the where-are-we-now question is the waste of thousands of person-hours in such a misguided effort, because there is no way of ever getting all the information anyway.

However well-intentioned, to ask *Where are we now?* is the first step down the slippery slope to failure. The question fails to challenge the assumptions underlying the mode of reasoning that has *caused the problems in the first place.*

Far more productive—and at the same time, ultimately less costly—would be to question the purposes of (challenge assumptions about) the way that the corporation manufactures its products, to expand the purposes of the way it designs its products, and to establish purpose arrays and solutions-after-next for scheduling its work.

As a Breakthrough Thinker, you must challenge the unsatisfactory status quo by examining the purpose of everything you do. Examine and change methodology that is based on current thinking. Challenge the unstated assumptions underlying the question *Where are we now?*

The second question, *Where do we want to be?* is also misguided. The correct question to ask is, Where do we want to be after that?

Above all, none of the three questions demands that corporate executives question the *purposes* of the activities of their corporations—*the critical issue* of any human endeavor.

One way to help pierce these steps in strategic planning is to treat each part of such an assignment as a problem for which Breakthrough Thinking can be used: environmental scanning (what are the purposes and so on), organizational assessment or design, vision statements, strategic planning, implementation, and performance evaluation. This provides an opportunity to push for your larger ends.

How to Get Started

What do you do next? Get started. In Breakthrough Thinking, as in any other undertaking that requires intuition as well as systematized knowledge, only practice will make perfect.

Fine, you say, but how do I begin?

Begin by beginning. Stop procrastinating. Learn about the enlightenment, hard work, and fun of Breakthrough Thinking.

Remember that culture is nothing more than the accumulated weight of individual actions and values. So only different individual actions can change the culture. As we said in the beginning, it's up to you.

Like riding a bicycle, skiing, dancing the waltz, or playing tennis, you are bound to feel awkward and insecure at first. Especially in the beginning of your life as a Breakthrough Thinker, you should remember one overriding truth: Wrong action in the right direction is better than no action at all.

In most groups and for most individuals, using Breakthrough Thinking produces the experience that University of

Chicago psychology professor Michael Csikszentmihalyi calls "flow."[7] A build-up of consciousness occurs, one that moves people to high levels of performance. The principles and process infuse people with psychic energy and attention. They begin to realize the excellent results that the process can lead to, and they lose their self-conscousness as the process continues. Immersion in the Breakthrough Thinking process can be exhilarating.

Even if at first you're clumsy, it is better to make mistakes in the practice of Breakthrough Thinking than to be apparently correct in the practice of old methodologies of problem solving. Whatever mistakes you make with Breakthrough Thinking, your solution will almost certainly be better than if you had not taken the risk of thinking this new way.

Develop a schedule for your project using the Breakthrough Thinking core steps (see the Process Worksheet, Table 11-1) and estimate the times you think ought to be allocated. Breakthrough Thinking projects need to be performed within time and cost limits, just as are conventional thinking projects. Yet the Breakthrough Thinking process allows you to avoid lateness and sloppiness wherever possible.

Most of us have used such project management techniques before, so the ideas of scheduling your time is familiar. The difference now is using the Breakthrough Thinking pattern and principles as the basis for that scheduling, including (if at all possible) the dates you set for betterment of your system or solution. In addition, everyone is familiar with the constant revisions of project schedules, so updating the schedule remains the same with the Breakthrough Thinking pattern, whether the need arises from mistakes in applying the principles or from ordinary slippage.

At least with Breakthrough Thinking, you always have a method for starting over again from scratch, asking again, asking always, asking above all about the expanded *purposes* of solving your problem and about what the next project activity will accomplish. Even if you find purposes that make no sense, you know the system of inquiry to follow. After a while—and sooner than you think—you too will become an expert.

Our emphasis in this book is on what you and every other person thinks—how to understand the basic *principles* as your new assumptions of thinking to create or restructure systems and to put them into practice through a flexible and iterative process. A great deal of computer software is now available to help you in certain parts of the Breakthrough Thinking process— generating ideas, assessing risks, making decisions, analyzing spread sheets, voting in groups, recording brainstorming sessions, and so on. However, we do not consider this software to be a critical part of Breakthrough Thinking.

Unfortunately, almost all these programs to date are based on conventional reasoning or at least on telling you that the program will substitute for your own thinking. These failings are their fatal flaws. You should never seek to automate your thinking, to substitute computers for human reasoning and understanding. Some of the programs may indeed supplement and augment your thinking; they can be used to provide stimuli to develop ideas *after* you know the focus purpose(s), to assess alternatives *after* you have developed solution-after-next options. But these are different uses than those adverstised.

At this time, the only software that we recommend for use with Breakthrough Thinking is called PLAN. This program prompts you about the core steps in the Breakthrough Thinking process; it lets you skip and later return to various steps; it cajoles you to expand your thinking; it keeps records of your thoughts and ideas. You may use other programs as needed when you think they might help, but never forget that Breakthrough Thinking means you have to think.

Iteration

In fact, applying the principles of Breakthrough Thinking to your problem actually makes your early errors useful to the perfection of the system or solution you come up with. Why? Because there are no automatic breakthroughs. Merely using the principles does not guarantee the best possible solution. What guarantees the best possible solution is the *reiterated use* of the Breakthrough Thinking principles *over time*.

The simple fact that you begin to search for an answer to your problem by focusing on purposes and solutions-after-next does not guarantee a breakthrough right away. Each of us has had to start over again on purposes or other Breakthrough Thinking principles while working on certain projects because the group suddenly felt that what it had done to date just did not seem valid. But since Breakthrough Thinking has principles that you can follow on the reiterated effort, compared to the conventional approach of exhortations to "try and try again" and "just get more information,"—your chances for success are even better now. In addition, you have learned a great deal from your previous work with purposes and solutions to help the second (and third) iteration.

Whatever you do when reiterating, don't go looking for whose fault it is. Don't try to fix blame. Simply begin the process all over again. Start over with purposes. Start over with solutions-after-next. It is neither necessary or possible that each time you apply a single principle of Breakthrough Thinking you reach the best possible solution. *Breakthroughs are generated by the iterative use of all seven of the principles over time.*

Keep coming back to the principles, stick to the Breakthrough Thinking perspective, and finally, over time, your breakthrough will gel. The real breakthrough may consist of the *series of changes* you make, not necessarily the first change.

Breakthroughs tend to be won *incrementally* by applying the principles often, in concert, and repeatedly. With each new effort, you're likely to get better and better results and increasingly advanced solutions that *in the aggregate* achieve the breakthrough you desire. Remember, contrary to the natural assumption, Breakthrough Thinking means more than producing a moment of epiphany, that "aha!" feeling.

So, especially when you're getting started, don't swing for a home run on every pitch. Try for singles and doubles. Move the runners around the base paths, advance your teammates toward homeplate. Then, soon enough, you'll score.

Implementation and Reiteration

The importance of seeking *incremental* as well as major changes through *reiteration of the process* relates directly to the need to consider early in the process your ability to *implement* the solution that you finally choose. From the start, as emphasized in the Breakthrough Thinking Process Worksheet, you have to ask yourself who's going to be involved in or affected by the solution.

Remember that successful designing is a sociotechnical process. Almost every system ever designed addresses the interrelationships of people and the technologies involved. Remember that, just as people and technology must work together, so must the technology you devise (your solution) function together with the people involved in its implementation.

For example, say you design a great self-cleaning oven, one that is both microwave and regular. A breakthrough? Maybe. But if you don't consider how people are going to use your invention—at the simplest level, their abilities to read its dials and knobs—your solution will almost certainly fail. No matter how elegant a technical solution it may be in the abstract, if people aren't happy with it or refuse to use it, it's never going to get the chance to solve the problem or do the job.

Just as people and machines have to work together to serve each other successfully, the process of designing any solution is also sociotechnical. As a Breakthrough Thinker—a solution designer and problem preventer—you will never be designing in a vacuum. You'll know that no expert alone can ever solve a problem successfully. Any successful solution must consider and satisfy those who would implement it.

This is not always easy or allowed for within current management and production systems, especially in the United States. A strategy for change takes more to succeed than a mandate from the corporate board. "Boards of directors increasingly react to unsatisfactory results by bringing in a new CEO from outside the organization," says Larry Greiner, professor of management and organization at the University of Southern California School of Business Administration. "In an effort to turn things around, these outsider CEOs do tend to make major changes. The problem is most of them fail."[8]

Instead, Greiner and his colleague, Arvind Bhambri, identify, as a result of a three-year study of a company, five systematic phases a new CEO should follow to make successful strategy more likely—phases very much in line with the principles of Breakthrough Thinking:

1. Establish credibility by demonstrating your expertise, preferably by quickly solving a short-term performance problem.

2. Develop a consensus among the top management team of where you want the company to go, along with a strategy for getting there. "This step is critical," says Greiner, "because in its absence each senior executive has a vision of his own in mind. Competing visions can cripple change."

3. Start to turn the vision into a reality by changing people, positions, and the corporate structure. Identify the key people who can make the vision come alive. "To lessen the probability of covert resistance from executives, it's best to confront them and collaborate with them in creating the new structure and their positions within it."

4. The top executives now communicate the new strategy to their own people, using a similarly collaborative approach.

5. Reinforce the strategy by making sure it filters down to the lowestlevels of the corporation. Make sure everything else in the company is consistent with the new philosophy, from training to rewards.[9]

Notice that the CEO considers first what he or she is trying to get accomplished, the *purpose*. Then, and only then, the CEO *develops consensus* as to where he or she wants the company to go. Long-term solutions-after-next and people design are the principles used, along with a strategy for turning vision into a reality closely related to the system matrix and betterment timeline. Get started with a "small win," but start. Waiting to solve the whole problem, even when you have a solution-after-next target in mind, is detrimental. Actions *are* needed to strive toward personal or organizational goals, even in the absence of complete understanding.

An enlightened CEO works a great deal on changing the perspectives of other key people. This is what we mean by *de-*

signing for implementability. This is the true power of effective executives, not the imposed authority that deprives others of understanding, contributions, and commitment. It sometimes takes longer to proceed this way. But by and large, the length of time it takes is not as critical as the fact that the job is getting done, the vision is becoming a reality, the desired change is actually taking place.

As Ralph H. Kilmann, consultant and professor of business at the University of Pittsburgh, emphasizes, isolated, quick-fix solutions no longer work in today's complex organizations. In fact, short-term, immediate-impact, ready-made solutions are almost always self-defeating. Paradoxically, the apparently clumsy, reiterative process of using Breakthrough Thinking principles is actually the best way to design.[10]

Reiteration is not necessarily clumsy. In fact, reiteration is part of the process of finding excellent solutions. Moreover, following the principles and process of Breakthrough Thinking, you now can reiterate more systematically.

More important than simple reiteration, however, more important than the process of elimination of solutions (trying it one way, then another, continually refining toward your SAN target and its reiteration), is to reiterate the process in the area where it will do the most good.

If you go through the conventional problem-solving process, you typically spend too much time collecting data that is not only ultimately useless, but also actually hinders your finding the best solution. How? Among other ways, it wastes time best applied to the process of elimination, the reiteration of *alternative solutions.*

Invariably, too much time is spent on collecting data about what goes on. Thus, any time left for reiteration of solutions is far too compressed. The time is misspent on data collection rather than on reiteration of the process of finding solutions.

It is far better to move quickly from the very beginning of your problem-solving process to find purposes. Know what you're going to try to accomplish. Know what your customer needs. Then move quickly toward the solution of your problem—seek the solution-after-next, the ideal system. Get the user involved. That ideal solution indicates the kind of information really needed, the data you're going to have to get. Then you'll no longer waste time collecting data.

Reiterating the process of Breakthrough Thinking inevitably provides you with alternative solutions, which are critical to your long-term success solving and preventing problems. Unfortunately, Americans typically don't try alternatives, usually because they do not *have* them.

Too often, people just throw up their hands and assume they can't do anything. "It's a lousy situation, and we have no choice but to let it keep going." Then all they've gained is a precise knowledge of just how lousy the situation really is. They don't even try to start solving the problem and getting to the basic purposes that need to be achieved.

The Japanese have, in fact, failed at a lot of things and failed often, but they also tend to have in hand alternative solutions. As a result, Japanese economic failures are not as serious as similar failures would be in the U.S. economy.

Why? Because the Japanese know what their alternatives are. Americans on the other hand—facing as they do the pressure to find an answer immediately—assume that a single, correct answer exists. If that single, correct answer fails, Americans tend not to have any other answers. Consequently, their failures are complete.

And that's the whole point of implementation and reiteration—not that you're automatically going to achieve a breakthrough but that you'll end up with at least one answer that you *didn't* use. These alternative solutions are critical. In fact, in many cases, they provide the breakthrough you're seeking.

Readiness

Your history and behavior pattern, as well as that of your organization, will influence the readiness to use Breakthrough Thinking. Some organizations, for example, have restrictive policies regarding the delegation of authority to nonmanagers, highly compartmentalized structure, limited communication among departments, stringent employment policies (sick leave, training, absenteeism), and so on. Any group or individual project will have an easier time introducing Breakthrough Thinking in an organization with less-restrictive policies on such factors.

Because an organization's level of readiness can be so variable, another way to get started with Breakthrough Thinking is to treat its introduction as a project in itself. A group could be formed, even informally to solve the problem of how to introduce Breakthrough Thinking into Organization X. Purposes and solutions-after-next would be identified and *action* taken as a result.

Possible solutions could range from you alone using Breakthrough Thinking only on your own projects to a policy statement that Breakthrough Thinking is the way we will solve all problems (including other alternatives that could be used independently—education sessions on Breakthrough Thinking for everyone, a continual betterment timeline program, a revamped organizational structure to promote lowered levels of decision making, and so on).

Warren Bennis includes these among his ten ways to avoid disasters during periods of change: "Recruit with scrupulous honesty.... Guard against the crazies [recruit change agents, not agitators]. Build support among like-minded people.... Don't allow those who are opposed to change to appropriate basic issues.... Know the territory [appreciate environmental factors].... Change is most successful when those who are affected are involved in the planning."[11]

Readiness conditions are going to be at different levels in each organization. The level or amount of each factor affects the organization's readiness. The ways Bennis mentions are themselves intricately associated with the degree of preparation of people for different ideas. They are also useful for you in your Breakthrough Thinking activities because they reiterate several of the principles. Furthermore, they emphasize that every moment is a period of change. The betterment timeline principle should change the readiness in any organization to a high level, especially to a high level of tolerance for the ambiguity and flexibility so needed now and for tomorrow.

Readiness is also related to the size of the problem. Changing the organizational structure to achieve a shift in market orientation or in competitive position is a much larger problem than changing a workplace layout. The large problem will need many iterations of the Breakthrough Thinking core steps for successive stages, as a means of preparing your organization for change.

Your own readiness for personal or company problems is obviously critical. Each of us begins (and ends) with what psychotherapists have identified as the four givens of life: each of us will die; each of us is alone (no other person can ever *know* what is in your head); none of us *knows* the meaning of life (we make many assumptions in asserting one or another explanation); and each of us *can* take actions to improve ourselves.

The uncertainties and fears these axioms unleash for us in daily life are great in number and profound in meaning. Each of us experiences feelings or beliefs about ourself and our abilities that can inhibit our actions and our effectiveness: isolation, impatience, ignoring of others, doubt about our abilities, tentativeness, and fear, to name a few. These and other psychological blocks can exist at various levels for each of us, and those with the most blocks need Breakthrough Thinking the most. Indeed, they need it right away, even though their readiness for it is lower.

So pull up your boot-straps and start your very next interaction with a person or group or problem by following the core steps of the Breakthrough Thinking process. Ask about purposes of the system or problem or issue or question. Expand those purposes.

Be sure you know what information or decision you want before you ask (purposes). Ask the right person(s) (people design). Ask about what you would do if you started all over again (solution-after-next).

Be prepared to give something in order to receive. Phrase your question or statement artfully, based on the Breakthrough Thinking principles and process. Request or invite participation rather than demanding it. Overcome your blocks to asking by expanding your purposes and those of the people you deal with. You just can't approach the problem in the same old way, not if you want to advance your readiness and increase your abilities.

In other words, concentrate on what needs to be accomplished, not on whether or not you are blocked in using your abilities. Psychologists Robert J. Sternberg and John Kolligian, Jr., point out that people overly concerned with how well they are performing will not succeed as much and will believe they are less competent than those who focus on the task at hand.[12] Task orientation—getting results, seeking performance, accomplishing purposes—is the attitude that psychologists believe will prove more fruitful than the self-concerned attitude called ego orientation.

Persistence and Determination

Regardless of your talent, education, and intelligence, so the old proverb goes, they will not provide you with success. Only persistence and determination are omnipotent.

Both persistence and determination are essential to Breakthrough Thinking. And Breakthrough Thinking is critical if your persistence and determination are to be more effective, more likely to obtain a payoff, and more efficient. The days when persistence and determination using conventional thinking were successful are long gone. New ways of exploring, inventing, and building are what Breakthrough Thinking provides to those who are determined to persist in achieving what Rosabeth Moss Kanter calls "the four F's—focus, flexibility, fast response, and friendly interaction."[13]

Trying Breakthrough Thinking's "software for your mind" may seem risky to you. After all, you are widely experienced in the conventional approach to problem solving, and you feel comfortable with it. But you are certainly aware of the great difficulties all of us face, including you, your organization, and your community. All approaches are risky; all involve making decisions that contain elements of risk. So the major question you have to answer is, Which method of reasoning provides the least risk in your attempt to achieve progress?

To help you answer that question, try three brief quizzes related to the results you (and your organization, community, and society) seek to achieve whenever you try to change, solve problems, design, plan, improve, re-engineer, or otherwise create or restructure solutions.

The first result you seek is the most effective recommendations, ones that are innovative, offer a high cost-benefit-ratio, are workable, and provide customer satisfaction. Now ask yourself these questions: Does the conventional problem solving process or thinking paradigm give you:

- Assurance of working on the right problem at the right time?
- An expanded solution space?
- Links to customer's purposes and target groups' needs?
- Opportunities for creativity in all project phases?
- Significantly better-than-expected benefits, innovative solutions, good economic return, high quality, and customer satisfaction?
- Built-in continual improvement?
- Advanced purposes and solution ideas to make you a leader in the competitive world?

The second result you seek is a high likelihood that your recommendations will be implemented. Does the conventional problem-solving process or thinking paradigm give you:

- Early stakeholder involvement so that implementation starts at the beginning and is supported throughout all changes?
- Ways to remove obstacles to simple solutions?
- Identification of all interfaces, risks, and consequences of proposed plans?
- Ability to cope with uncertainties, such as environment, economics, regulations, and external forces?

The third result you seek is a low cost of resources (people, money, equipment) and time taken to get the first two desired results. Does the conventional problem-solving process or thinking paradigm give you:

- Clutter-free reasoning?
- Less time than expected per project?
- Minimal but required information collection, reducing analysis-paralysis?
- Structure for the imaginative mind and freedom for the structured mind?
- Effective, continuing communication among the participants after a project is completed, thus leading to team building and open information exchange?

Based on the responses we've received from many project groups and audiences we've addressed, we believe your answers to these question are almost all *No!* If you now answer the questions with reference to the principles and process of Breakthrough Thinking, almost all your answers are going to be *Yes!*

Now answer for yourself, Which approach is riskier for you, your family, your organization, your community, your society? Continuing to use the outmoded thinking paradigm of the conventional approach is obviously dangerous to your problem-solving health. Conversely, Breakthough Thinking holds the promise of a better, happier, more productive, more effective life.

So do it. Start a Breakthrough Thinking project.

Actually trying the Breakthrough Thinking principles and process is better than ruminating endlessly, asking questions about their effectiveness and validity. The worst that can happen is that you revert to the old outmoded method of collecting "all the facts." Any process that might help you avoid that largely wasted effort is surely worth trying.

The successful people we studied reported that their intuitive process and values, detailed in previous chapters and embodied in Breakthrough Thinking, nonetheless required hard work. We agree. Nothing in this book says Breakthrough Thinking is easy. As the effective people we studied told us, in their lives, luck is spelled W-O-R-K.

We have confidence you will succeed. Remember: *Attitude is everything.*

NOTES
1. Benson R. Snyder, M.D., "Literacy and Numeracy: Two Ways of Knowing," *Daedalus* (Spring 1990), pp. 233–255.

2. James G. Greeno, "A Perspective on Thinking," *American Psychologist* Vol. 44, No. 2 (1989), pp. 134–141.

3. G. Hoffher, J. Moran, And G. Nadler, *Breakthrough Thinking in Total Management* (Englewood Cliffs, New Jersey: Prentice-Hall, 1994).

4. D. J. Isenberg, "The Tactics of Strategic Opportunism," *Harvard Business Review* (March-April 1987).

5. Lester Thurow, "A Weakness in Process Technology," *Science* 238 (December 18, 1987).

6. L. Thurow, *Head-to-Head: The Coming Economic Battle Between Japan, Europe, and America* (New York: Warner Books, 1993).

7. M. Csikszentmihalyi, *Flow: The Psychology of Optimal Experience* (New York: Harper & Row, 1990)

8. L. Greiner and A Bhambri, "New CEO Intervention and Dynamics of Deliberate Strategic Change," *Strategic Management Journal* (1989).

9. Ibid.

10. Ralph H. Kilmann, *Managing Beyond the Quick Fix* (San Francisco: Jossey-Bass, 1989).

11. Warren Bennis, *Why Leaders Can't Lead* (San Francisco: Jossey-Bass, 1989).

12. R. J. Sternberg and J. Kolligian, Jr., Eds., *Competence Considered* (New Haven, CT: Yale University PRess, 1993).

13. R. M. Kanter, *When Giants Learn to Dance* (New York: Simon & Schuster, 1989).

Chapter 12

Welcome to the Future

The definition of insanity is continuing to do
the same things and expecting different results.
Think smarter, not harder.

*I*n the twenty-first century, human "thinkability"
more than any other factor—even more than air, water, and
food—will be at a premium. The "invisible advantage" of the
quality of thinking will make the crucial difference in the performance of people and organizations.

The twenty-first century will be an age of unparalleled
creativity, an age in need of, demanding, and rewarding people
who apply the "full-spectrum creativity" concepts of Breakthrough Thinking. The thinking skills of individual human beings—not natural resources, capital, or technology (all of
which are even now available throughout the world)—will
make the crucial difference between success and failure, between those who lead and those who follow.

Why? Because Breakthrough Thinking provides a process
by which we can usefully and creatively convert information
and knowledge to practice, thus bridging the gap between our
technologies and our values. Breakthrough Thinking is the
road map to excellence. It is the method to cope with *Future
Shock* and *The Third Wave,* the means to take advantage of
Megatrends. Breakthrough Thinking is a specific, research-
backed, and application-tested concept that enhances the life
opportunities of individuals (and organizations) everywhere.

Benefits of
Breakthrough Thinking

Many people who have tried Breakthrough Thinking have related to us the characteristics that they believe summarize what its principles and process bring to any effort to solve problems, to create or restructure solutions. They say that Breakthrough Thinking:

- Identifies the uniqueness of each project.
- Treats each part of a project as a problem or opportunity.
- Investigates the problem-as-stated to determine the problem-to-work-on by expanding boundaries.
- Defines measures of quality and results that are actually important.
- Gets people to participate and develop their own solutions.
- Brings people together from many disciplines and departments.
- Builds in the concept of continual change.
- Shows the impact a solution idea will have on the larger environment.
- Emphasizes synthesis, not analysis.
- Focuses its search for solution(s) on opportunities in the future, not on problems in the past.
- Takes the attitude of the believer, not the doubter.
- Begins by asking, Are we doing the right thing? It does not ask, Are we doing things right?
- Initially generates a large solution space.
- Gives focus to the search for information, as opposed to the waste of time and energy inherent to "give me all you've got."
- Emphasizes useful implementation from the very beginning.
- Offers you a rich, multifaceted role in solving and preventing problems.

These responses conveyed to us informally by those who have used Breakthrough Thinking, as well as the formal research we have conducted, show the major benefits that Breakthrough Thinking provides. In addition, achieving the following benefits and results (see Chapter 11) is the major reason that Breakthrough Thinking gives you "a person's invisible advantage." Breakthrough Thinking:

- Removes obstacles to simple solutions.
- Forces a fresh look at options.
- Requires minimal data collection, thus reducing "analysis-paralysis."
- Produces answers that give much greater benefits (quality, economic return, timeliness, etc.).
- Requires much less time and cost for projects in developing these benefits.
- Promotes innovative thinking, the sort that seeks new products and major changes in systems and services.
- Gets you to recognize systems for the long term.
- Causes implementation of recommendations.
- Builds natural teams and personal interactions for the long term.

In a world flooded with information and knowledge, Breakthrough Thinking shows how the maxim "Knowing how to use knowledge is power" can be put into operation. Power requires the focus that Breakthrough Thinking provides, yet that knowledge and information alone do not.

Now consider your personal world. Are you:

- Setting up a meeting?
- About to telephone someone?
- Establishing performance goals?
- Completing a performance evaluation?
- Dissatisfied with a training course?
- Reviewing an equipment request?
- Working on a stalled Parents' Association committee?
- Stuck in a conventional meeting or on a conventional task force?

- Being told to "get all the facts"?
- Setting up family vacation plans?
- In the midst of a domestic quarrel?

Each of these "everyday" situations, each problem that "walks in the door," gives you the opportunity to improve your effectiveness by gaining the benefits of Breakthrough Thinking.

A New Beginning: Your Future with Breakthrough Thinking

One major outcome of your developing Breakthrough Thinking will be a basic change in your attitude toward today's problems and toward your own future. Your values and those of your organization will encompass breadth of vision and quality everywhere. With these new principles, you will gain the ability to contribute creatively at all levels of problem solving and prevention. You will engage people with a diversity of backgrounds (including customers) in project efforts. Your (and their) attitudes will open to continuing change, always considering a wide range of alternatives. You will discover faster, better, cheaper ideas for all activities and systems. Finally, in applying the Breakthrough Thinking principles, you'll come to realize that the process of purpose-directed problem solving will evolve further as you continue to apply it.

Developing Breakthrough Thinking is an ongoing challenge that commands our best efforts throughout our lifetimes, throughout generations of growth and change. Having become Breakthrough Thinkers, you who read this book and apply its principles will write its future chapters.

Breakthrough Thinking will allow you to look for breakthroughs continually—right from the start—for each new problem you confront. With greater assurance of success, you'll find a solution that is much more effective than one arrived at by conventional methods.

Consider your usual day at work or at home. It consists of many "standard" activities and problems that "walk in the door." How can you handle these most effectively? First, get the person who "walks in the door" with the problem to start talking about purposes and the purposes of that purpose, and so on. Often enough, identifying the focus purpose(s) leads directly to the insights that resolve the problem. If the purpose and context are satisfactory to all, then start asking about ideal systems and solutions-after-next. If the person brings with him or her a solution, ask about the other options considered before selecting the recommendation.

If the purpose(s) and solution appear satisfactory, then ask, "How would the system actually work if it were installed?" to be sure of all elements and dimension specifications and their inter relationships. If the purposes, solution-after-next target, and recommended system is workable, then ask, "How can the recommendation get installed?" Ask questions related to designing the installation plan with the key people, using the core steps of Breakthrough Thinking.

The solution you find might not be ideal. In fact, there are no single, "right" answers. But it will be much closer to a target ideal solution that represents your goals and your ideals. This solution will address real, immediate purposes and will prepare you for challenges still on the horizon.

In adopting this new approach to your problems, you will gain the ability and confidence to work constructively and purposefully. Systematically applying the seven principles of Breakthrough Thinking will inevitably increase your chances of and opportunities for success. You and the organization or group with which you work and interact will get more than before of the three types of breakthroughs—the "aha!" or innovative solution, far better results, and the actual implementation of good ideas.

You will no longer approach problems with the doubt— or even dread—that comes from dwelling on what's wrong. Instead, you'll find the power of belief, of positive action, not by some magic or superhuman gift, but by discovering in yourself and others the ability to take control of current circumstances and direct them toward significant ideals and solutions. In short, you'll learn the Breakthrough Thinking language of successful and innovative change.

Moreover, with Breakthrough Thinking you are able to re-solve one of the most difficult dilemmas that people face today in their *personal interactions* with others, whether at work, in organizations, within a family, or in a social setting, as com-pared to their expected *professional and organizational roles.*

Most of us are trained extensively in the latter, yet have lit-tle preparation for the former. The latter takes up much of peo-ple's time and, of course, produces the income essential to their sustenance. The former, however, takes up the majority of time for most people, even at work, especially as the family, friends, and social lives of individuals constitute a major influ-ence on the beliefs and values that they bring to an organiza-tion.

We are expected to use the conventional approach when handling problems in planning, designing, and improving for our organizations; we are expected to practice the hard-nosed, analytical "doubting game." At the same time, we are urged to deal positively with people, demonstrating the trust, flexibility, and optimism of the "believing game."

These are, of course, two fundamentally different ap-proaches to "people problems," which, ultimately, comprise what organizations actually are. This fundamental dichotomy explains, perhaps, why so many people so often fail when they use the conventional approach in their organizations and why others, those who practice "people skills," such as counseling, social work, and career guidance, tend to succeed a little more often in organizations, even when they use the conventional approach.

Breakthrough Thinking solves this dilemma. It provides the concepts that combine the best of what needs to be done in both professional and personal settings.

Who Applies
Breakthrough Thinking

Not everyone can personally benefit from the practice of Break-through Thinking *for every problem.* Research indicates that, at the lower end of the scale, five to eight percent of the population have no real ability to prevent and solve the problems of organizations and society. At the top end, another five to eight percent of the population, our best intuitive problem solvers, our most effective people—the ones we study—already practice Breakthrough Thinking for such problems without consciously trying.

Psychologists have identified more than one type of intelligence and shown that people vary in the types of intelligence they have as well as the "amount" in each type. Harvard University psychologist Howard Gardner has identified several types: linguistic, intrapersonal, logical/mathematical, musical, interpersonal, spatial, and bodily-kinesthenic.[1] A person with high levels of one type of intelligence may well be an intuitive Breakthrough Thinker in that particular area but inept while using the conventional approach in other areas. Thus, every person is capable of using Breakthrough Thinking in several areas of his or her intelligence. Moreover, the specified principles and process can also help gifted individuals better to explain how they actually think in their particular domains of intuitive expertise.

As one of us (Nadler) was reminded while attending a concert of the Los Angeles Philharmonic Orchestra, no one could teach Beethoven anything about thinking that he did not already know. If you doubt this assertion, simply listen closely to his Fifth or Ninth Symphony.

Although 85 to 90 percent of the world's population can benefit from Breakthrough Thinking in relation to a particular problem area, the people comprising the group in that percentage are not the same for each problem! Even Beethoven could have used Breakthrough Thinking for many other problems, making him a member of the 85 to 90 percent for planning personal financial solutions, for example.

This means that every person has the ability to use Breakthrough Thinking for many, if not all, of the varied problems he or she confronts. The successful people we studied, with their intuitive use of Breakthrough Thinking, frequently told us that they were glad to learn about the principles emerging from our research because they could then consciously use those principles to improve solution finding in other parts of their work and personal lives. They could now tell others precisely *how* they approach problem solving. But every situation does not call for Breakthrough Thinking.

Conductor Esa-Pekka Salonen, for example, and the orchestra musicians did not need to use Breakthrough Thinking as they played Beethoven's music. They needed only to practice and then perform certain well-honed skills to achieve a well- established purpose.

The preparation of a gourmet meal or the playing of a tennis match do not demand Breakthrough Thinking. For the most part, the uniqueness and purposes of these endeavors, even their solutions-after-next, are self-evident. If you have to design your kitchen or need to strategize how best to beat a certain opponent, however, Breakthrough Thinking is your ticket.

The fact is that, if change for the better is actually to occur, it's up to you. Assuming you're neither a genius nor a cretin, it will be you and people like you, more likely than not, who will practice and implement the seven principles of Breakthrough Thinking to prevent and to solve problems. This will make for happier lives, more creative and productive workplaces, and more responsive governments—in short, a better world.

It is essential that you rise to the challenge and champion innovation and modernization in your companies. You can be a leader in solving and preventing problems in the midst of the now normal, real-world chaos. This is so for many sound reasons:

- You, at whatever level you function in your organization, are close to some operating level that you understand, one where you can appreciate the benefits and interrelationships of proposed changes.

- You have many years left in your career, and you want to be associated with an innovative activity. You should *drive* hard for its success.

- You attend many professional meetings or have access to a vast amount of information that can stimulate you for many changes.

- You know Breakthrough Thinking, which can help bring the latest techonology into effective solutions that overcome the top management tendency to be overly conservative and suspicious of new technology.

Even if you are not the one "in charge," you *are* the one who knows how to practice Breakthrough Thinking. You can apply the principles first in your personal life, but you don't have to stop there.

In your family decisions; your church or neighborhood clubs; your fraternal or professional organizations; with colleagues in your workplace, company, or organization; with fellow citizens on the city, state, and national levels of political involvement; with like-minded members of groups working to solve problems of international and even global significance, *you* can forge a better future by applying the principles of Breakthrough Thinking you have learned. In most of these situations, the problems have familiar names—quality, productivity, health care, job satisfaction, crime, education, welfare, taxation, ecological balance, national security, leadership, energy, and other crises (oil spills, savings and loan bailouts, terrorism).

On the very personal front, Breakthrough Thinking can be instrumental in handling the frictions and feuds that arise in personal and family relationships. We're not experts in this area, but psychologists and therapists tell us that analyzing the wrongs—my parents favored my brother, my sister treated me badly, my neighbor lets his dog bark at night, my ex-spouse treats the children and me poorly—causes festering anger that is not conducive to problem resolution. It leads to fighting with others rather than getting results that at least make you feel better and at best bring two combative sides together.

Try asking the other person(s) involved in your dispute what purposes both of you want to achieve, what larger purposes you have, what purpose(s) you should focus on and accomplish, what solution-after-next options you have, and so on. If possible, get a Breakthrough Thinking facilitator to help (or go to a counselor who specializes in brief therapy, an approach that has several similarities to Breakthrough Thinking). The potential for real progress does exist. And you can do it.

In fact, the impact of applying Breakthrough Thinking to real, existing problems is potentially enormous and affects the personal, workplace, corporate, neighborhood, city, state, national, international, and global arenas. The problems within each of these arenas are too numerous to cover completely, but we will discuss a few of the major ones that influence national and international decision making. Can you think of others that Breakthrough Thinking could be used to solve or prevent?

TRADE AND FINANCE

In May of 1989, the administration of President George Bush—facing tremendous domestic political pressure in the development of new U.S. policy on international trade—defined Japan as one of the nations practicing "unfair trade" with the United States. In 1989, the Japanese were outraged at the threatened sanctions, which they perceived as a deliberate insult. Japan refused even to discuss the matter further. In 1993, with the change in presidential administrations, an attempt at negotiation was made, but nothing much was actually accomplished.

In addressing this problem of the U.S. trade deficit with Japan, apparently no one in Congress, which passed a 1989 trade bill, gave much thought to solutions-after-next. Nor did anyone bother to run the chosen "solution" through a system matrix to assess how to avoid the "law of unintended consequences" and possible complications of the chosen solution.

Rather than asking about the purposes of the current system, rather than involving the significant actors in this particular arena to address a present problem with reference to a common future, the Americans—seeking to fix the blame for their problems, as opposed to finding a solution—acted preemptorily and unilaterally from a patchwork of impressions and perceptions. The repercussions are still felt today, with no coherent and consistent policy toward Japan.

What different approach, which specific steps, might the Congress have taken to resolve more effectively the problem of the U.S. trade deficit?

EDUCATION

There can no longer be any doubt that the quality of public education in the United States today lags far behind that of many other industrialized nations in Europe and Asia. For example, surveys rank U.S. schoolchildren at the bottom of the scale in math when tested against South Korean, Canadian, Spanish, British, and Irish children.

At least part of the problem seems to be that what has been taught to, learned by, and rewarded in *teachers* has resulted in their adherence to sometimes mindless standards and generic rules. Such rigidity actually hinders their students' learning, rather than resulting in the teachers' dedication to helping students acquire knowledge and values.

Applying the principles of Breakthrough Thinking to elementary education systems, Nadler and his associates developed the SPARK program—Student Planned Acquisition of Required Knowledge.[2] SPARK demonstrates that the people design principle of Breakthrough Thinking can have a remarkably salutary effect on sixth- and seventh-graders. Students who were given responsibility for planning their own acquisition of required knowledge—and taught the process of Breakthrough Thinking that allowed them successfully to plan their education—did consistently better than other students in the quality and innovativeness of the final outcome. They produced poems, skits, debates, and interviews, not just the usual book reports.

The children had no difficulty understanding the different approaches needed to create or restructure solutions (Breakthrough Thinking) and to do research for developing generalizations (the conventional approach). Michigan State University professor Charles Anderson and Mary Budd Rowe, professor of science education at the University of Florida, observed: "Children begin to engage in the activities labeled 'higher-order thinking'—description, explanation, prediction, and control of the world around them—*before* they learn to memorize facts and reproduce them on demand [which] has little in common with meaningful uses of ... knowledge."[3]

Can you plan other ways to improve your local system of education?

LEADERSHIP

International foreign correspondent Stanley Meisler, who for more than twenty years reported for the *Los Angeles Times* from Africa, Spain, France, and Canada, wrote that he returned to the United States in 1988 to find a complacent, cowed America, at once both smug and scared.

"Perhaps the problem is leadership," Meisler noted. "Leaders of most industrial democracies have a breadth of intellect and experience, a moral strength and commitment to reason, that often seems lacking here. Perhaps the very power of our people undercuts leadership. U.S. leaders have to cater to the tastes and whims of the masses in ways that leaders in countries like France and Britain do not."[4]

Meisler is not alone in noting the penchant of American leaders for short-term "solutions" that respond more to their own personal self-interest in reelection than to the nation's real, obvious, and increasingly urgent problems.

Commentator Meg Greenfield argues for a return among political leaders to the "somewhat archaic" virtue of constancy. It is the antidote, she says, "not only to what is most fundamentally wrong with our politics and politicians, but also what both most desperately need, in fact, what real leadership consists of."

Constancy, says Greenfield, is not to be confused with blind stupidity and intractable pig-headedness. Constancy is something different. "It is being able to make a sound, deliberate choice and stick with it, being able to keep your eye on that large goal [purposes], while adjusting, if need be, to altered circumstances along the way. Above all, it is being principled and confident enough to withstand the pressures, the temptations of our distinctive craze-of-the-month politics."

Developing political leaders capable of constancy, she suggests, would go a long way toward obviating the complaints of American allies that U.S. leaders are "inclined to unpredictability, to swerving, mutually contradictory, and self-canceling enthusiasms." Greenfield urges Americans to vote for those who develop long-distance, long-term vision—those who, in the phrase of Martin Luther King, Jr., and Jesse Jackson, "keep their eyes on the prize."[5]

These are virtues developed in the practice of Breakthrough Thinking, especially in its insistence on the constant
questioning of purposes and seeking of solutions-after-next.

How would you apply the principles of Breakthrough
Thinking to enhance the political process that has the most direct impact on your own life?

The argument between political left and right in the United States—a dialogue dramatized exquisitely by Frances Moore
Lappe[6]—would be far more likely to elicit the success of a less-
divided, more moderate, less-ideological, and more thoughtful
body politic if the citizens who together comprise the nation
would begin their dialogue by questioning the purposes of
their society.

Especially when passions run so high, the application of
Breakthrough Thinking principles does not assure success, but
it does increase the probability of finding mutually acceptable
and thus long-term, successful solutions. Certainly, the old
methods of reasoning have for too long encouraged divisions
within the body politic in the defense of mutually exclusive positions, rather than the search for mutually held principles and
expanded common ground.

Indicative of this partisan split is the perennial argument
between American liberals and conservatives concerning the
value of social welfare programs versus the need to promote
corporate profits and thus the investment essential to an expanding economy.

"The U.S. corporate tax burden [combined profit and social security employer taxes] has been below the rates of Japan,
West Germany, Canada and France, so scratch that as an element of the trade crisis," wrote journalist Robert Conot in his
review of *America's Trade Crisis* by Congressman Don L.
Bonker, then chairman of the House Foreign Affairs Subcom-
mittee on International Economic Policy and Trade.

It is true, however, that virtually all industrial nations, with
the exception of the United States, levy hefty sales, value-
added and excise taxes that dampen consumption, and so
in effect act as a subsidy to exports. But it is also true that
all of the Western European nations use these revenues for

comprehensive social welfare systems far beyond anything in the United States. So what is taken with one hand is given back with the other.

But one cannot solve problems by simply throwing statistics at them, any more than by throwing money at them. We have the data from innumerable sources. What we need now from Bonker and persons like him in leadership positions is more incisive analyses, innovative thinking, and creative approaches to respond to those challenges.[7]

We suggest that the principles of Breakthrough Thinking form an excellent basis for the innovative and creative solutions demanded of today's political leaders. Of course, the search for far-reaching, long-term solutions is made more difficult in the hyper-responsive political climate of American democracy. In a political culture where congressional elections take place every two years—a system originally designed to ensure that elected officials remained accountable to the will of the people—the vast majority of those elected to the Congress can realistically afford to look ahead only as far as the next election.

Indeed, short-term solutions seem almost inherent to the American political process. But if so, the principles of Breakthrough Thinking can certainly provide the basis for, the process toward, and the possibility of visionary statesmanship.

Aid To Developing Countries

The United States has been very generous over the past forty-five years in supplying food and technical assistance to developing countries. Besides providing humanitarian aid in times of famine, natural disaster, and large-scale accidents, the United States has attempted to transfer technology to so-called Third World countries, which has been a fiasco. Billions of dollars of equipment and factories have been left rusting and wasting in the various countries to which they were transferred.

When Hibino took part in a Japanese program to improve the productivity of rural manufacturing companies in Kenya, he used the Breakthrough Thinking approach. He had to present

his case forcefully to experts from several social development organizations (the United Nations, the Japan International Cooperation Agency, and the U.S. Agency for International Development)
who insisted on using the "what's wrong" or conventional approach. They had already conducted extensive surveys and produced volumes of data. Yet not a single rural industry had been
developed.

By contrast, Hibino had each company use Breakthrough
Thinking to design its own system and thus identify for itself
what technology could be used. The resultant changes were
dramatic—the solutions chosen fit the company, the people
were anxious and willing to use what they themselves had designed, and future changes were identified.

The premise of the usual technology transfer rests on the
assumption that an answer that is good for me is good for you.
Obviously, this violates the uniqueness principle of Breakthrough Thinking and explains the failures so prevalent in organizations in both advanced and developing countries.

Corporate Productivity
and Competitiveness

In the corporate world as well, there is no dearth of problems
to be solved by Breakthrough Thinking. Among them are some
so deep-seated as to have become endemic.

One recent book attempts to define the nature and extent
of the dilemmas faced by American business.[8] In reviewing it,
Warren Bennis, consultant and distinguished professor of business administration at the University of Southern California,
noted:

[Its] list of weaknesses is the usual: outdated strategies,
short time horizons, technological weaknesses in development and production, neglect of human resources, failures
of cooperation, and government and industry at cross-pur-
poses.

Nevertheless, it is precisely at the level of change that
the study lets us down. For example, we are told that well-
run companies reduce the number of layers of manage-

ment and base their reward system on performance. Those are two sensible suggestions. They've been espoused for years—airport bookstores are filled with pop management books offering the same advice.

But what does it take for organizations to get from here to there? How do we get engineering schools to lengthen the typical four-year engineering program (as the report suggests) to make it more like law or medicine or any other professional school?

When MIT president Paul Gray, who commissioned the study, was asked this question, he replied that it would not happen quickly and would take place only when major engineering schools all agreed to do it at the same time.

Don't hold your breath.[9]

And yet, applied to any one of these many endemic problems, the principles of Breakthrough Thinking could surely keep us all from turning blue. What matters most is *how* successfully we can turn into practice the outstanding technologies we already have—the people skills and thinking needed to create or restructure solutions.

According to investment banker Jeffrey Garten, president of New York-based Eliot Group, management consultant Peter Drucker hits the nail squarely on the head in *The New Realities*.[10] Garten notes that "[Drucker shows] how real comparative advantage has far less to do with natural resources, the value of the dollar, or government subsidies but with how companies are organized and directed.

"At the base of *The New Realities* are two propositions. There is a crying need for new approaches to politics, economics, and management. And second, such innovation will have little to do with high-tech breakthroughs, but with *changes in the way we define problems and organize ourselves for work*" (emphasis added).[11]

Even the down-sizing or right-sizing so prevalent today illustrates the poor solutions of the past and the inappropriate approach used to achieve reduced payrolls and fewer middle managers. Breakthrough Thinking would develop the systems (whether radically redesigned or not) that operate most effectively with fewer people (recall the nurse-utilization case in Chapter 5). In addition, the systems principle of Breakthrough Thinking would identify much less stressful and time-consuming activities for those who remain. At the same time, it would help in determining and implementing the fairest and most equitable arrangements for those who leave.

As might be expected in an economy under siege, horror stories about badly defined problems and work organization abound. Not surprisingly, one of the most horrendous in recent memory—perhaps only because, like the elephant in the circus parade, it was so highly visible—concerns the U.S. automotive giant, General Motors Corporation.

As noted by commentator Robert J. Samuelson, even after a recent precipitous drop in the value of the dollar, the U.S. trade deficit still remained immense, roughly $120 billion a year. Even though Japan maintained a voluntary quota, which led them to export higher profit margin cars to the United States, Japanese cars were still imported in large quantities.[12]

Yet even as their market share declined because of the value that American consumers continued to place on the high quality of the restricted Japanese cars, even at increased prices, U.S. manufacturers chose also to increase prices and saw their own profits rise to all time highs.

U.S. automobile manufacturers, especially General Motors, took advantage of the voluntary restraint of their Japanese competitors to increase profits, rather than to increase market share by lowering prices or focusing on reducing the design-to-delivery cycle time and cost in order to produce cars actually competitive with the Japanese products. Highly touted rebates and similar marketing gimmicks and incentive schemes offered by American manufacturers to lure consumers were in fact ridiculous, says Samuelson. Even offering $1,200 rebates on their products, American manufacturers were still making their greatest profits in history, because they set prices so high in the first place.

At the same time, American automobile executives continued to complain that they needed protection against Japanese competitors who were steadily eroding the market share to which Americans had become accustomed. It seemed entirely to escape their consideration that U.S. market shares might increase greatly if they priced their (relatively poor quality) products lower.

Rather than stimulate demand by lowering prices, American manufacturers preferred to constrict supply by lobbying for continued restrictions against Japanese imports. General Motors in particular chose to give their shareholders short-term satisfaction. Even more satisfied were the high-salaried executives, who paid themselves huge bonuses based on their record profits, which they generously chose to mistake for performance.

The late 1980s and early 1990s continued this shortsightedness. Both General Motors and Ford showed tremendous profits through this period but chose to invest their money in acquisitions in areas only broadly related to the business of building automobiles—for example, aerospace, information technology, and information services—rather than in research and development and producing new products in their main line of business, vehicular transportation. These inept decisions were caused by poor planning (GM's investment in robotics as *the* answer, Ford's investment in aerospace) and by the conventional thinking that continued to permeate management (GM's not listening to suggestions that it change its self-defeating course).

Such ultimately self-destructive financial legerdemain would surely have been too shortsighted to pass for a viable solution-after-next in Breakthrough Thinking.

The picture through 1993 is not much prettier. Management still seeks the latest fad that it believes will solve its problems, obviously not realizing the truth of the uniqueness principle of Breakthrough Thinking. Each new fad *does* have worthy goals and aims, and the corporate executives involved with it *do* have honorable desires and values that motivate them to seek some plans and actions. Yet the way they go about their adoption of the fad leads them to fail. (Many studies have shown that most such fads have a success rate between 10 and 20 percent.)

For example, a fad of particular prominence in late 1993 is called Business Process Reengineering (BPR). It argues, as does Breakthrough Thinking, that simply fixing what's wrong is insufficient. But then BPR makes the arbitrary assumption that "a need exists for heavy blasting" of a given business process, while there may exist no assurance that the process actually needs to be re-engineered.

BPR also makes the arbitrary decision that other problems or processes do *not* need to be reengineered—a poor decision, in light of the many Breakthrough Thinking cases that began with an apparently small or mundane problem that, once viewed in the light of purpose expansion and solutions-after-next, came to require a much different, larger strategic (or "reengineered") solution.

The BPR fad recommends an approach that starts by analyzing what already exists, yet such a beginning demonstrably limits the identification of effective solutions and the likelihood of their implementation. It assures that a reengineered process is *the* single appropriate answer, yet such an assurance falls into the conventional trap of smugness and self-satisfaction when it should instead insist on a betterment timeline. BPR emphasizes the value of *fixing* business processes, instead of designing them correctly in the first place. It addresses only one aspect of business processes—reengineering—without realizing that other worthy goals might also be considered, such as Total Quality Management, self-directed work teams, computer integrated systems, and concurrent design. Moreover, BPR itself should logically cease to exist once all the business processes it wishes to address have been reengineered! All these characteristics are unmistakably those of a passing fad.

But problems of mismanagement are hardly limited to giant corporations. Failure to consider purposes and seek solutions-after-next, relying instead on the constant analysis and measurements of micro-managers, can have a devastating impact on an enterprise of any size, with painful consequences for all concerned.

As chronicled by Max Holland, the Burgmaster division of Houdaille Industries succumbed to a variety of woes characteristic of American manufacturing enterprises in the 1970s and 1980s.[13]

Founded in 1944 as a family-run business that began in the garage of Fredrick Burg, Burgmaster—maker of an ingenious turret-head drill that was particularly popular with the U.S. aerospace industry—became the target of a leveraged buyout by the notorious corporate raiders Kohlberg, Kravis, and Roberts in 1979.

Yale University professor of finance William N. Goetzman notes: "The halcyon years of Burgmaster were all too brief. In the merger mania of the 1960s, Burgmaster attracted a suitor: Houdaille Industries. By Holland's account, the Houdaille team of sharp-pencil men, armed with the latest time-motion studies, virtually managed the life out of Burgmaster. They quickly replaced its family-style management with a divisive corporate culture that discouraged technical innovation and dictated unworkable production schedules."

Bought out by KKR after a decade of economic stagnation, the Burgmaster division of Houdaille finally went under after "the desperate cash-flow requirements of the new KKR management stifled the development of new products and destroyed what was left of their reputation for quality workmanship."

The story of Burgmaster's disgrace, dissolution, and ultimate demise is a classic cautionary tale, says Goetzmann, about "what happens when a company's perspective shifts from a focus on quality products to a focus on quarterly reports to a focus on monthly cash flow."[14]

This sort of micromanagement, the attitude that gets all the details, analyzes all the data, and then tries above all to cut costs, ignoring the ongoing need for innovative solutions and systems. Fundamental purposes of the enterprise are ignored as the expectations of new stockholders and then the demands of new debtholders take precedence. Profits, not products, come to be considered paramount—and another industry dies.

By contrast, 3M Company—generally considered to be among the best-managed U.S. enterprises—has long followed management procedures designed to encourage and support the innovation that has made it world renowned for its constant development of successful new products. It eschews the typical American idea of good management—put the ideas of managers into the hands of labor. Though evolving independently, the organization and management of 3M Company and the principles of Breakthrough Thinking are remarkable in their similarity.

As noted in *Business Week,* 3M's minimization of corporate rules leaves plenty of room for experimentation. It consciously tolerates—even approves of and rewards—the innovative failures essential to ultimate success, in other words, solutions-after-next.

> Minnesota Mining and Manufacturing inventor Francis G. Okie was dreaming up ways to boost sales of sandpaper, then the company's premiere product, when a novel thought struck him. Why not sell sandpaper to men as a replacement for razor blades? Why would they risk the nicks of a sharp instrument when they could rub their cheeks smooth instead?
>
> The idea never caught on, of course. The surprise is that Okie, who continued to sand his own face, could champion such a patently wacky scheme and keep his job. But unlike most companies then—or now—3M Co. demonstrated a wide tolerance for new ideas, believing that unfettered creative thinking would pay off in the end.
>
> Indeed Okie's hits made up for his misses: He developed a waterproof sandpaper that became a staple of the auto industry because it produced a better exterior finish and created less dust than conventional papers. It was 3M's first blockbuster.[15]

What's more, sixty-six years later in 1988, some 32 percent of 3M's annual sales of $10.6 billion came from products introduced within the previous five years.

How does 3M do it? It instinctively practices the principles of Breakthrough Thinking, as codified in a few simple rules:

1. *Keep divisions small* (people-design and critical details). 3M division managers must know each staff member's first name. When a division gets too big, it is split up.

2. *Tolerate failure* (solution-after-next). By encouraging plenty of experimentation and risk taking, there are more chances for a new-product hit. The goal is that a division must derive 25 percent of sales from products introduced in the past five years.

3. *Motivate the champions* (uniqueness, purposes, solution-after-next, systems matrix, betterment timeline). When a 3M employee comes up with a product idea, he or she recruits an action team to develop it, a team recruited from the technical, manufacturing, marketing, sales and possibly finance areas.

   The team designs the product and figures out how to produce and market it. Then it develops new uses and line extensions. Salaries and promotions are tied to the product's progress. The champion has a chance to someday run his or her own product group or division.

4. *Stay close to the customer* (people design, purposes, solution-after-next). Researchers, marketers, and managers visit with customers and routinely invite them to help brainstorm product ideas.

5. *Share the wealth* (limited information collection). Technology, wherever its developed, belongs to everyone.

6. *Don't kill a project* (betterment timeline). If an idea can't find a home in one of 3M's divisions, a staffer can devote 15 percent of his or her time to prove it is workable. For those who need seed money, as many as ninety in-house grants of $50,000 are awarded each year.

Effective leaders and problem solvers tend to follow instinctively the seven principles of Breakthrough Thinking—a process that systematizes the attitudes and approaches that have made the 3M Company among the most successful enterprises in the world.

Masters of innovation, the people at 3M have devised their own system to nurture the flash of insight, the light bulb of creativity, that illumines the path to a better future. Other successful companies have developed their own sets of operating and strategic guides or rules that reinforce the Breakthrough Thinking concepts.

For example, Cabletron Systems, Inc., which has seen more than a 500 percent increase in the price of its stock since its first public offering in 1989, "invests only in what helps the business grow—develop local area networking hardware and software [purposes, solution-after-next, betterment timeline].... You can get as much work done in a small office as you can in a big one [solution-after-next, limited information collection].... No meeting lasts more than 20 minutes [limited information collection, people design].... No sit-down conference rooms [systems].... No travel on company time [systems].... Cheap desks [solution-after-next, systems, purposes].... The founders do not receive high salaries: we invest in engineers and sales-men. More than 100 of our employees make more than [the two founders] do [purposes, systems, people design].... Being a tightwad [stems from realizing that] overhead is like cancer. Once it gets started, it's hard to cut out." [16]

Similarly, the process and principles of Breakthrough Think-ing prepare your mind for and encourage innovation, allow you to harness brainstorms, seize the fleeting notion, develop from it the best possible solution to your own personal problems, and seek solutions to those problems that confront us all.

Regarding this issue of innovation, it seems to us worth re-emphasizing that the limited information collection principle of Breakthrough Thinking is not an excuse for a life of emotional and intellectual lethargy. The collection of excessive data as a substitute for and an obstacle toward the discovery of purposes and ultimately successful solutions is very different from a devo-tion to constantly accumulating knowledge and evolving educa-tion.

Breakthrough Thinking does not obviate the need to learn. Throughout our lives, it is essential to keep learning. But there is a distinct difference between the breadth and depth of knowledge characteristic of a liberal education and the collec-tion of analytical data that may or may not be applicable to the solution of the problem at hand.

In no way do we suggest that Breakthrough Thinkers be-come know-nothing airheads. Learning keeps the mind active and nourishes it as fertile ground for innovative, Breakthrough

Thinking. Access to bodies of knowledge, to learning and wisdom, must never be limited, only access to those random data that exist more as noise than as music.

Patronizing art museums, attending plays, reading books, listening to concerts, attending seminars unrelated to one's field of expertise or professional interests, acquiring knowledge unrelated to any particular project or problem, learning without any certainty that the knowledge you acquire will ever prove directly "useful," and similar pursuits are essential to the expansion of the human mind. As such, lifelong learning is critical to Breakthrough Thinking.

Research in Basic Thinking

In recent years, there has been an explosion in the technology applicable to and the fascination with research into the reasoning processes of human beings—in short, how we think. This has taken the form of debates over the nature of cognition and pattern recognition, the design and functions of the brain, and the definition (even the existence) of the mind.

Philosophers view the mind in terms of "cognitive functions" and thinking as the perfomance of various mental operations. In turn, they consider mental operations the manipulation of language symbols in the "right" way.

Our book, *Creative Solution Finding,* provides a great deal of background information on these issues. Chapter 6 of that book particularly addresses research into thinking. We discuss these issues in terms of, among others, the following topics: the human brain as a biological entity; classical models of thinking; modern conceptual perspectives; modes of thinking; intelligence, creativity, and intuition; the varieties of intelligence; dominant decision styles; different thinking patterns used for different purposeful activities; holistic versus analytical thinking; the need for flexibility; characteristic habits and approaches of expert problem solvers; inhibitions to effective thinking; right-brain/left-brain studies; teaching thinking; the reality of individual perception; and the power of vision.

While it is beyond the scope of this book—or perhaps any other—to deal with all of these profound questions, we note with interest the work of certain researchers because their findings may eventually improve Breakthrough Thinking. For example, Robert Sternberg, professor of psychology at Yale University, proposes three kinds of human knowledge: (1) What might be called *basic knowledge,* the knowledge acquisition component of intelligence that is usually measured by I.Q. and other intelligence tests; (2) *organizational knowledge,* the executive functions and experiential factors that recognize problems and organize our awareness of how to proceed; (3) what might be called *political and social intuition* or "street smarts," the wisdom that translates the procedural phases of the executive functions into performance and contextual inferences and relationships using the knowledge base.[17]

As we see it, Breakthrough Thinking is the guarantee of, and the shortcut between, the second and the third types of knowledge categorized by Sternberg. Breakthrough Thinking provides a learnable concept that ensures access to the sort of problem-solving methods practiced intuitively by successful people. It is an expression of adaptive competency, a contextual concept of intelligence, cognition, and thinking. Adaptive competency stresses the capacities to respond at all times of life with proactive resilience to challenges.[18]

Another area of research into thinking that intrigues us is the future of general systems theory. L. Raphael Troncale of the Institute for Advanced Systems Studies at California State Polytechnic University, cites thirty-three specific obstacles inhibiting current research in systems science. Suggestions for overcoming these obstacles are also presented as a prescription for improved progress in the field.[19]

Especially noteworthy, it seems to us, is the fact that many of the obstacles identified by Troncale are best addressed and overcome by the principles of Breakthrough Thinking. In particular, such obstacles as the need to transcend internal conflicts, transcend disciplinary specific training, form adequately transdisciplinary teams, produce consensus, increase networking, and connect people to computer data bases are particularly helped by Breakthrough Thinking. Future research in these areas points to changes in the methods of problem solving and prevention, which will help Breakthrough Thinking.

Research in the theory of design will eventually affect the philosophy and principles of Breakthrough Thinking. For example, efforts in cognitive modeling examine processes in the brain that can explain and predict how designers design. Our research is centered on the intuitive methods of recognized experts—that is, highly successful designers, especially so in the early phases of problem solving—this other research includes all practitioners of systems design. Inevitably, these findings will have an impact on Breakthrough Thinking.

We believe current research will demonstrate that the issue of design fixation is critical. How can a problem solver overcome his or her fixation on a solution that may prove to be the right solution to the wrong problem? We suggest that integrating the research on fixation into the search for a process of finding solutions-after-next may prove to be a major help in Breakthrough Thinking.

Teaching the skills of critical thinking has become a focus of interest in primary and secondary education. As outlined by Stephen Brookfield, critical thinkers can identify and challenge assumptions that underlie ideas, beliefs, values, and actions that others take for granted. Once these assumptions about context are identified, critical thinkers examine their accuracy and beliefs and try to imagine and explore alternatives. Imagining and exploring alternatives leads to reflective skepticism.[20]

Breakthrough Thinking shows how to do critical thinking that leads to analysis and exposition. The research into critical thinking skills, however, should provide insights into changes in some Breakthrough Thinking techniques.

These and other similar developments are indicative of ongoing research that is sure to have an impact on the further development of Breakthrough Thinking. We are hardly unique in our interest in the field of cognition and problem-solving processes. An entire range of endeavors, as well as the research of gifted design practitioners and others, has and will continue to form the basis for our own research.

Research in
Breakthrough Thinking

Our research investigates the specific attributes and characteristics of experts—the most successful planners, executives, designers, engineers, and other problem solvers. It examines the opinions of these experts as to how they categorize, combine, and coordinate the different aspects of their often intuitive problem-solving methods and design processes to arrive at remarkably successful solutions. Chapter 9 of our book, *Creative Solution Finding*, covers this research in detail.

We then compare the intuitive methods of the experts to those of the everyday practitioner. Our goal is to discover what is different in the intuitive processes of the expert and the everyday practitioner, so that we can identify more clearly those methods, aids, and techniques that intuitive experts use in their problem-solving processes.

Other research we have recently undertaken relates to the sociotechnical processes of Breakthrough Thinking—that is, how best to involve people with each other, and with each other's ideas, in the activities of problem solving and prevention, as well as how best to involve these people with the technical accoutrements that facilitate the process, such as computers, data bases, and communications systems. The key to this research seems to involve how best to facilitate and enhance these sociotechnical processes.

One method we now employ is an interactive computer program (PLAN), which we use to train our students in the process of Breakthrough Thinking. The program (itself being constantly improved and developed) prompts the students to consider ever-larger purposes, find their relationships, compare the purpose statements for hierarchical ranking, and decide which purpose to pursue.

We expect that this research will lead to improvements in the methods whereby data are stored and presented. This, in turn, will enhance the process of identifying purposes and placing them in hierarchies. The same methods could be used to generate stimuli for individuals or groups of problem solvers to be more creative.

Whether or not this research will ultimately affect the principles of Breakthrough Thinking remains uncertain. We think not, but we know enough to keep an open mind. In any case, methods of applying the principles will surely be improved.

Remember that Breakthrough Thinking itself includes the seeds of its own change. These are found in certain questions that remain to be answered—for example, how best to find ever-larger purposes and how to identify better solutions-after-next. We don't yet have enough answers to these questions, but in the answers that those questions generate will be found the seeds of change in Breakthrough Thinking.

How long the principles and process of Breakthrough Thinking will prove useful to humanity no one can say. Just as the research approach (scientific inquiry) has been refined but has not changed fundamentally in some 400 years, these principles for creating or restructuring systems—designed as a method of preventing and solving problems—may last a long time too. We hope so. In any case, 400 years of human utility seems a worthy goal for our endeavors.

To this end, Breakthrough Thinking is open and evolving. Far from indicating a current deficiency in the principles or process, this ongoing research emphasizes the fact that Breakthrough Thinking encourages and is itself authentically open to change.

The Future for Breakthrough Thinking

Significantly, the behavior characterized pejoratively as childlike is also that often exhibited by writers, actors, painters, composers, and other particularly creative people. Americans first coming to know the Japanese culture also sometimes make the mistake of denigrating the exceptionally creative Japanese as being exasperatingly childlike.

Yet this very attitude of openness and wonder is precisely what allows artists and other creative people to become particularly successful in solving their problems—in short, reaching breakthroughs in their thinking. The Japanese, in fact, are notorious for never saying no, always leaving open the possibility of alternative solutions.

In a sense, this is a way to play the believing game. To be childlike is to remain open, to let the imagination roam freely— not to categorize—to be willing to try something new. The principles of Breakthrough Thinking provide the mechanism and the modes of reasoning that allow anyone to be similarly and successfully childlike.

Breakthrough Thinking is *not* a program or a new fad to be installed in your organization. Many groups decide that something is wrong or missing and then go out to get *the* program or programs to fix it (they haven't heard of the uniqueness principle). Companies are spending billions of dollars on programs to improve quality, install new or replace old equipment, develop new incentive and reward programs, restructure the organization, get total employee involvement, reengineer business processes, and change the organization culture.

These programs go by names such as: Total Quality Management, Benchmarking, Total Productivity Program, Broadbanding Pay Levels, Computer Integrated Manufacturing, Organizational Design, Performance Management, High-Involvment Management, Information Systems, Concurrent Engineering.

Business Week, the American Electronics Manufacturers Association, and other study groups consistently report that the results of these programs are hardly noticeable. Less than one-third of the electronic manufacturers who set up extensive quality programs reported any major changes in results.

On July 6, 1993, the *Wall Street Journal* reported in a front-page article entitled "The Best Laid Plans: Many Companies Try Management Fads, Only to See Them Flop," that the success rate of such programs is quite low. As noted earlier, employees and customers rate the effectiveness of such management fads at between 10 and 20 percent. The reported satisfaction rate of even the executives involved is well below one-third. What's more, the increasingly desperate executives lurch from one fad to another because the effectiveness of the current favorite is invariably poor. Indeed, these programs seem to be implemented as the "flavor of the month."

Similarly poor results have occurred in the "information age" acquisition of computers in order to control and manage data in the office. Too often, the technology acquired has had the opposite effect, generating even more information *on paper* (which was supposed to disappear) and causing enormous difficulties in assimilating increased amounts of electronic data.

Even the new emphasis on customer service and satisfaction is undermined by the misplaced priorities of most organizations. For example, customer service managers have been found to receive the lowest percentage pay increases of all executives. What message does that send about an organization's purposes and priorities?

The only benefit that may exist in these fashionable programs relates to the education and training of workers in new technology and techniques that the programs may contain. Companies in the United States schedule less than a half day of training per employee per year, whereas the rest of the industrialized world schedules more than twelve. Yet the *Wall Street Journal* reports that, even while exposed to relatively so little training, American workers are complaining: "Stop the Fads. No more posters, seminars, and training classes."

The real problem is that none of these programs and techniques provides a *process* by which to implement solutions. We submit that what managers and executives concerned with quality, productivity, and competition ought to be considering is Business Process Reengineering: The Breakthrough Thinking Approach to Get Results; Total Quality Management: The Breakthrough Thinking Approach to Get Results; Employee Involvement: The Breakthrough Thinking Approach to Get Results; Organizational Design: The Breakthrough Thinking Approach to Get Results; and so on. Only in this way can existing techniques and technologies become actually applicable to the unique situations they are expected to address.

You can start using Breakthrough Thinking right away without waiting for a program to get under way. Each of us knows the goals to seek and the results to achieve—effectiveness, quality, productivity, implementation, computer-integrated manufacturing, low cost and time to get results, automated information systems, worker participation, and so forth.

Since each of us is always dealing with problems we want to solve or prevent, all that is necessary—as we noted in Chapter 11—is to do it. *How* you go about problem solving and reaching your own and organizational goals *can* make a big difference. Each person in the organization can use Breakthrough Thinking to manage his or her performance, for example, so that a fad program and its attendant staff would not be needed. Breakthrough Thinking is a way of removing the barriers to real progress. It breaks the addiction to fads.

Ian Mitroff, professor of business policy and director of the Center for Crisis Management at USC's Graduate School of Business noted: "Nothing less than a total redesign of our institutions is needed, so that we and they can not only react, but prevent these crises from occurring in the first place. If we do not, then the mega-crisis may be the only area of production in which the United States will continue to lead the world."[21]

In his book, Thomas Hughes says that the taming of invention in America is but one symptom of a larger theme. As reviewed in *Science* magazine by George Wise, that larger theme is to define a nation where, over time, "heroes gave way to system builders. Edison, with his vision of electrifying America, was succeeded by utility magnate Samuel Insull, with his systems that build and diversify electrical load to lower cost. Inventor Henry Ford gave way to mass-production master Henry Ford."[22]

"With success comes narrowing," writes Wise. "Technological momentum, one of Hughes' favorite concepts, not only moves mountains. It also digs ruts into which systems settle. Worse, it forecloses on the future: 'Mature systems suffocate nascent ones.'"[23]

Or, as Bertrand Russell is supposed to have said: "As techniques increase, wisdom fails."

Breakthrough Thinking is a way to get out of the rut, or better yet, avoid ruts in the first place. As noted by Peter Drucker, the best companies continually research to surpass their own successes.[24] For example, when Dupont's nylon became so successful in the late 1940s, the company was already trying to develop new synthetic fibers to replace it.

Organizational psychologist Kate Ludeman asserts that "the reason that the work ethic—producing goods and services through long hours of hard work—no longer serves America well, is that the work environment found in most American companies discourages people from 'working from the heart,' from caring about the job they do and the people with whom they work. As a result, the work environment—the way we manage and define our jobs—discourages what we used to call 'labors of love.'"[25]

We believe that by involving people with each other positively in the search for solutions to their common problems, the process and principles of Breakthrough Thinking can contribute significantly to the recovery of this long-lost love. Not only would people then recover satisfaction in their jobs and personal lives, they would perform far more productively.

Imagine the power that you derive by asking questions about purposes and solutions-after-next, the confidence of considering the uniqueness of each and every situation, the capacity for leadership that follows from seeking solutions-after-next and limiting the collection of information, the positive influence you will have on others in light of the principles and process of Breakthrough Thinking (as opposed to the negative impact of demands and orders), and the wisdom obtained throughout such exchanges.

Author Charles Garfield comments: "[Peak performers] are leaders not because they care so much for the trappings of dominance, but because they care so much for results: Make things happen toward goals, consistent with a mission, while developing oneself in the process."[26]

Developing Breakthrough Thinking is one sure way to realize your own—as well as your group's or company's—peak performance. Breakthrough Thinking improves your ability to view and understand each problem, opportunity, project, or activity in a much more productive and effective way. It allows you to share your thoughts and ideas with others in a way that allows you all to grow. It provides personal empowerment. It gives you the ability to learn and reorganize, to purposefully change and change again. It encourages you to tackle the problem or seize the opportunity, not simply to label it as stress or anxiety and try to ignore it.

There *is* hope. There *is* a set of principles and a process you can use to solve your problems. At least—since there are no final, complete, and total answers, rather only *changes* that include the seeds of their own future change—there *is* a way in which you can *continually approach the solution* of your problems. Strategic thinking is available.

Breakthrough Thinking itself tells you that the principles and process can be arranged flexibly to fit your own circumstances and style. For example, several of our colleagues rearrange the order of the seven principles to fit their own beliefs about what needs to be emphasized first. One associate puts them in this order: purposes, limited information collection, solution-after-next, systems, uniqueness, people design, and betterment timeline. Another prefers this order: betterment timeline, purposes, solution-after-next, uniqueness, systems, people design, and limited information collection. A third starts with systems and then the rest, in the order we prefer to present them. As emphasized in Chapter 11, the Breakthrough Thinking principles and process are very flexible.

Do these changes make any ultimate difference in how well Breakthrough Thinking is adopted and used? Of course not. In order to be most effective, the assumptions and concepts of Breakthrough Thinking must fit your own unique perspective. They are the way of being pragamatic in the modern world—sensitive to context, focus on purposes and outcomes, openness to uncertainty, and willingness to make do.[27] Based on the principles and process, you change the way you *think* when you create or restructure systems and solutions.

You must change the way you seek solutions. Conventional approaches have produced too many difficulties, crises, and failures. They need to be replaced.

If you want to achieve the significant changes that you and others need, you must achieve "a paradigm shift in thinking." You must reprogram the computer between your ears with Breakthrough Thinking's "software for your mind."

"In *The Lessons of History*," Garfield notes, "Will and Ariel Durant observe: 'The future never just happened. It was created.' If that is true for societies and organizations, it is true as well for individuals."[28] The noted Oxford and Yale historian Michael Howard is even more direct in showing how history is no infallible guide to success, no formula for each situation, no shortcut to wisdom.[29]

As Breakthrough Thinkers, our task—and our talent—is to accomplish nothing less than to create the future, to bridge the gap between human knowledge and practice. Not only must we find ways to convert knowledge to practice, we must also traverse the chasm between, on the one hand, our values and aspirations and, on the other, the reality of our daily lives.

We know now that technology alone—especially computers, artificial intelligence, neural networks, virtual reality, and telecommunications—is not sufficient. What is needed, and the crucial question, is *how* to convert technology to practice.

How can ordinary people be empowered to overcome the abuses of power and the arrogance of position inherent to a corporate culture in which top American executives pay themselves far more than their Japanese counterparts, by whom they are consistently outperformed? One way is the practice of the principles of Breakthrough Thinking.

Although American executives tend to blame the Japanese competitive advantage on the high level of U.S. labor costs, in fact, U.S. workers average less per hour than do Japanese workers. In any case, labor as a percentage of overall costs continues to *decrease* with each passing year. As Garfield states unequivocally: "The fact is, people are a resource, not a cost. The Japanese have accepted that, and we have not."[30]

"The surest path to economic decline, for a nation or a business, is to blame others for your problems," noted commentator Robert J. Samuelson.[31] The Excuse Industry, as he calls it, is "the collection of corporate executives, interest groups, and their political and intellectual allies who are constantly finding excuses to explain why U.S. industry isn't faring well...."

This pernicious habit, a result of the conventional approach to creating or restructuring systems and solutions, can be broken by Breakthrough Thinking. Surely, placing blame doesn't solve problems, even though those seeking the excuses assume those whom they perceive to be at fault should solve the problem by changing. In other words, placing blame is simply another search for the ever-elusive quick fix, the bane of contemporary Western society.

Now, having read this book, having learned the principles and process of Breakthrough Thinking, you are an inestimable resource in solving your vexing personal problems, as well as preventing and solving problems that plague the world.

As you apply the principles of Breakthrough Thinking, we believe that you will come to realize that Breakthrough Thinking itself will evolve further as you continue to apply it. Why? Because a Breakthrough Thinker is not just up-to-date. Rather, he or she is constantly looking toward and actively planning for the future, achieving the "flow" of involved enjoyment, the feeling of control and psychic reinforcement described as "optimal experience."[32]

As Breakthrough Thinking advances along its own betterment timeline, improving Breakthrough Thinking will be an ongoing challenge that commands our best efforts throughout our lifetimes, throughout generations of human growth and change. In a society—a world community—of Breakthrough Thinkers, what challenge could be insurmountable?

THE BEGINNING
Uniqueness
Purposes
Solution-After-Next
Systems
Limited Information Collection
People Design
Betterment Timeline

NOTES
1. Howard Gardner, *Multiple Intelligences: The Theory in Practice* (New York: Basic Books, 1993).

2. M. Norton, W.C. Bozeman and G. Nadler, *Student Planned Acquisition of Required Knowledge* (Englewood Cliffs, N.J.: Educational Technology Inc., 1980).

3. K.C. Cole, "Science Under Scrutiny," Special Education Section, *New York Times* (January 7, 1990).

4. Stanley Meisler, "Coming Home to Find a Smug, Scared America," *Los Angeles Times* (June 4, 1989).

5. Meg Greenfield, "Down With 'Leadership,'" *Newsweek* (January 25, 1988).

6. Frances Moore Lappe, *Rediscovering American Values* (New York: Ballantine Books, 1989).

7. Robert Conot, Review of Don L. Bonker, *America's Trade Crisis, Los Angeles Times* (November 27, 1988).

8. Michael Dertouzos, Richard K. Lester, Robert M. Solow, and the MIT Commission on Industrial Productivity, *Made In America: Regaining the Productive Edge* (Cambridge, Mass: MIT Press, 1989).

9. Warren Bennis, Review of Dertouzos et al, *Made In America, Los Angeles Times* (June 4, 1989).

10. Peter Drucker, *The New Realities* (New York: Harper & Row, 1989).

11. Jeffrey Garten, Review of Drucker, *The New Realities, Los Angeles Times* (June 4,1989).

12. Robert J. Samuelson, *Newsweek* (February 20, 1989).

13. Max Holland, *When the Machine Stopped: A Cautionary Tale From Industrial America* (Boston, Mass.: Harvard Business School Press, 1989).

14. William N. Goetzman, *Los Angeles Times* (March 26, 1989).

15. Russell Mitchell, "Masters of Innovation," *Business Week* (April 10, 1989).

16. Craig Benson, "Setting a Tone with Battered Desks," Forum in the Business Section, *New York Times* (September 29, 1991).

17. Robert J. Sternberg, *Beyond IQ: A Triarchic Theory of Human Intelligence* (London: Cambridge University Press, 1985).

18. D.L. Featherman, N.F. Marks and C.A. Caldwell, "Mind, Self and the Aging Society," Working Paper, University of Wisconsin-Madison (Department of Sociology, August 1989).

19. L. Raphael Troncale, "The Future of General Systems Research: Obstacles, Potentials, Case Studies," *Systems Research* 2. No. 1 (1985).

20. Stephen Brookfield, *Developing Critical Thinkers* (San Francisco: Jossey-Bass, 1987).

21. Ian Mitroff, "In a Modern World, Our Responses Are Way out of Date," *Los Angeles Times* (March 3, 1989).

22. Thomas Hughes, *American Genesis: A Century of Invention and Technological Enthusiasm* (1870-1970) (New York: Viking, 1989).

23. George Wise, *Science* 244 (May 19, 1989).

24. Peter Drucker, *Wall Street Journal* (May 30, 1989).

25. Kate Ludeman, "Bosses, Embrace Your Workers," *New York Times* (May 14, 1989).

26. Charles Garfield, *Peak Performers* (New York: W. Morrow, 1986).

27. N. Nohria and J. D. Berkley, "Whatever Happened to the Take-Charge Manager," *Harvard Business Review*, January-February 1994.

28. Garfield, op. cit.

29. M. Howard, *The Lessons of History* (New Haven, Conn.: Yale University Press, 1991).

30. Garfield, op. cit.

31. Robert J. Samuelson, "The Excuse Industry," *Newsweek* (December 11, 1989).

32. Michael Csikszentmihalyi, *Flow: The Psychology of Optimal Experience* (New York: Harper & Row, 1990).

Afterword

In another few years, we plan to publish a third edition of this book (version 3.0 along the betterment timeline). For inclusion in this future work, we would like to consider your own case histories using Breakthrough Thinking. Whether corporate executive, elected official, middle manager, or private citizen, as you use the principles and process of Breakthrough Thinking, won't you take the time to write us concerning your own breakthrough experiences?

Thank you.

Professor Gerald Nadler
Industrial and Systems Engineering
University of Southern California
Los Angeles, CA 90089-0913
USA

Professor Shozo Hibino
Chukyo University
16-20 Nishijima
Moriyama Nagoya
JAPAN 463

INDEX